AUTOBODY
REFINISHING
HANDBOOK

AUTOBODY REFINISHING HANDBOOK

ANDRE G. DEROCHE

*Instructor in Autobody
Repairing and Painting,
Red River Community College
Winnipeg, Manitoba, Canada*

PRENTICE HALL, Englewood Cliffs, New Jersey 07632

Library of Congress Cataloging-in-Publication Data

DEROCHE, A. G.
    Autobody refinishing handbook.

    Includes index.
    1. Automobiles—Painting. I. Title.
TL154.D43 1988   629.2′6   87–11409
ISBN 0-13-054198-2

Editorial/production supervision and
    interior design: Tom Aloisi
Cover design: Diane Saxe
Manufacturing buyer: Lorraine Fumoso

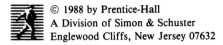 © 1988 by Prentice-Hall
A Division of Simon & Schuster
Englewood Cliffs, New Jersey 07632

Printed in the United States of America

10 9 8 7 6 5 4 3 2 1

ISBN 0-13-054198-2 025

Prentice-Hall International (UK) Limited, *London*
Prentice-Hall of Australia Pty. Limited, *Sydney*
Prentice-Hall Canada Inc., *Toronto*
Prentice-Hall Hispanoamericana, S.A., *Mexico*
Prentice-Hall of India Private Limited, *New Delhi*
Prentice-Hall of Japan, Inc., *Tokyo*
Prentice-Hall of Southeast Asia Pte. Ltd., *Singapore*
Editora Prentice-Hall do Brasil, Ltda., *Rio de Janeiro*
Whitehall Books Limited, *Wellington, New Zealand*

The author would like to dedicate this book to his children Mark and Kimberley, and to all young people who have the fortitude and determination to become qualified painters and improve their living standards.

Contents

Preface

This book was written for a number of reasons: for the student or apprentice beginning in the automotive refinishing trade; for instructors in comprehensive high schools, trade schools, and colleges; for experienced painters who have not been able to keep up with the changes that are occurring so quickly, to enable them to catch up and increase their skills and earn a better living; for personnel connected with automotive refinishing in body shop management or insurance claims departments who wish to broaden their information background; and to familiarize personnel in autobody paint shops with paint equipment and safety rules for the painter.

Automotive refinishing, like any other trade or occupation, is made up of the theory of why and how the work is done and the skill development needed to develop a qualified person. Skill development requires that certain operations be done over and over until they can be done with no errors and become a habit.

A qualified painter must be able to accomplish in a safe manner all the operations and methods described and be able to respond easily to all the Review Questions given at the end of each chapter.

Chapter 1 describes the needs of the refinishing trade and gives a history of paint coatings. It describes the methods a paint shop uses to make a profit and maintain a good clientele. It also describes the paint systems used in Japan, Europe, and the North American continent, how serial numbers are read, and trim and color codes and how they are used to mix or order paint from suppliers. The methods that paint manufacturers, jobbers, and representatives use to help keep the qualified painter up to date are described.

Chapter 2 describes types of spray booths, the need to service them, and how. Compressors, a vital part of the operation, are described and how they work and how to take care of them are covered. Air transformers and hoses are described as to type, pressure drop, and methods of use. Due to the amount of isocyanates being used today, paint respirators are described as to their use for protection and sanitation. The use of infrared baking equipment to dry paint is also covered.

Chapter 3 describes many types of spray guns; atomization and vaporization; how to clean, lubricate and, most important of all, adjust them; and how to recognize the different parts and learn to use them. The troubleshooting section describes how to detect what is wrong and how to fix it. Finally, spraying techniques and practice methods are covered.

Chapter 4 introduces the many different types of abrasives, their backing, and methods of grading the abrasives both in North America and Europe. All the methods of using the different abrasives to perform different tasks by hand or by machine are covered.

Chapter 5 covers the different types of refinishing materials used, how to determine the condition of the surface, sandblasting, paint removers, and general clean-up of the substrate. The use of the different primers, thinners, reducers, and specialty items is discussed. Information on masking materials and problems, as well as how to mask, is included.

Chapter 6 covers the metal conditioning of the substrate, priming the surface, and sanding the surface. Shop repair materials are covered to explain how they should be used. The different types of top coats and color are discussed and explained.

Chapter 7 covers the methods used when repainting a vehicle from the start to the cleaning, stirring of paint, reduction, and applying the paint film. Acrylic enamel and lacquer base coat/clear coat systems are explained, as well as the rubbing and polishing of a paint film.

Chapter 8 explains how to spot repair using acrylic lacquer or acrylic enamel and the very important subject of matching colors, either by spray gun methods or by the tinting of colors. The information on tinting is from manufacturers' tinting information tables.

Chapter 9 explains how to paint plastics and recognize the different types and the international plastic codes. The troubleshooting of paint failures and the installation of adhesive backed moldings, wood grain, and striping tape are also covered.

References made to the Occupational Safety and Health Act (OSHA) in this textbook are not a complete covering of OSHA regulations affecting the automotive refinishing trade. The purpose of providing excerpts of OSHA regulations is to familiarize painters with the methods and regulations that are in force to protect them and their health. These references cover OSHA regulations that were in effect before November 1978.

If the student, tradesperson, or representative reading this text desires to learn about auto body repairing, *The Principles of Auto Body Repairing and Painting,* by A. G. Deroche and N. N. Hildebrand, is available from Prentice Hall, Inc., Englewood Cliffs, New Jersey.

Andre G. Deroche

Acknowledgments

The author wishes to express his sincere thanks to all the people at the following companies who helped him to make this book possible.

BASF Inmont, Inc.
Binks Manufacturing Co. of Canada Ltd.
Black & Decker of Canada Inc.
Canadian Industries Limited of Canada
Devilbiss of Canada Ltd.
Ditzler Automotive Finishes Division of PPG Industries
Du Pont of Canada and the United States
Mitchell Information Services, Inc.
Martin Senour, Inc., USA

Sikkens B.V., Sassenheim, Holland
Sherwin Williams of Canada Ltd.

The author would also like to thank Steve Chanas, Edward Debeuckelaere, Orest Dobinsky, B. J. Small, and W. L. Williams, all members of the Red River Community College staff; and the following members of the paint equipment and paint material industry: Richard Kozicki, Sherwin Williams, Inc. Canada; Kurt Bazel, Sherwin Williams, Inc. USA; Doug Dilts, Du Pont of Canada; Wayne Penhall, Ditzler of Canada; Les Hargeaves, BASF Inmont Canada; and Bill McLeod, ABS Warehouse Ltd.

CHAPTER ONE

The Automotive Refinishing Trade

SAFETY HINTS

A well-ventilated, safe, and clean shop will keep the skilled personnel healthy; they are the most precious assets.

Well-lighted and neat working areas encourage and improve the performance of employees.

The shop should be kept free from debris, rags, and old parts; a fire could be a calamity.

Never more than a day's supply of paint materials should be outside of an approved storage area.

Hands should always be washed before eating or smoking.

Aisles and walkways should be kept free of tools, creepers, or any other object that might cause somebody to trip or stumble.

All floors should be kept clean, and paint, oil, or other materials should be cleaned up immediately. Any holes in the floor should be repaired.

The world rolls on wheels, whether it is trains, automotive vehicles, airplanes, or even the military forces of each country that are used for defense—they all roll on wheels. When these wheels slow down, the economy and activity of a country usually slow down, bringing with it slight recession or even depression in its economic stability. Whatever the type of vehicle, they all have one thing in common—paint. Paint is used to give them beauty, as well as to protect them and make them last longer.

It is well known that the different colors preferred by the buying public influence the sale of vehicles, whether automobile, truck, recreational vehicle, or motorcycle. In fact, the list is endless as paint is used on practically everything that is bought by the general public.

The number of vehicles brought to different types of paint shops to be repainted is staggering. The amount of money spent by companies, governments, and the general public to refurbish their vehicles is enormous.

To understand the refinishing of today's vehicles, a person should look to the past to understand the technological advances used today. Before 1924, it took almost a month for an auto manufacturer to paint a car. These vehicles were refinished by brushing on oil-based primers, followed by coat after coat of a mixture of lamp black or other pigments and varnish. Each coat had to dry before it could be rubbed with pumice and water. This type of finish would usually last about a year and then turn dull and was often badly cracked.

Then lacquer called Duco, composed of simple formulas based on hard resins, plasticizers, and nitrocellulose, was introduced by Du Pont; this finish revolutionized the industry. It quickly replaced the old methods of refinishing. It was durable and dried quickly in a matter of hours, and this enabled manufacturers to greatly increase production. It could be applied quickly with a spray gun for the first time in history. Between 1926 and 1928, chalk-resistant white pigments became available.

In 1930, an alkyd improved lacquer coating was introduced on the market; this type of lacquer contained a coconut alkyd resin instead of the hard resin and pigments. This improved the resistance to the sun, providing less chalking and dulling.

In 1929 an alkyd enamel called Dulux was introduced by Du Pont; this was an extremely tough finish and needed no compounding, because it dried to a full gloss. This material was especially suitable for the requirements of trucks and automobiles. The enamel used on production assembly lines was a baking type that contained either urea or melamine resin. This enabled manufacturers to cure the paint by baking the paint for 30 minutes at 250°F or 125°C. This type of paint was used by many motor vehicle manufacturers for many years until the super enamels were produced. In 1932 new color pigments were introduced, and constant improvements have provided the new, durable, glamour colors used in modern finishes.

As we look back, we see the tremendous steps that have been made in the paint industry. In 1956, Lucite, a thermoplastic acrylic lacquer, was introduced by Du Pont. In 1963, thermoset acrylic enamels were pioneered by Sherwin-Williams and were used by Chrysler, Ford, and American Motors on their production lines. Some of this material is still used but the formula has been refined and modified. In 1970 a new type of enamel called thermoset acrylic enamel was introduced to the paint field.

In the early 1970s, new coating systems were being used by General Motors, Chrysler, Ford, and American Motors. The coatings are a nonaqueous dispersion type; this means that the pigment and resin are dispersed in a nonsolvent like gasoline. This type of paint is applied on the car surface and when baked the heat fuses the particles together to give a normal coating appearance. This method in no way changes the end product, as it is still an acrylic finish and only the method of application on the vehicle is different.

In the middle 1970s, new antipollution laws that regulated manufacturers required the development of new methods of application, and new materials appeared on the assembly line. The main problem was to get rid of the solvents in the paint. This was achieved by using high-solid coatings sprayed from the gun as 100% solids. Powder coatings are applied by electrostatic spray; this dry form of coating is applied and then baked at a high temperature to fuse the particles. Also, waterborne acrylic enamels that use water to carry the coating to the surface to be painted were developed; the water is forced off with high-temperature baking.

In the late 1970s the industry saw the start of the use of basecoat/clearcoat on foreign-built vehicles. This technology and its new methods are rapidly being put to use in vehicle assembly plants in North America.

1-1 THE NEEDS OF THE TRADE AND A DESCRIPTION

Since we live in a world in which paint plays such an important role, many industries are required to service us. Some of these are the manufacturers of paint, refinish equipment, and the miscellaneous materials that are required to keep the refinish industries going. All these industries are needed to supply paint and all the necessary items that are used each working day.

The most important person in refinishing is the qualified painter, who must have a thorough knowledge of the craft to be able to use the many different types of materials on the marketplace. Qualified painters must be able to achieve good color matches as well as make necessary repairs flawlessly.

To the general public, a qualified painter is a person who applies paint. Little do the majority know that to be a master a painter must spend many long hours mastering the requirements of the craft. The painter must know the fundamentals of the preparation required as well as understand the paint problems that will be encountered during the work day. Knowledge of spray equipment, spray guns, air pressures, and spray booths, in fact all equipment used during the day, must be at his or her fingertips. The painter must be able to identify the type of paint on the surface to be repaired to be able to match Original Equipment Manufacturer (OEM) finishes or after-market paint surfaces. The qualified painter must be able to use the many different types of paints and systems that are on the market and be able to match the existing vehicle paint color that is being refinished.

There are different types of shops in which a painter will work; the most common is a refinish shop that is part of a collision shop. Then there are the high-volume, lower-cost shops, and last but not least are the custom paint shops, which do high-quality work and are very expensive.

Depending on the location, paint shops have to meet local as well as state or provincial and federal laws and safety codes. These codes and laws provide the requirements of zoning, local requirements, and also the workplace and safety ordinances or acts. To be able to operate, the shops are usually licensed by the proper authority and must follow the requirements established in the particular area or country.

1-2 HOW A PAINT SHOP OPERATES

When a vehicle needs painting as a result of collision or just general deterioration of the paint film, the customer usually gets estimates from a few shops. Some shops, due to attitude and high-quality standards of paint refinish work, provide an estimate, but the price for the job could be higher. Other shops may charge less, and some high-volume shops offer specials at certain times of the year.

When the customer comes to the shop, he or she is usually met by the owner or the person in charge of giving estimates. The estimator examines the vehicle and notes on an estimate form the work required on each panel if either collision or other damage is present. The estimator totals the amount of labor for body repairs and painting time, which may be found in flat-rate manuals. The material charge for both body repair and painting is usually a percentage or a fixed amount of dollars per labor hour. The rate for materials is higher for painting than for body repairs, because the cost of these materials is much greater.

Depending on whether the vehicle has to be completely refinished or just a partial repaint has to be done, the cost will vary considerably from one vehicle to another. Let us consider the estimate that is written up for a complete paint job, which is usually called a color coat. The estimate could call for 12.0 to 18.0 hours of labor time, which is multiplied by the shop labor rate to get a total labor time. Then the material for the paint work is added to the estimate of labor for the painting, which gives a total for the particular job that is then given to the customer.

Generally, the head painter in the shop is responsible for ordering all necessary paint materials and supervising apprentices in all aspects of their different tasks. The painter prepares the paint materials for different vehicles as required. He or she either finishes preparing or supervises the final preparations of the panels requiring painting before the appropriate color is applied.

The painter paints the vehicle or supervises apprentices while painting the vehicles so that the work is properly done. The painter is responsible for either unmasking and cleaning the vehicle after the paint has dried or supervising the apprentices so that the vehicle is ready for delivery to the customer in a satisfactory, clean condition. The painter is also responsible for seeing that all equiment is kept clean and in good working condition and put away everyday at closing time. The painter must also assign and supervise the cleaning of the paint shop, as well as the spray booth and paint mixing area.

To better understand the refinish trade and how it is organized, it is important to know that the many manufacturers and suppliers must abide by laws, codes, and regulations made by federal, state, provincial, county, or municipal governments. The vehicle refinisher buys all paint, usually from OEM suppliers. Spray equipment and the miscellaneous paint material required are all bought from the appropriate suppliers as required.

The paint used on a factory production line, which moves continuously, is different from what is used in the refinish trade. The production line has a high bake oven system, which bakes the paint applied on the vehicles at a set temperature for the required amount of time. The paint is applied mainly by robot spray guns or bells, and only the areas that the robots cannot reach are done by expert painters.

The intensive technological changes that the automotive industry is going through due to downsizing of automobiles, which was caused by energy shortages and increasing air pollution requirements, have also affected paint manufacturers. Coating systems have been developed or altered to meet air-pollution regulations enforced by government agencies. When painting must be done on a vehicle, the type of OEM materials must be properly identified.

1-3 CURRENT PAINT SYSTEMS

Japan

In the current system in Japan, the metal treatment used is a zinc phosphated steel applied in a seven-stage system. The primer is an electrodeposited polyester primer in a dip tank that is baked 30 minutes at 340°F or 171°C. The surface or sealer coat is a melamine polyester resin surfacer, usually applied by an automatic electrostatic bell system. This surfacer is baked for 30 minutes at 290°F or 143°C and then wet sanded with 400 to 500 or P800 to P1000 grit sandpaper.

Japanese companies use both melamine alkyd and acrylic baking enamels, as are used in some North American plants. The paint is applied by using state-of-the-art robotic application equipment by reciprocating disc, which is known as turbo bells or minibells. Some of the solid topcoat colors have clearcoats, which sometimes have dye or pigmentation added to them.

When applying metallic colors, the Japanese mostly use a basecoat/clearcoat system of applying metallic paint. Whatever the method of application employed by the Japanese, baked acrylic enamel is used. The basecoat is allowed to flash for 2 to 4 minutes in a high-air-velocity spray booth and then the clearcoat is applied. This paint and clearcoat system is then baked 30 minutes at 290°F or 143°C. On-assembly-line repairs are made using the same type of OEM paint, which is baked by infrared heating systems.

The Toyota company uses a three-stage paint system, which is a pearlescent-type coating using a solid basecoat color. Then it is covered with a mica-filled second coat of clear, and then a final clearcoat is applied over all.

Europe

The metal treatment is a seven-stage zinc phosphate application; then polybutadiene-type primer or powder is electrodeposited and then baked for 30 minutes at 350°F or 176°C. The solid color of super-enamel is baked for

30 minutes at 290°F or 143°C. The metallics are all basecoat/clearcoat; the basecoat is a CAB polyester.

United States and Canada: Ford, Chrysler, AMC, and GMC Trucks

The metal treatment is a seven-stage zinc phosphate system used on steel and zincrometal, which is followed by one of the following two systems: A polyester or epoxy ester primer is applied using electrodeposition and then baked for 30 minutes at 400°F or 240°C. When an electrodeposition system is used, an epoxy ester surfacer is applied by the spray system and then baked for 30 minutes at 350°F or 176°C and then wet sanded with 400 or P800 sandpaper.

There is also a new Uniprime version of the E-Coat system that builds a high thickness and thus allows the primer-surfacer step to be completely eliminated. Some Ford plants are using a polyester basecoat, which is followed by an acrylic clearcoat. Other Ford plants use the new high-solids clearcoat enamel system. The automatic electrostatic bell is used for applications in the newer,. modified plants. Some plants, however, are still using conventional spray guns with different combinations of air atomizing and electrostatic systems. Hand spray gun operations are still used for "cutting in" around different body openings that robots cannot reach or to spray dry or thin coats at the end of the spray line before baking. But most plants have by now shifted to an automatic robotic paint application system.

General Motors

The metal treatment is a seven-stage zinc phosphate system on steel and zincrometal. The priming is done by electrodeposition almost exclusively, except in the case of plastic and fiber-glass bodies; this primer is baked for 30 minutes at 350°F or 176°C. The type of primers are either epoxy esters or polyesters.

The surfacer is an epoxy ester type applied by air atomized electrostatic guns, which is then baked for 30 minutes at 350°F or 176°C; this surfacer is then wet sanded with 400 or P800 grit sandpaper.

The topcoat used in some plants at General Motors is a reflow acrylic lacquer. The first coat is force dried 30 minutes at 200°F or 93°C; then the second coat is applied and baked 30 minutes at 200°F or 93°C. This high heat causes the acrylic lacquer total film thickness to reflow, which gives an excellent high-gloss appearance.

Some General Motors plants have used a waterborne acrylic baking enamel, which was baked at 350°F or 176°C. Because of the use of the water in this particular system, the spray booths had to be air conditioned to be able to control the temperature and humidity. This control of the system was the substitute for faster or slower solvents used in a conventional system.

For the future at General Motors plants, electrodeposition will be used as their primer and they will gradually shift to Uniprime type to eliminate extra priming steps. The use of surfacers will gradually be phased out except on plastic-bodied cars, where they are used to get a good surface profile on the plastic panels.

General Motors, with its many plants, is using a staging system to help reduce total solvent emissions. In the first step they changed from a 12% solid-solution lacquer to a 17% and then to a 27% dispersion lacquer. The dispersion lacquer is similar to latex; the paint is in a nonsolvent like gasoline. The only difference is that in latex the paint is suspended in water.

General Motors will gradually convert from dispersion lacquer to basecoat/clearcoat enamel as it builds new plants and remodels old plants. The dispersion lacquer must have a proper baking cycle to form a good film. The biggest difference with dispersion lacquer is its poor solvent resistance and more mottling and orange peel in the paint film. Many of these vehicles will look like baked enamel but are actually painted with dispersion lacquer. Most truck plants use a conventional baked acrylic enamel, but the minivans use a basecoat/clearcoat system.

Production Line Painting

The following is an overview of production line painting in automotive plants. Metal preparation is a fairly uniform procedure among all manufacturers. They use a multistage pretreatment system that utilizes an acid wash and a water rinse. After having been thoroughly dried off in an oven, a bondizer is applied that leaves a phosphate film, which is an ideal surface for the adhesion of primers.

Most manufacturers use electrocoat primer immersion of the entire body. This coat is usually a composition of epoxy and urethane material. This is usually followed by a sprayed polyester prime coat. Automotive primer-surfacers are usually applied from 1.2 to 1.5 mil or 3.1 μm to 3.8 μm thick over electrocoated bodies to fill imperfections and surface defects in the metal. Wet sanding is used to sand this primer; it is then wiped with an alcohol and water mixture to remove fingerprints and wiping streaks.

On most production lines, items such as door jambs, rear compartments, and engine compartments are hand sprayed by painters using hand-held air atomizing electrostatic guns. All the spray booths are down-draft water wash design, which removes all overspray down through floor grates. This system is the most efficient for keeping overspray off the vehicles and the booth and atmosphere free of paint overspray without creating draft and turbulence air problems.

Most assembly line paint lines use a rotary disc type of application. These are usually referred to as turbobells or minibells; this name is derived from the bell-shaped hood that encloses the disc mechanism. This system allows the paint to be fed full bodied onto a spinning disc. The centrifugal pressure or force created by the spinning disc throws the paint off in a fine mist; it also charges the paint with an electrical positive charge. The vehicle body is grounded (negative) and therefore sets up an attraction that draws or attracts most of the paint to the body. The big advantage of the rotary disc is that it will apply paint with a very high solids content. Thus less solvent is used and expelled up exhaust stacks, which creates less air solvent pollution. The paint is usually shipped in special tanks that hold 200 to 500 gallons or 700 to 1890 liters, instead of in drums. This paint is pumped into the assembly plant's paint reservoirs from the tanks.

Some bell systems use shaping air, which is a stream of air that helps to direct the paint mist and to adjust the fan as required. Some bells produce almost an invisible fog, while others produce a noticeable fog. Paint operators are usually stationed outside the spray booths at electronic consoles. These operators monitor the painting through the windows of the booth as the vehicle bodies move on the paint line. Color changes and variations in body shape are accommodated by the computer, which picks up the information from the build order as the vehicle approaches the paint spray booth. The computer signals the bell units as they move over the surface of the particular body at a distance of 8 to 15 in., or 20 to 38 cm, and shuts them off when paint is not required.

Ford. The Ford basecoat/clearcoat system is a polyester basecoat and an acrylic enamel clear topcoat. A rotary cone rather than a flat disc is used to apply the basecoat, with a certain amount of atomizing air for basecoat. The clearcoat is applied by bell units that use centrifugal force only. Usually the basecoats have a film thickness of 0.7 to 0.8 mil or 1.8 μm to 2.0 μm and the clearcoats are 1.5 mils or 3.8 μm. They are baked at 250°F or 121°C for 20 minutes.

General Motors. This company's dispersion lacquer plants (thermoplastic acrylic lacquer) use painters for the areas that must be "cut in" with hand-held air atomized electrostatic spray guns. The main body is usually sprayed by automatic electrostatic guns or bell-type rotary disc sprayers. The body film build is usually

3.2 to 5.0 mils or 8.1 μm to 12.7 μm; the sheet-metal-system film build is 2.8 to 4.0 mils or 7.1 μm to 10.1 μm. The flash-off time between coats is 1 to 3 minutes and the reflow bake is 2.5 minutes at 335°F or 168°C after allowing 7 minutes for the vehicle body to warm up.

High-Solids Enamel Plants (Thermosetting Acrylic Enamel). This material is applied by bell units and the first coat is approximately 1.0 mil or 2.5 μm; flash-off time is 1 to 1½ minutes. The second coat is also approximately 1 mil or 2.5 μm with a flash-off time of 1 to 1½ minutes. The third coat is an additional 0.7 mil or 1.8 μm approximately, which is applied for metallics as a blend coat and is sprayed by hand-held spray guns. The flash time is 5 to 8 minutes before the oven, where the body of the vehicle has 7 minutes of heat-up time, followed by 15 minutes of baking at 250°F or 121°C.

Basecoat/Clearcoat Plants (Thermosetting Acrylic Enamel). These plants usually use air atomizing automatic spray guns on the basecoat. This is followed by the clearcoat, which is applied by the bell system, as indicated in Table 1-1. The flash-off time is 6 to 8 minutes before the vehicle body enters the oven, and then it is heated for 7 minutes and baked for 15 minutes at 250°F or 121°C.

At the Corvette Plant, manual operations are used throughout. Body filling, surfacing, and sanding operations are all done by hand. The primer used, called Polane and manufactured by Sherwin-Williams, as well as the basecoats and clearcoats, is applied with hand-held atomizing spray guns.

The basecoat/clearcoat systems at Chrysler and AMC basically use the same procedure as GM. The nonclearcoat colored vehicle bodies usually use a "wet out" area near the end of the paint line, where a painter with a hand-held spray gun checks and touches up any areas that do not have good gloss level.

Most manufacturers used exterior skins of steel that are hot galvanized on their 1986 models. Some manufacturers used steel that was galvanized on both sides and for others only the exterior of the panels was galvanized. This basically covers the types of paint materials used by the manufacturers as well as their methods of applying and baking the surfaces.

Paint Suppliers

Many paint manufacturers supply paint to the vehicle manufacturers, but there are additional paint manufacturers who supply the refinish trade with a complete line of refinish materials. The paint materials are supplied by the paint companies to regional warehouses, which

TABLE 1-1

	Nonmetallics (mils)	Metric Units	Metallics (mils)	Metric Units
First coat (basecoat)	0.4–0.8	1.0–2.0 μm	0.4–0.5	1.0–1.3 μm
Second coat (basecoat)	0.4–0.8	1.0–2.0 μm	0.2–0.3	0.5–0.76 μm
Third coat (clearcoat) Flash time: 1 to 5 min	0.7–0.9	1.8–2.3 μm	0.8–1.0	2.0–2.5 μm
Fourth coat (clearcoat)	0.7–0.9	1.8–2.3 μm	0.8–1.0	2.0–2.5 μm

in turn sell these materials to jobbers, which distribute this material to their respective customers. These customers are mainly autobody repair and paint shops.

Paint companies have representatives in all their different regions; these representatives advise the jobbers and their customers on how to use their materials. They are a vital link for the paint industry as they are factory trained, and this qualifies them to help keep the jobbers and paint customers up to date. The paint material supplied to OEMs is not quite the same as the materials supplied out in the field. The materials supplied to OEMs are similar in pigments, but the resins are made to be baked at high temperatures, and the materials used in the field are meant to air dry.

Paint companies also offer training by sending out highly qualified painting instructors who hold paint training programs in different cities. The jobbers' customers are invited to these training programs to enable their staff to keep up to date on the yearly changes in materials and their methods of application. Also many programs are offered by colleges and vocational education centers where apprentices are trained to fill the jobs that are available in the industry.

1-4 IDENTIFICATION OF SERIAL NUMBERS AND PAINT CODES

Before a painter orders paint from the jobber or mixes it on the shop's mixing system, he or she must be able to identify the year of the vehicle. The vehicle identification plate (Figs. 1–1 through 1–10) is located on the

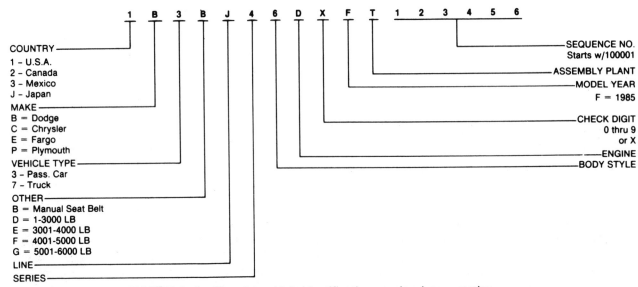

CHRYSLER CORP. 1985
PASSENGER CARS/FWD TRUCKS

LOCATION – UPPER LEFT SIDE OF INSTRUMENT PANEL, ALSO IN CENTER PORTION OF BOTTOM ROW OF BODY CODE PLATE

Vehicle Identification Plate contains 17 characters interpreted as follows:

1 B 3 B J 4 6 D X F T 1 2 3 4 5 6

COUNTRY
1 – U.S.A.
2 – Canada
3 – Mexico
J – Japan
MAKE
B = Dodge
C = Chrysler
E = Fargo
P = Plymouth
VEHICLE TYPE
3 - Pass. Car
7 - Truck
OTHER
B = Manual Seat Belt
D = 1-3000 LB
E = 3001-4000 LB
F = 4001-5000 LB
G = 5001-6000 LB
LINE
SERIES

SEQUENCE NO.
Starts w/100001
ASSEMBLY PLANT
MODEL YEAR
F = 1985
CHECK DIGIT
0 thru 9
or X
ENGINE
BODY STYLE

FIGURE 1-1 Chrysler vehicle identification number interpretation. *(Courtesy of Mitchell Information Services, Inc.)*

CHRYSLER CORP. PASSENGER CARS

BODY CODE PLATE — 1981-83

LOCATION — The body code plate is located on the left front fender side shield or wheelhousing or on the
upper radiator support.

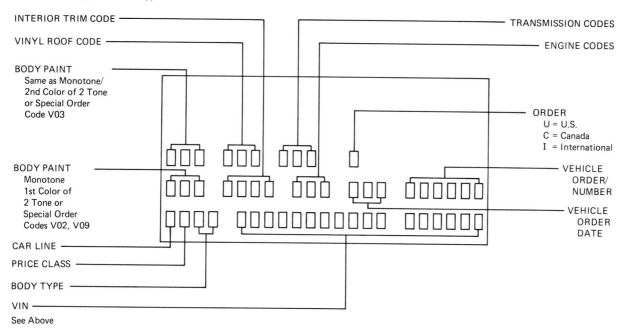

BODY CODE PLATE — 1984 PASSENGER CARS/FWD TRUCKS

LOCATION — The body code plate is located on the left front fender side shield or wheelhousing or on the
upper radiator support.

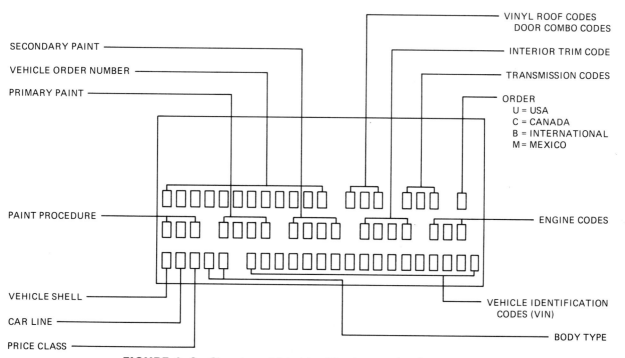

FIGURE 1-2 Chrysler vehicle identification number interpretation.
(Courtesy of Mitchell Information Services, Inc.)

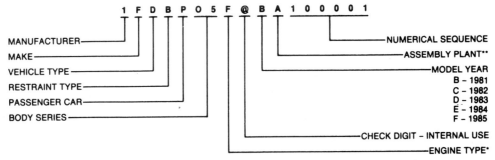

FIGURE 1-3 Ford Motor Company vehicle identification number. *(Courtesy of Mitchell Information Services, Inc.)*

FORD - LINCOLN - MERCURY
1981-85

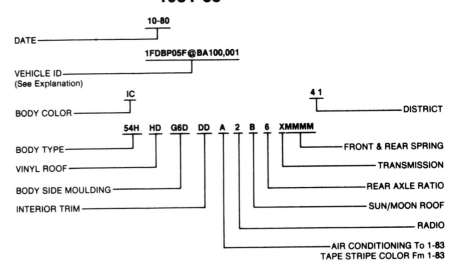

FIGURE 1-4 Ford vehicle identification label. *(Courtesy of Mitchell Information Services, Inc.)*

BUICK

LOCATION – UPPER LEFT SIDE OF INSTRUMENT PANEL VISIBLE THROUGH WINDSHIELD.

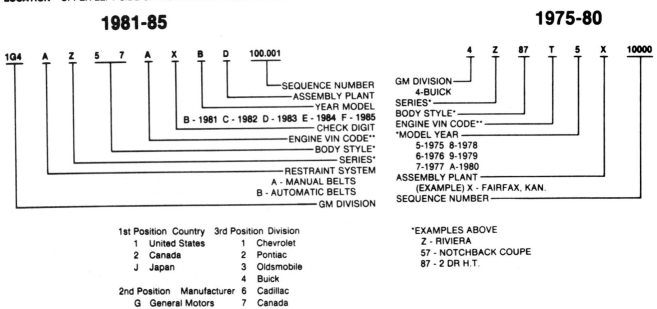

FIGURE 1-5 General Motors vehicle identification number. *(Courtesy of Mitchell Information Services, Inc.)*

AMERICAN MOTORS

1981-85

LOCATION – PLATE ATTACHED TO THE UPPER LEFT CORNER OF INSTRUMENT PANEL AND BOTTOM LINE OF METAL PLATE ATTACHED TO THE UPPER LEFT CORNER OF THE FIREWALL UNDER THE HOOD.

Typical VIN interprets as follows:

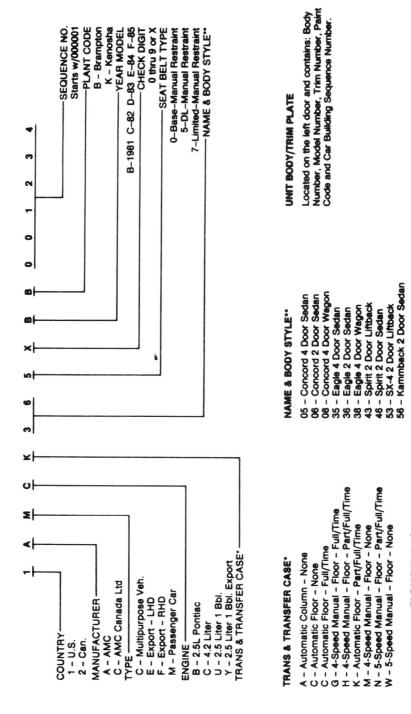

1 A M C 3 6 5 X B 0 0 1 2 3 4

COUNTRY
1 – U.S.
2 – Can.

MANUFACTURER
A – AMC
C – AMC Canada Ltd

TYPE
C – Multipurpose Veh.
E – Export – LHD
F – Export – RHD
M – Passenger Car

ENGINE
B – 2.5L Pontiac
C – 4.2 Liter
U – 2.5 Liter 1 Bbl.
Y – 2.5 Liter 1 Bbl. Export

TRANS & TRANSFER CASE*

SEQUENCE NO.
Starts w/000001

PLANT CODE
B – Brampton
K – Kenosha

YEAR MODEL
B-1981 C-82 D-83 E-84 F-85

CHECK DIGIT
0 thru 9 or X

SEAT BELT TYPE
0–Base–Manual Restraint
5–DL–Manual Restraint
7–Limited–Manual Restraint

NAME & BODY STYLE**

TRANS & TRANSFER CASE*

A – Automatic Column – None
C – Automatic Floor – None
C – Automatic Floor – Full/Time
G – 4-Speed Manual – Floor – Full/Time
H – 4-Speed Manual – Floor – Part/Full/Time
K – Automatic Floor – Part/Full/Time
M – 4-Speed Manual – Floor – None
N – 5-Speed Manual – Floor – Part/Full/Time
W – 5-Speed Manual – Floor – None

NAME & BODY STYLE**

05 – Concord 4 Door Sedan
06 – Concord 2 Door Sedan
08 – Concord 4 Door Wagon
35 – Eagle 4 Door Sedan
36 – Eagle 2 Door Sedan
38 – Eagle 4 Door Wagon
43 – Spirit 2 Door Liftback
46 – Spirit 2 Door Sedan
53 – SX-4 2 Door Liftback
56 – Kammback 2 Door Sedan

UNIT BODY/TRIM PLATE

Located on the left door and contains: Body Number, Model Number, Trim Number, Paint Code and Car Building Sequence Number.

FIGURE 1-6 American Motors Company vehicle identification numbers. *(Courtesy of Mitchell Information Services, Inc.)*

PAINT COLOR CODE LOCATIONS

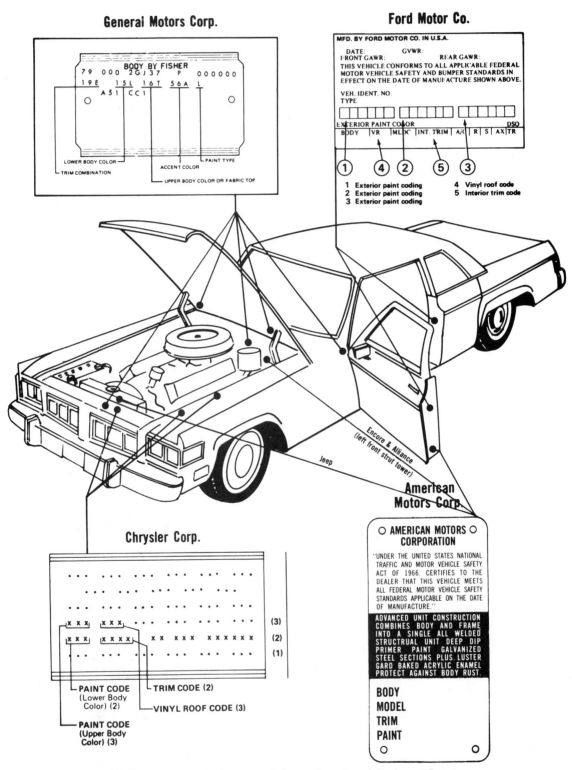

General Motors Corp.

BODY BY FISHER
79 000 2GJ37 P 000000
19 E 15L 16T 56A L
A 51 CC 1

LOWER BODY COLOR
TRIM COMBINATION
ACCENT COLOR
PAINT TYPE
UPPER BODY COLOR OR FABRIC TOP

Ford Motor Co.

MFD. BY FORD MOTOR CO. IN U.S.A.
DATE: GVWR:
FRONT GAWR: REAR GAWR:
THIS VEHICLE CONFORMS TO ALL APPLICABLE FEDERAL
MOTOR VEHICLE SAFETY AND BUMPER STANDARDS IN
EFFECT ON THE DATE OF MANUFACTURE SHOWN ABOVE.

VEH. IDENT. NO.
TYPE

EXTERIOR PAINT COLOR   DSO
BODY | VR | ML | DC | INT. TRIM | A/C | R | S | AX | TR

① ④ ② ⑤ ③

1 Exterior paint coding   4 Vinyl roof code
2 Exterior paint coding   5 Interior trim code
3 Exterior paint coding

Encore & Alliance
(left front strut tower)

Jeep

American Motors Corp

Chrysler Corp.

(3)
(2)
(1)

PAINT CODE
(Lower Body
Color) (2)
TRIM CODE (2)
VINYL ROOF CODE (3)
PAINT CODE
(Upper Body
Color) (3)

○ AMERICAN MOTORS ○
CORPORATION

"UNDER THE UNITED STATES NATIONAL
TRAFFIC AND MOTOR VEHICLE SAFETY
ACT OF 1966. CERTIFIES TO THE
DEALER THAT THIS VEHICLE MEETS
ALL FEDERAL MOTOR VEHICLE SAFETY
STANDARDS APPLICABLE ON THE DATE
OF MANUFACTURE."

ADVANCED UNIT CONSTRUCTION
COMBINES BODY AND FRAME
INTO A SINGLE ALL WELDED
STRUCTRUAL UNIT DEEP DIP
PRIMER PAINT GALVANIZED
STEEL SECTIONS PLUS LUSTER
GARD BAKED ACRYLIC ENAMEL
PROTECT AGAINST BODY RUST.

BODY
MODEL
TRIM
PAINT

FIGURE 1–7 Manufacturers information plate location. *(Courtesy of Sherwin-Williams Automotive Finishes, Inc./Finitions Automobile Sherwin-Williams, Inc.)*

1986 General Motors Service Parts Identification Label

In 1986 GM will have a Service parts Identification Label that will identify the color used on the various models. The color will be identified by the regular Color Code and a Fisher "WA" part Number. In addition it will also indicate the type of paint on the vehicle such as indicated by the sample sticker shown here. Location of stickers vary depending upon the model. The following represents the various Body Styles and the location of the sticker.

Service Parts Identification   **DO NOT REMOVE**

1G1AZ3799ER157148
ARL A02 A65 B6Y B9A B9K C60 D1B D35 E5Z E6E E9Z FLT GU1 JM7
K19 K64 LC3 MX1 M31 NA5 NB1 QMX VK3 VC2 VY1 VY4 V73 Y19 ZJ7
6BJ 62L 62U 67D 671 679 7BJ 8HJ 9HJ

DIS. LACQUER WA-L8240 U8240

PRINTED IN U S A   PART NO. 14065987

LABEL LOCATIONS

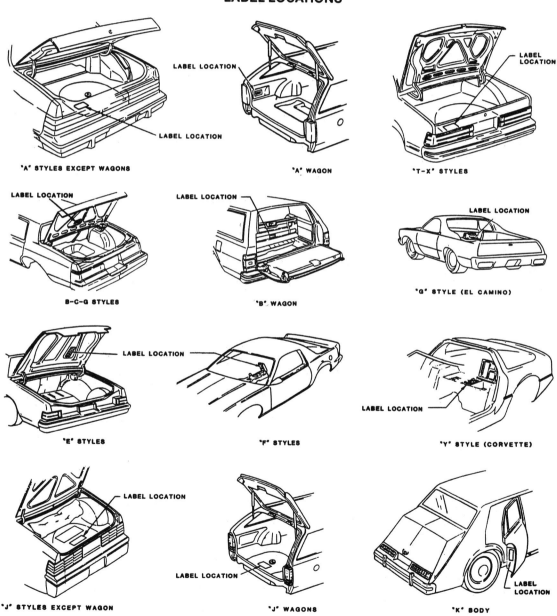

FIGURE 1–8 General Motors paint information plate location. *(Courtesy of Sherwin-Williams Automotive Finishes, Inc./Finitions Automobile Sherwin-Williams, Inc.)*

EUROPEAN IMPORT

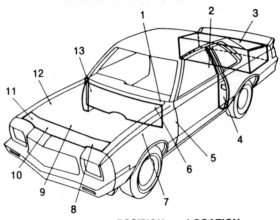

MODEL	POSITION	LOCATION
ALFA ROMEO	3	Luggage Compartment – Underside
AUDI	3	Luggage Compartment – Underside
BMW	12	Wheelhouse – Right Side
CAPRI	12	Wheelhouse – Right Side
FIAT Strada	7	Engine Compartment – Left Side
131/Brava	11	Radiator Support – Right Side
X1/9	3	Luggage Compartment – Underside
124/128	–	Not Available
FIESTA 1978-79	11	Radiator Support – Right Side
1980	13	Firewall – Right Side
JAGUAR	4	Front Door – Left Side, Rear Face
	9	Engine Compartment – Front
LANCIA	4	Lock Pillar – Left Side
	5	Hinge Pillar – Left Side
	9	Engine Compartment – Front
MERCEDES-BENZ exc	10	Radiator Support – Center
250/280SL	7	Wheelhouse – Left Side
MG	–	Refer to Owner's Manual
PEUGEOT	7	Engine Compartment – Left Side
PORSCHE 911/912	3	Engine Compartment – Rear XMember
	5	Hinge Pillar – Left Side
924	7	Engine Compartment – Left Side
	5	Hinge Pillar – Left Side
928	4	Lock Pillar – Left Side
944	7	Engine Compartment – Left Side
RENAULT Le Car	12	Wheelhouse – Right Side
18i	7	Shock Tower – Left Side
R15/R17	7	Wheelhouse – Left Side
R12	7	Wheelhouse – Left Side
Fuego	7	Shock Tower – Left Side
ROVER	–	Not Available
SAAB 900	10	Engine Compartment – Front
	12	Wheelhouse – Right Side
99	7	Wheelhouse – Left Side
TRIUMPH	6	Firewall – Left Side
VOLKSWAGEN Scirocco	3	Luggage Compartment – Rear Panel
Rabbit exc	3	Luggage Compartment – Floor Panel
Convertible	3	Luggage Compartment – Underside
	3	Cross Panel Behind Seat – Left Side
Pickup	2	Cab Panel – Behind Driver Seat
Super Beetle	10	Behind Spare Tire
Bug	5	Hinge Pillar – Left Side
Vanagon	1	Dashboard – Under Left Side
Dasher	3	Luggage Compartment – Floor Panel
Jetta	3	Luggage Compartment – Rear Panel
Quantum	3	Luggage Compartment – Floor Panel
VOLVO 1975-80	10	Radiator Support – Center
	13	Firewall – Right Side
1981-85	12	Wheelhouse – Right Side

FIGURE 1–9 European import paint location plate. *(Courtesy of Mitchell Information Services, Inc.)*

JAPANESE IMPORT

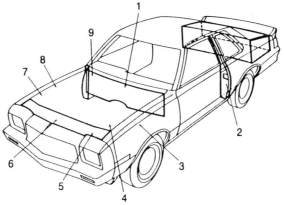

MODEL		POSITION	LOCATION
ARROW		5	Radiator Support – Left Side
CHALLENGER 1978-82		5	Radiator Support – Left Side
	1983	4	Hood – Left Underside
CHAMP		3	Fender Apron – Left Side
CONQUEST		1	Engine Compartment – Center
COLT 1974-82		3	Fender Apron – Left Side
	1983-84	5	Radiator Support – Left Side
COLT VISTA		4	Hood – Left Underside
COURIER		2	Lock Pillar – Left Side
		5	Radiator Support – Left Side
		8	Fender Apron – Right Side
DATSUN/NISSAN		6	Radiator Support – Center
		8	Fender Apron – Right Side
		9	Engine Compartment – Right Side
DODGE D50		5	Radiator Support – Left Side
HONDA		2	Lock Pillar – Left Side
ISUZU		6	Radiator Support – Center
LUV 1972-80		1	Engine Compartment – Center
	1981-82	6	Radiator Support – Center
MAZDA		5	Radiator Support – Left Side
		8	Fender Apron – Right Side
		9	Engine Compartment – Right Side
MITSUBISHI Starion		1	Engine Compartment – Center
Montero/Pickup		5	Radiator Support – Left Side
Cordia/Tredia		7	Fender Apron – Right Side
OPEL		–	Not Available
SAPPORO 1978-82		5	Radiator Support – Left Side
	1983	4	Hood – Left Underside
SUBARU		6	Radiator Support – Center
TOYOTA Passenger		1	Engine Compartment – Center
Truck		7	Fender Apron – Right Side

FIGURE 1-10 Japanese import paint location plate. *(Courtesy of Mitchell Information Services, Inc.)*

upper left side of the instrument panel, which is visible through the windshield (Figs. 1-1, 1-3, 1-5, and 1-6). This is true for all manufacturers.

The body code plate is located usually on the left front fender side shield or the upper radiator support. The body code plate gives the information that the painter needs to order the paint required for the body paint, vinyl roof, and interior trim code (Figs. 1-2, 1-7, and 1-8).

The other information that the painter requires is usually found on the left front door under the lock or on the door lock pillar (Fig. 1-4).

1-5 COLOR CHARTS AND CHOOSING COLORS FROM THE CODE

When the painter checks the body plate for the paint job code, he or she must be able to determine what these codes mean. For example, Fig. 1-7 from General Motors shows 19E as the trim combination, 15L is the color of the lower body section, 16T is the upper body color or the fabric top, 56A is the accent color, and L shows that it is lacquer. If the letter E is shown as the paint type, it is acrylic enamel, and the letter W shows that a waterborne acrylic enamel was used. Other manufacturers use a similar system. All that is needed is to study the body code plate on these vehicles.

A trouble light or flashlight is sometimes needed to find these body plates. Often a rag is needed to clean the body plate to make it legible. Once the numbered code is found, write it on a piece of paper with the make and year of the vehicle. The painter can then check the proper chart in the color code book and find the proper color number for the particular paint job. Figures 1–11 and 1–12 are typical color sample sheets as received from paint manufacturers.

Paint manufacturers supply color charts every year as new vehicles appear in dealer lots. By using the color charts, a painter can readily identify (Fig. 1–13) and communicate with the jobber as to the availability of the particular color required or the need to mix it on the mixing system in the shop. Color code books cover all the manufacturer's vehicles, whether made in North America, Europe, Japan, or South Korea. It is wise to have a binder for North American production of automobiles and trucks and separate binders for imports. Jobbers usually supply color code books to their customers at no cost.

The color code number should be checked and the color identified; the color is the proper one if the sample on the color chip matches the finish on the vehicle. Sometimes the body plate is not present on the vehicle or not legible; the painter should then be very careful when selecting the proper paint code number. Some vehicles have been repainted a different color, and unless a paint change number or color sticker is on the vehicle where it is readily accessible (Fig. 1–14), it can be very difficult and frustrating to find the proper color. The painter will have to go from page to page until he or she finds a color that matches the color on the vehicle. It may be necessary at times to find an approximate color and tint it to match.

Once the color number has been selected, the painter must find the color either in a color code paint formula book or use a microfiche on a projector (Figs. 1–15 and 1–16).

There is a difference between the paint used on the outside and on the inside of the car. Outside colors are glossy, and for the interior they are flat in driver-vision areas and usually semigloss for the other areas. These color finishes should always be used so that they match the vehicle's inside colors; they should never be interchanged. The flat colors are used to prevent glare in the driver's vision areas. Some manufacturers do not use color chips to identify interior colors; they use trim code, color name, and stock number.

If it is impossible to obtain the trim color, it is possible to flatten the color by adding a flattening compound to the color. The painter should then test spray the color and let it dry; then the true amount of gloss will be seen. A different amount of flattening additive must be used for lacquer or enamel; read the directions on the can label.

Before ordering or mixing the paint required for a particular job, it is prudent on the painter's part to double-check the code number. Then the painter must figure out how much paint is required and of what type. If the painter makes an error in color number, the paint will be the wrong color and therefore a loss for the shop unless it is a factory-packaged color. Jobbers will not take back a mix of paint if the painter orders the wrong code; therefore, the shop loses the money it costs to mix the paint.

Once the paint code number has been verified, the painter can mix the paint in the paint shop mixing system (Fig. 1–17).

1–6 SHOP SAFETY RULES

1. A well-ventilated, safe, and clean shop will keep the skilled personnel healthy; they are the most precious assets.

2. Well-lighted and neat working areas encourage and improve the performance of employees.

3. When spray painting, always wear a respirator of the appropriate type for the materials used, especially when using isocyanates.

4. The shop should be kept free from debris, rags, and old parts as a fire could be a calamity.

5. All paint and solvents should be stored in approved cabinets or in storage rooms that have explosion-proof lights and adequate ventilation.

6. Never more than a day's supply of paint materials should be outside of an approved storage area.

7. All solvent drums must be grounded and bonded to containers while being used.

8. High-flash paint solvents should always be used when possible.

9. NO SMOKING signs should always be posted in spray areas or any other critical area. Any spray area should be 20 feet or 7 meters from flames, electric motors, sparks, or any other ignition source. All spray areas should be free of hot surfaces, and any lamps in the spray area should be enclosed and guarded. Any electrical drying apparatus must be properly grounded and vented.

General Motors Corp. 1986 Colors
Buick • Cadillac • Chevrolet • Corvette • Oldsmobile • Pontiac

EXTERIOR (AL) Currently available Factory Packaged in Acrylic Lacquer (34 prefix)
(AE) Currently available Factory Packaged in Acrylic Enamel (35 prefix)

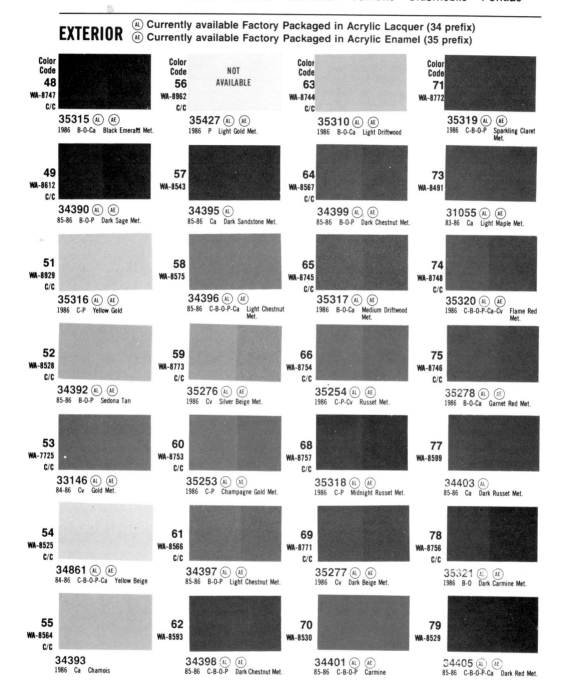

Color Code 48 WA-8747 C/C	Color Code 56 WA-8962 C/C NOT AVAILABLE	Color Code 63 WA-8744	Color Code 71 WA-8772
35315 (AL) (AE) 1986 B-O-Ca Black Emerald Met.	35427 (AL) (AE) 1986 P Light Gold Met.	35310 (AL) (AE) 1986 B-O-Ca Light Driftwood	35319 (AL) (AE) 1986 C-B-O-P Sparkling Claret Met.
49 WA-8612 C/C	57 WA-8543	64 WA-8567 C/C	73 WA-8491
34390 (AL) (AE) 85-86 B-O-P Dark Sage Met.	34395 (AL) 85-86 Ca Dark Sandstone Met.	34399 (AL) (AE) 85-86 B-O-P Dark Chestnut Met.	31055 (AL) (AE) 83-86 Ca Light Maple Met.
51 WA-8929 C/C	58 WA-8575	65 WA-8745 C/C	74 WA-8748 C/C
35316 (AL) (AE) 1986 C-P Yellow Gold	34396 (AL) (AE) 85-86 C-B-O-P-Ca Light Chestnut Met.	35317 (AL) (AE) 1986 B-O-Ca Medium Driftwood Met.	35320 (AL) (AE) 1986 C-B-O-P-Ca-Cv Flame Red Met.
52 WA-8528 C/C	59 WA-8773 C/C	66 WA-8754 C/C	75 WA-8746 C/C
34392 (AL) (AE) 85-86 B-O-P Sedona Tan	35276 (AL) (AE) 1986 Cv Silver Beige Met.	35254 (AL) (AE) 1986 C-P-Cv Russet Met.	35278 (AL) (AE) 1986 B-O-Ca Garnet Red Met.
53 WA-7725 C/C	60 WA-8753 C/C	68 WA-8757 C/C	77 WA-8599
33146 (AL) (AE) 84-86 Cv Gold Met.	35253 (AL) (AE) 1986 C-P Champagne Gold Met.	35318 (AL) (AE) 1986 C-P Midnight Russet Met.	34403 (AL) 85-86 Ca Dark Russet Met.
54 WA-8525 C/C	61 WA-8566 C/C	69 WA-8771 C/C	78 WA-8756 C/C
34861 (AL) (AE) 84-86 C-B-O-P-Ca Yellow Beige	34397 (AL) (AE) 85-86 B-O-P Light Chestnut Met.	35277 (AL) (AE) 1986 Cv Dark Beige Met.	35321 (AL) (AE) 1986 B-O Dark Carmine Met.
55 WA-8564 C/C	62 WA-8593	70 WA-8530	79 WA-8529
34393 1986 Ca Chamois	34398 (AL) (AE) 85-86 C-B-O-P Dark Chestnut Met.	34401 (AL) (AE) 85-86 C-B-O-P Carmine	34405 (AL) (AE) 85-86 C-B-O-P-Ca Dark Red Met.

Most colors available via the Intermix System in Enamel **33**- prefix: Acrylic Lacquer **34**- prefix: Acrylic Enamel **35**- prefix.
C/C Clear Coat Finish **C**-Chevrolet **B**-Buick **O**-Oldsmobile **P**-Pontiac **Ca**-Cadillac **Cv**-Corvette
Check microfiche for formula and cost suffix.

FIGURE 1–11 General Motors exterior colors. *(Courtesy of Sherwin-Williams Automotive Finishes, Inc./Finitions Automobile Sherwin-Williams, Inc.)*

General Motors Corp. 1986 Colors

Buick • Cadillac • Chevrolet • Corvette • Oldsmobile • Pontiac

INTERIOR

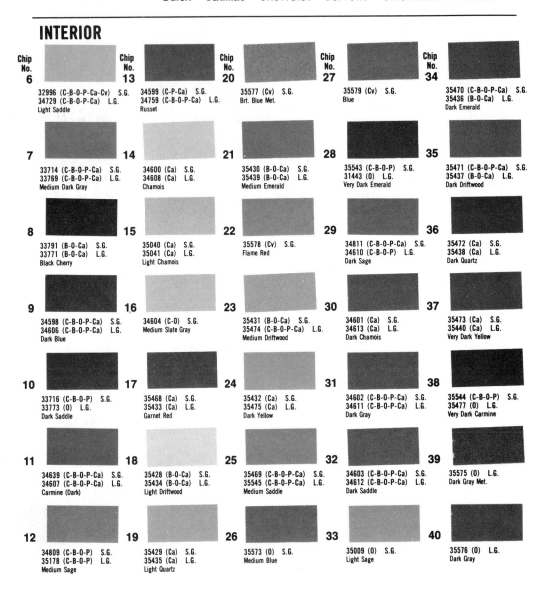

Chip No. 6	Chip No. 13	Chip No. 20	Chip No. 27	Chip No. 34
32996 (C-B-O-P-Ca-Cv) S.G. 34729 (C-B-O-P-Ca) L.G. Light Saddle	34599 (C-P-Ca) S.G. 34759 (C-B-O-P-Ca) L.G. Russet	35577 (Cv) S.G. Brt. Blue Met.	35579 (Cv) S.G. Blue	35470 (C-B-O-P-Ca) S.G. 35436 (B-O-Ca) L.G. Dark Emerald
7 33714 (C-B-O-P-Ca) S.G. 33769 (C-B-O-P-Ca) L.G. Medium Dark Gray	**14** 34600 (Ca) S.G. 34608 (Ca) L.G. Chamois	**21** 35430 (B-O-Ca) S.G. 35439 (B-O-Ca) L.G. Medium Emerald	**28** 35543 (C-B-O-P) S.G. 31443 (O) L.G. Very Dark Emerald	**35** 35471 (C-B-O-P-Ca) S.G. 35437 (B-O-Ca) L.G. Dark Driftwood
8 33791 (B-O-Ca) S.G. 33771 (B-O-Ca) L.G. Black Cherry	**15** 35040 (Ca) S.G. 35041 (Ca) L.G. Light Chamois	**22** 35578 (Cv) S.G. Flame Red	**29** 34811 (C-B-O-P-Ca) S.G. 34610 (C-B-O-P) L.G. Dark Sage	**36** 35472 (Ca) S.G. 35438 (Ca) L.G. Dark Quartz
9 34598 (C-B-O-P-Ca) S.G. 34606 (C-B-O-P-Ca) L.G. Dark Blue	**16** 34604 (C-O) S.G. Medium Slate Gray	**23** 35431 (B-O-Ca) S.G. 35474 (C-B-O-P-Ca) L.G. Medium Driftwood	**30** 34601 (Ca) S.G. 34613 (Ca) L.G. Dark Chamois	**37** 35473 (Ca) S.G. 35440 (Ca) L.G. Very Dark Yellow
10 33716 (C-B-O-P) S.G. 33773 (O) L.G. Dark Saddle	**17** 35468 (Ca) S.G. 35433 (Ca) L.G. Garnet Red	**24** 35432 (Ca) S.G. 35475 (Ca) L.G. Dark Yellow	**31** 34602 (C-B-O-P-Ca) S.G. 34611 (C-B-O-P-Ca) L.G. Dark Gray	**38** 35544 (C-B-O-P) S.G. 35477 (O) L.G. Very Dark Carmine
11 34639 (C-B-O-P-Ca) S.G. 34607 (C-B-O-P-Ca) L.G. Carmine (Dark)	**18** 35428 (B-O-Ca) S.G. 35434 (B-O-Ca) L.G. Light Driftwood	**25** 35469 (C-B-O-P-Ca) S.G. 35545 (C-B-O-P-Ca) L.G. Medium Saddle	**32** 34603 (C-B-O-P-Ca) S.G. 34612 (C-B-O-P-Ca) L.G. Dark Saddle	**39** 35575 (O) L.G. Dark Gray Met.
12 34809 (C-B-O-P) S.G. 35178 (C-B-O-P) L.G. Medium Sage	**19** 35429 (Ca) S.G. 35435 (Ca) L.G. Light Quartz	**26** 35573 (O) S.G. Medium Blue	**33** 35009 (O) S.G. Light Sage	**40** 35576 (O) L.G. Dark Gray

Most colors available via the Intermix System in Enamel **33**- prefix;   Acrylic Lacquer **34**- prefix;   Acrylic Enamel **35**- prefix.
C/C Clear Coat Finish   **C**-Chevrolet   **B**-Buick   **O**-Oldsmobile   **P**-Pontiac   **Ca**-Cadillac   **Cv**-Corvette
Check microfiche for formula and cost suffix.   **S.G.**-Semi-Gloss   **L.G.**-Low Gloss

FIGURE 1–12   General Motors interior colors. *(Courtesy of Sherwin-Williams Automotive Finishes, Inc./Finitions Automobile Sherwin-Williams, Inc.)*

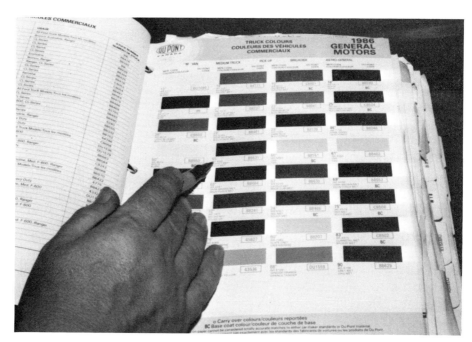

FIGURE 1–13 Choosing the color by code.

FIGURE 1–14 Change of color sticker.

FIGURE 1–15 Microfiche projector.

MIX BASE		$\frac{1}{8}$ GAL.	$\frac{1}{4}$ GAL.	$\frac{1}{2}$ GAL.	$\frac{3}{4}$ GAL.	1 GAL.
758S	Drier	22	44	88	132	176
723A	Violet	29	58	116	174	232
705A	Black	62	124	248	372	496
724A	Blue	93	186	372	558	744
710A	Med. alum.	458	916	1832	2748	3664

B8503A2C
GROUP: 02 SUFFIX: 0830 DATE: 85-03-13-3C

MAKE: 1985 GM

COLOR: LT. BLUE MET. 25

LUCITE B8503L
DULUX D8503D

NOTE: BEST POSSIBLE MATCH

FIGURE 1-16 Paint formula. *(Courtesy of Du Pont Canada)*

(a)

(b)

FIGURE 1-17 (a) Mixing system. (b) Mixing system with scale.

10. Adequate ventilation must be provided to remove any solvent fumes.

11. The right type of fire extinguishers must be placed in strategic locations, and they should be checked periodically to be sure they work.

12. Care should be used to prevent spilling of solvents or liquids.

13. Hands should always be washed before eating or smoking.

14. Always read directions on labels to find the safe way of using products and for first aid instructions.

15. Aisles and walkways should be kept free of tools, creepers, or any other objects that might cause somebody to trip or stumble.

16. All floors should be kept clean; any paint, oil, or other materials should be cleaned up immediately, and any holes in the floor should be repaired.

17. Used cloth or paper towels should be stored in a covered container and then removed from the shop at day's end and stored in a proper garbage bin or tank.

18. Always wear safety goggles to protect the eyes from flying objects, particles, and splashing liquids.

19. Always wear the appropriate respirator or dust filter masks when painting, machine sanding, or sandblasting. These respirators or dust filters protect your lungs from the harmful effects of solvents, dust, and fine silica sand dust.

20. If at all possible, wear safety shoes; they have a metal insert that prevents injuries to the toes from falling objects.

21. Always place safety stands under the axles of a vehicle that is jacked up and block the wheels.

REVIEW QUESTIONS

1-1. What are the duties of a qualified painter?

1-2. What special knowledge does a painter require?

1-3. How does a paint shop operate?

1-4. What type of paint system is used in Japan?

1-5. What type of paint system is used in Europe?

1-6. What type of paint system is used by Chrysler?

1-7. What type of paint system is used by General Motors?

1-8. What digit on the vehicle identification plate signifies the year on a Ford-manufactured vehicle?

1-9. Where is the paint code found on a vehicle built by General Motors?

CHAPTER TWO

Spray Booths and Equipment

SAFETY HINTS

When spray painting, always wear a respirator of the appropriate type for the materials used, especially when using isocyanates.

NO SMOKING signs should always be posted in spray areas or any other critical area. Any spray area should be 20 feet or 7 meters from flames, electric motors, sparks, or any other ignition source. All spray areas should be free of hot surfaces, and any lamps in the spray area should be enclosed and guarded. Any electrical drying apparatus must be properly grounded and vented.

The right type of fire extinguishers must be placed in strategic locations, and they should be checked periodically to be sure they work.

2-1 SPRAY BOOTHS

A spray booth is an investment that will pay many dividends, which include a clean environment for painting, increased productivity, and a safe working environment for the painter. Many factors are used to determine what type of spray booth is required. These include the type of work that will be done in them, the type of materials used in the spraying operation, and the different code requirements regarding air velocity, air replacement, exhaust stacks, and lighting.

Basically, the booths used are the water-wash and the paint-arrestor type (Figs. 2–1 and 2–2). Water-wash booths use a type of air washing action to trap the paint particles. A water-wash booth delivers cleaner air to the atmosphere, and thus less pollution, as well as a constant air velocity that results in a better ventilation system.

A booth that uses disposable paint-arrestor filters is usually suited for limited or interrupted spray operations, such as a refinish shop where paint use is moderate. Moderate consumption would include minimal overspray, and the amount of paint being sprayed would not exceed 2 gallons per hour. These booths work best when the coating used does not dry too rapidly. If the materials sprayed can react chemically with each other, a water-wash system must be used.

The paint-arrestor type of booth removes airborne paint particles from the spray booth exhaust air by using a disposable paint-arrestor filter. These filters must be of a good quality and must be changed as required; otherwise they choke off the air to the exhaust fan. In a booth

with interlocks, a pressure differential switch shuts off the compressed air when insufficient air is going up the stack. The OSHA code requires that filters be examined after each period of use, and if any clogged filters are present, they must be discarded and replaced immediately.

The OSHA code also requires that the clogged filters must be removed and placed in a water-filled container or a safe detached location and disposed of at the end of the day's work. In some areas a draft gauge must be installed to meet code requirements (Fig. 2–3). This draft gauge or manometer should be installed on the side of the booth; the pilot tube is placed on the intake side and the other tube on the exhaust side of the filter stack to indicate there is a pressure differential or drop across the filter bank. After new filters are installed, a reading should be taken on the manometer and noted. The filter media will need replacement when a ½-in. or 0.635-mm increase is indicated on the manometer. This is caused by the air movement through the filters diminishing due to restricted passages in the filter media.

The paint-arrestor filters are made from a fire-retardant treated paper, and the holes are formed into a diamond-shaped configuration. Several thicknesses of paper are sewed together; therefore, as air flows through the filter media it is forced to move back and forth and sheds the paint particles on the filter media through centrifugal force. The sizes of the holes in the first sheet of paper on the filter are the largest, and they get progressively smaller toward the back of the filter.

Usually two filters are used in each frame present in the filter bank exhaust; they are usually placed one

FIGURE 2-1 Paint-arrestor filter bank used in cross-draft spray booth.

against the other with the small holes toward the inside of the exhaust filter bank (Fig. 2-4). A grid is used on the inside to help hold and prevent the filter from collapsing, and one grid is on the outside to hold the filters in place. The two most common sizes are 1 × 20 × 25 in. (2.5 × 51 × 63 cm) or 1 × 20 × 20 in. (2.5 × 51 × 51 cm).

When the filters need to be changed (Fig. 2-5), the grid is removed, the filters are removed, a new filter is inserted at the back, the filter that was on the back is

FIGURE 2-2 Paint-arrestor filter bank used in down-draft spray booth.

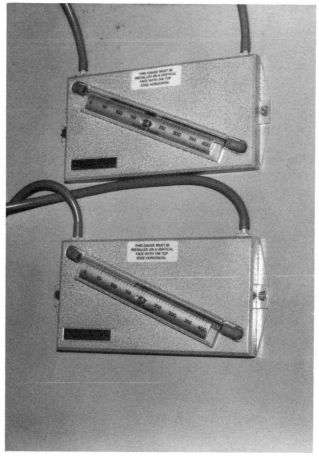

FIGURE 2-3 Dual draft gauge used in down-draft spray booths.

installed on the front, and the grid is replaced. The reason that they are changed in this fashion is that the greater portion of the paint is on the side facing the inside of the booth.

This method of changing the filters cuts the cost in half and is still very effective in cleaning the air. The filter bank area must be cleaned of all residue dried paint before completing the filter change. An accumulation of dried paint inside the filter bank could cause spontaneous combustion if the right conditions were present. The old filters must be disposed of according to code in a safe and appropriate manner.

The paint-arrestor-type spray booth is less expensive to buy, is lighter, and is easier to install. In many states, provinces, and cities, it is required by code that the booths be equipped with a sprinkler system of sufficient capacity and with proper location of sprinkler heads. The electric and building codes must also be followed, and consulting the local authorities can save a purchaser or contractor many headaches as well as money. These authorities can help advise as to what equipment is necessary, what electrical and fire preven-

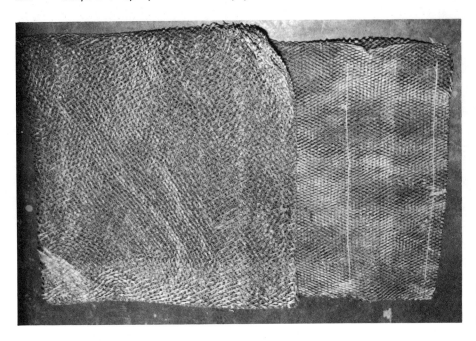

FIGURE 2-4   Filter media shown with opposite sides, showing the different size holes in the material.

tion codes to follow, and the location of the spray booth in the paint shop. These regulations are usually in line with the National Fire Protection Association (NFPA) and the Occupational Safety and Health Act (OSHA) in the United States. In Canada they must meet Canadian Standards approval (CSA).

Many cross-draft booths (Fig. 2-6) are used in North America, and only lately have changes been made to this design. One change is the semi-down draft (Fig. 2-7) in which the air is drawn from the upper levels of the shop. This air is usually cleaner and is pulled through filters located in a plenum on the roof of the spray booth. This air plenum is equipped with a baffle so that the air is distributed evenly and smoothly over the vehicle.

In the cross-draft spray booth the air is drawn through filters installed in the doors. The air travels horizontally along the vehicle and is exhausted by an exhaust fan. Figure 2-6 shows a typical cross-draft spray booth.

These booths leave a lot to be desired, especially since the air velocity must be adequate to remove paint fumes and provide a safe working environment, but yet

FIGURE 2-5   Changing the filters.

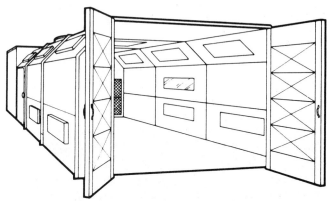

FIGURE 2-6   Cross-draft spray booth. *(Courtesy of DeVilbiss Canada Ltd.)*

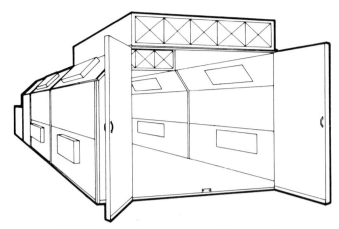

FIGURE 2–7 Semi-down-draft booth. *(Courtesy of DeVilbiss Canada Ltd.)*

FIGURE 2–8 Intake door air filters.

low enough to allow for a good paint job. OSHA and NFPA require a design velocity of 100 feet per minute (FPM) or 30.48 meters per minute (MPM).

The speed at which this air moves makes it difficult for the intake air filters to remove all the dust that is pulled into the booth by the exhaust fan in a negative pressure booth. The intake air filters are a self-sealing type and are designed to be efficient at an air velocity of 125 FPM (38 MPM) at 75°F or 21.1°C (Fig. 2–8). They are made from a soft, pliable polyester fabric coated with a special adhesive material to provide superior dust-trapping capabilities. They are held in a built-in reinforcing frame without a perforated metal facing, which would reduce air flow.

The life expectancy of the intake filters varies according to the amount of air going through them and the temperature of the air. The higher the velocity and temperature, the quicker the filter material will break down and start shedding fibers. Therefore, a program suited to the particular shop conditions must be followed as to when these filters have to be replaced.

The filters are provided to give a smooth, even flow of clean air, which in turn envelopes the vehicle being painted and carries away spray fumes and evaporating solvents. These filters are available in different sizes, but the most popular sizes are 2 × 20 × 20 in. (5 × 51 × 51 cm) or 2 × 20 × 48 in. (5 × 51 × 122 cm).

In recent years a new type of booth has been used in North America. It is called a down-draft spray booth (Fig. 2–9) and was developed in Europe. The down-draft spray booth is designed on the same principle as automotive production line down-draft booths. The replacement air passes through filters in the ceiling (Fig. 2–9b) and flows around the vehicle and through gratings in the floor (Fig. 2–10).

This varies from conventional spray booths where the air flow is from one end to the other across the vehicle. The air flow pulls the overspray down and away from the painter into the pit instead of along the length of the vehicle being sprayed. This minimizes the chance of overspray and contaminants collecting on a freshly painted vehicle and spoiling the finish. This type of spray booth gives superior quality to the painted vehicle and draws the overspray away from the painter; it gives a finish comparable to an original factory finish. Due to the better filtration system and different air flow, it helps to eliminate the two major causes of unsatisfactory refinish jobs: airborne dirt and a bad painting environment.

A variation of the down-draft booth is the DeVilbiss Concept/Cure Spray booth (Fig. 2–11). This booth operates the same as a down-draft spray booth in the paint application phase. But after the spraying operation is completed, the painter does not have to move the vehicle for the curing stage. The curing stage is initiated by the painter by flipping a lever and then selecting the temperature and time.

The purging of the solvents from the booth atmosphere and changing the cycle to a high temperature air flow is automatically carried out by pre-programmed controls. The curing time varies from 20 to 30 minutes, which depends on the type of paint used

(a)

(b)

FIGURE 2-9 (a) Down-draft spray booth. *(Courtesy of De-Vilbiss Canada Ltd.)* (b) Filtration media for down-draft spray booth.

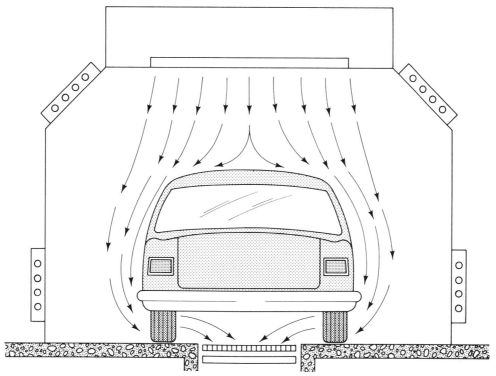

FIGURE 2-10 Air flow in a down-draft booth. *(Courtesy of De-Vilbiss Canada Ltd.)*

and the size of the vehicle. The booth controls are preset for each temperature and curing time to ensure consistent results.

The fresh air used is about 10% and is heated and mixed with recirculated air, maintaining a steady temperature without using an excessive amount of fuel. The air is filtered at all times; therefore, the car is not ex-

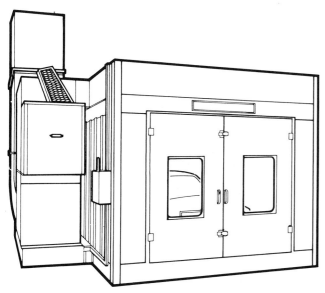

FIGURE 2-11 Concept cure spray booth. *(Courtesy of DeVilbiss Canada Ltd.)*

posed to any dust-laden air. Air flows through the spray booth in the same direction except that much less air flows when the booth is in the curing phase.

A spray booth should have walls that are smooth; this will eliminate dust clinging to them. The booth should be fireproof and should have an unobstructed working area as well as an access door so that the painter can go to and from the spray booth without opening large doors. The spray booth must have a lighting system that provides enough intensity and uniformity to produce good working conditions. Fluorescent light fixtures are usually used as they provide more uniform illumination and are much more economical to operate than incandescent light fixtures providing the same level of illumination.

Booths installed in the United States are equipped with vaportight fluorescent lights. Booths installed in Canada are equipped with four-tube open-light-type fixtures. Explosion-proof lighting, switches, and interlock must also be provided to meet electrical codes as required.

OSHA Spray Booth Regulations

Booth Construction. Spray booths shall be substantially constructed of steel not thinner than No. 18 U.S. gauge, securely and rigidly.

Each spray booth having a frontal area larger than

9 square feet or 0.84 square meter shall have a metal deflector not less than 2½ in. or 6.4 cm deep installed at the upper outer edge of the booth over the opening.

Booth Installation.   The floor surface of a spray booth and operator's working area, if combustible, shall be covered with noncombustible material.

Space within the spray booth on the downstream and upstream sides of filters shall be protected with approved automatic sprinklers.

Electrical wiring and equipment shall conform to the provisions of this paragraph and shall otherwise be in accordance with subpart S or this part (National Electrical Code).

Spray booths shall be so installed that all portions are readily accessible for cleaning. A clear space of not less than 3 feet or 91 cm on all sides shall be kept free from storage or combustible construction.

Illumination Regulations.   When spraying areas are illuminated through glass panels or other transparent materials, only fixed lighting units shall be used as a source of illumination. Panels shall effectively isolate the spraying area from the area in which the lighting unit is located, and shall be of a noncombustible material of such nature or so protected that breakage will be unlikely.

Portable electric lamps shall not be used in any spraying area during spraying operation.

The exhaust stack is required to ventilate the booth to the outside and this stack must be of the same size and diameter as the fan. The exhaust stack should discharge vertically to provide adequate exhaust air flow and must be high enough to meet the code. The exhaust stack must be built with sheet metal of sufficient gauge thickness to meet the code. When an exhaust stack is run horizontally through a side wall, a strong wind could drastically reduce the exhaust-air velocity in the booth.

Air Exhaust Regulations.   The average air velocity over the open face of the booth (or booth cross section during spraying operations) shall not be less than 100 linear feet per minute or 30.5 meters per minute. Visible gauges or audible alarm or pressure-activated devices shall be installed to indicate or ensure that the required air velocity is maintained.

Mechanical ventilation shall be kept in operation at all times while spraying operations are being conducted and for a sufficient time thereafter to allow vapors from drying coated articles and drying finishing material to be exhausted.

Exhaust ducts shall be constructed of steel and shall be substantially supported. If exhaust ducts without dampers are installed, they shall be maintained so

TABLE 2-1

Diameter	U.S. Gauge No.
Up to 8 in. (20 cm) inclusive	24
Over 8 in. to 18 in. (20 to 46 cm) inclusive	22
Over 18 in. to 30 in. (46 to 76 cm) inclusive	20
Over 80 in. or 203 cm	18

that they will be in full open position at all times the ventilating system is in operation. Exhaust ducts shall be protected against mechanical damage and have a clearance from unprotected combustible material of not less than 18 in. or 46 cm. Air exhaust from spray operations shall not be directed so that it will contaminate makeup air being introduced into the spraying area or other ventilating intakes, nor directed so as to create a nuisance. Air exhausted from spray operations shall not be recirculated.

Ducts shall be so constructed as to provide structural strength and stability at least equivalent to sheet metal of not less than the thicknesses shown in Table 2-1.

The proper type of fire extinguishers must be provided to meet fire prevention codes (Fig. 2-12).

In any new installation it is recommended and in some areas it is law that all new booths be provided with an air makeup unit that is capable of heating all replacement air used in the booth. Figure 2-13 shows a typical new installation, as well as the air movement inside the booth. The type of system shown is a positive

FIGURE 2-12   Fire extinguishers.

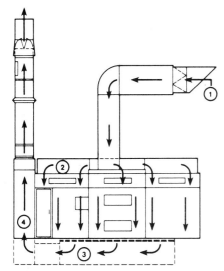

FIGURE 2-13 Typical new installation. *(Courtesy of DeVilbiss Canada Ltd.)*

type of installation; that is, slightly more air enters the booth than is exhausted according to code. This provides for a controlled environment, less dirt to contend with, and a controlled air temperature.

Air Replacement Regulations. Clean fresh air shall be supplied to a spray booth or room in quantities equal to the volume of air exhausted through the spray booth.

Means for heating makeup air to any spray booth shall be provided in all places where the outdoor tem-

perature may be expected to remain below 55°F (12.7°C) for appreciable periods of time.

As an alternative to an air-replacement system complying with the preceding, general heating of the building may be employed provided that all occupied parts of the building are maintained at not less than 65°F (18°C) when the exhaust system is in operation.

To have a proper air balance, the air replacement must be designed to deliver fresh, filtered, and heated air into a spray booth or building. To determine the air replacement requirements, multiply the exhaust fan rated capacity, in cubic feet per minute or cubic meters per minute, by 20. (This is based on three changes of air per hour: 60 min/3 = 20.) Using this calculation on a standard crossdraft booth, we would use 180,000–250,000 cubic feet of exhaust air, depending on the velocity code requirements governing the amount of air exhausted per minute. This can be found by multiplying the height × width of the booth times the velocity code requirements. OSHA and NFPA require manufacturers to design for velocities of 100 feet per minute or 31 meters per minute while spraying operations are being carried out. If the shop area (width × length × height) is less than the amount of cubic feet of air exhausted, an air-replacement unit should be installed. Figure 2–14 shows a typical air-replacement unit.

All booths have an exhaust fan that must be of sufficient capacity to meet the requirements of the NFPA and OSHA codes and must be installed to meet the National Electrical Code. These fans are designed in different models or sizes for different amounts of air

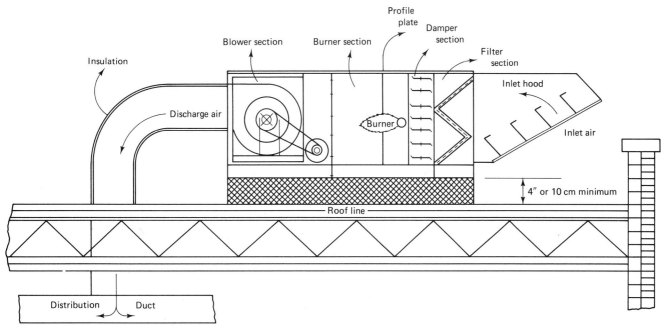

FIGURE 2-14 Typical air-replacement unit. *(Courtesy of DeVilbiss Canada Ltd.)*

FIGURE 2-15 Typical exhaust fan. *(Courtesy of DeVilbiss Canada Ltd.)*

is built to run up to a maximum rated speed and this should never be exceeded. If more exhaust is required, a larger fan must be installed. The blades should be checked periodically for cleanliness; if paint has accumulated on them, it should be cleaned off by gentle scraping, taking care not to damage the blades. Paint remover should not be used on aluminum blades as it could damage the metal if it is not neutralized properly.

Cleanliness. To keep the spray booth in a good operating shape when painting is to be done, it is important that the floor be swept and washed if required. The floor can be dampened to help keep dust problems to a minimum. The booth should be kept free of unrequired materials, such as parts, water buckets, brooms, squeegees, dust pans, and trash cans. Hoses should always be hung on hose hangers and not laid on the spray booth floor.

All filters, whether intake or exhaust, should be changed as required, and all door seals should be kept in good repair so that dust will not come through open gaps. The glass lenses, fluorescent fixtures, and spray booth walls should be kept in a clean condition.

movement. The fan has one-piece, nonsparking, balanced air-foil-type blades, which can move the large amounts of air required with minimum horsepower for high efficiency and economy (Fig. 2–15).

The fans are built to create the least possible amount of noise as they are running. If noise is a nuisance factor, a large fan turning slower will decrease noise decibels. Servicing is quite simple as the belts are enclosed in a housing that keeps them clean and prolongs their life for a long, smooth, operating time. The fan has permanently lubricated ball bearings that can be used in temperatures up to 225°F or 107°C. A fan

2-2 AIR COMPRESSORS

A compressor is the lifeline of the spray-finishing industry. It serves one main purpose; it compresses air, which operates sanding machines, cleaning and dusting equipment, and the spray gun. An air compressor is designed to supply air continuously at a determined pressure and a minimum volume in cubic feet (liters) per minute. There are two general types: the single-stage compressor and the two-stage compressor. The single-stage compressor can also be a diaphragm type (Fig. 2–16) or a piston type.

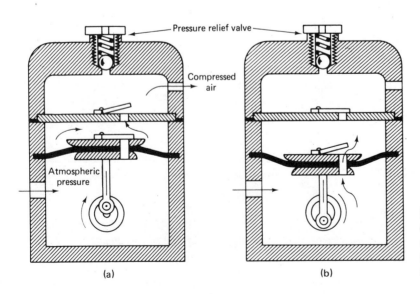

(a)   (b)

FIGURE 2-16 Diaphragm-type compressor. (a) Compression upstroke. (b) Intake downstroke. *(Courtesy of Binks Manufacturing Company of Canada Ltd.)*

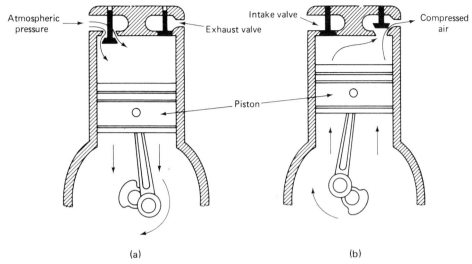

FIGURE 2-17 Piston-type air compressor (single stage). (a) Intake downstroke. (b) Compression upstroke. *(Courtesy of Binks Manufacturing Company of Canada Ltd.)*

Diaphragm-type compressors are small and portable and are used where a low volume of air is needed. The diaphragm in the compressor is moved up and down in the chamber by a rod attached to a reciprocating crankshaft and the diaphragm. This rod pulls and pushes the diaphragm up and down; this action causes the required valves to open and close at the appropriate time in each cycle to release compressed air into an air line. These compressors are oilless and therefore can be used to deliver clean air to an air-supplied mask as long as the equipment meets National Institute of Occupational Safety and Health (NIOSH) and Mining Enforcement and Safety Administration (MESA) requirements.

Piston-type compressors are available as either stationary units anchored to a floor or as a portable outfit that can be moved to the particular job. A piston-type compressor is much like an automotive engine that pulls outside air on the downstroke with the intake valve open. Then, as the crankshaft turns to go to the upstroke or compression stroke, the intake valve closes; then the exhaust valve opens as the piston comes up and releases compressed air to a cylinder or hose as required (Fig. 2-17).

Single-stage Compressor

A single-stage compressor can be of single or twin-cylinder design (Fig. 2-18). Air is drawn from the atmosphere and is compressed in one stage to final tank pressure. The transition of the air is from the atmosphere through the compressor aftercooler and then through the check valve to the supply tank. The single-stage compressor is generally used where a 100 psi or 690 kilopascal (kPa) maximum or less is desired. Single-stage compressors can be used at over 100 psi (690 kPa)

pressure, but their efficiency is considerably less and they are a great deal more costly to operate. As a rule, this type of compressor is approximately 60% efficient.

Two-stage Compressor

A two-stage compressor has a large cylinder where the air is compressed to an intermediate pressure and then delivered through an intercooler to a small cylinder (Fig. 2-19a). Here it is compressed to its final pressure and then delivered through an aftercooler to the air receiver.

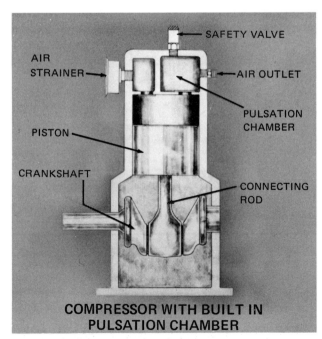

COMPRESSOR WITH BUILT IN PULSATION CHAMBER

FIGURE 2-18 Single-stage compressor. *(Courtesy of DeVilbiss Canada Ltd.)*

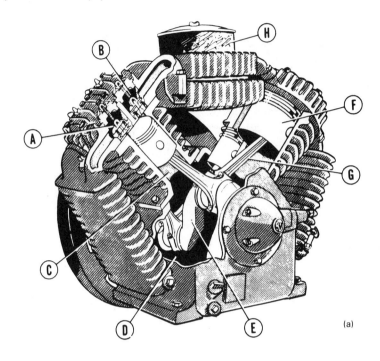

(a)

(b)

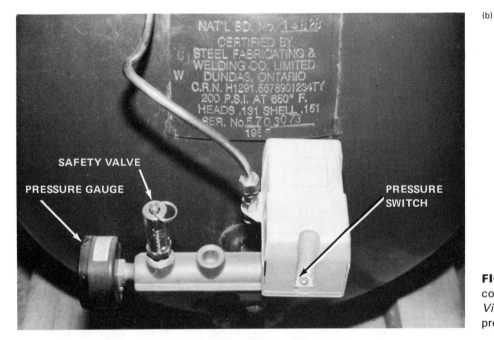

SAFETY VALVE

PRESSURE GAUGE

PRESSURE SWITCH

FIGURE 2-19 (a) Two-stage compressor. *(Courtesy of DeVilbiss Canada Ltd.)* (b) Automatic pressure switch.

Two stages are used when pressure exceeds 100 psi (690 kPa). The advantage of a two-stage compressor after 100 psi (690 kPa) is reached is higher efficiency; for example, at a working pressure of 200 psi (1380 kPa), 80% efficiency is achieved. The higher pressure also permits faster operation of tools, more air stored in the air receiver, and greater air delivery. The volumetric efficiencies of average single- and two-stage compressors are shown in Table 2-2.

Automatic Pressure Switch

Most compressors are equipped with an automatic pressure switch, which is a pneumatically controlled electric switch used for starting and stopping electric motors at required minimum and maximum pressures. These cut-in and cut-out switches are available for different requirements and are used when it is convenient and economical to start and stop the motor. A compressor that

TABLE 2–2

Volumetric efficiencies of air compressors

Single Stage	
Maximum working pressure in lb (kPa)	Efficiency (%)
75 (518)	75
100 (690)	70
125 (862)	65
150 (1035)	60
Two Stage	
100 (690)	80
125 (863)	80
150 (1035)	80
175 (1210)	80

runs intermittently for less than 60% of the time should be controlled with a pressure switch (Fig. 2–19b).

A compressor driven by an electric motor has a switch called a motor starter. This switch is designed to provide overload protection or other necessary electrical controls used for starting motors of different sizes. The design of the switch varies according to different motor sizes and current characteristics. The selection and installation of such switches should only be made by a qualified electrician.

Small motors are usually protected by fuses, and thermal overload relays are used on the starting devices on large motors. Relays with time-delay features are recommended so that the circuits will not be opened by overloads of short duration, which are not harmful enough to damage the motor. All compressors except the smaller types that operate from a standard wall socket should have overload protection.

Centrifugal Pressure Release Valve

Most compressors are equipped with a centrifugal pressure release device. This device allows the motor to start up and gain momentum before engaging the load or pumping air against pressure (Fig. 2–20). When the compressor slows down and as the crankshaft rotates more slowly, steel balls (Fig. 2–20a) move toward the center where they wedge against a cam surface, forcing the cam outward. This opens a valve (Fig. 2–20b) that bleeds air from the line connected to the check valve. With the air pressure bled from the pump and aftercooler, the compressor can start up free of back pressure until it gets up to speed. When normal speed is reached, the balls move out by centrifugal force, releasing the cam and closing the valve, and air is again pumped into the air receiver.

Selecting and Air Compressor

The two main types of air compressors can be driven electrically or by gas; they can be stationary or portable, horizontal or vertical, air-cooled or water-cooled. The type chosen depends on a particular shop's requirements.

In selecting an air compressor, the size is determined by listing all the equipment that is operated by air. How much air will each require, and how many hours will each piece operate in an 8-hour day? Then

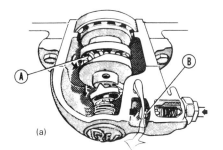

(a)

FIGURE 2–20 View of exploded CPR valve: (a) shows steel balls that are used to wedge against cam surface; (b) shows valve where air is released. *(Courtesy of DeVilbiss Canada Ltd.)*

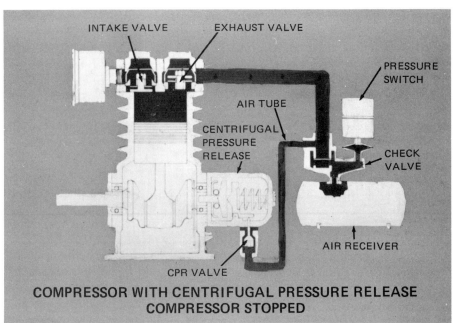

(b)

select a compressor that will cope with the air requirements with approximately 10% surplus.

The emphasis must be placed on cooling, because keeping a compressor operating as cool as possible is the major factor in determining efficiency. It is very important to select the right size so that the compressor will run intermittently throughout the day and therefore run cooler.

To find the proper size of compressor needed, consult Tables 2–3 and 2–4. When the total amount of air for the shop has been tabulated and the highest pressure used found, consult Tables 2–5 and 2–6 to find the right size of compressor.

OSHA Compressor Regulations

All new compressor receivers must be constructed in accordance with the 1968 edition of the ASME Boiler

TABLE 2–3

Operating consumption and air requirements chart (English units)

Device	Air pressure range (psi)	Average free-air consumption (CFM)
Air filter cleaner	70–100	3.0
Air hammer	70–100	16.5
Body polisher	70–100	2.0
Body sander	70–100	5.0
Brake tester	70–100	3.5
Carbon remover	70–100	3.0
Car rocker	120–150	5.75
Car washer	70–100	8.5
Dusting gun (blowgun)	70–100	2.5
Engine cleaner	70–100	5.0
Fender hammer	70–100	8.75
Grease gun (high pressure)	120–150	3.0
Hoist (1 ton)	70–100	1.0
Hydraulic lift[a]	145–175	5.25
Paint spray gun (production)	70–100	8.5
Paint spray gun (touch-up)	70–100	2.25
Pneumatic garage door	120–150	2.0
Radiator tester	70–100	1.0
Rim stripper	120–150	6.0
Spark plug cleaner	70–100	5.0
Spark plug tester	70–100	0.5
Spray gun (undercoating)	70–100	19.0
Spring oiler	70–100	3.75
Tire changer	120–150	1.0
Tire inflation line	120–150	1.5
Tire spreader	120–150	1.0
Transmission and differential flusher	70–100	3.0
Vacuum cleaner	120–150	6.5

Source: Courtesy of DeVilbiss Canada Ltd.
[a]For 8000 lb capacity. Add 0.65 cfm for each additional 1000 lb capacity.

TABLE 2–4

Operating consumption and air requirements chart (metric units)

Device	Air pressure range (psi)	Average free-air consumption (CFM)
Air filter cleaner	480–690	85
Air hammer	480–690	467
Body polisher	480–690	57
Body sander	480–690	141
Brake tester	480–690	99
Carbon remover	480–690	85
Car rocker	830–1035	163
Car washer	480–690	241
Dusting gun (blowgun)	480–690	71
Engine cleaner	480–690	141
Fender hammer	480–690	248
Grease gun (high pressure)	820–1035	85
Hoist (900 kg)	480–690	28
Hydraulic lift[a]	1000–1210	149
Paint spray gun (production)	480–690	241
Paint spray gun (touch-up)	480–690	64
Pneumatic garage door	830–1035	57
Radiator tester	480–690	28
Rim stripper	830–1035	170
Spark plug cleaner	480–690	141
Spark plug tester	480–690	14
Spray gun (undercoating)	480–690	539
Spring oiler	480–690	106
Tire changer	830–1035	28
Tire inflation line	830–1035	42.5
Tire spreader	830–1035	28
Transmission and differential flusher	480–690	85
Vacuum cleaner	820–1035	184

Source: Courtesy of DeVilbiss Canada Ltd.
[a]For 3630-kg capacity. Add 18.4 liters/min for each additional 454-kg capacity.

and Pressure Vessel Code Section. All receivers must also be equipped with safety valves, which must be constructed, installed, and maintained according to the ASME Boiler and Pressure Vessel Code, Section VIII, 1968. This safety valve protects the receiver or storage tank, air lines, and equipment against excessive pressure.

Compressor Belts.   Where running compressor belts that are exposed and are 42 in. or 107 cm from the floor, these belts shall be fully enclosed by appropriate belt guards.

Installation of a Compressor

A stationary compressor is usually used in the shop; therefore, the unit should be bolted at its proper location to prevent it from moving (Fig. 2–21). Electrical

TABLE 2–5

Compressor capacity chart (English units)

| Compressor (psi) | | Free air consumption of total equipment (cfm) | | Compressor[c] (hp) |
Cut in	Cut out	Average service station or garage use[a]	Continuous operation[b]	
80	100	Up to 6.6	Up to 1.9	½
		6.7–10.5	2.0–3.0	¾
		10.6–13.6	3.1–3.9	1
		13.7–20.3	4.0–5.8	1½
		20.4–26.6	5.9–7.6	2
		30.5–46.2	8.8–13.2	3
100	125	46.3–60.0	13.3–20.0	5
		60.1–73.0	20.1–29.2	7½
		73.1–100.0	29.3–40.0	10
		100.0–125.0	40.1–50.0	15
120	150	Up to 3.8	Up to 1.1	½
		3.9–7.3	1.2–2.1	¾
		7.4–10.1	2.2–2.9	1
		10.2–15.0	3.0–4.3	1½
		15.1–20.0	4.4–5.7	2
140	175	Up to 11.9	Up to 3.4	1
		12.0–18.5	3.5–5.3	1½
		18.6–24.2	5.4–6.9	2
		24.3–36.4	7.0–10.4	3
		36.5–51.0	10.5–17.0	5
		51.1–66.0	17.1–26.4	7½
		66.1–88.2	26.5–35.3	10
		88.3–120.0	35.4–48.0	15

Source: Courtesy of DeVilbiss Canada Ltd.

[a]These figures are not to be regarded as the capacity of the compressor in free air output but instead they are the combined free air consumption of all the tools in the shop, as well as tools anticipated for future added equipment. A factor has been introduced to take into account intermittent operation of tools likely to be in use simultaneously in the average shop or service station.

[b]These figures are to be employed when the nature of the device is such that normal operation requires a continuous supply of compressed air. Therefore, no factor for intermittent operation has been used, and the figures given represent the compressor capacity in free air output.

[c]Do not use a compressor of less than 1½ hp if the pneumatic equipment includes a lift of 8000-lb capacity.

connections must be made by a qualified electrician; then the air line from the shop should be connected to the receiver. The compressor should be installed in a cool, clean area that has access room for maintenance or repair.

A compressor crankcase should be filled with a good grade of oil to the proper level; use SAE 10 for ordinary conditions and SAE 20 for temperatures above 100°F (37.8°C). The oil should be changed every 2 or 3 months and the level should be checked every week. The bearings on the electric motor should be oiled weekly unless they are life-lubricated bearings.

The belt should be checked for proper tension and alignment so that proper power transmission is achieved. All dust should be blown away from the cooling fins, including the intercooler and aftercooler. The air-intake strainer should be cleaned once a week. The safety valve handle on the tank should be lifted at least once a week to check that it is functioning properly. The flywheel should be checked for tightness on the crankshaft. The tank should be drained of moisture every day, especially in high-humidity areas (Fig. 2–21).

A compressor, if properly cared for, will last a long time; but if trouble develops, consult the manufacturer's manual supplied to the purchaser.

2–3 AIR TRANSFORMER

A transformer (Fig. 2–22) is a device that condenses air, oil, and moisture; regulates and strains the air; and provides outlets to which spray guns, dusters, and the like, can be connected. The transformer separates the oil and moisture by mechanical means and air expansion, allowing only clean, dry air to reach the spray gun. If any moisture or oil passes through the spray gun onto the freshly painted surface, it will ruin the paint finish. Therefore, a transformer is required in the refinishing field.

A transformer regulator controls pressure at the

TABLE 2-6

Compressor capacity chart (metric units)

Compressor pressures per kPa	Free air consumption of total equipment (liters/min)		Compressor (watts)
Cut in to Cut out	Average service station or garage use[a]	Continuous operation[b]	
550–690	Up to 187	Up to 53.8	374
	190–297	56.6–85	558
	300–385	87.8–110	746
	388–575	113–164	1,120
	578–753	167–215	1,492
	865–1300	249–374	2,238
690–862	1305–1700	376–566	3,730
	1725–2065	569–826	5,600
	2066–2832	829–1130	7,460
	2832–3540	1135–1420	11,190
830–1035	Up to 107	Up to 31.1	374
	110–206	34–59.5	558
	210–286	62.4–82	746
	290–424	85–122	1,120
	427–567	125–161	1,492
966–1210	Up to 337	Up to 96.2	746
	340–524	99–150	1,120
	526–685	153–195	1,492
	688–1030	198–294	2,238
	1035–1445	298–482	3,730
	1446–1870	484–748	5,600
	1871–2490	750–1000	7,460
	2500–3400	1002–1360	11,190

Source: Courtesy of DeVilbiss Canada Ltd.

[a]These figures are not to be regarded as the capacity of the compressor in free air output but instead they are the combined free air consumption of all the tools in the shop, as well as tools anticipated for future added equipment. A factor has been introduced to take into account intermittent operation of tools likely to be in use simultaneously in the average shop or service station.

[b]These figures are to be employed when the nature of the device is such that normal operation requires a continuous supply of compressed air. Therefore, no factor for intermittent operation has been used, and the figures given represent the compressor capacity in free air output.

gun to give the desired atomization. The transformer regulator has a gauge that shows main line pressure and a gauge for working pressure. It also has outlets for main line pressure and outlets for working pressure, such as used when painting a vehicle. The regulator knob adjusts the working air pressure, and a drain is attached to the bottom of the cylinder. Transformers are usually hooked up off the main line at least 25 ft or 7.75 m from the compressor. The workings of a transformer are relatively simple. The air enters at the back of the transformer main pressure line. By adjusting the pressure regulator knob until the desired pressure is reached, a diaphragm opens that allows air to pass through a metal filter. Water separators and baffle condensers clean the air of its impurities and then it passes out through the regulated side to the spray gun. Drain the transformer daily if necessary.

If the transformer cannot stop all the oil in the air line, it is necessary to install a filter such as in Fig. 2–23, which uses a roll of double toilet paper as a medium to remove oil from the air. Filters must be checked regularly, and when a bit of oil is present on the intake side, the element should be changed.

Coalescing oil removal filters are available to remove oil and water vapors and dirt particles from the compressed air. Some of these filters are available as submicron filters, which coalesce oil aerosols and remove them from the lines. The filtered air will contain less than 0.1 ppm of oil by weight. The life of the filter cartridge is exceptionally long when removing aerosols and is designed for 99.999% efficiency. A filter designed to remove any remaining oil vapor and its taste and odor must be used when the air is to be used for breathing purposes. To remove carbon monoxide from compressed air, there are units available on the market that will clean the air for breathing purposes.

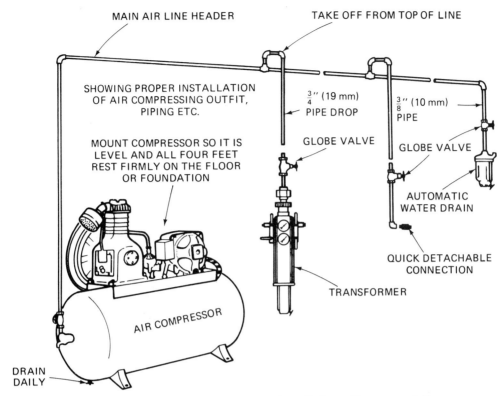

MAIN AIR LINE HEADER

TAKE OFF FROM TOP OF LINE

SHOWING PROPER INSTALLATION
OF AIR COMPRESSING OUTFIT,
PIPING ETC.

$\frac{3}{4}''$ (19 mm)
PIPE DROP

$\frac{3}{8}''$ (10 mm)
PIPE

MOUNT COMPRESSOR SO IT IS
LEVEL AND ALL FOUR FEET
REST FIRMLY ON THE FLOOR
OR FOUNDATION

GLOBE VALVE

GLOBE VALVE

AUTOMATIC
WATER DRAIN

QUICK DETACHABLE
CONNECTION

TRANSFORMER

AIR COMPRESSOR

DRAIN
DAILY

FIGURE 2-21 Typical compressor installation. *(Courtesy of De-Vilbiss Canada Ltd.)*

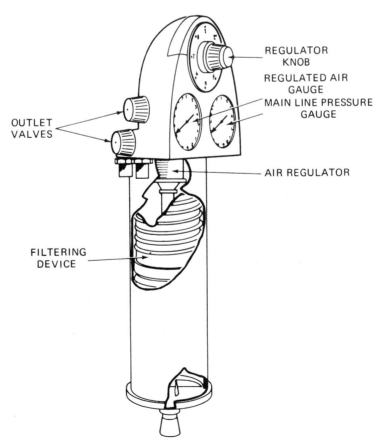

REGULATOR
KNOB

REGULATED AIR
GAUGE

MAIN LINE PRESSURE
GAUGE

OUTLET
VALVES

AIR REGULATOR

FILTERING
DEVICE

FIGURE 2-22 Typical transformer. *(Courtesy of DeVilbiss Canada Ltd.)*

FIGURE 2-23   Typical air filter.

Installation of Air Transformers

The air transformer should be bolted securely to the spray booth or to some similar sturdy object near the operator for convenience in reading the gauges and operating the valves. It should be installed at least 25 ft or 7.75 m from the compressor and the take-off should always be from the top of the air line. Piping should slope toward the compressor air receiver or a drain leg installed at the end of the air line or at the end of each branch to provide for drainage of moisture from the air line (Fig. 2-24). The reason the air line is sloped is to control the water in the air line. Humid air condenses to water when the air is compressed. If some of the water is allowed to get through the system and on a paint job, it will ruin it. Therefore, it is necessary to drain the compressor, receiver, drain leg, and transformer as often as required. Use piping of sufficient size for the volume of air passed and the length of pipe used (Tables 2-7 and 2-8). The pipe must always be of the recommended size or larger. Otherwise, excessive pressure drop will occur.

2-4   HOSES

Fluid Hose

Two types of hoses are available in the finishing industry: an air hose and a fluid hose. A fluid hose is always black in color with a special solvent-resisting liner that

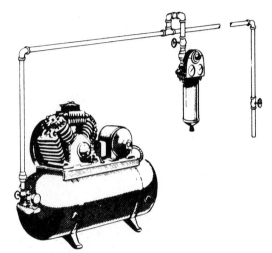

FIGURE 2-24   Piping of sufficient size must be used. *(Courtesy of DeVilbiss Canada Ltd.)*

TABLE 2-7

Minimum pipe size recommendations (English units)

| Compressing outfit | | Main air line | |
Size (hp)	Capacity (cfm)	Length (ft)	Size (in.)
1½ and 2	6–9	Over 50	¾
3 and 5	12–20	Up to 200	¾
		Over 200	1
5–10	20–40	Up to 100	¾
		Over 100 to 200	1
		Over 200	1¾
10–15	40–60	Up to 100	1
		Over 100 to 200	1¾
		Over 200	1½

Source: Courtesy of DeVilbiss Canada Ltd.

TABLE 2-8

Minimum pipe size recommendations (metric units)

| Compressing unit | | Main air line | |
Size (watts)	Capacity (liters/min)	Length (m)	Size (mm)
1120 and 1492	170–255	Over 15	190.6
2238 and 3730	340–566	Up to 61	190.6
		Over 61	254
3730–7460	566–1130	Up to 30.5	190.6
		Over 30.5 to 61	254
		Over 61	318
7460–11,190	1130–1700	Up to 30.5	254
		Over 30.5 to 61	318
		Over 61	382

Source: Courtesy of DeVilbiss Canada Ltd.

is almost impervious to all common solvents in paints, lacquers, and other finishing materials that readily attack ordinary composition hose.

Figure 2–25 shows a typical fluid hose construction; the inner tube is made from carefully selected materials that resist the effects of the materials that will pass through it. The braid insert is made up of one or more layers of strong fabric braid bonded to the inner tube and the outer jacket. The braid insert gives the hose strength for resisting high work pressures and good flexibility. The outer cover protects the hose from damage by oil, chemicals, abrasion, water, and general exposure. For production finishing, ⅜-in. (10-mm) hose is used for large guns. For maintenance finishing, ½-in. (13-mm) ID (inside diameter) hose is used for large guns and ⁵⁄₁₆-in. (8-mm) ID hose is used for smaller outfits.

Air Hose

Air hoses (Fig. 2–26) are constructed similarly to fluid hoses except the inner liner is a different material such as nitrile rubber (buna N). The braid is of similar material to the fluid hose and the outside cover is neoprene or natural rubber. The outer cover is usually red and can be smooth or corrugated; some hoses are built with a special static wire between the outer cover and the braid. This is used to remove static electricity and ground the equipment being used. Inexpensive orange

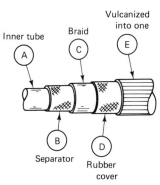

FIGURE 2–25 Fluid hose two-braid construction. *(Courtesy of DeVilbiss Canada Ltd.)*

braid hose is also available; this is usually used on small outfits. Using the improper size of hose will result in an excessive drop in air pressure, which will starve the spray gun.

Tables 2–9 and 2–10 should be consulted to find the proper size of hose. Too often a spray gun is blamed for functioning improperly when the real cause of trouble is an inadequate supply of compressed air at the gun. The most commonly used hoses for spray guns are 35 to 50 ft (10 to 15 m) long, ⁵⁄₁₆-in. (8-mm) ID, and ⅝-in. (16-mm) OD (outside diameter).

Pressure drops in hoses are caused by the friction of the flowing air against the walls of the hose in a re-

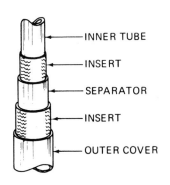

TWO-BRAID CONSTRUCTION

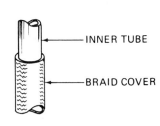

BRAID COVERED TUBING

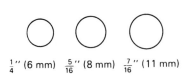

AIR HOSE SIZES

FIGURE 2–26 Air hoses and their construction. *(Courtesy of DeVilbiss Canada Ltd.)*

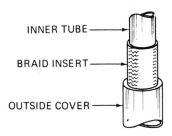

ONE-BRAID CONSTRUCTION

TABLE 2-9

Air pressure drop (English units)

Size of air hose (ID)	Air pressure drop at spray gun (lb)					
	5 ft Length	10 ft Length	15 ft Length	20 ft Length	25 ft Length	50 ft Length
¼ in.						
At 40 lb pressure	6	8	9½	11	12¾	24
At 50 lb pressure	7½	10	12	14	16	28
At 60 lb pressure	9	12½	14½	16¾	19	31
At 70 lb pressure	10¾	14½	17	19½	22½	34
At 80 lb pressure	12¼	16½	19½	22½	25½	37
At 90 lb pressure	14	18¾	22	25¼	29	39½
⁵⁄₁₆ in.						
At 40 lb pressure	2¼	2¾	3¼	3½	4	8½
At 50 lb pressure	3	3½	4	4½	5	10
At 60 lb pressure		4½	5	5½	6	11½
At 70 lb pressure	4½	5¼	6	6¾	7¼	13
At 80 lb pressure	5½	6¼	7	8	8¾	14½
At 90 lb pressure	6½	7½	8½	9½	10½	16

Source: Courtesy of DeVilbiss Canada Ltd.

stricted fitting, which is used by mistake or lack of knowledge. The smaller the inside diameter and the longer the hose, the more pressure drop that will be present. The painter must understand that, although the regulator shows 60 psi (414 kPa) of working pressure, the pressure at the end of a 50-ft (15.3-m) hose of ⁵⁄₁₆-in. (7.9-mm) ID that is attached to a spray gun will only be able to deliver 48½ psi (374.6 kPa) of air pressure, which is a drop of 11½ psi (79.4 kPa). Pressure drop in a hose can be checked with a gauge at the gun outlet to determine the pressure available (Fig. 2-27).

Hose Connections

All hoses are usually equipped with reusable hose connections so that they can be connected to various units. Figure 2-28 shows typical hose connectors.

When a hose starts to leak at a certain area, it can be cut and shortened if the area is a short piece near the end. But if it is near the center, a hose splicer is used to repair the hose. The hose is cut at the leak and the splicer is put in place following the instructions available with the splicer kit. All these connectors, splicers,

TABLE 2-10

Air pressure drop (metric units)

Size of air hose (ID)	Air pressure drop at spray gun (kPa)					
	1.53 m Length	3.05 m Length	4.58 m Length	6.10 m Length	7.63 m Length	15.3 m Length
6 mm						
At 276 kPa pressure	41	55	65	76	88	165
At 345 kPa pressure	52	69	83	97	110	123
At 414 kPa pressure	62	86	100	115	131	214
At 482 kPa pressure	74	100	117	134	155	234
At 551 kPa pressure	84	114	134	155	175	255
At 620 kPa pressure	97	129	152	174	200	272
8 mm						
At 276 kPa pressure	15.5	19	22.4	24.1	27.6	58.6
At 345 kPa pressure	20.7	24.1	27.6	31	34.5	69
At 414 kPa pressure	25.9	31	34.5	38	41.4	79.4
At 482 kPa pressure	31	36.2	41.4	46.6	50	90
At 551 kPa pressure	38	43	48.3	55	60	100
At 620 kPa pressure	44.8	52	58.5	65.5	72.5	110

Source: Courtesy of DeVilbiss Canada Ltd.

FIGURE 2-27 Checking pressure drop of air pressure between regulator and spray gun.

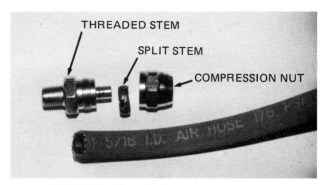

FIGURE 2-28a Typical hose connectors.

FIGURE 2-28b Connecting a spray gun to hose and using a quick coupler.

double nipples, and quick connectors are available from your local paint supply store.

Hoses are usually connected to air tools by using a quick connector (Fig. 2-29). These couplers are either attached to the hose by a threaded connector or the quick connector has a part to fasten it on the hose built into it (Fig. 2-30).

To repair a hose with this type of connector, the air pressure is shut off. Then the fitting is loosened with the appropriate wrenches and the nut slid back on the hose. The brass split ring is slipped back on the hose using a flat-blade screwdriver. Then the hose is pulled out of the fitting and cut past where it is damaged. To reinstall, reverse the order of the steps required to take it apart.

To make a hose last, a great amount of care must be given to it. It should never be dragged over sharp objects, tools, or abrasive surfaces. A severe end pull should not be applied to it as neither the hose nor connectors are built for this abuse. The hose should never be used at higher pressure than it was designed for. It should not be run over by heavy machinery or kinked severely. It should always be kept clean and always hung on appropriate hangers when not in use.

OSHA Regulations Regarding Pressure Hoses

All pressure hoses and couplings must be inspected at regular intervals according to use. The hose and coupling must be tested with the hose extended and under the maximum in-service operating pressure. Any hose

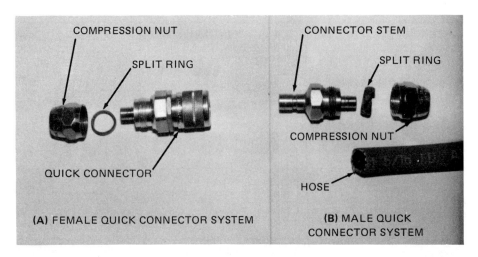

FIGURE 2-29 Quick connectors.

FIGURE 2-30 Quick connectors attaching blowgun to hose.

FIGURE 2-31 Typical blowgun.

or coupling showing deterioration, leakage, or weakness in its carcass or coupling must be withdrawn from service and repaired or discarded. Both air and fluid hoses are classified as pressure hoses.

Blowguns

Blowguns are used extensively in a shop to blow dust away or to help dry a vehicle. Figure 2-31 shows a typical blowgun. Many blowguns are built using lightweight, heavy-duty plastic, which is corrosion and rust resistant, and use a squeeze-type trigger. Great care must be used with a blowgun as a person can injure himself or herself or another person with careless use. The air stream should always be directed away from people so that dust or chips will blow away from them. Always wear safety glasses or goggles. Never use the blowgun to blow air directly against the body and never allow foreign matter to enter the operator inlet hoses.

OSHA regulations state that compressed air is not to exceed 30 psi (207 kPa) when the nozzle orifice is blocked and air pressure to the gun is 100 psi (690 kPa).

2-5 RESPIRATORS

Due to lack of knowledge or just carelessness, many painters are endangering their means of earning a livelihood by not wearing respiratory protection. The different materials present in the workplace and the many airborne chemicals, dust, and elements that are inhaled can damage the lungs severely. Some chemicals also irritate the skin and eyes, and some are absorbed by the skin into the body.

Some possibly harmful elements found in paint are antimony, barium, cadmium, nickel, and selenium. When paint hardeners and gloss improvers are used, isocyanates are introduced into the air that a painter breathes. Therefore, it is of great importance that breathing protection be worn as required.

When working in dusty conditions or when power sanding or dry sanding is done, a dust mask, such as in Fig. 2-32, should always be worn. This is a mechanical-type respirator that removes dust and solid particles from the air a person breathes. The respirator covers the nose and mouth and when covered with dust is thrown away. With vacuuming or light brushing, masks can be

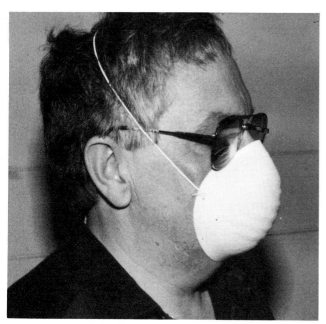

FIGURE 2–32 Dust mask.

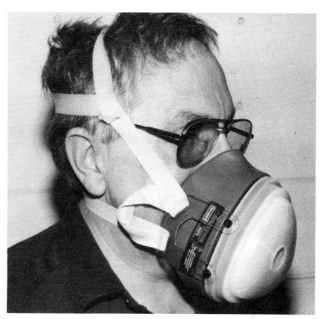

FIGURE 2–33 Disposable paint respirator.

cleaned so that they last longer. When the respirator is clogged with dust from filing plastic or fiber glass, it should be discarded. Masks should only be stored in a clean box or cupboard for proper hygiene. For best results, use dust masks that fit properly and have been approved by NIOSH (National Institute of Occupational Safety and Health), MESA (Mining Enforcement and Safety Administration), or CSA (Canadian Standards Approval).

The respirators most generally used for painting are made to protect against the general types of paints, such as lacquers, and enamel mists and organic vapors. If they fit properly, these respirators protect the painter from inhaling vapor and paint mists that can damage the lungs. These respirators must be air-purifying types with built-in air-purifying filter elements. The filters are approved by NIOSH (National Institute of Occupational Safety and Health)/MSHA (Mine Safety and Health Administration). They have a label with the approval no. TC-23C-354. They can be used until the smell or taste of paint vapor comes through the element.

This type of respirator is meant to be used where air is moving, such as in a spray booth, and should never be used in an enclosed area where there is no air movement. Figure 2–33 shows a throw-away type of respirator with a prefilter. Figure 2–34 shows a respirator with twin cartridges elements, which are changed as required.

After the respirator has been fitted on the painter's head by adjusting the stretchable elastic straps, it should be checked for proper fit. The inhalation covers

are plugged by using a hand (or hands for twin cartidges), and the painter inhales deeply. If the respirator moves against the face when inhaling, a proper seal has been formed. When exhaling with the covers still covered, the respirator should move away from the painter's face. If the respirator lets air bleed through between the face and the respirator, the painter has a poor fit. A poor-fitting respirator must never be used as it endangers the painter's health. Painters in many areas are

FIGURE 2–34 Respirator with disposable cartridge. *(Courtesy of DeVilbiss Canada Ltd.)*

not allowed to wear a beard because it prevents a good seal between the face and respirator. These types of respirators are available through most paint jobbers and equipment suppliers.

When polyurethane additives or any type of paint using a catalyzed finish that has isocyanates in it is being used, only vapor/particulate respirators recommended by a jobber and meeting NIOSH approval should be used. Always follow manufacturer's recommendations as to the type of respirator to match the job.

Typical Warning Labels on Paint Cans Containing Isocyanate Chemicals. *WARNING FLAMMABLE.* Keep away from heat, sparks, and open flame. *WHEN MIXED WITH ENAMEL TYPE OF PAINT, VAPOR HARMFUL. MAY CAUSE ALLERGIC SKIN OR RESPIRATORY REACTION. MIXTURE CONTAINS ALIPHATIC ISOCYANATES.* Individuals with chronic respiratory problems or prior allergic respiratory reaction to isocyanates must not be exposed to vapor or spray mist containing isocyanates. Do not breathe vapor or spray mist. Do not get in eyes, on skin or clothing. *USE ONLY WITH ADEQUATE VENTILATION.* If engineering and administrative controls of air contaminants are not feasible, wear a positive-pressure air line respirator (TC-19C NIOSH/MSHA or equivalent) during application and until work area has been exhausted of all vapor and spray mist. FIRST AID. In case of skin contact, flush with plenty of water; for eyes, flush with plenty of water for 15 minutes and get medical attention. If affected by inhalation of vapor, remove to fresh air; if swallowed *CALL PHYSICIAN IMMEDIATELY. DO NOT INDUCE VOMITING.*

In many areas the only type of protection approved for the painter when using polyurethane additives is the hood (Fig. 2–35), a complete face mask (Fig. 2–36), or a half-mask (Fig. 2–37).

These types of respirators are positive-pressure types and must be used at all times when spraying paints that have polyurethane additives in them. These respirators can be used when spraying in areas that are enclosed as they are supplied with clean, pure air at all times.

Manufacturers can supply to jobbers all the equipment that meets NIOSH standards for clean, pure, breathable air. The hood or respirator must be labeled with the NIOSH approval nos. TC-19C-174 and TC-19C-175. All the components must meet the code, such as the regulator, waist belt assembly, air supply hoses (25 ft or 7.6 m), and air regulators. The air line used by the hood or respirator cannot use the same source as the spray gun. The air used for the respirator must meet the

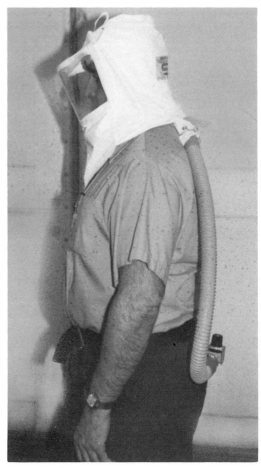

FIGURE 2–35 Hood air-fed respirator.

FIGURE 2–36 Complete full-facepiece pressure respirator.

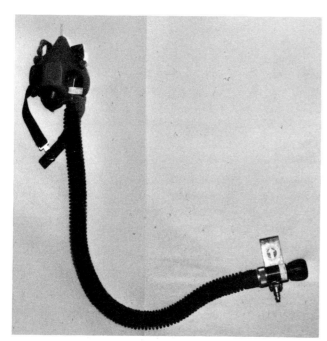

FIGURE 2-37 Half-facepiece pressure respirator.

Breathing Air Standards (maximum allowable contaminant level)		
Contaminant	OSHA	CSA
Carbon monoxide (ppm)	20	5
Carbon dioxide (ppm)	1000	500 ± 25
Oil (condensed) hydrocarbons (mg/m³)	5	1
Odors and tastes	Slight	Slight

FIGURE 2-38 Breathing air standard, allowable maximum contaminant level.

standards set by OSHA or CSA (Fig. 2-38); these guidelines set rigid purity standards for compressed air used.

The piston, oil-lubricated-type compressor, if used to supply the air required for hoods or respirators, can produce carbon monoxide if it overheats. To prevent this, a constant monitoring analyzer must be installed in the air line for breathing; also, a high-temperature alarm is installed on the compressor itself. Filtration units are also offered by industry to clean the air of any oil, water, or carbon monoxide.

In many shops a small oilless compressor is used; these vary from a diaphragm-type oilless piston to an oilless turbine type driven by an electric motor (Fig. 2-39).

The type and number of hoods or respirators used determine the type and size of air system required. The compressor air intake must be located so that only clean fresh air is drawn into the compressor. Great care must be taken to place the intake away from engine exhaust, chemical processes, and dust sources. The air should be checked often to assure its purity.

The hood and full facepiece are worn as required

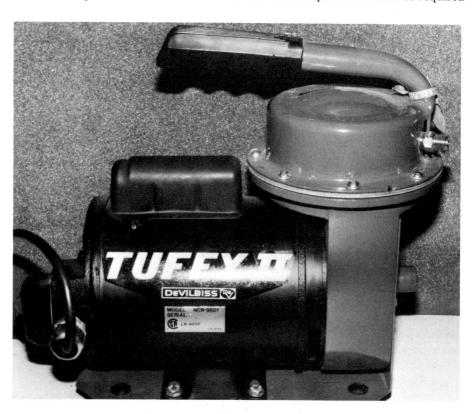

FIGURE 2-39 Small diaphragm compressor.

by code to protect the painter's lungs, eyes, and face from toxic chemicals, dust, and paint vapors. The half-mask respirator is used where eye protection is not required. This respirator protects the lower part of the face and the lungs from hazardous vapors, dust, and chemicals. The same air system must be used for both systems.

Before donning the respirator or hood, connect the hose to the air supply, put the waist belt on and tighten it snuggly, and clip on the regulator. Don the hood over the head if a hood is used and attach as required. If the full-facepiece respirator is used, extend the bottom two headstraps to their full length. First, the chin is inserted into the facepiece; then the headstraps are pulled over the head and down as far as they will go. For the half-mask, place it against the face and connect the upper two straps behind the head; make sure the straps are above the ears. Then the lower straps are connected behind the head.

Lower straps are tightened first; then the upper straps. The straps must be tight enough so that the facepiece or half-mask is held securely enough to prevent leakage. They must not be so tight as to make the mask uncomfortable to wear. The full facepiece or half-mask air hose is attached to the regulator on the waist belt and the regulator is plugged into the hose line. The respirator is then ready for use when the regulator pressure is adjusted as required.

Remember that these different types of respirators are for respiratory protection only in areas or atmospheres not immediately dangerous to health or life and from which a painter can escape without the aid of a respirator.

The air-supplied respirator must be inspected for defects after each use; if defective, it must be repaired immediately. It should then be cleaned, disinfected, and stored properly to assure that it is kept in satisfactory working condition. The lens can be protected during use by applying a replaceable throw-away lens on the full facepiece.

The regulator should be connected to the breathing air source at 30 to 125 psi (0.21 to 86 kPa); then the respirator is put on to check if ample quantities of air are being delivered without fluttering and are free flowing. Then all hoses should be checked for cracks, leaks, abrasion, and fitting for tightness.

For sanitary reasons, all respirators should be cleaned and disinfected after each use even if they do not look dirty. Use a proper cleaning solution that contains detergent and an effective disinfectant. With the solution heated to 140° to 160°F (60° to 71°C), the respirator is immersed top first into the cleaning solution. It must only be immersed until the exhalation valve is covered. Do not get the cleaning solution inside the mask

hose. Then, using a soft brush, brush the respirator gently until it is clean.

The respirator or half-mask is then rinsed in a clean water bath and allowed to air dry. Mild heat of less then 160°F (71°C) can be used to speed up the drying. Use only a lint-free towel to dry the respirator. Caution must be used when cleaning the lens not to scratch it through careless or abusive handling. Usually, detergents are adequate to remove adhering grime; if stubborn stains or deposits are present, denatured alcohol or mild solvent can be used. The solvent must not be allowed to come in contact with rubber parts and must only be used in well-ventilated areas.

All the required supplies and all breathing apparatus are available from suppliers, and all these suppliers must meet NIOSH and CSA standards and requirements.

OSHA Respirator Regulations

When effective engineering controls are not possible, or while they are being instituted, appropriate respirators shall be used pursuant to the following requirements. The respirator furnished shall provide adequate respiratory protection against the particular hazard for which it is designed in accordance with standards established by competent authorities. The U.S. Department of Interior, Bureau of Mines, and the U.S. Department of Agriculture are recognized as such authorities.

When an operator must be positioned in a booth downstream of the object being sprayed, an air-supplied respirator or other type of respirator approved by the Bureau of Mines, U.S. Department of the Interior, or specified for the material being sprayed should be used by the operator.

2-6 INFRARED BAKING EQUIPMENT

To speed up the drying of enamels, many shops have installed infrared baking equipment. Many cars are refinished in enamel because it is a cheaper process than using lacquer. Enamel dries to a hard glossy finish and needs no polishing after painting. The baking units can range from a single bulb to portable units that do only a section to traveling ovens that are used in either a spray booth or a specially ventilated drying room (Fig. 2-40). The traveling ovens usually go back and forth on tracks; the movement is reversed by stop plates that are placed at the proper distance on the floor for the size of the object being force-dried (Fig. 2-41). Air movement must always be maintained in the booth when the oven is used. If the oven is in a special drying room, the car is put in it for the required drying time.

FIGURE 2–40 Infrared baking equipment. *(Courtesy of DeVilbiss Canada Ltd.)*

There are different drying temperatures. Although varying somewhat with different materials, the distinctions generally recognized in the trade are as follows:

1. *Air-drying temperature:* less than 100°F (37.8°C). Air-drying temperature causes the vaporization of the solvents, which normally takes from 8 to 10 hours.
2. *Force-drying temperature:* from 100° to 180°F (37.8° to 82.2°C). In force-drying, the automobile is placed in a convection-type oven. By movement of the heated air, heat is trans-ferred to the painted surface. The surrounding air must always be hotter than the vehicle. Air temperature is generally 165°F (73.2°C).
3. *Baking temperature:* above 200°F (93.3°C). Baking temperature, in contrast to radiant heat sources, gives off energy in the form of infrared rays. The air between the source and the object does not absorb an appreciable amount of this radiated energy. In an infrared oven, as soon as the lamps are turned on, the radiated energy is immediately transformed into heat upon reaching the painted surface, which instantly becomes hotter than the surrounding area. Metal temperature is 220°F (104°C).

Enamel jobs will be ready for delivery in approximately 30 minutes when they are baked out. Lacquer-based undercoats and color coats are ready to sand or polish after 10 minutes in any weather. Enamel topcoats have better gloss, hardness, and color life when they have been baked in temperatures of 200°F (93.3°C) or more. Lacquers also usually have a better gloss if they are baked.

Improved Quality

Although the *drying from the inside out* aspect of infrared baking has been somewhat oversold, it is definitely true that infrared does have penetrating power and that this penetration of the paint film itself results in more uniform drying. There is also less possibility of surface pigment discoloration and much better flow-out, since paint film temperatures of from 200° to 230°F

FIGURE 2–41 Traveling baking equipment. *(Courtesy of DeVilbiss Canada Ltd.)*

(93.3° to 110°C) are practicable with infrared equipment in the refinishing field. The quality of enamels is greatly improved due to the considerable amount of polymerization (a curing of the resins) that takes place during short baking cycles. Baked enamels are harder and more durable and have considerably longer color life.

After an infrared treatment, lacquer-based primer surfacers are dried much faster and allow easier sanding. Similarly, a force-dried lacquer color coat has better gloss with less rubbing. Infrared drying ensures fewer comebacks and rework because of improperly dried undercoats or finish coats.

One of the characteristics of lamp-type infrared units is the fact that different colors and materials have varying abilities to absorb near-infrared energy. Light colors require a somewhat longer drying time than dark ones because a part of the energy is reflected rather than absorbed. Similarly, certain parts of automobiles, such as glass, plastics, and adhesives, have very poor infrared absorptive characteristics compared to paint or metal. This characteristic of near infrared permits the actual baking of the paint film on a car with temperatures in excess of 200°F (93.3°C) without any damage whatsoever to the more critical parts, such as glass, plastics, or the gasoline in the tank.

A smaller type of oven requires a longer time to dry a paint job. Drying-time information should be obtained from the distributor who sells the equipment.

WARNING: Vehicle manufacturers recommend that on-board computers be removed from vehicles if temperatures are likely to exceed 176°F (80°C). This could occur in paint booth dryers, ovens, or in any heating or welding done with a torch or any electric welding equipment.

OSHA Regulations Regarding Drying

Freshly sprayed articles shall be dried only in spaces provided with adequate ventilation to prevent the formation of explosive vapors. In the event adequate and reliable ventilation is not provided, such drying spaces shall be considered a spraying area.

Automobile refinishing spray booths or enclosures, otherwise installed and maintained in full conformity with this section, may alternately be used for drying with portable electrical infrared drying apparatus when conforming with the following:

1. Interior (especially floors) of spray enclosures shall be kept free of overspray deposits.
2. During spraying operations, the drying apparatus and electrical connections shall not be located within the spray enclosure or in any other location where spray residues may be deposited thereon.
3. The spraying apparatus, the drying apparatus, and the ventilating system of the spray enclosure shall be equipped with suitable interlocks so arranged that:
   a. The spraying apparatus cannot be operated while the drying apparatus is inside the spray enclosure.
   b. The spray enclosure will be purged of spray vapors for a period of not less than 3 minutes before the drying apparatus can be energized.
   c. The ventilation system will maintain a safe atmosphere within the enclosure during the drying process, and the drying apparatus will automatically shut off in the event of failure of the ventilating system.

OSHA Regulations Regarding Infrared Drying

All electrical wiring and equipment of the drying apparatus shall conform with applicable sections of Sub Post S of this part (National Electrical Code). Only equipment of a type approved for Class 1, Division 2 hazardous locations shall be located within 18 in. or 46 cm of floor level. All metallic parts of the drying apparatus shall be properly electrically bonded and grounded.

The drying apparatus shall contain a prominently located, permanently attached warning sign indicating that ventilation should be maintained during the drying period and that spraying should not be conducted in the vicinity if spray will be deposited on the apparatus.

REVIEW QUESTIONS

2-1. Why is a spray booth used when painting vehicles?

2-2. What is the amount of lineal feet or meters of air a spray booth must average in a cross section when painting?

2-3. When must exhaust filters be changed and how are they disposed of?

2-4. How are arrestor-type filters replaced in a paint spray booth?

2-5. What is a down-draft booth and how does it work?

2-6. What type of filter is used in a cross-draft booth?

2-7. What is an air makeup unit and when is it required?

2-8. How must an exhaust fan be cleaned?

2-9. Name two types of compressors.

2-10. What is the efficiency of a two-stage compressor?

2-11. What is an automatic pressure switch?

2-12. What is a centrifugal pressure release valve?

2-13. How far should a transformer regulator be from the compressor?

2-14. Why should an air line slope back toward the compressor?

2-15. What is meant by pressure drop?

2-16. How is a fluid hose constructed?

2-17. What is the pressure drop in a 50 ft (15 m) long hose with an ID of 5/16 in. (79 mm) when the pressure is set at 60 psi (413 kPa) at the transformer?

2-18. What is used to attach equipment to an air hose?

2-19. What is a blowgun used for?

2-20. What type of respirator is used for general paint work?

2-21. What type of respirator is used when painting with paint that has isocyanates in it?

2-22. What is the force-drying temperature used in a convection oven?

CHAPTER THREE

Spray Guns

A paint spray gun is a tool built with great precision to enable it to do a good job of applying paint, if it is in the hands of qualified, experienced painters. The paint spray gun needs proper handling, cleaning, and lubrication if it is to last and do the job properly. The qualified painter must master the use, repair, and troubleshooting of the spray gun. The apprentice under supervision must learn to dismantle the gun carefully and inspect each part and know its function, as well as reassemble it.

The qualified painter has mastered the techniques required to enable the spraying of a multitude of different materials. He or she has mastered the manual dexterity and movements required when spraying, which include movement of the body as well as the arm, elbow, wrist, hand, and fingers. The qualified painter has developed good depth perception as to the distance of the gun from the surface to be painted. The spray stroke is started at the right time and location and must move at the right speed to apply an appropriate thickness of paint. The painter is able to adjust himself and the gun for the many types of jobs that will have to be done, such as overall painting, panel painting, or spot repair. The painter is able to spray panels of many different shapes and sizes and produce good quality work.

3-1 TYPES OF SPRAY GUNS

A spray gun is a mechanical means of bringing air and paint together. It atomizes or breaks up the paint stream into a spray and by ejection applies a coating to a surface to preserve and beautify. This is accomplished by moving air and paint through different passageways in the gun body until they meet at the fluid tip and air cap (Figs. 3-1 and 3-2). When the air and paint meet, the air breaks up or atomizes the paint and the air stream hits the area to be painted and applies the paint to the surface in a controlled pattern. When sprayed on thickly enough, the paint particles join together and form a film that is smooth and without any blemishes.

Spray guns are precision instruments. They are constructed as accurately and tested as carefully as precision tools and gauges. When completely assembled, each spray gun is tested for general operation. It is adjusted for atomization, spray pattern size, and uniformity with the paint and accessory equipment for which the gun was designed. If given a reasonable amount of care, it will produce good results for years. Neglect and carelessness are responsible for the majority of spray gun difficulties.

A wide choice of spray guns is available. A pro-

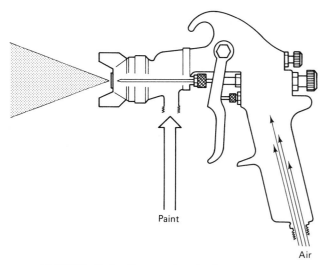

FIGURE 3–1 Conventional air spray gun. *(Courtesy of Binks Manufacturing Co.)*

duction-type gun should be chosen, whether it be used on a suction cup attachment or pressure-type equipment. Smaller guns are used for spot spraying and touch-up. When used for complete overall refinishing, these smaller guns are not fast enough to make the job profitable.

The way in which the paint is supplied to the nozzle of the spray gun will decide if it is a suction-feed or pressure-feed type. These two types can be further subdivided into bleeder and nonbleeder and external and internal mix guns.

Suction Feed

Suction feed is designed to create a vacuum and thus draw the material from the container, better known as the suction cup. This system is generally limited to 1 quart (1 liter) and used only with paint (Fig. 3–3). A vacuum is created when the trigger is pulled, allowing air to flow out of the orifice surrounding the fluid tip. The paint is then pulled from the container out through the fluid passage. This vacuum is augmented by the opening in the lid of the fluid container, allowing atmospheric pressure to exert itself on the material. On suction-type guns the fluid tip will always protrude approximately 1/32 in. (1 mm) beyond the air cap (Fig. 3–4).

Pressure Feed

In this type of system, the material is placed in a closed container to which direct air pressure is admitted. A hose leads from the container to the spray gun and the paint is thus forced through the spray nozzle. This method is employed where large quantities of the same color are used; it is slightly faster than the suction feed. A paint container can be from 2 quarts to 60 gallons (2 to 227 liters). It has a gauge on the container to show the pressure at which the diaphragm is set to let air exert pressure on the material. On pressure-type guns, the fluid tip does not extend beyond the air cap (Fig. 3–5).

Bleeder Type. *Bleeder* means an intentional discharge of air from the spout of the gun that prevents

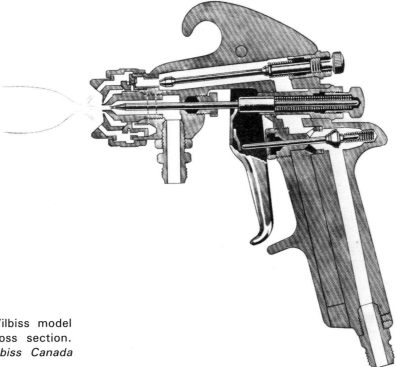

FIGURE 3–2 DeVilbiss model JGA spray gun cross section. *(Courtesy of DeVilbiss Canada Ltd.)*

FIGURE 3-3 Vacuum created at air cap. *(Courtesy of DeVilbiss Canada Ltd.)*

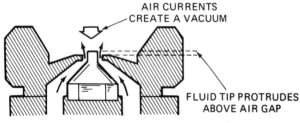

FIGURE 3-4 Suction or gravity feed cap. *(Courtesy of DeVilbiss Canada Ltd.)*

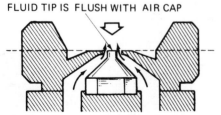

FIGURE 3-5 Pressure feed cap. *(Courtesy of DeVilbiss Canada Ltd.)*

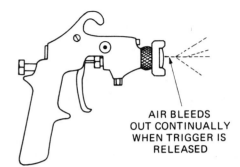

FIGURE 3-6 Bleeder-type system. *(Courtesy of DeVilbiss Canada Ltd.)*

air pressure from building up in the hose. This type of gun is used where there is no pressure control device, such as an automatic unloader or pressure switch on the compressor. The air valve on this gun is designed to remain open even after the trigger has been released, shutting off the fluid (Fig. 3-6).

Nonbleeder Type. This type of gun is used when air is supplied from the tank or compressor having pressure control. The gun is equipped with an air valve that shuts off the air as well as the fluid when the trigger is released. This gun is used in automotive maintenance work in applying industrial finishes and is more popular than the bleeder type (Fig. 3-7).

External Mix. As the name implies, the air and the fluid are mixed outside the air cap (Fig. 3-8).

Internal Mix. With this method, the air and fluid are mixed inside the air cap. It should be remembered, however, that this gun is limited to slow-drying materials that will not build up and dry inside the cap (Fig.

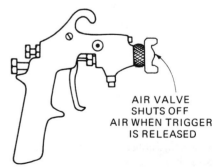

FIGURE 3-7 Nonbleeder-type system. *(Courtesy of DeVilbiss Canada Ltd.)*

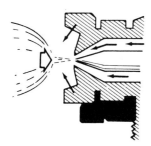

FIGURE 3-8 External mix. *(Courtesy of DeVilbiss Canada Ltd.)*

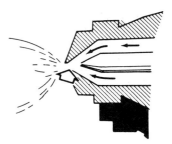

FIGURE 3-9 Internal mix. *(Courtesy of DeVilbiss Canada Ltd.)*

3-9). The only advantage of internal mix over external mix is less overspray. Internal mix always involves pressure feed equipment.

Spray Gun Parts

The paint and equipment suppliers have many different types as well as makes of spray guns. A spray gun should be chosen by quality of the product, service for parts, and reputation of the manufacturer.

An apprentice student must learn how a spray gun is constructed and how it works. Figure 3-10a shows a typical Binks spray gun with the parts labeled to help an apprentice learn the name of the parts. Figure 3-10b shows a typical DeVilbiss spray gun and names the principal parts.

An air atomizing spray gun uses compressed air to break up material into small droplets and to give direction to these droplets. The spray gun has two valves that start and stop the flow of compressed air and fluid. The mixing of the air and the material can take place outside the spray gun between the horns of the air nozzle or cap. This is called external mix atomization (Fig. 3-8). When the mixing of the air and material takes place inside the air cap or nozzle of the spray gun, the term internal mix is used (Fig. 3-9).

An apprentice must learn, in a class room situation if possible, how a spray gun is taken apart and reas-

FIGURE 3-10 (a) Typical Binks spray gun. *(Courtesy of Binks Manufacturing Co.)* (b) Cross section of typical DeVilbiss model JGA spray gun. *(Courtesy of DeVilbiss Canada Ltd.)*

KEY: 1, Air cap; 2, fluid needle packing; 3, fluid tip; 4, trigger bearing stud; 5, air valve spring; 6, fluid feed valve; 7, spreader control valve; 8, air valve; 9, fluid inlet; 10, gun body (or handle); 11, trigger; 12, air inlet; 13, air valve packing (leather); 14, fluid needle; 15, fluid needle spring; 16, baffle; 17, fluid needle packing nut.

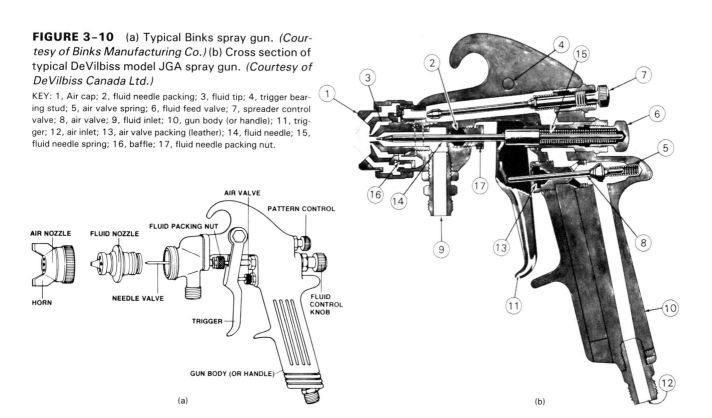

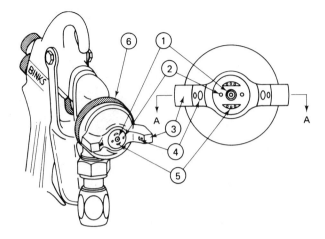

1. Round opening around fluid tip
2. "Containment holes"
3. "Horns" of air cap
4. Pattern control holes
5. "Auxiliary" holes
6. Air cap retaining ring

FIGURE 3-11 Air cap or nozzle construction. (Courtesy of Binks Manufacturing Co.)

sembled, as well as how to troubleshoot any problems that may occur. Before the spray gun is disassembled, the proper wrenches and gaskets should be available. Great care must be taken not to damage threads or parts, and the gun should be protected by a rag if held in a vise.

Air Caps

The first part usually removed is called the air cap or air nozzle, and it is held on the gun body by threads. It is unscrewed to remove and screwed back on when reassembled; do not overtighten or it may jam on the body. The purpose of the air cap or nozzle is to direct air jets to atomize the fluid and give the droplets the velocity required to reach the surface to be painted. The external mix air cap or nozzle is the most common type used today (Fig. 3-11). In external mix, air is ejected through spreader horns through a center orifice and, sometimes, auxiliary orifices (Fig. 3-12).

Multiple jets have five, seven, nine, or more orifices, a center orifice, one in each horn, plus twin auxiliary jets. The size of the air cap is determined by the type of material being sprayed and the air requirements. Multiple jets offer better atomization for viscous materials, such as synthetics and heavy-bodied lacquers (Fig. 3-13).

The air cap or nozzle breaks up the paint material and also helps to form the spray fan as the air and material are propelled to the surface to be painted. Equal and opposing forces of air coming from the holes in the center and horns of the cap form the desired spray fan. The containment, auxiliary, and angular holes of the air cap (Figs. 3-11, 3-12, and 3-13) provide better atomization of the material being sprayed. When a hole in the horn gets plugged, the spray pattern is thrown off balance, giving the shape of a partial circle; this causes the

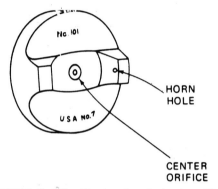

FIGURE 3-12 Conventional air cap. *(Courtesy of DeVilbiss Canada Ltd.)*

paint fan to be moved toward the sides affected. An air cap or nozzle and all the holes in it must always be kept very clean before, during, and after spraying operations.

Air caps or nozzles must be chosen with great care so that they match both the fluid tip and needle. The greater the amount of holes in the air cap, the greater the amount of compressed air that will be used. Check

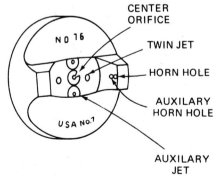

FIGURE 3-13 Multiple-jet air cap. *(Courtesy of DeVilbiss Canada Ltd.)*

TABLE 3–1

Matched equipment part numbers for spray guns and air consumption (DeVilbiss Equipment)

Spray gun	Fluid tip	Fluid needle	Air cap	Diameter of fluid tip (in.)	(mm)	CFM at: 40 psi	50 psi	60 psi	Max. pattern (in.)	CMM at: 276 kPa	344 kPa	413 kPa	Max. pattern (cm)
Standard production spray guns: Suction feed													
MBC-510	AV601EX	496DEX	36	0.070	1.77	8	11	12.8	12	0.226	0.311	0.362	30.5
JGA-502	AV601EX	496DEX	36	0.070	1.77	8	11	12.8	12	0.226	0.311	0.362	30.5
MBC-510	AV601EX	496DEX	30	0.070	1.77	9	11	12.8	12	0.254	0.311	0.362	30.5
JGA-502	AV601EX	496DEX	30	0.070	1.77	9	11	12.8	12	0.254	0.311	0.362	30.5
MBC-510	AV601EX	496DEX	43	0.070	1.77	10	12	14.5	12	0.283	0.339	0.410	30.5
JGA-502	AV601EX	496DEX	43	0.070	1.77	10	12	14.5	13	0.283	0.339	0.410	30.5
JGA-502	AV601EX	496DEX	80	0.070	1.77	10	12	14.5	13	0.283	0.339	0.410	33
MBC-510	AV601EX	496DEX	80	0.070	1.77	10	12	14.5	13	0.283	0.339	0.410	33
JGV-560	AV601EX	496DEX	80	0.070	1.77	10	12	14.5	13	0.283	0.339	0.410	33
Standard production spray guns: Pressure feed													
MBC and JGA	601FX	a	765	0.0452	0.108	10	12		16	0.283	0.339	0.362	40.6
MBC and JGA	601FX	a	74	0.0452	0.108	9	10		4	0.254	0.283		10.1
MBC and JGA	601FX	a	704	0.0452	0.108	12	15		12	0.339	0.424		30.5
MBC and JGA	601FX	a	705	0.0452	0.108	11	13		9	0.362	0.368		22.8
MBC and JGA	601FX	a	54	0.0452	0.108	7	8		9	0.198	0.226		22.8
Small spray guns: Suction feed													
EGA-502	608E	406E	395E	0.070	1.77	5			7	0.141			18.8

ᵃUse MBC-444 or JGA-402.

Tables 3–1 and 3–2 for the proper match. The annular ring or the space between the fluid tip and the air cap gives off a column of air to surround the fluid stream (Fig. 3–11). The fluid coming from the fluid tip expands and mixes with the air coming from the annular ring of the air cap; this causes first-stage atomization.

On pressure feed guns the air cap usually contains a second set of holes set 90° from the containment holes (Fig. 3–11). These holes are called angular converging holes and they cause second-stage atomization. These additional air passages add an additional force to help atomize the fluid stream, because in a pressure feed sys-

TABLE 3–2

Matched equipment part numbers for spray guns and air consumption (Binks Equipment)

Spray gun	Fluid nozzle	Fluid needle	Air nozzle	ID of fluid nozzle (in.)	(mm)	CFM at: 30 psi	50 psi	70 psi	Max. pattern (in.)	CMM at: 206 kPa	344 kPa	482 kPa	Max. pattern (cm)
Standard production spray guns: Suction feed													
7	36	38	36SD	0.070	1.77	7.8	11.5	15.2	10.5	0.22	0.33	0.56	27
18	66	65	66SD	0.070	1.77	7.9	12.1	18	10.5	0.22	0.34	0.56	27
62	66	365	66SD	0.070	1.77	7.9	12.1	18	10.5	0.22	0.34	0.56	27
69	66	565	66SH	0.070	1.77	7.9	12.1	18	10.5	0.22	0.34	0.56	27
BBR	A072	AB	AS17	0.073	1.85	7.8	11.5	15.2	12	0.22	0.33	0.56	30
Standard production spray guns: Pressure feed													
7	33	33	33PE	0.040	1.02	10.1	15	20	10	0.286	0.424	0.566	25
18	63B	63A	66PE	0.046	1.15	9.5	15	20	13	0.269	0.424	0.566	33
62	63B	363A	66PE	0.046	1.15	9.5	15	20	13	0.269	0.424	0.566	33
69	63C	563A	66PE	0.052	1.32	9.5	15	20	13	0.269	0.424	0.566	33
BBR	A061	A047	AP19	0.059	1.50	9.0	16	21	13	0.254	0.453	0.594	33
Small spray guns: Suction feed													
15	78	78	78S	0.052	0.132	4.2	6.9		8	0.118	0.195		20
26	78	78	78SD	0.040	0.102	2.8	4.0		8	0.079	0.113		20

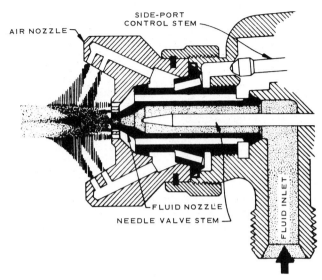

FIGURE 3-14 Air and material flow. *(Courtesy of Binks Manufacturing Co.)*

tem the fluid must come out of the fluid tip at a higher rate than for a siphon type of a gun. Air movement at this area creates an air cushion at the face of the air cap to help keep the face of the air nozzle clean.

The air passageways in the horns are called side port jets, and the air coming out of them strikes the fluid stream just ahead of the second-stage atomization point. The primary use of side port air jets is to shape the air and fluid stream into the required fan or spray pattern shape (Fig. 3-14). The size of this fan is controlled by the spreader control valve.

Fluid Tips

Fluid tips meter and direct the material into the air stream. They provide a self-aligning concentric ball and cone seat for the air cap and equalize the air leaving the center orifices of the cap (Fig. 3-15). In selecting a fluid

tip, consideration should be given to several factors. Heavy, coarse material requires large-nozzle-size tips to eliminate clogging. Very thin material that sags readily is applied at low atomizing pressure with a small nozzle to prevent excessive material application.

The fluid tip must fit the air cap properly so as to balance the amount and shape of the spray fan. When the trigger is pulled, the fluid needle gives off a round, controlled stream of paint to be atomized by the air cap. The fluid tip is the seat for the fluid needle, which shuts off the paint when the trigger is released. Fluid tips and needles are made to fit each other in matched sets and are available in many sizes (Tables 3-1 and 3-2).

Fluid Needles

Fluid needles control the amount of material flow and always carry the same number as the fluid tip; that is, FF tip with FF needle, EX tip with EX needle (Fig. 3-16). The fluid needle controls and limits the amount of fluid going through the fluid tip as controlled by the trigger. This needle is adjustable by adjusting the setting on the fluid control knob. How to make this adjustment is one of the first things to learn (Fig. 3-16).

The fluid needle is kept sealed to the body by a fluid needle packing, and it uses a fluid needle packing nut to keep it tight and sealed. To prevent leakage, the packing nut is tightened by finger pressure or the appropriate wrench. The packing must be lubricated with a nonsilicone oil and must be tight against the fluid needle, while still allowing it to move freely. The fluid needle spring is used to return the fluid needle to the shut off position when the trigger is released.

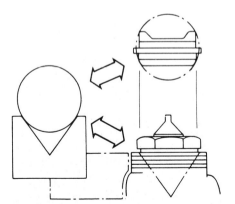

FIGURE 3-15 Self-aligning concentric ball and cone seat. *(Courtesy of DeVilbiss Canada Ltd.)*

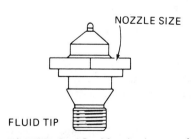

FIGURE 3-16 Matched set of fluid needle and fluid tip. *(Courtesy of DeVilbiss of Canada Ltd.)*

Fluid Needle Adjustment. This adjustment controls the movement of the fluid needle and meters the amount of material through the nozzle. This valve is generally used with at least the first thread in sight. The fluid feed valve or control knob is used to control the amount of fluid going through the fluid tip when the trigger is pulled back. When the fluid control is turned clockwise all the way in, the fluid cannot leave the fluid tip. When it is turned counterclockwise until one thread shows, it is then wide open. Between both these adjustments a multitude of adjustments can be made by the painter as required for the particular job to be done. This adjustment is considered one of the two most important adjustments performed on a spray gun.

Spreader Adjustment Valve

The spreader adjustment valve controls the amount of air allowed to the air horns. This adjustment is used when changing from a round spray pattern to a flat elliptical pattern or any desired pattern in between. The spreader control valve or pattern control valve is used to control the amount of air going through the horn holes of the air cap and controls the height and width of the spray pattern. When the air spreader control is closed completely clockwise, the spray forms a small round pattern (Fig. 3–17a). When spot repairing or blending with solvents is required, a medium-sized spray pattern must be obtained by adjusting the spreader con-

trol (Fig. 3–17b). When the spray gun is used for normal painting, a full fan is used; this requires that the spreader control be turned counterclockwise till the first thread shows (Fig. 3–17c). This produces a spray pattern between 10 and 12 in. (25 and 30 cm) high without splitting in the center when sprayed 8 in. (20 cm) away from the surface. This adjustment is the next most important adjustment to the fluid feed on the spray gun.

The trigger is used to open both the fluid and air valve. The trigger has two positions; the first opens the air valve and the gun works as a dusting gun only. When opened up more, it contracts the fluid needle and moves it back from the fluid tip as required, allowing paint to come out of the gun. The trigger is designed so that two fingers are used on it while the other two are holding the handle on the gun body.

The trigger bearing stud and screw hold the trigger attached to the body of the spray gun.

Air Valve

The air valve in the gun body controls the air and is opened or closed by the pull and release of the trigger. The air valve is used to control the amount of air through the spray gun; the more it is open the more compressed air that moves through the gun.

Some air valves use leather or plastic as a packing, and others use a tapered metal-to-metal seal. If the valve leaks and it has a seal, the valve should be tightened

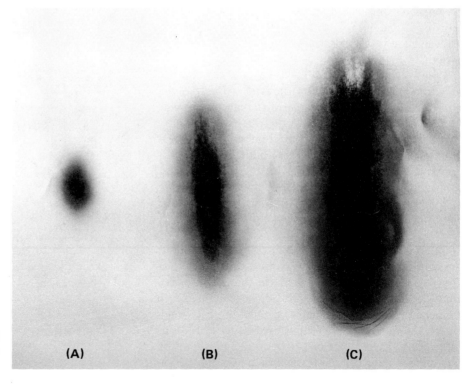

FIGURE 3–17 Different-sized spray patterns. (a) Small. (b) Medium. (c) Full Size.

(A)   (B)   (C)

slightly. An air valve spring is used to close it when the trigger is released.

Gun Body

Gun bodies are usually made from a hard, tough aluminum alloy. They are designed to be easy to balance and handle and are very durable. The gun body is designed with a hook at the top of it, and it is the principal part to which all other parts are fitted. The handle is shaped to be comfortable when held in the hand, and it fits the two fingers holding it as it is being used. It can last a lifetime if properly cared for.

The fluid inlets on the gun are made so that the fluid hose of a pressure pot or the tube of the paint cup of a suction feed can be attached to it. This inlet guides the material to passageways to reach the fluid tip. All fluid inlet connections must be tight; otherwise, spray gun operations will be faulty. The fluid inlet has a thread that is usually ⅜ in. (9.5 mm) NPS.

At the base of the gun handle is a threaded hole for an air line adapter; the size of the threads is ¼ in. (64 mm) NPS. A threaded connector or a quick connector is usually attached to this adapter.

Baffle

The baffle ensures an even distribution of air inside the air cap; this baffle is situated at the front of the gun where the spray head is located. On some spray guns the baffle is a removable part, while on others the baffle is engineered into the design of the spray head of the spray gun. The purpose of the baffle and spreader control valve are to control the size and shape of the spray pattern.

Tables 3–1 and 3–2 show the type of fluid needle, fluid tip, and air caps used on different spray guns. These parts are matched to work with certain combinations in the spray gun. The part numbers are the parts recommended by manufacturers to be used in their equipment. The tables also provide the amount of air used by different air caps at different pressures.

Fluid Containers

Fluid containers come in different sizes and materials. There are two general types of cups, a cup for the suction feed and a cup or container for the pressure feed gun. These containers come in different materials, such as metal, glass, and plastic. The small 1- to 6-ounce (50- to 180-milliliter) glass cup is used on air-brush-type spray guns. The 1-quart or 1-liter metal cup is used on suction feed guns (Fig. 3–18), which are the most com-

(a)

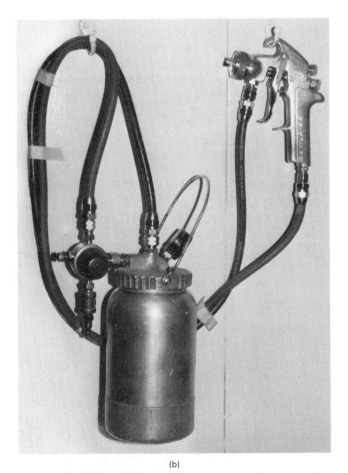

(b)

FIGURE 3–18 (a) Suction-feed spray cup assembly. (b) Typical 2-quart remote pressure cup.

monly used. The 2-quart (2-liter) metal cup, as well as larger containers, is used with pressure feed equipment. Plastic 1-quart (½-liter) cups are used on some gravity fed spray guns.

On suction feed guns, the cup is attached to the fluid inlet by using a clamping device on the fluid tube, which attaches to the two pins on the gun cup. The fluid tube also holds the lid of the paint cup. The lid has a vent hole that lets air enter the spray cup to allow atmospheric pressure to push the fluid through the spray gun. The suction cup cover must always be installed with the vent at the back of the gun, that is, close to the handle. This reduces the possibility of the fluid dripping out through the vent hole while spraying horizontal surfaces. This hole must always be kept clean. Many newer types of covers have a dripless feature built into them. The cover has a gasket that is made of either leather or rubber to form a seal between the cover and the cup.

The fluid tube is usually positioned on the cup cover assembly in a position so that it faces the front of the gun. These types of cups are designed with systems for quick attachment and removal from the tube assembly. To install a Binks cup, it is positioned to engage the clamp hooks on the cover with its two side lock pins; then the wing nut is tightened clockwise to hold the cup. To disassemble, the procedure is reversed by turning the wing nut counterclockwise, and the cup is disengaged from the cover.

With a DeVilbiss gun cup (Fig. 3-18a), the clamp is tightened and loosened by using a half-turn swivel cam. This clamp secures the cup to the cover when it engages the lock pins on the cup properly. When the cup locking pin is engaged into the hooks of the clamp lever and cam assembly, the cam is turned 180° to tighten the cup to the fluid tube assembly. To disassemble, reverse the procedure. Before lifting the gun from the work area after engaging and tightening the cup, always check to see if it is attached and properly secured.

The 1- to 2-quart (1- to 2-liter) cup containers on a pressure feed gun usually use a threaded cup and receiver to join them together. The 1-quart (1-liter) cup is usually attached to the spray gun, whereas the 2-quart (2-liter) cup is attached by using short hoses. On larger containers the gun is attached by means of hoses and metal pipe to the container. When using pressure equipment, air is used to force the material to the spray gun.

The 2-quart pressure remote cup has an air regulator on the lid (Fig. 3-18b) and a gauge as well as a bleed valve to permit removal of the cup when spraying is finished. This regulator is used to regulate the pressure on the fluid in the cup to usually around 5 to 15 psi (35 to 100 kPa) as required for the type of material to be sprayed. The regulator transformer regulates atomizing air pressure to the spray gun. The cup is connected to the gun by using two hoses, one for air and the other for the fluid.

The pressure feed offers some advantages over the suction feed type of gun. The spray gun is light and easy to handle, and the remote cup is usually tied to a belt. It allows the painter to adjust with precision the right ratio of fluid to air for quality control. The spray gun will give a large, full spray pattern and excellent atomization. Since it uses a larger container, the painter does not have to stop as often to refill, thus speeding up the work. The only drawback is that the cup assembly and gun must be cleaned meticulously; otherwise, it can be troublesome. It is really a spray gun that should be used by one painter only.

The pressure feed attached cup on the spray gun is available with a regulator or without. On the regulator type, the pressure can be varied according to material to be sprayed; the pressure registers on the gauge. This prevents excessive pressure buildups. Some models also have a valve to control the atomizing air through the gun.

The nonregulator type (Fig. 3-19) has no pressure-controlling devices; only a bleeder relieves the pressure when spraying is finished. This type of gun uses the same pressure on the fluid as for atomizing; it is usually used on small outfits. Never overpressurize the cup as it could damage it.

FIGURE 3-19 Nonregulated pressure-feed gun.

A different type of spray gun that has appeared on the market is the gravity fed type (Fig. 3–20). This gun is quite common in Europe. It is used mainly for applying heavy-bodied, catalyzed, two-component, high-build primer surfaces or for small areas such as touch-ups and blend areas. Its construction is similar to a suction feed gun except that it is fed by gravity.

3–2 ATOMIZATION AND VAPORIZATION

A spray gun in operation produces atomization and vaporization. Atomization is the process of breaking up the solids in the paint and depositing these solids on the surface in the form of tiny spheres or globules (Fig. 3–21). Vaporization is the gassing off of the thinners or reducers in the paint, a process that takes place between the gun and the surface being coated (Fig. 3–22). It is

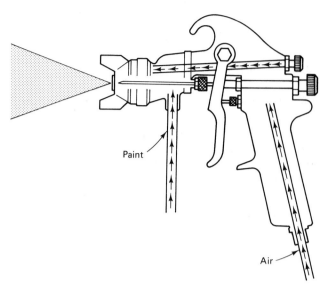

FIGURE 3–21 Atomization of paint. *(Courtesy of DeVilbiss of Canada Ltd.)*

important for the spray gun to atomize the material properly; therefore, maximum atomization is desirable. Vaporization, which results in a loss of paint thinner or solvent, is not desirable; therefore, it should be held to a minimum. This brings us to the basic rule in spray painting. A production gun should be held 6 to 8 in. (152 to 203 mm) away from the surface being coated. There is one exception, however—metallic colors, for which the gun is held 12 to 14 in. (305 to 356 mm) away when applying the final coat (Fig. 3–23).

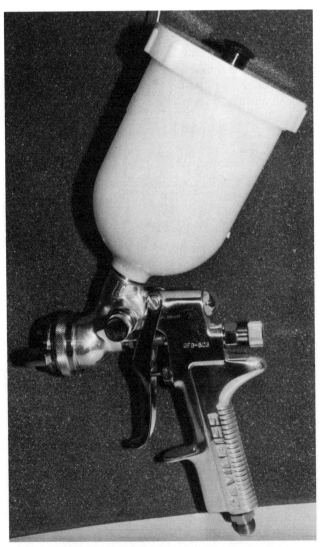

FIGURE 3–20 Gravity-feed spray gun.

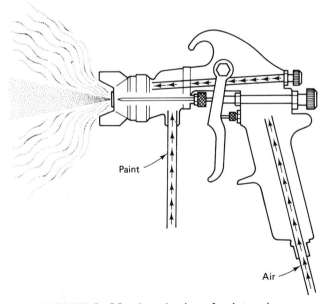

FIGURE 3–22 Atomization of paint and vaporization of thinner. *(Courtesy of DeVilbiss Canada Ltd.)*

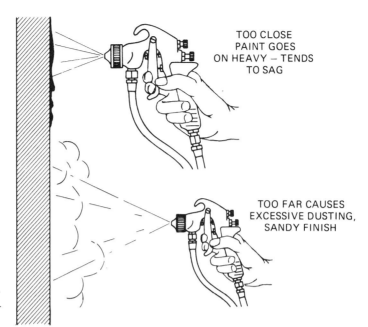

FIGURE 3-23 Improper spraying distance. *(Courtesy of DeVilbiss Canada Ltd.)*

A number of fundamental motions in the use of the spray gun are very important and must be followed if a good finish is to be obtained. The importance of gun distance is the major cause of poorly painted articles. A good guide to correct gun distance is to use the span of a person's hand, which will be approximately 8 in. (203 mm). If the gun is held too close, flooding will result. If held too far, excessive overspray and dry spray occur (Fig. 3-24). The next thing to consider is the speed of the gun as it is moved across the surface to be painted. Most operations require the application of a full coat of material. This means that the gun should be moved fast enough to obtain production but slow enough to put on a good finish. A definition of a wet coat is *all the paint that can hang on a vertical surface without sagging* (Fig. 3-25).

Proper Stroking and Triggering of the Spray Gun

To achieve proper stroking, the gun must at all times be held perpendicular to the surface being coated. If the gun is tilted, there will be a flooding condition nearest the gun and dry spray at the bottom of the pattern (Fig. 3-26).

Triggering is the method used when beginning or ending a spray stroke. A spray gun is designed with two pressures on the trigger—first and second. In first pressure, the air is allowed to pass through the gun by opening only the air valve. The second pressure pulls the fluid needle back, allowing the material to enter the airstream.

At the start of a stroke, the trigger is pulled back all the way and the gun is moved only the length of the

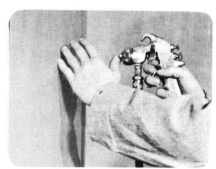

FIGURE 3-24 Proper spraying distance. *(Courtesy of DeVilbiss Canada Ltd.)*

panel, or within the comfortable reach of the operator. The trigger is then released back to first pressure and the gun is placed in position to begin another stroke. If the operator does not release the trigger at the end of each stroke, there will be a buildup of paint at each end, which may result in sags (Fig. 3-27).

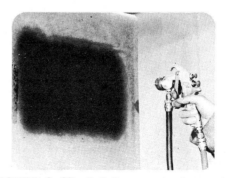

FIGURE 3-25 Full flow coat of material. *(Courtesy of DeVilbiss Canada Ltd.)*

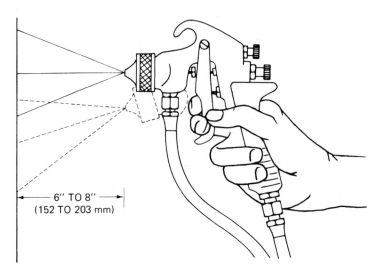

6" TO 8"
(152 TO 203 mm)

FIGURE 3-26 Spray gun should be held perpendicular to the surface as shown here by solid lines. Tilting the gun up or down gives an uneven spray pattern. *(Courtesy of DeVilbiss Canada Ltd.)*

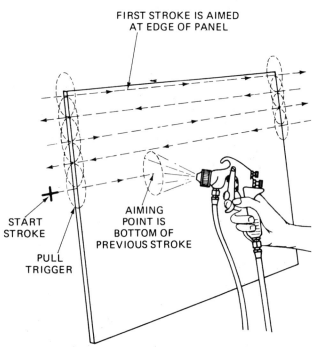

FIRST STROKE IS AIMED AT EDGE OF PANEL

START STROKE

PULL TRIGGER

AIMING POINT IS BOTTOM OF PREVIOUS STROKE

FIGURE 3-27 When spraying a panel, use alternate right and left strokes, triggering the gun at the beginning and end of each stroke. The spray pattern should overlap one-half the previous stroke for smooth coverage without streaks. *(Courtesy of DeVilbiss Canada Ltd.)*

The spray gun should be moved with a steady, deliberate pass at approximately 1 ft per second. The spray gun should never stop moving or the sprayed coat will drip and run. Generally, the work is started at the top of an upright surface such as a door panel. The spray gun air cap should be level with the top of the surface to be painted. This means that the upper half of the spray pattern will be applied on the masking paper. The

second pass is made in the opposite direction with the air cap level with the lower edge of the previous spray pass pattern. Thus one-half of the pattern overlaps the previous spray pattern and one-half is sprayed on the unpainted area.

The spraying continues in this back and forth system, and at the end of each pass the spray gun is lowered one-half the top-to-bottom width of the spray gun pattern. The last pass is made with the lower half of the spray pattern below the surface of the article being painted. The procedure just described is called a *single coat*. If a double coat is to be applied, the same procedure is repeated. This system is usually used when applying lacquer topcoat. Flash-off time of several minutes must be given to allow the solvents to evaporate and the finish to dull slightly between coats. Some paint manufacturers recommend that, when painting lacquer, topcoats should be sprayed cross coated; that is, half of the coats of paint are applied at right angles to the other coats.

Overlapping, Banding, and Arcing

When spraying, always overlap the area 50%. Overlapping is accomplished by aiming the air horns directly at the bottom or top of the last spray stroke; otherwise, streaks will appear on the sprayed surface. This is particularly true when metallic paint is sprayed (Fig. 3-28).

If the painter has only one panel to paint on an automobile, it should be banded at the edges (Fig. 3-29). This method reduces the amount of overspray that reaches the surface to be painted. Either this overspray is exhausted through the exhaust fan or it falls on the spray booth floor. The painter sprays a band at each end of the panel vertically; then the panel is sprayed with horizontal strokes. The painter triggers the gun at

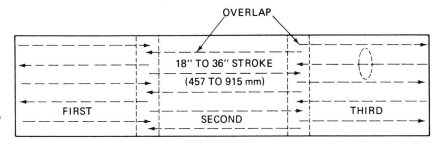

FIGURE 3-28 Long work is sprayed in sections of convenient length, each section overlapping the previous by 4 in. (102 mm). *(Courtesy of DeVilbiss Canada Ltd.)*

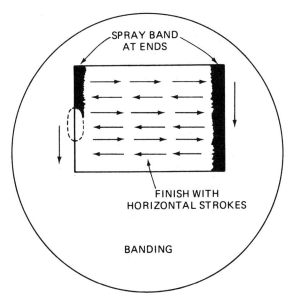

FIGURE 3-29 Vertical bands sprayed at the ends of a panel prevent overspray from horizontal strokes. *(Courtesy of DeVilbiss Canada Ltd.)*

the appropriate time in the stroke. The bands help overcome any arcing that could be present in the stroke. This method will give a good flow out of the painted surface and cut the waste of material. It is well known that approximately 30% of the material is wasted, especially if proper triggering and gun stroking are not applied to the job by the painter. The stroke must always be a smooth and steady movement by the painter at all times.

Arcing means that the gun is swung in a stroke in which the gun may be 6 to 8 in. (152 to 203 mm) from the surface in the center of the swing, but at the end of the stroke it could be perhaps 16 in. (406 mm) away from the surface. The results are an excessive overspray and poor flowing out of the painted surface (Fig. 3-30). When spraying a radius or curved surface, the gun must follow a path that has the same radius as the surface being coated, maintaining the correct gun distance. For slender work, adjust the spray pattern to fit the job—avoid excessive overspray. Spray technique is the most important phase of spray painting, and the various rules

and methods just outlined should be practiced until they become fixed working habits.

Feathering

Feathering is a control used by painters during blending and spot repairs. To feather a spray gun means that, when the spray gun is approaching the area requiring paint, the trigger is pulled back gradually. This allows paint to come gradually out of the gun. The trigger is pulled back more where more paint is required in the blend or spot area, and then the trigger on the gun is feathered again to cut off the paint volume. Depending on the area to be painted, such as from a door edge to the middle of the panel, the spray gun is feathered at the end of the stroke. If the repair is from the center toward the edge, the spray gun is feathered at the start. If the repair is done in the middle of a wheel opening, hood edge, or trunk lid, this situation could require that the spray gun be feathered at the start and end of the stroke.

When spraying a level surface (Fig. 3-31), the spraying should always be started on the near side and gradually worked out to the far side as shown. This is essential when lacquer is sprayed, since lacquer overspray landing on wet paint will dry sandy or rough. The gun is sometimes tilted a certain amount for some level surfaces, but where practical the spray gun can and should be held at as near a right angle to the surface as possible.

Tilting the Gun

When a spray gun with a suction feed cup attachment is used on a job that requires the spray gun to be tilted, the painter must take care to ensure that the tilt is not excessive. Otherwise, the paint material may clog or drip out of the air vent in the cup lid. The lack of atmospheric pressure on the paint in the cup will stop the fluid flow. DeVilbiss has available a plastic diaphragm to put on top of the gun cup for the nondripless cup lid to prevent the paint from dripping from the vent hole. To prevent leaks that can occur between the paint cup and the lid from dripping on the painted surface, it is some-

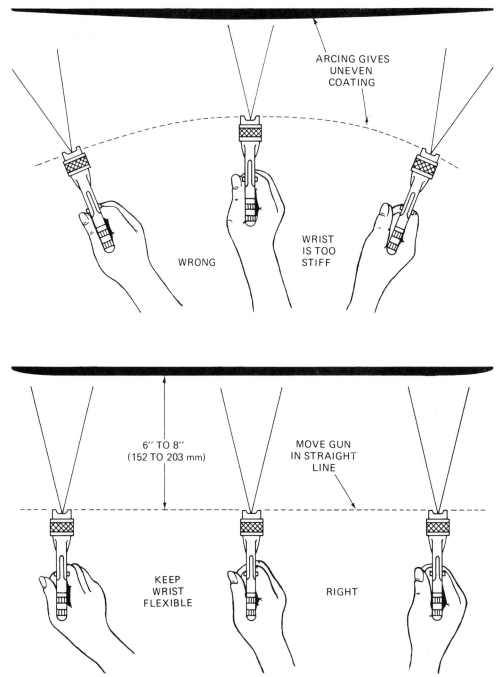

ARCING GIVES
UNEVEN
COATING

WRONG

WRIST
IS TOO
STIFF

6″ TO 8″
(152 TO 203 mm)

MOVE GUN
IN STRAIGHT
LINE

KEEP
WRIST
FLEXIBLE

RIGHT

FIGURE 3–30 Proper spraying motion gives accurate, even coverage of paint film on surface. *(Courtesy of DeVilbiss Canada Ltd.)*

times necessary to tie or wrap a rag or towel around the cup and secure it with masking tape until the spray application is finished. Different makes of cups on the market have a dripless feature built into them.

When it is required to spray at an upward angle for any appreciable amount of time, the complete cup should be rotated on the gun fluid inlet through a 180° turn. This allows the air vent to be in front of the fluid inlet tube and the fluid pick-up tube in the cup where

it curves, allowing the pick-up tube to reach the material when the gun is tilted.

Edges and Corners

When it is required to spray a panel on the edges as well as on the face, a modified banding technique is used (Fig. 3–32). One stroke is applied along each edge; this coats the edges and bands the face of the panel at the

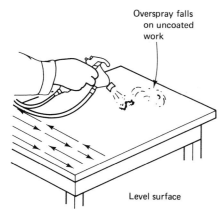

FIGURE 3-31 Start at near edge to avoid overspray on coated work. *(Courtesy of De-Vilbiss Canada Ltd.)*

FIGURE 3-32 Banding edges and corners. *(Courtesy of DeVilbiss Canada Ltd.)*

same time. When painting boxes, the outside corners of the boxes or cabinets are done using a similar method (Fig. 3-33).

Inside corners should be sprayed square on, as shown in Figs. 3-34 a and b. This technique will not apply a uniform coat but it is fast and practical. When it is important that an even coating be applied to each face of the corner it should be done as in Fig. 3-34b. After a vertical stroke to paint the corner, short horizontal strokes are used to cover the area adjacent to the corner to avoid double-coating or overspraying the adjoining surface.

When slender work has to be sprayed, it is im-

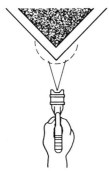

FIGURE 3-33 Adjoining surfaces are banded with one stroke of the gun. *(Courtesy of DeVilbiss Canada Ltd.)*

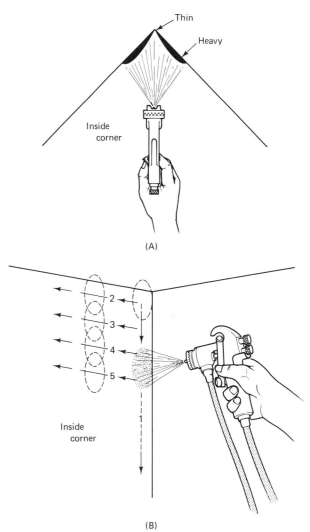

FIGURE 3-34 (a) Spraying directly into the corner gives an uneven coating but is satisfactory for most work. *(Courtesy of DeVilbiss Canada Ltd.)* (b) Spraying each side of the corner separately gives an even coating. Use vertical spray pattern. *(Courtesy of DeVilbiss Canada Ltd.)*

portant to make the spray pattern fit the job (Fig. 3-35). Either a smaller horizontal pattern or a large vertical fan spray will give complete coverage without excessive overspray. On the other hand, do not spray with too small a pattern.

When spraying such items as fences, iron grilles, and similar work, it should be done to get the most paint material on the largest area with each stroke. A picket fence should be sprayed with a single up-down angle stroke on each side. Intricate work or a wire fence should also be sprayed at an acute angle (Fig. 3-36). It is helpful to use a shield behind the wire, which will deflect the paint and help coat the back of the work.

When spraying around work like a flat round disc,

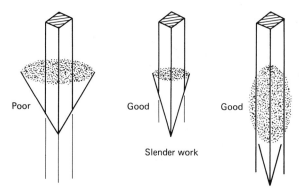

FIGURE 3–35 Avoid excessive overspray; adjust the spray gun pattern to fit the job. The center illustration shows the best method for this type of work. *(Courtesy of DeVilbiss Canada Ltd.)*

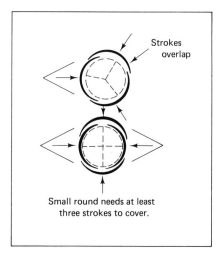

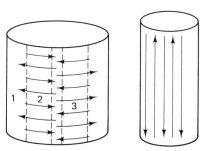

FIGURE 3–37 Use a round spray or vertical fan pattern for table legs or similar round surfaces. On larger round work, curve the strokes to conform with the surface. *(Courtesy of DeVilbiss Canada Ltd.)*

it should be sprayed just like any other plane surface, first banding the edge and then spraying the center. Large cylinders are usually painted using the same method as for a flat panel, except the strokes are shorter (Fig. 3–37). A cylinder of small diameter is more efficiently sprayed using lengthwise strokes (Fig. 3–37).

When spraying with a spray gun it is important that there be no wasted motion. Wasted motion is wasted time and material, which can be very costly. An analysis should be made of each painter's work to determine what improvements can be made in working methods. Many suggestions can be made to the spray gun operators that will enable them to reduce fatigue that is caused by the way they work. If the benefits are explained to the operators when the motion study analysis is done, their cooperation should be easily obtained. If a careful study is made, a significant savings in operations is possible, and perhaps higher production from the spray finishing equipment.

3–3 CLEANING SPRAY GUNS

Cleaning the spray equipment can be easily done if a few simple rules and procedures are established. On the suction-feed gun, loosen the cup from the gun; while the fluid tube is still in the cup, unscrew the air cap two complete turns, hold a rag over the cup, and pull the trigger. This process diverts the air pressure to the fluid or passageways, forcing the material back in the cup. Then empty the cup of the material and replace with thinner. Usually about 1 pint (½ liter) of thinner will be adequate; spray the thinner through the gun the same as paint (Fig. 3–38). The suction action lifts the material out of the cup and through the fluid tube and flushes the thinner down through the fluid passageway inside the gun. The air cap is then taken off the gun and carefully cleaned with a soft bristle brush, such as a toothbrush, using thinner if necessary (Fig. 3–39). Avoid

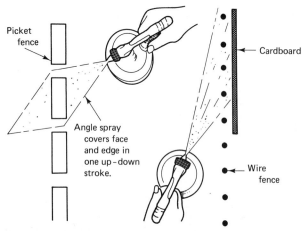

FIGURE 3–36 Open work is usually sprayed at an angle to cover as much of the work as possible with each spray gun stroke. *(Courtesy of DeVilbiss Canada Ltd.)*

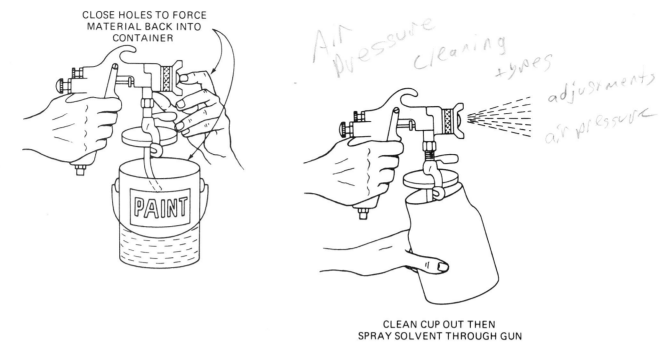

CLOSE HOLES TO FORCE
MATERIAL BACK INTO
CONTAINER

PAINT

CLEAN CUP OUT THEN
SPRAY SOLVENT THROUGH GUN

FIGURE 3-38 Cleaning the suction-feed spray gun. *(Courtesy of DeVilbiss Canada Ltd.)*

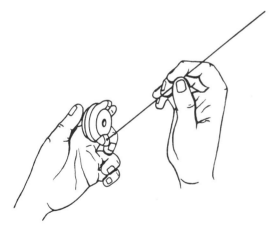

FIGURE 3-39 Cleaning the air cap. *(Courtesy of DeVilbiss Canada Ltd.)*

placing the entire gun in thinner, for this will wash out the lubrication in the various packings in the gun and contaminate the inside air passageways. Consequently, the gun will operate either inefficiently or not at all.

Pressure Feed

On the pressure-feed gun, additional steps are involved. The first operation is to blow back the system. This is done by releasing the pressure in the paint container and undoing the container from the top. Now go up to the spray head and hold a cloth over the front end of the gun and pull the trigger. Since the cloth is restricting the airflow to the atmosphere, the air will turn around and push the paint from the gun through the fluid hose back into the paint container. This blow-back can also be accomplished by unscrewing the air cap retaining ring three full turns and pulling the trigger.

This blowing-back operation is done to empty the paint out of the gun and fluid hose. Remove the paint from the pressure paint container and pour in 1 quart (1 liter) of the thinner or reducer used for thinning the material. It will not be necessary to atomize, so the atomization air can be turned off. Pull the trigger, thus allowing the thinner to be forced by pressure back through the hose and gun. Any paint that may have accumulated on the outside of the gun should be wiped off with a thinner rag or brush.

A hose cleaner, which saves both time and thinner, is available to do this same fluid tube and gun cleaning operation. It is important to remember that all spray equipment should always be clean. Any paint used should be properly strained before going into the system to avoid plugging up the inside of the fluid tip in the spray gun (Fig. 3-40).

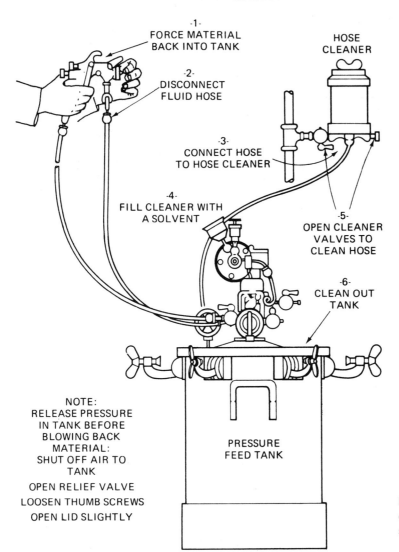

CLEANING SPRAY GUN-PRESSURE FEED

-1-
FORCE MATERIAL
BACK INTO TANK

HOSE
CLEANER

-2-
DISCONNECT
FLUID HOSE

-3-
CONNECT HOSE
TO HOSE CLEANER

-4-
FILL CLEANER WITH
A SOLVENT

-5-
OPEN CLEANER
VALVES TO
CLEAN HOSE

-6-
CLEAN OUT
TANK

NOTE:
RELEASE PRESSURE
IN TANK BEFORE
BLOWING BACK
MATERIAL:
SHUT OFF AIR TO
TANK
OPEN RELIEF VALVE
LOOSEN THUMB SCREWS
OPEN LID SLIGHTLY

PRESSURE
FEED TANK

FIGURE 3-40 Using hose cleaner to clean fluid hose and spray gun. *(Courtesy of DeVilbiss Canada Ltd.)*

Spray Gun Lubrication

The spray gun needs to have a number of its parts lubricated at regular intervals, depending on how often it is used. The fluid needle packing, the air valve stem, and the trigger bearing screws should be oiled. The fluid needle packing should occasionally be softened with oil. The fluid needle spring should be coated with light grease (Fig. 3-41).

3-4 HOW TO PAINT WITH A GUN

A production type of spray gun can either be suction or pressure and is used in the refinishing of a panel or a whole body. If the gun is a suction feed, it will probably have a fluid tip with an orifice of 0.070 in. (1.78 mm)

or larger, up to 0.085 in. (2.1 mm), if faster application is desired. Different sizes of air caps use different amounts of air. An air cap to fit a 0.070-in. (1.78-mm) fluid tip will use approximately 12 cubic feet (340 liters) of air at 60 psi (414 kPa).

On certain makes of pressure-feed guns, the same size of air cap and fluid tip can be used. A pressure-feed gun usually needs a slightly lower air-atomizing pressure than the suction feed because all the air that goes through the air cap is solely used to atomize the paint.

Spray guns used in shops have two controls that must be adjusted before painting (Fig. 3-42). These controls are used by the painter to control the amount of fluid and pattern of the spray. When the spreader-adjusting valve is closed, no air reaches the horns in the air cap, and the result is a round spray pattern. The spreader-adjusting valve should be opened enough so

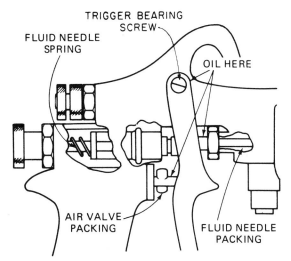

FIGURE 3-41 Points of lubrication. *(Courtesy of DeVilbiss Canada Ltd.)*

that a proper spray pattern is formed to suit the job to be done.

The fluid valve, when closed, stops the paint from entering the air-stream coming out of the air cap. This valve should only be opened for the amount of paint that is required for the job. For spot work, use only a minimum flow; for painting a panel, a maximum flow is used.

The painter or apprentice will have to decide what type of gun is required for the particular job. A small gun should be used if access to the job or paint work is limited. A large production gun, either suction feed or pressure feed, is usually used for most types of work. The equipment used could also depend on what equipment the shop has available unless the painters or apprentices have their own spray guns.

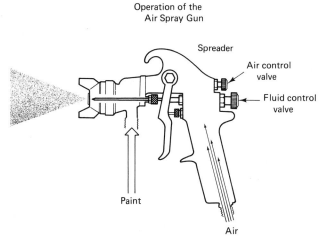

FIGURE 3-42 Fluid- and air-control valves. *(Courtesy of Binks Manufacturing Co.)*

To get satisfaction from a spray gun, it must be equipped with the proper fluid needle, fluid tip, and air cap (see Tables 3-1 and 3-2). These are chosen by the type of materials that will be sprayed and the rate of the fluid flow required. The air cap is chosen by the size of the area to be painted, type of material, speed required, fluid feed method, quality of finish, and amount of compressed air available.

The air supply required by most production guns in automotive painting is measured in cubic feet per minute (cubic meters per minute). A typical spray gun air cap consumes a lot of air depending on the pressure used (see Tables 3-1 and 3-2). The air delivered to the spray gun must be clean and regulated to the required pressure for the materials to be used.

The apprentice painter must learn to adjust the spray gun so that the amount of paint being used is balanced by the height of the spray fan and the amount of air being used.

It is important that the apprentice painter learn to use proper techniques when learning to paint. Proper techniques are a little harder to learn and to practice than bad techniques; bad techniques are sometimes a sign of lack of interest in the work and a poor attitude. Learning to paint consists of learning the theory of using the spray gun to its full potential, such as adjustments of the spray gun, application of the paint material, and how to obtain the best results. Theory is learned by studying textbooks and manuals, attending classes and clinics, and asking questions that make sense.

To develop the skill area, the apprentice must practice the different methods of holding and using the spray gun under many conditions. The apprentice must practice until very little thought has to be given on how to adjust and use the spray gun properly; the apprentice is proficient when he or she can do this by habit. The apprentice must also learn to use many different materials, such as epoxy material, lacquer, enamel, and different paint systems, under all necessary conditions used in the refinishing industry.

Spray Gun Adjustments

The painter or apprentice must know the basic adjustments for the spray gun before applying paint on a vehicle. The painter adjusts the spray gun so that the spray gun produces the proper spray pattern. The air cap can be used in two different positions; to adjust this, the air cap retaining ring is turned a half a turn. If a perpendicular (straight up and down) spray fan is desired, the air horns are adjusted so that they are in a horizontal position; this is the position most used by painters. The air cap retaining ring is then tightened securely but not overtightly. The other adjustment is when the spray pattern is horizontal and the horns are in the vertical position.

Three main patterns are used (Fig. 3–17). The full open pattern is used for complete paint jobs or large panels. The medium pattern is used mainly for spot repairs and blending with solvents. The small round pattern is used for small spots that require a fast material build up or for special repairs used sometimes when refinishing. The spray gun should be held as in Fig. 3–43, with two fingers on the trigger and the other two fingers and thumb holding the handle.

Pressure

The air pressure used at the gun is adjusted to the required pressure at the regulator on the transformer, taking into consideration the pressure drop caused by the hose. The pressure that should be used on different products varies according to the manufacturer's recommendation. Table 3–3 can be used if the recommended pressures are not known. The pressure used must sometimes be increased or decreased, depending on the viscosity of the material that is to be sprayed. If the pressure used is too low, the surface will be rough or have an orange peel effect. Too high an air pressure

FIGURE 3–43   Proper method of holding the spray gun.

will cause overatomization, resulting in dry spray and orange peel, because the air forces too much of the solvent to evaporate. The result will be a poor flow-out of the painted surface.

The spray gun cup is filled with the appropriate paint material, the air line is connected to the spray gun, and the air pressure is adjusted as required. The air cap is positioned for the horizontal position; then the retaining ring is tightened. The spreader control valve is opened counterclockwise to its full open position (Fig. 3–44a). The fluid control valve is then opened counterclockwise to its full open position, which is with one thread on the fluid valve adjustment screw visible (Fig. 3–44b).

Hold the gun the required distance from a suitably masked off area in the spray booth or a special spray stand in the vertical position. Spray material with a horizontal fan for the required time to flood the area of the spray pattern. Watch how and where the runs develop; if the runs are at both ends it shows that too much paint material is being applied there (Fig. 3–45). This is called a split pattern and is caused by too high an atomizing pressure, fan control too wide open, or overreduced paint.

If the air pressure is correct and the material is not overreduced, turn the air control valve slightly clockwise and retest the spray pattern. If the paint runs unequally for the length of the pattern, close the air control valve again and then retest. This is repeated until a run of equal volume lengthwise is created on the paper for the spray pattern test. If the pattern is too heavy at the center (Fig. 3–46), turn the fluid valve clockwise half a turn and repeat the flooding test to see where the paint run develops. If it is still too heavy at the center, close the fluid valve a little more and open the spreader control valve counterclockwise half a turn and retest the spray pattern. These adjustments are repeated until the spray pattern will flood and run down equally for the whole length of the pattern.

When spraying spot repairs, the spray gun is adjusted from a barely open position to a half or more open position (Fig. 3–47). This is governed by the size of the spot repair, and usually the smallest fan is used when possible. The gun controls should only be opened or closed by half-turns and are usually set at a midpoint of their range of adjustments. The spray pattern must be tested until the right size of pattern is obtained for the spot repair.

Some paint techniques require a dry spray adjustment. In dry spraying the spray gun releases just enough paint in a small pattern so that it is almost dry when it hits the panel. This is used to apply some primers that could lift or swell the sand scratches of a fresh finish that was defective. The paint applied in this manner is

TABLE 3-3

Spray gun air pressure chart

REFINISH MATERIAL	AIR PRESSURE RANGE (p.s.i.)												
	20	25	30	35	40	45	50	55	60	65	70	75	80
ACRYLIC LACQUERS													
Acme Pro-Kril				▓	▓	▓							
Ditzler Duracryl				▓	▓								
Dupont Lucite (Overall Refinishing and Panel Repair)					▓	▓							
Dupont Lucite (Spot Repair)	▓	▓	▓	▓									
Martin Senour Acrylic Lacquer				▓	▓								
R-M Alpha-Cryl				▓	▓								
Rogers Acrylic Lacquer				▓	▓								
Sherwin Williams Acrylic Lacquer				▓	▓								
Sikkens Auto Fine						▓	▓						
ACRYLIC ENAMELS													
Acme Acrylic Enamel (Non-metallic)							▓						
Acme Acrylic Enamel (Metallic)									▓				
Ditzier Delstar (Overall)								▓	▓				
Ditzler Delstar (Spot Repair)						▓							
Dupont Centari (Overall and Panel Repair)							▓	▓	▓	▓			
Dupont Centari (Spot Repair)			▓	▓									
Limco							▓	▓					
Martin Senour Acrylic Enamel (Non-metallic)							▓	▓					
Martin Senour Acrylic Enamel (Metallic)									▓				
Nason Acrylic Enamel							▓	▓					
R-M Miracryl 2 (Standard Colours)						▓	▓	▓					
R-M Miracryl 2 (Base Coat)					▓	▓							
Rogers Acrylic Enamel (Non-Metallic)							▓	▓					
Rogers Acrylic Enamel (Metallic)									▓				
Sherwin Williams Acrylyd (Non-metallic)							▓						
Sherwin Williams Acrylyd (Metallic)									▓				
URETHANES													
Acme Miralon									▓	▓	▓		
Ditzler Deltron					▓	▓	▓						
Ditzler Durethane					▓	▓	▓						
Dupont Imron (Non-metallic)							▓						
Dupont Imron (Metallic)										▓	▓		
Martin Senour Nitram									▓	▓	▓		
R-M Bonacryl							▓	▓					
Rogers Monarch									▓	▓			
Sherwin Williams Sunfire 421									▓	▓			
Sikkens Auto Cryl									▓	▓			
SYNTHETIC ENAMELS													
Acme Fleet X (With 61 Reducer)								▓	▓				
Acme Fleet X (With 62 Reducer)							▓	▓					
Acme Fleet X (With 65 Reducer)				▓	▓								
Ditzier Ditzco								▓	▓				
Dupont Dulux							▓	▓					
Limco							▓	▓					
Martin Senour Synthol (With 8004 Reducer)							▓	▓					
Martin Senour Synthol (With 8005 Reducer)							▓	▓					
Martin Senour Synthol (With 8008 Reducer)					▓	▓							
Nason Astron and Nasco									▓	▓	▓		
R-M Super-Max							▓	▓					
Rogers Synthacote (With 4061 Reducer)								▓	▓				
Rogers Synthacote (With 4062 Reducer)							▓	▓					
Rogers Synthacote (With 4065 Reducer)					▓	▓							
Sherwin Williams Kem Transport (With 179 Reducer)								▓	▓				
Sherwin Williams Kem Transport (With 183 Reducer)							▓	▓					
Sherwin Williams Kem Transport (With 6220 Reducer)					▓	▓							
	138	172	207	241	276	310	345	379	414	448	483	517	552
	AIR PRESSURE RANGE (kPa)												

(a)   (b)

FIGURE 3-44   (a) Spreader air-control valve adjustments. (b) Fluid-control valve adjustments.

FIGURE 3-45   Flooding test-split spray pattern.

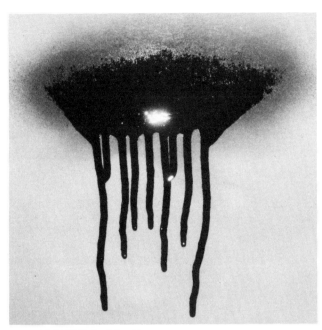

FIGURE 3-46 Heavy center spray pattern.

dry enough to be wiped with a tack rag to remove dust and loose overspray. This technique is used to do spot repairs, as described in Chapter 7. The fluid needle and spreader control are closed completely; they are then opened just enough so that just a slight amount of material comes out of the gun with a small, round spray pattern. The trigger is pulled back and the material is applied in a circular motion, keeping the gun 6 in. (15 cm) from the surface. The air line pressure is the same

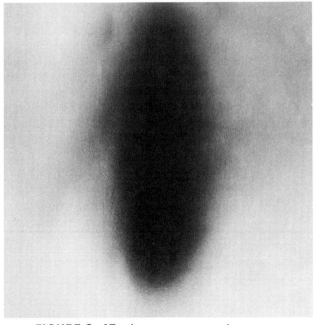

FIGURE 3-47 Average spot repair pattern.

as used when applying the material in the conventional method. Approximately every 10 seconds the application is stopped to observe the smoothness of the application and to tack off the surface. If the material is too dry, increase material flow and recheck the application. If the material that is going on is too wet, the distance of the gun is increased a bit or the fluid control valve is turned slightly clockwise to reduce the flow of material. The application is rechecked and the material is tack wiped again; this is an important step, which must be repeated often when doing this type of work. The work is finished, as explained in Chapter 7, according to the paint system being used.

It is important to remember when spraying that the appropriate type of respirator should be worn at all times. The general type is used for general paint work that has no isocyanates and an approved respirator when using paint that contains isocyanates.

3–5 TROUBLESHOOTING

Sags or *runs* (Fig. 3–48) are caused by holding the gun too close to the surface, the viscosity of paint being too low, or the speed of stroke being too slow. Other causes are strokes overlapping too much or not using enough air pressure.

Dry spray (Fig. 3–49) is caused by the air pressure being too high, the viscosity of the paint being too high, the speed of stroke being too fast or not overlapping enough, or the gun being held too far away from the panel.

Proper flow-out (Fig. 3–50) results when correct air pressure is used, the viscosity of the paint is right, the spray gun is used with the proper stroke and proper overlapping, and the gun is held at the proper distance from the panel.

Excessive orange peel is caused (Fig. 3–51) by the viscosity of the paint being too high, using too high or too low air pressure, or using a poor reducer or thinner.

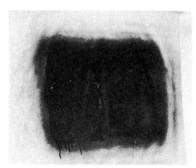

FIGURE 3-48 Sags or runs on panel. *(Courtesy of DeVilbiss Canada Ltd.)*

FIGURE 3-49 Dry spray on panel. *(Courtesy of DeVilbiss Canada Ltd.)*

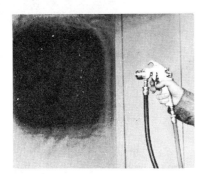

FIGURE 3-50 Proper flow-out of paint on panel. *(Courtesy of DeVilbiss Canada Ltd.)*

FIGURE 3-51 Excessive orange peel on panel. *(Courtesy of DeVilbiss Canada Ltd.)*

The first thing a painter must do once the mixed paint is in the gun cup is to check the spray pattern (Fig. 3-52). The fluid valve is opened to give sufficient flow, and then the spreader adjustment is opened to get the proper spray pattern. If the gun does not give the proper spray pattern, the painter must know what is causing this:

1. When the spray pattern is top heavy, it is the result of horn holes being partially plugged, an obstruction on the bottom of the fluid tip, or dirt on the air cap seat or fluid tip seat (Fig. 3-53).

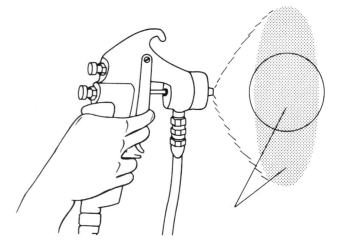

FIGURE 3-52 Adjusting the spray gun for normal spray pattern. *(Courtesy of DeVilbiss Canada Ltd.)*

2. When the spray pattern is bottom heavy, it is caused by horn holes being partially plugged, an obstruction on the top side of the fluid tip, or dirt on the air cap seat or fluid tip seat (Fig. 3-53).
3. Heavy right-side pattern is caused by right-side horn holes being partially clogged, dirt on right side of the fluid tip, or on the twin jet air cap by the right jet being clogged (Fig. 3-54).
4. Heavy left-side pattern is caused by left-side horn holes being partially clogged, dirt on left side of the fluid tip, or on the twin jet cap by the left jet being clogged (Fig. 3-55).
5. Heavy center pattern is caused by too low a setting of the spreader adjustment valve, or with twin jet cap by too low an atomizing pressure or the material is too thick; with pressure feed equipment, too high a fluid pressure for the atomization air being used or the material flow is in excess of the normal cap's capacity. The nozzle could be too large or too small for the material used (Fig. 3-56).
6. Split spray pattern is due to air and fluid not being properly balanced. Reduce the width of the spray pattern by means of the spreader adjustment valve or increase fluid flow (Fig. 3-57).

Remedies for 1 to 4

To determine if the obstruction is on the air cap or fluid tip, make a test spray pattern: rotate the air cap half a

TOP HEAVY

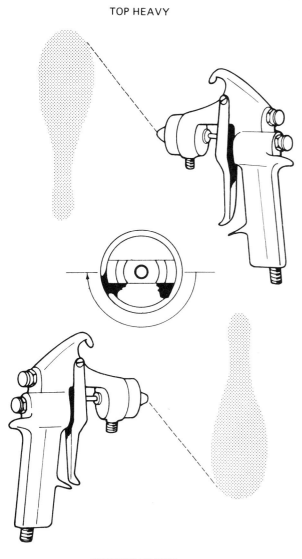

BOTTOM HEAVY

FIGURE 3-53 Faulty spray patterns. *(Courtesy of DeVilbiss Canada Ltd.)*

FIGURE 3-54 Heavy right-side pattern. *(Courtesy of DeVilbiss Canada Ltd.)*

FIGURE 3-55 Heavy left-side pattern. *(Courtesy of DeVilbiss Canada Ltd.)*

FIGURE 3-56 Heavy center pattern. *(Courtesy of DeVilbiss Canada Ltd.)*

FIGURE 3-57 Split spray pattern. *(Courtesy of DeVilbiss Canada Ltd.)*

turn and spray another pattern. If the defect is inverted, the obstruction is on the air cap; but if it is not inverted, the obstruction is on the fluid tip. Clean the air cap and check the fluid tip for a fine burr or dried paint inside the opening.

Remedies for 5 or 6

If the adjustments are out of balance, readjust atomizing pressure, fluid pressure, and spray width adjustment until the desired spray is obtained.

The causes of a jerky or fluttering spray (Fig. 3-58) are lack of sufficient material in the container, the container is tipped at an excessive angle, there is an obstructed fluid passageway, the fluid tube could be loose or cracked, or the fluid tip or seat could be damaged. These conditions apply both to a suction- or pressure-feed gun. The following conditions only apply to a suction feed. The material viscosity is too high or the air vent in the cup lid is clogged. The coupling nut or cup lid could be loose, dirty, or damaged. The fluid needle packing nut is either dry or loose, or the fluid tip is resting on the bottom of the cup.

3-6 PRACTICE SPRAYING

The best way to get the feel of handling a spray gun is by using it. The wrist, arm, and body must be able to flex at the right time. Therefore, practice spraying panels with the gun, using water as the fluid. When painting panels, a certain method should be used to save material and time.

Remember that the spray gun should be held the proper distance, be as perpendicular as possible to the surface, and follow the contours of the body or panel.

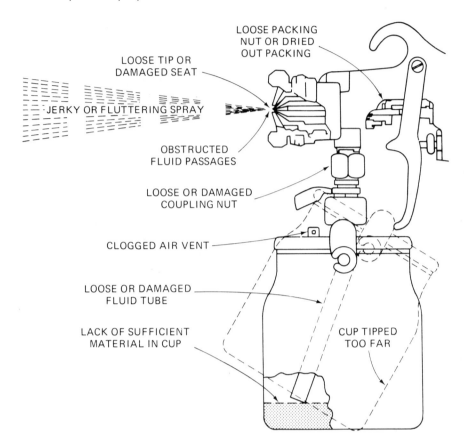

LOOSE PACKING
NUT OR DRIED
OUT PACKING

LOOSE TIP OR
DAMAGED SEAT

JERKY OR FLUTTERING SPRAY

OBSTRUCTED
FLUID PASSAGES

LOOSE OR DAMAGED
COUPLING NUT

CLOGGED AIR VENT

LOOSE OR DAMAGED
FLUID TUBE

LACK OF SUFFICIENT
MATERIAL IN CUP

CUP TIPPED
TOO FAR

FIGURE 3-58 Causes of jerky or fluttering spray. *(Courtesy of DeVilbiss Canada Ltd.)*

A smooth and steady motion must be used; the speed of travel must be just right to cover the surface properly. Overlapping of the previous stroke must be 50%, and no arcing of the gun must be done at the start or finish of the stroke.

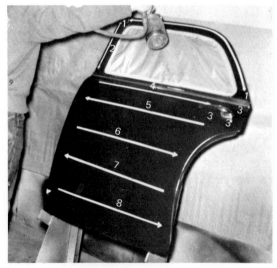

FIGURE 3-59 Spraying a door.

Spraying a Door

The top of the door frame is painted first and then the painting proceeds down toward the bottom of the door. If only one door is painted, the edges should be banded; also, care must be taken when spraying near the door handle, for a little too much paint will cause a sag to occur (Fig. 3-59).

Spraying a Fender

The hood edge and the body flange of the fender are done first, then the front part around the headlight, and then the crown, progressing downward to the bottom (Fig. 3-60).

Spraying a Quarter-Panel

The edges should be done first; then the painter should stand halfway along the panel and spray the panel in long, continuous strokes. If this is impossible, divide the area in half. Great care must be paid to the overlapping at the center when it is done with this method. If too much paint is loaded in the center, a sag will occur (Fig. 3-61).

FIGURE 3-60   Spraying a fender.

Spraying a Hood

The cowl edge is done first and then the front of the hood. Next, standing along the side of the fender, start at the center and progress toward the edge; both sides are done the same way (Fig. 3-62).

Spraying a Turret Top

To paint a top, a painter usually stands on a bench to be able to reach the center of the top. The windshield edge is done first on one side; then painting progresses from the center to the outer edge. The back and side are done after one side is completed. The other side is done using the same method (Fig. 3-63).

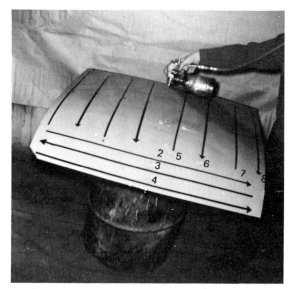

FIGURE 3-62   Spraying an engine hood.

Complete Refinishing

When refinishing a car completely, the order in which the different sections of the car are painted may vary and this is left to the preference of the painter. Generally, however, in the cross-draft booth the sections farthest from the exhaust fan are painted first. This procedure keeps a minimum amount of spray dust from settling on the already painted sections and results in a glossier finish. The turret top is painted first (Fig. 3-64). Then the doors on either the right or left side of the car are painted. Next the rear quarter-panel on the same side is painted, followed by painting the deck lid and trunk lower panel. The opposite side of the car is painted starting at the quarter-panel and then the doors and

FIGURE 3-61   Spraying a quarter-panel.

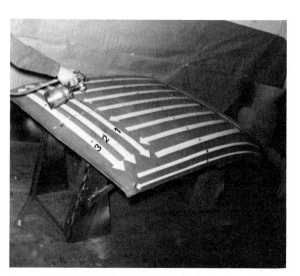

FIGURE 3-63   Spraying a turret top.

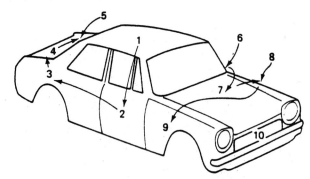

FIGURE 3-64 Spraying a complete automobile in cross-draft spray booth.

front fender. The hood, grille shell, valance, and opposite fender are painted last.

In a down-draft booth, since the air is moving from the ceiling down toward the pit under the vehicle, a painter must change methods. To be able to keep the edge of the paint film wet, the roof should be painted first, and then the hood and the trunk lid. Then the right side is painted, followed by the lower trunk panel and then the left side moving toward the front, which is finished last (Fig. 3–65).

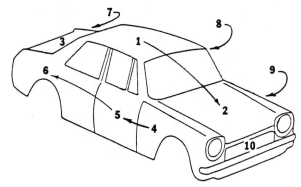

FIGURE 3-65 Spraying a complete automobile in down-draft spray booth.

REVIEW QUESTIONS

3-1. Describe how a spray gun brings paint and air together.

3-2. Describe the difference between an air cap on a suction-feed gun and a pressure-feed gun.

3-3. Name three types of spray guns.

3-4. Where does the air and material meet in an internal-mix spray gun?

3-5. What is the purpose of an air cap or nozzle?

3-6. Is it necessary that the fluid tip and fluid needle be matched?

3-7. What is the purpose of multiple jets in an air cap?

3-8. What is meant by containment holes in an air cap?

3-9. How must a fluid tip and air cap fit together?

3-10. How is the fluid flow adjusted on a spray gun?

3-11. What is the purpose of the spreader-adjustment valve on a spray gun?

3-12. What is the purpose of the air valve on a spray gun?

3-13. What is the purpose of a baffle on a spray gun?

3-14. How many cubic feet of air per minute or cubic meters per minute does a JGA-502 with an 80 air cap use?

3-15. What is the purpose of multiple jets in an air cap?

3-16. Describe how a fluid cup is held on a DeVilbiss spray gun.

3-17. What size of containers are used on a suction-feed spray gun?

3-18. How is a gravity spray gun fed the paint material?

3-19. What is the average size of the portable pressure-fed spray gun?

3-20. What is meant by atomization?

3-21. What is meant by vaporization?

3-22. In general, how far should a production gun be held from the surface when spraying (a) 4 to 6 in. (102 to 152 mm); (b) 6 to 8 in. (152 to 204 mm); (c) 12 to 14 in. (305 to 357 mm)?

3-23. What is meant by overlap?

3-24. What is meant by arcing?

3-25. What is the main difference in painting in a cross-draft booth compared to a down-draft booth?

CHAPTER FOUR

Abrasives and Power Tools

SAFETY HINTS

Always wear safety goggles to protect the eyes from flying objects, particles, or splashing liquids.

Always wear the appropriate respirator or dust filter masks when painting, machine sanding, or sandblasting. These respirators or dust filters will protect your lungs from the harmful effects of solvents, dust, and fine silica sand dust.

If at all possible, wear safety shoes; they have a metal insert that will prevent injuries to the toes from falling objects.

Always place safety stands under the axles of a vehicle that is jacked up and block the wheels.

4-1 ABRASIVES

An abrasive is any hard, sharp material that will wear away a softer, less-resistant surface when the two are rubbed together. The term abrasive is generally applied to sharpening stones, grinding wheels, and, when used on flexible backings, coated abrasives.

Seven different minerals are used in the manufacturing of abrasives today. Four minerals, flint, garnet, iron oxide (crocus), and emery, are classified as natural mineral abrasives because they are used in their natural state. The remaining three, aluminum oxide, zirconia alumina, and silicon carbide, are classified as synthetic mineral abrasives because they are manufactured.

Flint or flint quartz is found in large quantities all over the world, but not all flint can be used as abrasives. The best type for this purpose varies in color from a dull gray to a faint pink. The lumps, when crushed, break up into sharp crystals that are graded as to size and fastened to paper by means of an adhesive, giving us what is commonly called flint sandpaper. This paper does not, however, hold its sharpness for very long.

In addition to being an abrasive, garnet (in its larger, purer forms) is used as a semiprecious stone in making jewelry. The smaller, more imperfect stones are crushed. The crystals formed are also graded and fastened to paper by means of an adhesive. Garnet possesses toughness and hardness that are second only to diamond. When garnet breaks down, each break produces new sharp edges. It is this breaking down that gives garnet sandpaper its superior cutting action and longer life.

Emery, because of its great hardness, is used in the form of powder, grain, or larger masses for grinding and polishing. It is black and composed of iron oxide and corundum (aluminum oxide). When emery is crushed, its grain shape is more rounded than either flint or garnet. For this reason, emery sandpaper is more frequently used as a polishing paper than for cutting. Iron oxide (crocus) is a very soft natural abrasive; it is red in color.

Silicon carbide is a synthetic mineral made by processing a mixture of sand and carbon in an electric furnace. Its crystals are very hard and sharp (needlelike); when first manufactured, it was used for polishing gems. As manufacturing costs dropped, however, its use as an abrasive in the manufacture of sandpaper increased. This bluish-black abrasive is very effective for sanding low-tensile metals, plastics, copper, aluminum, and paint materials. When used with water it becomes an excellent material for sanding primer-surfacers, sealers, paint, or fiber-glass products and for featheredging and scuffing between coats.

Aluminum oxide, another synthetic mineral, is produced from a form of clay called bauxite; it is mixed with coke and iron filings and heated to a high temperature in an electric arc furnace. The resulting reddish-brown material is then crushed. The crystals formed are coarse and chunky, do not break very readily, and can therefore withstand greater working strains. Aluminum oxide is especially suited for cutting and grinding operations on steel and other hard surfaces and it is considered the toughest and longest lasting of all abrasives.

Zirconia alumina is a rugged synthetic (nonmetal) abrasive that provides a free, cool cut and is used for removing rugged stock applications. It has a blockier but sharper grain than aluminum oxide. Due to its microcrystalline structure, it permits controlled breakdown and self-shaping. This bluish-gray abrasive is only available in coarse grits from 24 to 80 or P24 to P80.

Zirconia alumina is very well suited for the heavy grinding of ferrous and nonferrous metals, the planing of wood, and the shaping and sanding of body filler.

Of the preceding abrasives, flint emery and crocus are more suitable for household use, while garnet, silicon carbide, zirconia, and aluminum oxide are used extensively in industry. In repairing and refinishing autobodies, silicon carbide, zirconia, and aluminum oxide abrasives are the most commonly used.

Coated abrasives have flexible backings that are made of either rope or Kraft paper cloth or a combination of paper and cloth. Rope paper backings are made from old rope and are the strongest paper backings available. Kraft paper backings are made from wood pulp and are used where a weaker paper backing can be employed.

Paper backings are provided in four weights. The A weight is the most pliable and lightest; it is used on finishing paper and is designed mostly for hand-sanding operations. The C and D weights are usually used where more stiffness and strength are required. These papers are usually used on hand or light portable machine operations. The E weight is a cylinder paper that is stiff, strong, and of high tensile strength. It is usually supplied in roll, disc, or belt form for machine use.

Cloth backings are supplied in only two weights. The J weight is a flexible light cloth used in light machine- or hand-sanding operations. The X weight is stronger and heavier and has a more stretch-resistant backing; it is used in belt and disc form where stock removal is of first importance.

Fiber combination backing is a combination of X weight cloth with a strong blue-gray vulcanized fiber. It is mostly used on portable disc sander operations where high speeds and severe strains are encountered, such as body solder removal, deburring, and rough grinding of welds. The fiber backing is durable and strong and is used mainly on heavy-duty disc operations on frame and body metal.

The abrasives placed on backing are crushed and then put through steel rollers. The grit is screened and graded for size. Grit sizes are designated by symbols or mesh number, or both. Abrasives used in autobody repairing all employ the mesh number in describing the grit size. The finer grits, called *flour,* are graded by the sedimentation or the air-flotation process. Abrasive particles or grains are then cleaned chemically or by heating, thereby removing any surface contaminations that would result in poor bonding with the adhesive.

Different types of adhesives are used to fasten or affix the abrasive to the different backings. *Hide glue* is a flexible strong adhesive used primarily on dry hand sanding or light mechanized sanding operations, such as between coat sandings or for featheredging paint.

The *modified bond* has an inert filler added to hide glue to provide a denser, more heat-resistant bonding agent. This type is usually used for more severe dry sanding operations on body metal and paint.

The *resins* used are of the thermosetting synthetic type; they are used as bonding agents so as to overcome the effect of heat caused by fast machine sanding. Resin bonds are used in belt and disc grinding for heavy cut down and high production on body frames, bumpers, and metal parts.

The *resin modified* has an inert filler added to the resin adhesive to increase the resistance to heat of the bond. This occurs in heavy stock removal of rough surfaces, such as in contouring.

The *resin and varnish* is used as the fastening or bonding agents in the manufacture of waterproof paper used in wet sanding operations.

An *open-coat* type of disc or paper indicates between 50% to 70% coverage of the backing surface by the abrasive grain. Open-coat types of disc and paper abrasives will resist loading and are effective when used on materials such as aluminum, plastics, body solder, and paint. The *closed-coat* type of disc or paper indicates that the abrasive grains completely cover the surface of the backing material used. It is used for severe operations requiring heavy pressures and high removal rates. A closed-coat abrasive type on the backing will increase its life on rugged applications.

Elecroplating is one method used to apply the abrasive grain to the adhesive spread backing. The individual grits are firmly embedded, with the sharpest points erect and evenly spaced. The other method used is *gravity coating;* the abrasive is applied downward from a controlled hopper to form a uniform measured layer of grains on the adhesive. Gravity coatings are usually used for heavy stock removal materials. The material is then transferred to a drying room on drying racks. After drying, it is wound into very large rolls from which a variety of abrasive items, such as sandpaper and sanding disks and belts, is then cut.

The flexibility of the product is the method of being able to adapt the particular product to the required operations. The term *flexing* best describes the method of controlled fracturing of the bonds at either a 45° or 90° angle in uniform segments. A nonflex is a stiff material in which bond layers have only slight fracturing and therefore it is seldom used. A flex 90, which is a single flex, is a material that can be flexed 90° in the length direction. Thus the coated abrasive is flexible in one direction but stiff in the other.

A *flex 45* is a coated material that can be flexed lengthwise at two 45° angles. Thus the material can be flexed in two directions. A *flex 90 plus flex 45* is known as a triple flex and is a combination of the two standard flexes to give it the greatest flexibility for irregular or sharp corners.

The two most commonly used sandpapers for preparing surfaces on vehicle bodies are the wet and dry silicon carbide type and the dry sanding aluminum oxide type. Silicon carbide is a closed-coat type of abrasive, while aluminum oxide is usually open coat.

As much as 50% to 75% of the time in a paint shop is spent sanding different types of materials. The most straightforward repair system consists of at least three important stages of sanding. The first sanding is done on the repair area; then the primer-surfacer and filler must be sanded. Then the total area that is to be painted must be sanded. A type of work that is done so frequently must be important; the time spent in sanding considerably influences the final result. Thus the painter or apprentice greatly influences the quality of the paint work by the care given to the sanding job. If it is not done properly, there will be lack of paint adhesion, sand-scratch marks and a generally poor appearance, and poor durability of the paint work.

The painter or apprentice must know what grits are used to do certain types of work. Table 4-1 shows that there are approximately 22 different grain particle sizes or grits, which range from 12 or P12, which is the coarsest, to 600 or P1200, the finest. The coarser grits are used for rougher or more rugged applications, and the finer grits are used for finishing or polishing applications. Table 4-1 is also a comparison chart for all these grits. It aligns the grading system used in North America with the European grading system.

Sandpaper can vary considerably, and the type of sanding material will vary according to the purpose for which it is used, that is, whether it is dry, wet, heavy, or light sanding work. The painter and especially the apprentice should take a piece of sandpaper and look at it carefully. The first thing that is seen and felt is the grit. The grit adheres or is held to the backing firmly by means of a special glue.

Figure 4-1 shows that a piece of sandpaper is made of grit, glue, and backing. Any of these components will vary according to the purpose for which the sandpaper is to be used. For example, the difference could be in using either aluminum oxide or silicon carbide grits. The differences between these two types of material are illustrated in Figs. 4-2 and 4-3.

The coding of sandpaper in Table 4-1 refers to the number of grains over a certain area of paper; the higher the number, the finer the sandpaper will be (Fig. 4-4). When comparing sandpaper from different manufacturers, the numbers do give a guide to the coarseness of each type of paper. But there are differences in the actual grit coarseness, although the same number may be used by different manufacturers. This is especially true

TABLE 4-1

Grit comparision chart

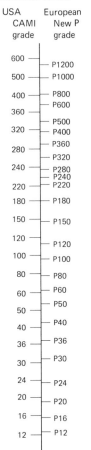

USA CAMI grade	European New P grade
600	P1200
500	P1000
400	P800
360	P600
	P500
320	P400
280	P360
	P320
240	P280
	P240
220	P220
180	P180
150	P150
120	P120
100	P100
80	P80
60	P60
50	P50
40	P40
36	P36
30	P30
24	P24
20	P20
16	P16
12	P12

Source: Sikkens B.V., Sassenheim, Holland.

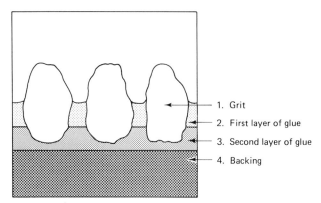

FIGURE 4-1 Sanding material is made up of four components; the first layer of glue ensures adhesion of the grit to the backing. The second layer of glue ensures good cohesion of the grit. *(Courtesy of Sikkens B.V., Sassenheim, Holland)*

1. Grit
2. First layer of glue
3. Second layer of glue
4. Backing

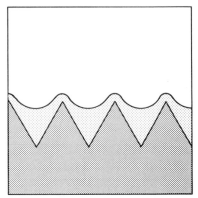

FIGURE 4-2 The sanding scratch caused by aluminum oxide shows less steep cuts, which are wider apart in the substrate than silicon carbide grit. Consequently, a finish applied to such a substrate shows a major wave (scratch mark). *(Courtesy of Sikkens B.V., Sassenheim, Holland)*

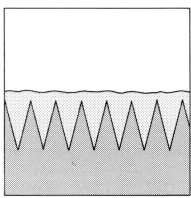

FIGURE 4-3 The sanding scratch caused by silicon carbide is steep and the edges are close together. Consequently, the finish has less of a gap to bridge, so that a smooth surface is obtained. *(Courtesy of Sikkens B.V., Sassenheim, Holland)*

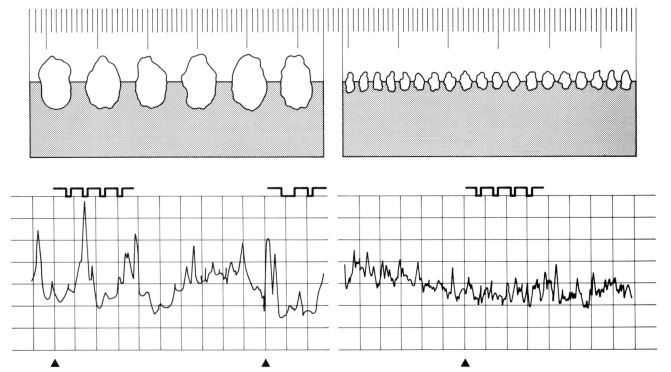

FIGURE 4-4 The coding of sandpaper is intended to indicate the number of grains on a certain area. The higher the number, the finer the sandpaper. The difference in grit coarseness is illustrated in the drawings. The profilogram depicts similar pictures of 280 or P320 and 360 or P500. *(Courtesy of Sikkens B.V., Sassenheim, Holland)*

TABLE 4–2

Comparison of grit codes used by different manufacturers

Old code waterproof	FEPA's new code waterproof	Manufacturer A waterproof Type 1	Manufacturer A waterproof Type 2	Manufacturer B waterproof	Manufacturer C waterproof	Manufacturer D waterproof	Manufacturer A dry
600	P1200			P600			
500	P800–P1000	P1200		P500	500		
400	**P500–P600**	**P1000**	**P800**	**P400**	**P600**	**P500**	**P400**
360	P400	P800	P600	P360	P500	P400	P360
320	P320	P600	P500	P320	P400	P360	P320
280	P280	P500					
etc.							

Source: Sikkens, B.V., Sassenheim, Holland.

The table compares the various grit codes used by different manufacturers. The starting point is the fact that the various types actually have the same coarseness, but differ so much in numbering that misunderstandings are likely to occur. So you have been warned.

in the finer types of sandpaper; the differences are apparent in the coarseness of the scratch marks. As long as one manufacturer's papers are used, the numbering will give a picture of the relative coarseness of the grit (Table 4–2).

Table 4–2 clearly shows the differences in the coarseness of sandpaper from manufacturer to manufacturer. The profilograms of Fig. 4–5 show the differences of the different papers. Thus once the painter has chosen a type of sandpaper, the same type should be purchased again to attain the same quality work. The numbering system is not an absolute guarantee for the coarseness of the sanding grit.

Only the experience of the painter can or should direct the choice and type of sandpaper purchased. If a change is contemplated, a small area on an old panel should be sanded with both makes or types of sanding material and then covered with a dark paint. This test should allow the painter to see the differences in the sand-scratch patterns.

A misconception exists that a coarse sanding material will do the work quicker; consequently, sandpaper that is too coarse is often used. Poor results, such as sand-scratch marks in the finish, come from too coarse

a paper. For a particular job, care should be taken to choose sandpaper that is the finest grade that will do the job.

4–2 HAND AND POWER SANDING TOOLS

Although we are in the power equipment age, a lot of sanding must still be done by hand. Sanding close to edges and moldings and concave and convex areas requires hand sanding to produce a job of high quality.

Sanding Aids

There are many types of sanding aids, such as hard, pliable rubber blocks, flexible rubber blocks like squeegees, soft rubber foam pads, and speed files. Figure 4–6 shows two different sizes of hard, pliable rubber blocks. These blocks are used to sand and featheredge paint on fairly flat areas (Fig. 4–7). These blocks can also and should be used when sanding glazing putty so as to give a straight surface after the sanding is done properly (Fig. 4–8).

The two sanding blocks in Fig. 4–6 are of different

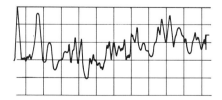

Profile of sandpaper of
make A — FEPA no. P400

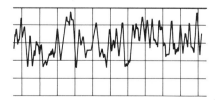

Profile of sandpaper of
make B — US no. 400

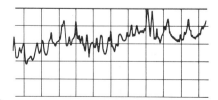

Profile of sandpaper of
make A — FEPA no. P800

FIGURE 4–5 Graphs of sandpaper profiles from same manufacturer, different numberings as well as profiles. *(Courtesy of Sikkens B.V., Sassenheim, Holland.)*

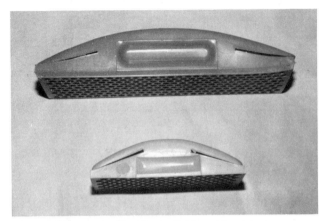

FIGURE 4-6 Hard pliable rubber blocks.

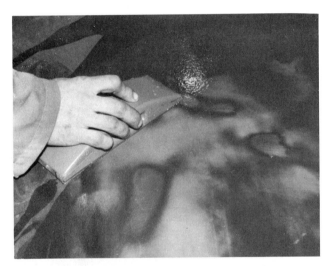

FIGURE 4-7 Featheredging area using a sanding block.

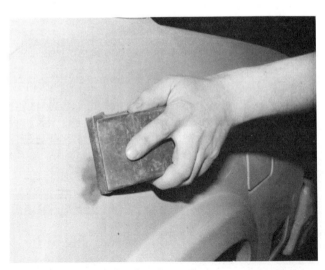

FIGURE 4-8 Sanding glazing putty with block.

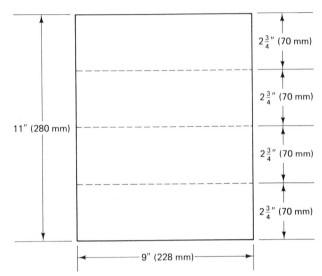

FIGURE 4-9 Cutting a sheet of sandpaper to fit short sanding block.

sizes; the smaller is 2¾ × 5½ in. (7 × 14 cm) and the longer block is 2⅞ × 9½ in. (7 × 24 cm). The smaller block can use single strips cut four times from a 9 × 11 in. (23 × 28 cm) sheet as in Fig. 4-9.

The longer block uses the same 9 × 11 in. (23 × 28 cm) sheet of sandpaper except it is cut as in Fig. 4-10. The sanding blocks are used to spread the cutting action of the sandpaper uniformly over the panel being sanded. This should eliminate highlights, which can be caused by fingers. The sanding block should only be used on low crown or nearly flat panels, because, due to its rigidity, it cannot bend or flex to follow contours. The

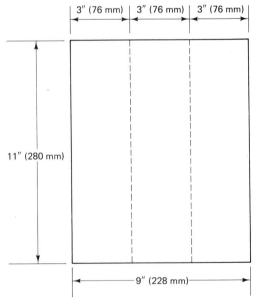

FIGURE 4-10 Cutting a sheet of sandpaper to fit long sanding block.

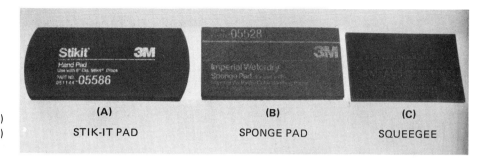

FIGURE 4–11 Sanding pad. (a) Stik-it pad. (b) Sponge pad (c) Squeegee.

(A)
STIK-IT PAD

(B)
SPONGE PAD

(C)
SQUEEGEE

sanding block is designed to hold the strips of sandpaper by short nails embedded in the bottom of the block, which are revealed when one of the upper lips, which are on each end, is lifted. The sanding block is designed to be used for both wet and dry sanding operations.

Figure 4–11 shows a Stik-It® hand pad, a sponge pad, and a squeegee. The stik-it pad is used with the round stik-it sheet from the rolled aluminum oxide dry sandpaper. The sponge pad uses wet or dry sandpaper from a sheet cut in half (Fig. 4–12). These are usually used with a half-sheet folded twice, producing three distinct working surfaces. The sponge pads are used by painters to help spread the sanding pressure uniformly, especially when doing concave or convex surfaces (Fig. 4–13).

The squeegee (Fig. 4–11) can be used also as a sanding block and it is fairly flexible. It can be used for either wet or dry sanding by wrapping it with sandpaper of the appropriate size. It is also used to wipe off the water and slush in wet sanding operations to check on the progress of the work. The squeegee is mostly used to apply plastic filler or glazing putty when required.

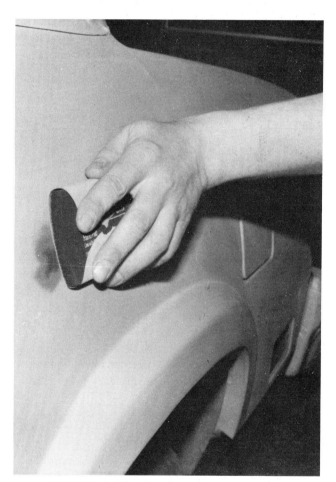

FIGURE 4–13 Sanding with sponge pad.

The long speed file (Fig. 4–14) is used both to sand plastic fillers and to sand glazing with a production paper; it is used to sand fairly flat, long panels. The reason for its use is that because of its length it can sand a panel, leaving a nonwavy finish if done properly. It is used by pushing and pulling fairly straight ahead and is also slid down at a slight angle.

Sanding without Aids

When sanding by hand without a pad, it is important that the sandpaper be held properly. The sandpaper is

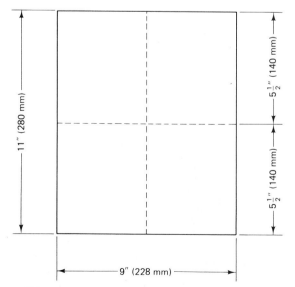

FIGURE 4–12 Cutting a sandpaper sheet in halves or quarters.

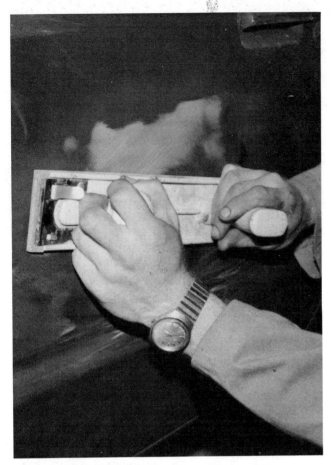

FIGURE 4-14 Sanding with speed file.

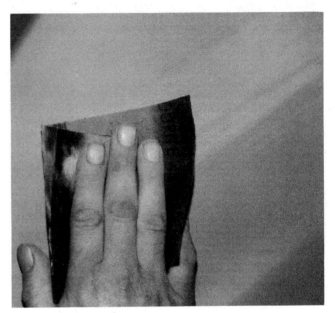

FIGURE 4-15 Holding and using sandpaper.

If a small area remains to be sanded, avoid the temptation of using an old piece of sandpaper. The old piece could be a coarse sandpaper grit worn smooth through use. It could feel quite smooth, but it is certainly dangerous to use as some grit could conceivably leave sand-scratch marks.

Sandpaper Characteristics

The sanding grades recommended in Table 4-3 relate to wet or dry sanding. When wet sanding by machine or by hand, one number finer grit is used for machine

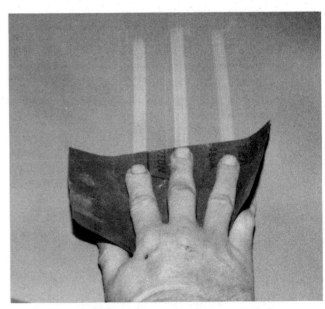

FIGURE 4-16 Fingers too far apart.

held in position by holding it with the thumb and the hand as it is laid on a flat surface and also between the fingers as in Fig. 4-15. By holding it in this fashion the sandpaper can be slid by hand at a slight angle crosswise back and forth, applying even pressure to sand the area properly. The sandpaper can also be held between the thumb and hand or third finger and little finger. Sanding with this method prevents sanding grooves in the paint surface.

Sandpaper should not be held and moved lengthwise as in Fig. 4-16 as this will leave wide unsanded and sanded grooves.

Figure 4-17 shows that the paper is held properly, but with sanding occurring in the direction in which the fingers are pointing, grooves will result, even if they are fewer.

When manually sanding down the last coat of primer-surfacer, a sponge block is very helpful as it distributes the pressure over the whole piece of paper (Fig. 4-18). Using this method reduces the amount of sand scratches; there is also less chance of bull's-eyes or contour mapping showing up in the painted surface. The surface will be smoother.

sanding, and by hand, one number finer than for machine sanding. Polyester materials should be dry sanded as they are sensitive to moisture. When doing regular sanding, the choice is usually up to the painter. Dry sanding creates a lot of dust but the results can be seen immediately. When wet sanding, the painter must wait until the surface has dried to see the effect of the work. The sanding mud is washed off, creating no dust and leaving a superior finish for a quality job. The water used not only carries away the sanding mud but also provides a lubricant for the grit, making it last longer with no clogging.

Table 4-3 shows the most common types of grits used when preparing a vehicle for metal repair and paint refinishing.

When using the 9 × 11 in. (23 × 28 cm) sheets of sandpaper to sand a vehicle either by hand or orbital sander, the sandpaper has to be cut to fit the purpose. The paper is usually cut by folding it in the appropriate place, bending it, and giving it a very sharp crease; it is then bent over the other way and the crease is applied at the same place. After doing this, the paper will usually rip at the crease when pulling pressure is applied on the sheet. Figure 4-19 shows how to cut the paper for use on an orbital sander or for sanding with a smaller type of block. For hand sanding some painters cut or fold the 9 × 11 in. (23 × 28 cm) sandpaper sheet in quarters (Fig. 4-20). It can be used in this fashion for wet or dry hand sanding.

Sandpaper can be purchased in a multitude of sizes and types and for different uses, from the round 5, 6, or 8 in. (13, 15, or 20 cm) adhesive-coated backing, to the rectangular 3⅔ × 9 in. (93 × 228 mm); see Fig. 4-21. In fact, any size used in the paint and body in-

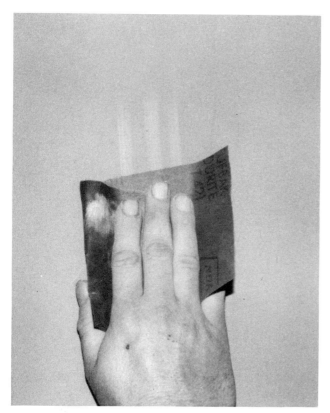

FIGURE 4-17 Sanding shows finger grooves.

FIGURE 4-18 Sanding primer-surfacer with sponge pad.

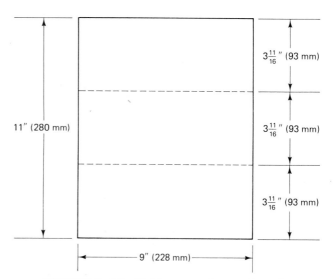

11″ (280 mm)

$3\frac{11}{16}$″ (93 mm)

$3\frac{11}{16}$″ (93 mm)

$3\frac{11}{16}$″ (93 mm)

9″ (228 mm)

FIGURE 4-19 Cutting a sandpaper sheet in three.

TABLE 4–3

Most commonly used abrasives for metal repair and paint refinishing

General abrasives types:	Sandpaper sheets	Sandpaper discs	
	Silicon carbide (closed coat), 9 × 11 in. or 23 × 28 cm	Aluminum oxide (close coat), 9 × 11 in. or 23 × 28 cm	Aluminum oxide (open coat), 5, 6, 8 in. or 13, 15, 20 cm

Paint sanding abrasives:

	USA CAMI Grade / European New P Grade	USA CAMI Grade / European New P Grade	USA CAMI Grade / European New P Grade
Fine	600 — P1200 / 500 — P1000 / 400 — P800, P600	600 — P1200 / 500 — P1000 / 400 — P800, P600	
Medium	360 / P500 / 320 — P400 / P360	360 / P500 / 320 — P400 / P360	P500 / 320 — P400 / P360
Coarse	280 / P320 / 240 — P280, P240, P220 / 220	280 — P320 / 240 — P280, P240 / 220 — P220	280 — P320 / 240 — P280, P240 / 220 — P220

Glazing, plastic and metal repair abrasives:

	USA CAMI / European New P	USA CAMI / European New P	USA CAMI / European New P
Fine	180 — P180 / 150 — P150	180 — P180 / 150 — P150	180 — P180 / 150 — P150
Medium	120 — P120 / 100 — P100 / 80 — P80	120 — P120 / 100 — P100 / 80 — P80	120 — P120 / 100 — P100 / 80 — P80
Coarse	60 — P60 / P50 / 50 / 40 — P40 / 36 — P36 / 30 — P30	60 — P60 / P50 / 50 / 40 — P40 / 36 — P36 / 30 — P30	60 — P60 / P50 / 50 / 40 — P40 / 36 — P36
	24 — P24 / 20 — P20	24 — P24 / 20 — P20	
Very coarse	16 — P16 / 12 — P12	16 — P16 / 12 — P12	

dustry is available from paint jobbers in sleeves of 100 sheets or even broken lots.

The size and grit of sandpaper, as in Fig. 4–21, is used on an orbital machine, either air or electric driven. This type of machine is called an orbital sander and can be used for many different purposes, such as sanding paint and fillers and featheredging.

Another type of material used is a general-purpose scuff pad, which is 6 × 9 in. (152 × 228 mm). These can be used to scuff door jambs and even painted surfaces. They are sold in three different types of abrasiveness: heavy, medium, and light. These pads can be torn to different sizes and are used for dry scuffing of surfaces (Fig. 4–22).

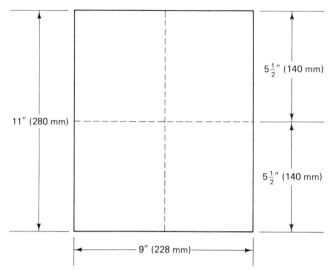

FIGURE 4-20 Cutting or folding a sheet of sandpaper in quarters.

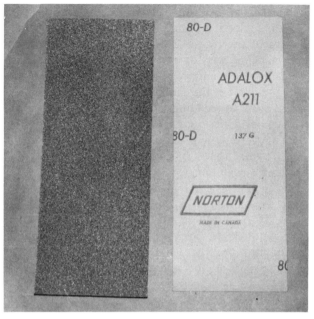

FIGURE 4-21 Production paper 80D or P80, $3\frac{2}{3} \times 9$ in. (93 × 228 mm).

Sanding Methods

The painter or apprentice must always be careful when sanding, especially when dry sanding operations are done. Approved breathing protection must be worn at all times; otherwise, a lot of dust will be inhaled into the lungs. This dust, which may come from paint, plastic fillers, glazing putty, and even the abrasive as it wears, can and will do tremendous damage to the lungs. You should always wear adequate protection because good health is your greatest asset.

As mentioned before and shown in Fig. 4-15, the paper must be held properly and the hand must go back and forth smoothly in fairly long strokes if possible. Paint should never be sanded in a circular motion because this could possibly leave circular marks in the new finish. Paint should always be sanded lengthwise as much as possible; this will not leave marks or scratches in the finish if done properly. The pressure on the sandpaper should be kept at a minimum; usually a light pressure is all that is required. Too much pressure on the

FIGURE 4-22 Scuffing door jambs with pad.

sandpaper may cause the backing to tear, and the grit will tend to load up and wear out faster and cause scratches in the finish. This method is used whether hand, machine, wet, or dry sanding is being done. At certain times it is necessary that the fingers exert most of the pressure on the sandpaper; this is usually when sanding close to moldings, the drip rail, and narrow parts such as upper door frames.

The best sanding method for large areas is usually a straight line, as this blends with adjacent areas. But sometimes a slight change is required to level a surface quickly, and this is achieved by using a slight cross-cutting stroke. The cross-cutting stroke is usually done with a 30° to 35° sliding motion, keeping the block or the finger direction fairly straight ahead. This method is used quite often when sanding glazing and plastic fillers with a speed file or sanding block.

Wet Sanding

When wet sanding a panel or vehicle, the work must start from the highest point. The necessary supplies should be at hand—appropriate sandpaper, sanding block if required, a pail of clear water, a hand sponge, and a suitable squeegee. The sandpaper and sponge are immersed in the water; then wet the higher area to be sanded first with the sponge and, if possible, leave the sponge on the appropriate area so that the water will run from it slowly. The sandpaper is held or folded as required and held by the proper hand grip or sanding block. The stroke of the hand should be just long enough to be comfortable, around 2 ft (61 cm). An area of 2 × 2 ft (61 × 61 cm) can be worked at one time usually fairly easily. The whole area is rubbed as often as required to dull the shiny surface of the paint and give the old paint tooth or small scratches to which new paint can adhere. Remember not to bear down on the sandpaper and to allow the grit to do the work. Water is fed to the sanding area by squeezing the sponge as required.

The sanding is stopped periodically and the surface is wiped dry using a squeegee. This allows the person doing the sanding to see if the job is being well done. Examine the surface at an angle to see if it is dull and smooth and all orange peel has been removed. The sandpaper is kept clean by dipping it frequently in clean water; use only as much water as is required to keep the area clean. When using a sanding block, it is important to check that the grit of the sandpaper is not sanding only a narrow area, with spaces in between the strokes. This is prevented by using a slight sliding motion on the sanding block; the block should not be used to sand paint on high-crown or convex areas.

The progress of the sanding job is checked fre-quently by wiping with the squeegee. The sandpaper must be changed as required when the grit wears down and no appreciable sanding is being accomplished. The sanding of an area is accomplished when the old paint film is dull and smooth and no orange peel is present. The work progresses from one adjacent area to another until the whole vehicle is sanded. The wet sanding operation should always be started at the highest point; then the vehicle is sanded and cleaned as the job continues in a downward fashion. By doing this, the vehicle is partially dry and clean when the sanding is completed.

When completed, the vehicle is cleaned with clean water and a sponge and wiped dry with a suitable towel or chamois or allowed to dry by itself. Sometimes, to speed up the drying action, compressed air is blown on the surface while drying with a towel. After this is completed, the floor in the sanding area should be cleaned of excess water and sanding residue.

4–3 POWER SANDING TOOLS

Dry Sanding

When dry sanding a vehicle, most of the work is done by a sanding machine, such as used in Figs. 4–23a and b.

Orbital sanders are used extensively in such autobody refinishing operations as featheredging, sanding, and polishing. They are manufactured in various sizes and models (light, standard, and heavy duty) and operate on either electricity (Fig. 4–23b) or compressed air. Those operating on compressed air can be used in wet as well as dry sanding operations; electrically operated oscillating sanders can only be used in dry sanding operations. They oscillate at anywhere from 3400 to 4500 orbits per minute and are generally equipped with pads that hold one-third of a 9 × 11 in. (227 × 279 mm) abrasive sheet of paper; they make it possible for a painter to perform featheredging, sanding, and polishing operations many times faster than manually.

The straight-line sander is primarily used by an autobody repairperson when sanding down the larger repaired areas on autobodies that are inaccessible and very difficult to metal-finish without the use of small amounts of plastic filler or body solder. The sander is operated by compressed air and works with a back and forth straight-line stroke. It is equipped with a long, wide backing pad that is fitted with clamps to hold 2¾ by 17½ in. (70 × 445 mm) strips of sandpaper.

NOTE: For better operation and longer life, pneumatic tools should be lubricated regularly with the correct lubricant and operated at air pressures no higher than recommended by the manufacturer.

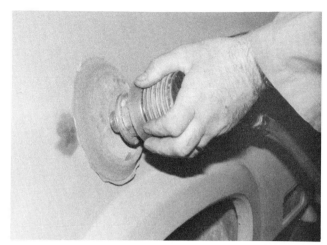

FIGURE 4–23a Using dual-action random orbit sander.

FIGURE 4–23b Using a rectangular pad vibrator.

The dual-action random orbit sander uses a 5-in (13-cm) disc (Fig. 4–24a). The larger disc is used on a sander polisher, and it has a 8-in. (20-cm) diameter (Fig. 4–24b). These discs are used to hold sandpaper that has an adhesive-backed coating. This type of equipment is used extensively in the trade. Discs are used to sand paint as well as to featheredge broken areas. The rectangular orbital sander can be used to sand and featheredge paint with the appropriate type of paper.

When any type of sanding is to be done, the appropriate types of backing should always be available; these include different types of blocks, sponge rubber pads, homemade blocks such as rectangular wood blocks or small sections of squeegees, or wooden paint paddles.

The appropriate type and grit of sandpaper should be available, silicon carbide for wet sanding and open-coat aluminum oxide for dry sanding. Usually, two dif-

FIGURE 4–24 Disc pads. (a) Stik-it, 6 in. (155 mm). (b) 8 in. (205 mm).

ferent grit sizes are used when sanding; the grits used are usually determined by the preference of the painter or apprentice. Remember, also, that, when sanding thermoplastic acrylic finishes or any material that is sensitive to high temperatures, the heat will cause the paint coating to melt easily and to plug the grit on the sandpaper. It is often necessary to use less air pressure on air-driven tools so that they turn slower and create less heat. Dual action sanders offer a combination of the features of the rotary sander and the surface sander. With each motion, the sanding disc of the eccentric rotary sander also makes an eccentric movement (Fig. 4–25). With strong pressure applied to the sander, the first movement is braked but the eccentric movement will continue, so the machine will sand like a surface sander.

Refer to Table 4–4 to determine the type and grit of sandpaper to use. When dry sanding, the best abrasive to use is usually an open-coat aluminum oxide sandpaper.

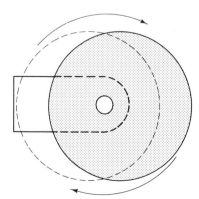

FIGURE 4–25 Sanding movement of an eccentric rotary sander. Less heat is developed. *(Courtesy of Sikken B.V., Sassenheim, Holland)*

TABLE 4–4

Disc grit numbers for portable sander

Disc types:

#	Coat	Description
#1	OPEN OR CLOSED COAT	DISCS ALUMINUM OXIDE GREEN BACK (Preferred) BLUE BACK ALSO AVAILABLE
#2	OPEN COAT ONLY	LUBE-KUT SILICON CARBIDE DISCS OR SHEETS
#3	OPEN COAT ONLY	LUBE-KUT ALUMINUM OXIDE DISCS OR SHEETS
#4	WATERPROOF PAPER	SILICON CARBIDE (Preferred) ALUMINUM OXIDE ALSO AVAILABLE CLOSED COAT ONLY G.M.
#5	OPEN COAT ONLY	ALUMINUM OXIDE DRY BACK PAPER DISCS OR SHEETS
#6	OPEN COAT ONLY	METAL RESIN CLOTH CUT SHEETS
#7	OPEN COAT ONLY	SILICON CARBIDE DRY BACK SHEETS
#8	CLOSED COAT ONLY	METAL CLOTH SHEETS (ALSO AVAILABLE FOR CRANKSHAFT BELTS)
#9	WATERPROOF CLOTH	BELT ONLY FOR GLASS EDGING SILICON CARBIDE

ORIGINAL FINISHES TO BE REFINISHED / REPAINTED FINISHES TO BE REFINISHED

System	Operation	ACRYLIC LACQUER — G.M.	ACRYLIC ENAMEL or SYNTHETIC ENAMEL	ACRYLIC LACQUER (repainted)	ACRYLIC ENAMEL & SYNTHETIC ENAMEL (repainted)
ACRYLIC LACQUER SYSTEM	HAND SAND	#2. (Preferred) 220-A 240-A DRY / #4. 360-A 400-A WET	#2. (Preferred) 280-A 320-A DRY / #4. 360-A 400-A WET	#2. 320-A DRY / #4. 400-A WET	NOT RECOMMENDED
ACRYLIC LACQUER SYSTEM	ORBITAL MACHINE SAND	#2. 280-A 320-A	#2. 240-A 280-A	HAND SAND PREFERRED	TEST FIRST!
ACRYLIC ENAMEL SYSTEM	HAND SAND	#2. (Preferred) 280-A 320-A DRY / #4. 320-A 360-A 400-A WET	#2. (Preferred) 280-A 320-A DRY / #4. 360-A 400-A WET	SAME AS O.E.M. ACRYLIC LACQUER	SAME AS O.E.M. ENAMELS
ACRYLIC ENAMEL SYSTEM	ORBITAL MACHINE SAND	#2. 240-A OR 320-A (SEAL WITH A.E PR. SEALERS)	#2. 240-A (on sides) 320-A (on horizontals)	SAME AS O.E.M. ACRYLIC LACQUER	SAME AS O.E.M. ENAMELS
SYNTHOL ENAMEL SYSTEM	HAND SAND	#2. (Preferred) 220-A DRY / #4. 320-A WET	#2. (Preferred) 220-A DRY / #4. 280-A 320-A WET	SAME AS O.E.M. ACRYLIC LACQUER (SEAL WITH 8098 SEALER)	SAME AS O.E.M. ENAMELS
SYNTHOL ENAMEL SYSTEM	ORBITAL MACHINE SAND	#2. 280-A (SEAL WITH 8098 SEALER)	#2. 220-A 240-A	SAME AS O.E.M. ACRYLIC LACQUER (SEAL WITH 8098 SEALER)	SAME AS O.E.M. ENAMELS

MACHINE SANDING (Flat—Disc—Orbital Sanders)

Category	DRY-HAND ROUGH SAND	DRY-HAND FINISH SAND	WET-HAND ROUGH SAND	WET-HAND FINISH SAND	Disc Recommendation
PRIMER SURFACER	#2. (Preferred) 220-A 240-A / #5. SAME GRITS / #7. SAME GRITS	#2. (Preferred) 280-A 320-A 400-A / #5. 280-A / #7. 280-A 320-A 360-A 400-A	#4. 180-C 220-A 240-A OR ALUMINUM OXIDE WATERPROOF MAY BE USED	#4. 280-A 320-A 360-A 400-A OR ALUMINUM OXIDE WATERPROOF MAY BE USED	#2. 150-A, 180-A, 220-A, 240-A—ROUGH 240-A, 280-A, 320-A—FINISH (Preferred) / #4. CUT SHEETS AVAILABLE—WET
PLASTIC BODY FILLERS	#6. 24-X, 36-X / #5. 36-E, 36-D, 40-D, 60-D, 80-D / #3. 60-D, 80-D (FOR FILE BOARD)	#5. 120-C, 150-C, 150-C, 180-A, 220-A / #2. 150-C, 150-A, 180-A, 220-A	NOT RECOMMENDED	NOT RECOMMENDED	#2. 80-A, 100-C, 100-A, 120-A, 150-A, 150-C / #6. / #5. SAME AS DRY HAND / #3. (FINER GRITS AVAILABLE)
METAL FINISHING	#6. 24-X, 36-X (FOR FILE BOARD)	#8. GRITS AVAILABLE FROM 50 GRIT TO 320 GRIT	NOT RECOMMENDED	NOT RECOMMENDED	#1. 5", 7", 9" DISCS 16, 24, 36—ROUGHING 50, 60, 80, 120—FINISHING
FEATHER EDGING	#3. 60-D, 80-D / #5. 60-D, 80-D	#2. 100-C TO 400-A / #5. 100-C TO 280-A	NOT RECOMMENDED	#4. 280-A 320-A 360-A 400-A OR ALUMINUM OXIDE WATERPROOF MAY BE USED	#3. / #2. / #5. ALL GRITS TO SUIT APPLICATION
GLASS EDGING & FINISHING	—	—	—	—	#9. BELT SIZES (WET) 3" x 24", 4" x 106", 4" x 118", 4" x 132"

A1428

Courtesy of Martin Senour Ltd.

A great deal of paint sanding and featheredging is done with machines. These machines speed up the work but they must be used properly. They should always be run with as much of the pad as possible rubbing on the surface; running them at a partial angle is very hard on the bearings and could cause premature failure. Very little pressure is required on the machine; let the weight of it put pressure on the flat surfaces so that the grit will cut properly. Remember, air-driven tools require lubrication at certain intervals; follow manufacturer's recommendations.

The term *scuff sanding* is used often and it means to make a surface smooth, dulling the film, or it may be just a light sanding to show imperfections in newly sprayed primer. Scuff sanding can be used on thermosetting and thermoplastic paint as well as air-dry enamels and lacquers. Scuff sanding is done to make slight grooves in the surface to give enamel-type paint mechanical adherence. Lacquer-type paint will adhere by a chemical bond when the thinner used reflows the old lacquer beneath it, but should be sanded to remove imperfections in the paint film.

The proper grit must be used, and open- or closed-coat sandpaper may be used because scuff sanding does not require too much sanding. The sandpaper is handled in the conventional straight line manner to remove the gloss and imperfections. The sandpaper should be checked often for cutting power; if it is loaded with paint, a stiff whisk broom or wire brush can be used to clean it. If it does not come clean, change to a new sheet of sandpaper.

When sanding a vehicle with a machine, the same technique can be used as for wet sanding. That is, start at the highest point and then work downward. The machine cannot be used to do everything, because when near moldings or sharp convex and concave areas it is necessary to work by hand (Fig. 4–26).

An approved dust mask must be worn when doing dry sanding because of the dust it creates. This dust should not be blown off in the shop with compressed air as it will only spread and settle on all flat surfaces and be inhaled by fellow workers. The dusty surfaces should be wiped off or blown off only when the vehicle is in a booth.

Featheredging

When preparing an old finish, it is necessary to prepare all broken paint areas; this is commonly known as featheredging. Featheredging is the wearing down of the paint film at a broken surface to a taper; this is done to help provide a flawless finish. A proper featheredge usually extends 1 to 2 in. (2.5 to 5 cm) for each coat of paint on the vehicle.

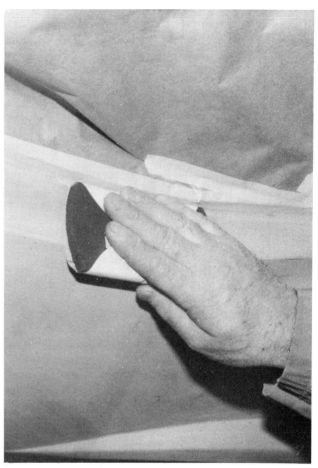

FIGURE 4–26 Hand dry sanding.

Two types of grits are usually used when featheredging by hand or machine sanding. The sandpaper should be selected according to Tables 4–3 and 4–4. Usually machine sanding is done as it is much quicker. The sanding starts at the break in the paint film and moves back usually as far as is required, or 1 to 2 in. (2.5 to 5 cm) per coat of paint (Fig. 4–27). Then a finer grit is used to sand over the area done with the coarser grit; a good practice is not to go more than 100 points from the coarse grade to the fine grade, using the same quality of sandpaper. If the sandpaper is too fine, it will be hard to sand away the deep sand scratches caused by the coarse sandpaper (Fig. 4–28). Sanding done with the finer sandpaper is sometimes called *back sanding*. This sanding is done with either a dry or wet sanding method, by hand or machine. The paint edges surrounding the metal spot are sanded with the appropriate sandpaper until the edge is invisible to the touch. No break or ridge should be felt by the fingers between the paint and metal (Fig. 4–29). The slightest ridge will show through the new topcoat and this will contour the work. Remember that sanding must progress well back into the paint to attain a gradual slope to the bare metal.

The feathered edges have been sanded with too coarse sandpaper. Touching up such areas takes much time and incurs the risk of contour mapping.

Preparation of the substrate with P60 or 60 to 80 grit paper is all right. Apply the polyester filler to the bare metal areas only.

The feathered edges have been sanded with P120 or 120 to 150 grit paper. This is an excellent substrate for the surfacer which is intended to cover polyester knifing filler and feathered edges.

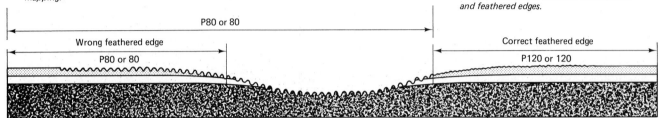

Sanding with too coarse sandpaper may cause contour mapping.

Think of the subsequent coat. Just sand the feathered edges of the spot-filled areas with paper of the same grit as you will use for sanding the subsequent coat.

FIGURE 4-27 Sanding for featheredge. *(Courtesy of Sikkens B.V., Sassenheim, Holland)*

When taking a mighty leap in grit coarseness (over 100 points), you only remove the tops. Deep scratch marks will remain.

A repair area sanded with P80 grit paper. This is a good substrate for coarse sanding material.

By including the intermediate stage of sanding with P150 or 150 grit paper, a greater part of the tops is sanded off. Final sanding with P240 or 280 grit paper will result in a fine, smooth substrate.

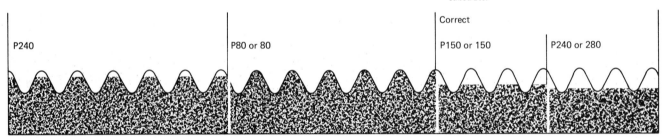

No mighty leaps from one grade to another.

FIGURE 4-28 Side view of a sanded area with different grits of sandpaper. *(Courtesy of Sikkens B.V., Sassenheim, Holland)*

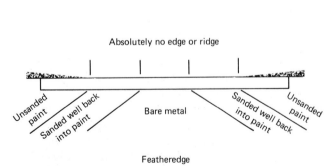

FIGURE 4-29a Side view of prepared feather-edge.

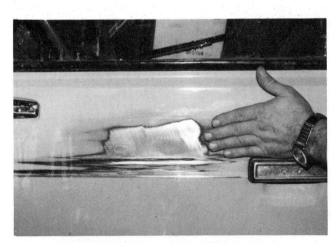

FIGURE 4-29b Feeling featheredge.

Three different types of power sanders are generally used in autobody repair shops today—the disc, the oscillating, and the dual-action sander. All are driven by either electricity or compressed air and are used in performing the many grinding, sanding, buffing, and polishing operations required before a damaged vehicle is restored to its original shape and appearance.

Disc sanders are manufactured in either 7-in. (178-mm) standard or 7- and 9-in. (178- and 229-mm) heavy-duty models. They are light in weight and have extra-powerful motors that run at high no-load speeds ranging from 4200 to 5000 rpm. The heavy-duty models eliminate the possibility of overheating when they are subjected to extra-heavy sanding for a prolonged period of time and will maintain a constant speed even when under heavy pressure.

Disc sanders are available with round, flexible, and molded rubber backing pads in 5-, 7-, and 9-in. (127-, 178-, 229-mm) diameters. When the sanding disc used on the backing pad becomes worn out and dull at its outer edge, it can be cut down to a somewhat smaller-sized disc with a fresh cutting edge by using a special tool called a disc trimmer (Fig. 4–30).

Method of Attaching Backing Pad and Sanding Disc

The rubber-molded backing pad has a metal hub that threads onto the sander spindle, marked B in Fig. 4–31. The spindle is kept from turning while the backing pad

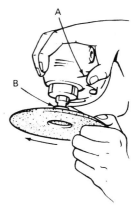

FIGURE 4–31 Holding spindle while removing disc. *(Courtesy of Black & Decker, Inc.)*

is turned onto it by depressing the spindle locking button marked A. The pad should be turned down all the way on the spindle and firmly tightened by hand—not by running the motor. The sanding disc, which is marked B in Fig. 4–32, is then laid on the rubber backing pad marked A, and the clamp nut marked C is placed on the spindle with the flange up. The clamp nut, after having been started one or two turns, is then turned into the metal hub until tight by holding the backing pad with one hand and the sanding disc with the other. The disc is turned clockwise until the clamp nut is completely turned down. The clamp nut is kept from turning in the center hole of the sanding disc because of the gripping action of the abrasive on the clamp nut. A wrench, which can also be used for tightening and removing the sanding disc (Fig. 4–33), is available as an accessory.

Using the Disc Sander

Electric disc sanders are equipped with *off-on* switches of the plunger, toggle, or compression type, depending on the manufacturer. The disc sander is lifted from the floor and held by grasping the control handle firmly with

DISK TRIMMER

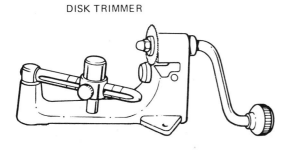

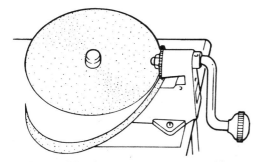

FIGURE 4–30 Grinder disc trimmer. *(Courtesy of Black & Decker, Inc.)*

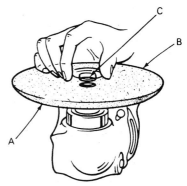

FIGURE 4–32 Putting disc-holding nut in pad. *(Courtesy of Black & Decker, Inc.)*

FIGURE 4-33 Tightening disc-holding nut with wrench. *(Courtesy of Black & Decker, Inc.)*

one hand and the side handle with the other. The side handle can easily be changed for either left- or right-hand use, whichever is most natural and comfortable for the repairperson. The disc sander is turned *on;* the disc is kept off the work and sufficient room for it to revolve freely is allowed. It is then held against the work and moved across its surface with long, sweeping, back and forth strokes, with just enough pressure to keep it from chattering and bouncing. The application of heavy pressure on the disc sander will not increase its cutting action; rather, it will slow it down and greatly reduce the life of the abrasive.

To operate the disc sander at maximum efficiency, it must be held against the work at an angle of approximately 20° so that the maximum amount of abrasive makes contact with the work and yet does not affect the smooth cutting action of the disc sander (Fig. 4-34).

Where sanding operations are performed using only the outer edge of the abrasive disc (Fig. 4-35), a rough-cut, burred, and often deeply gouged surface is obtained. On the other hand, if the disc sander is held directly flat against the work (Fig. 4-36), the sanding action is very rough and bumpy and the disc sander is hard to control.

Selection of Sanding Discs. Two types of sanding discs are employed in metal finishing and feather-

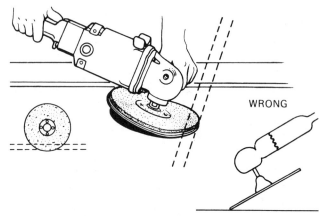

FIGURE 4-35 Using grinder in the wrong position. *(Courtesy of Black & Decker, Inc.)*

edging, open-coat and closed-coat abrasive discs (Fig. 4-37). Open-coat abrasive discs are designed for removing heavy coats of paint, glazing putty, and plastic filler from metal surfaces and for work on wood and other coarse fibrous materials having a tendency toward *loading up* the sanding disc. They are manufactured in various grits (see Table 4-5) ranging from #16 (P16), very coarse; #24 (P24), coarse; #36, #50, and #60 (P36, P50), fine; and #80 (P80) to #120 (P120), very fine, abrasive discs, which are used primarily in featheredging. Closed-coat abrasive discs are designed for metal finishing. Number 16 (P16), very coarse, and #24 (P24), coarse, grit discs are used for grinding and rough cutting in metal repair work. Grinding not only removes paint and rust (Fig. 4-38), but also outlines the damaged area for the repairperson. After the disc sander has been carefully passed over the entire lower portion of the panel, all surface irregularities are clearly visible. Bare metal areas indicate high spots, while areas where the paint has not been removed indicate low spots.

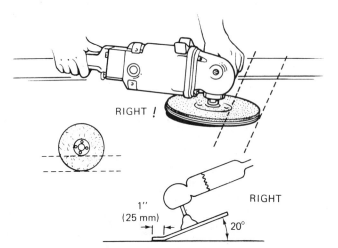

FIGURE 4-34 Using grinding disc in proper position. *(Courtesy of Black & Decker, Inc.)*

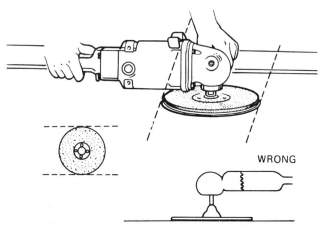

FIGURE 4-36 Using grinder in the wrong position. *(Courtesy of Black & Decker, Inc.)*

(A)   (B)

FIGURE 4–37 Different arrangement of grit. (a) Closed coat. (b) Open coat.

TABLE 4–5
Disc grit numbers for portable sander

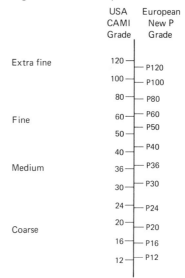

The low spots are raised by further dinging and bumping of the area, frequently passing the disc sander over it to check for high and low spots until a large percentage of the paint has been removed and the size of the low spots has been minimized. The panel is then more accurately rechecked by cross-filing it, and any remaining low spots are raised with the pick hammer. When this step has been completed, the repaired metal is disc-sanded again, first with #36 (P36), fine, grit abrasive disc, which is followed by a #50, #60 (P50, P60), or even a #80 (P80), very fine, grit disc (Fig. 4–39). Finishing the metal in this manner removes the disc scratch pattern left from previous disc sanding and polishes it, keeping the costs of refinishing materials and preparatory work down to a minimum.

To obtain the best quality finishes, it is recommended that disc grinding, sanding, and polishing be done in steps. If, on a particular job, a #24 (P24) grit open-coat sanding disc was first used to remove the paint, it should be followed by crosscutting the area with a #36 (P36) closed-coat sanding disc and finished by sanding the area (polishing) with a #50, #60, #80 (P50, P60,P80) closed-coat disc. The removal of metal in disc-

sanding operations should be kept at a minimum so that the original strength and thickness of the sheet metal are maintained as much as possible.

Any size grit closed-coat disc may be used for crosscutting, sanding, and polishing; however, it depends entirely on the job and the type of refinishing materials used in its repair.

Safety Precautions for Disc Sanding

When using the disc sander, or when in the immediate area where one is being used, the repairperson should protect the eyes by wearing either grinding goggles or plastic eye shields.

Always notify others near you before starting disc-sanding operations.

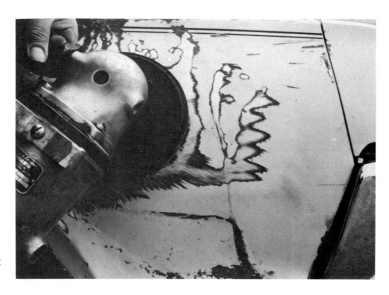

FIGURE 4–38 Removing paint with disc grinder.

FIGURE 4-39 Finish grinding with fine grit disc.

Loose-fitting clothes and long neckties should not be worn when using a disc sander.

The portable disc sander should always be started off the job and should be stopped on the job.

Before connecting the disc sander to the power supply, make sure that it is grounded properly and that it is in its correct position (sanding disc facing up), with the operating switch in the *off* position.

Before operating the disc sander, make sure that the disc is installed properly, and when changing from one disc to another, make sure that the lead is *pulled out* from the power supply. This will prevent accidental starting of the sander while discs are being changed.

When the sander is not in use in metal finishing, it should be laid on the floor to prevent accidental dropping and breaking.

When using the disc sander near drip moldings, sharp panel edges, loose clips and bolts, lap-joint con-structions, and badly rusted-out panels, great care must be exercised to prevent the sanding disc from being caught and torn, which often causes serious injury to the operator. This can be prevented when disc sanding potentially dangerous areas by switching the disc sander on and off and allowing the built-up momentum to do the sanding, or by operating the disc sander in such a way that the sanding disc does not rotate or turn into the edge of the metal but away from it instead (Fig. 4-40).

Disc Sanding Methods

Sanding the Crown Surface on a Fender. On a crown area, disc sanding should always be done with long, sweeping, back and forth strokes along the crown, as shown by the dashed lines in Fig. 4-41. Disk sanding is started at the top of the crown. The disc sander is

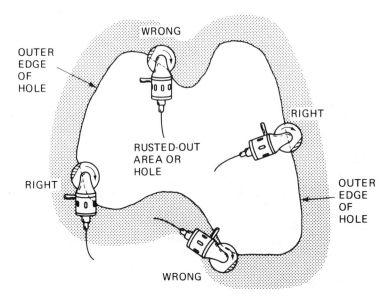

FIGURE 4-40 Disc sanding around a rusted-out area or hole.

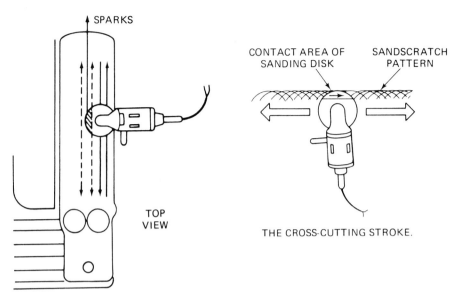

FIGURE 4–41 Proper power sanding strokes.

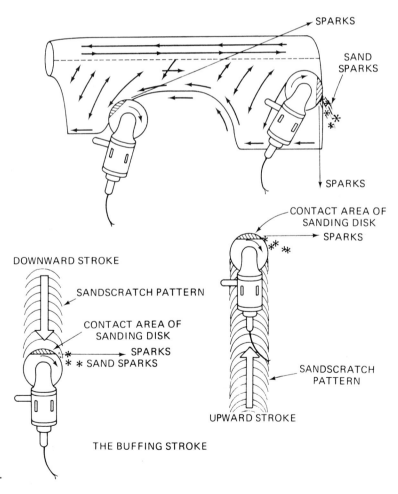

FIGURE 4–42 Buffing stroke.

moved from left to right in making the first forward stroke, with just a slight amount of pressure being exerted on the sanding disc.

At the end of the forward stroke, the return stroke is started immediately without any hesitation or stopping by passing the disc sander over the already sanded surface, but in the opposite (right to left) direction and without applying any pressure whatsoever on the sanding disc.

If disc sanding is done in this manner, generally called a *crosscutting* stroke (because of the intricate crisscross sand scratch pattern it creates), the return stroke will remove any burrs left by the cutting action of the abrasive disc in the preceding forward stroke and will result in a smoothly sanded surface.

It will be noticed that the area of contact between the abrasive disc and the crown is much smaller than when disc sanding flat surface metals. Therefore, the second and all subsequent forward and return strokes must be spaced more closely together and must be more numerous before a crown area has been completely covered and smoothly sanded.

Sanding the Side of a Fender. After the crown area of the fender has been sanded, the entire fender, including the headlight opening, can also be disc-sanded. Disc sanding is started at the top or lower edge of the crown area, as shown by the dashed line in Fig. 4–42. With the application of a small amount of pressure, the sander is moved down the side of the fender up to about 1 in. (25 mm) of the bottom edge. It is then moved up again over the same area, but without applying any pressure on the sanding disc. This procedure, generally called a *buffing* stroke (used in the fast removal of paint and the sanding down or leveling of flat and low-

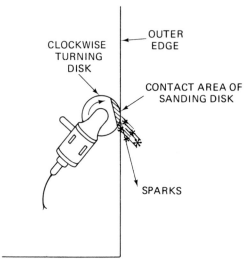

FIGURE 4–43 Proper sanding methods near edges.

crowned surfaces), is continued until the whole side of the fender has been completely sanded. All outer edges at the rear and bottom, as well as the wheel-opening fender flange, are sanded by holding the disc sander in such a position that the abrasive disc turns in a direction away from the particular edge being sanded and the sparks given off shoot away from the fender instead of onto it (Fig. 4–43). This method will prevent the sanding disc from turning into and catching the edge of the fender, shattering, and causing personal injury to the repairperson as well as others in the area.

The flange on the front of headlight openings and surrounding surfaces must be sanded very cautiously. These surfaces are generally sanded by utilizing the built-up momentum of the disc sander after it has been turned *on* and then immediately turned *off*.

FIGURE 4–44 Using cone mandrel with abrasive cone sleeve.

Hard-to-reach concave surfaces around headlights, fender flanges, and trim moldings are quite frequently sanded by changing the flat backing pad and sanding disc for a cone mandrel and abrasive cone (Fig. 4-44).

Sanding a Door. An automobile door is sanded in much the same way as a fender. The crown area of the door is sanded first, starting at the top near the glass opening and gradually working down, using the cross-cutting strokes until the crown has been completely sanded (Fig. 4-45). The flatter, lower portion of the door panel is sanded next, to within approximately 1½ in. (38 mm) of its outer edges, using long up-and-down vertical buffing strokes and the same procedure described for sanding the side of a fender. Notice how flat the disc sander is held, with just a slight curving motion as it is moved first down and then up, as the sanding is carried out. The outer edges of the door, like the fender, are sanded so that sparks run away from the door, which will prevent the disc from cutting into the outer edge of the panel.

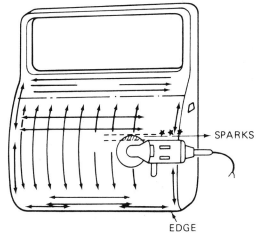

FIGURE 4-45 Grinding a door.

REVIEW QUESTIONS

4-1. What is an abrasive?

4-2. Name three natural mineral abrasives.

4-3. What abrasives are classified as synthetic?

4-4. Briefly describe how silicon carbide and aluminum oxide are made.

4-5. What abrasives are most commonly used in the repairing and refinishing of automobiles?

4-6. Which of the synthetic abrasives is the toughest and longest lasting, (a) aluminum oxide or (b) silicon carbide?

4-7. From what materials are the flexible backings on coated abrasives made?

4-8. Describe briefly how coated abrasives are made.

4-9. What is meant by open coat?

4-10. What is meant by closed coat?

4-11. Explain the three sanding stages.

4-12. What does the number stamped on the back of sandpaper mean?

4-13. Describe how a sheet of sandpaper is cut in three equal parts.

4-14. What can a squeegee be used for?

4-15. How is the sandpaper held when sanding by hand?

4-16. Describe how a vehicle should be wet sanded.

4-17. Describe why sandpaper should not be used in a circular motion.

4-18. Describe the stroke of the hand when sanding paint.

4-19. Orbital sanders are used extensively in what kind of repair operations?

4-20. Can orbital sanders, driven by electricity, also be used in wet-sanding operations?

4-21. What type of orbital sander can be used in both wet- and dry-sanding operations?

4-22. What size of sandpaper is used on an orbital sander?

4-23. Can featheredging, sanding, and polishing operations be performed much faster (a) by hand or (b) with an orbital sander?

4-24. Are polishers used in featheredging operations? If so, what changes must be made, and what type of abrasive is used?

4-25. Can featheredging be done faster or slower by means of a polisher rather than an orbital sander?

4-26. How is wet or dry featheredging done by hand?

4-27. What type and grit of sandpaper are used (a) in wet featheredging? (b) in dry featheredging?

4-28. What type of sandpaper is used in sanding primer-surfacers?

4-29. How is glazing putty generally sanded, and what type of sandpaper is used?

4-30. What type of sandpaper is used in preparing the old painted surface of an automobile for refinishing (a) in enamel? (b) nitrocellulose or acrylic lacquer?

4-31. How should the disc sander be started, and how should it be stopped when it is no longer required?

4-32. What necessary precautions should be taken before the disc sander is connected to the power supply?

4-33. Why should the lead be pulled out of the power supply when the sanding disc is being changed?

4-34. How can accidental dropping and breaking of the disc sander be prevented when it is not being used?

4-35. What areas on an automobile need special care when being power sanded?

4-36. Describe and illustrate with a sketch the proper method used in disc sanding a fender.

CHAPTER FIVE

Refinishing Materials

SAFETY HINTS

It is common knowledge that accidents are usually caused by negligence. Only by paying careful attention to accident causes can they be reduced. Many products used in a body shop are highly combustible—lacquers, reducers, thinners, and many other dangerous chemicals. Moreover, because the vehicles are sometimes dismantled in assemblies, they clutter up the floor or the alleys between the cars.

Combustibles are always a fire hazard and the containers holding such products as thinners, reducers, and paints should be kept closed and stored in fireproof cupboards. There should also be no welding or smoking close to the paint area, and proper signs signifying such restrictions should be prominently displayed. All painting should be done in a spray booth with exhaust fans that meet the requirements of local laws.

The majority of refinishing complaints arise from the fact that almost everyone tries to find the universal product, the shortcut, the cure-all—when no such method or item exists.

Each product is formulated for a specific purpose and must be used and handled in such a way as to fit properly into the complete refinishing system. This holds true in every stage of the refinishing procedure, from the beginning of the job, when the refinisher tests the condition of the surface to be painted, until the final coat of refinish material is dry and the job is ready for delivery to the customer.

The complete refinishing procedure is divided into five well-defined stages:

1. Examination and testing of the surface
2. Surface preparation and conditioning
3. Selection and preparation of materials
4. Application of the products
5. Final finishing touch

5–1 DETERMINING THE CONDITION AND TYPE OF PAINT FILM

With all the changes in types of refinishing materials, a painter should attend seminars and read technical bulletins to keep up to date. When a vehicle comes into the paint shop, the condition and type of finish or material must be examined very carefully. Remember that the best paint will not provide satisfaction, durability, and gloss if the surface on which it is applied is not perfectly prepared.

The vehicle should be washed with a detergent solution and rinsed with clean water and allowed to dry. Then the painter examines the paint surface and, using knowledge gained through experience, determines if the paint is in good or poor condition or a combination of both.

A surface in good condition would be a surface that has faded paint, off-color panels, stone bruises, small scratches in the paint, and small rusted areas caused by the broken paint film. These vehicles are usually completely repainted or spot repaired if the damage is not too severe. If it is to be completely repainted, it means that the paint film is sound and only needs the minimum of work and paint to restore it to a glossy looking vehicle; this is called a color coat.

A surface in poor condition might be due to the paint cracking because the film is too thick. Or the vehicle could have a series of dents, scrapes, deep surface rust, or rusted through panels. The body must be repaired, the affected paint surface removed entirely down to the metal surface, and the vehicle completely refinished properly step by step.

First the painter must carefully check the finish; a magnifying glass is excellent to find defects such as crazing, cracking, and splitting of the paint film. Surface rust or blisters should be examined carefully with a sharp instrument, and peeling paint should be checked with sandpaper for adherence to the old paint film. A small area can be compounded with a grit polish and a rag to check if the gloss is easy to restore and for the penetration of rust or chemical stains into the paint film.

The next step is to determine whether the old finish is lacquer or enamel. Lacquer color coats can be determined by wetting a cloth with a good grade of thinner and wiping it over the surface. If the paint dissolves after a few rubs, you can be almost certain it is lacquer.

To find out if it is nitrocellulose or acrylic lacquer, test with perchlorethylene on a rag. If some color comes off the old finish, it is acrylic; if it does not come off, it is nitrocellulose. On the other hand, if there is no color transfer, it is enamel.

If the finish is lacquer, certain precautions must be taken in preparing the car to prevent swelling of the old coat if it is to be recoated with lacquer. Swelling usually occurs where sanding has been done, and unless the new solvents are prevented from reaching the old surface, no amount of care will prevent the sanding scratches from showing.

The appearance and durability of a new paint job depend on the quality of the work done on the old paint surface to which it is applied. This is why all phases of the work required must be done at the right time and properly to achieve good results. First, the surface must be cleaned of contaminants such as oil, grease, wax, silicone, tree sap, tar, dirt, and rusted areas. Then comes surface preparation, which is important because this is the part of the job that prepares the foundation for the paint job. A painter cannot expect a new coat of paint to correct defects such as sand scratches, poor featheredging, glazing defects, and poor body repairs. Paint is meant to beautify and protect whatever it is applied to and please the customer and owner, not to correct defects.

To prepare a surface in good condition is much easier than preparing a surface in poor condition. Use of the proper procedures at the right time will give a surface without defects regardless if the topcoat is acrylic lacquer, alkyd enamel, acrylic enamel, or urethane enamel.

To wash the vehicle, use a pressure washer if possible (Fig. 5-1); if not available, use a mild detergent and hose. Do not wash the vehicle outside when the sun is shining or the water will leave marks. Once the vehicle has dried, the surface must be cleaned with a degreaser and dewaxer; see Table 5-1 for the appropriate product. If used properly, these products will remove silicones, grease, oil, wax, and some other contaminants. The product is applied liberally with a rag to an area that is comfortable to work with (approximately 3 × 4 ft or 914 × 1220 mm); then another dry rag or paper towel is used to wipe it dry while the degreaser is still wet (Fig. 5-2). The rag or shop towel should be turned over to present a new surface for wiping. If properly done, this should go a long way to prevent fisheyes; change rags or shop towels after doing each section as they are contaminated; never touch the spout of the can when pouring degreaser on the rag or towel. If it is touched, whether by fingers or contaminated shop rags or towels, the rest of the degreaser will also be contaminated. Throw all contaminated rags or shop towels into an approved garbage container. Solvents such as naphtha are sometimes used, but naphtha is a poor wax solvent and will not remove embedded wax. When no more scum comes off on the rag, it can be assumed that the wax and grease remover has dissolved all the old wax and floated it up to where it can be removed.

The third step is to featheredge stone bruises,

FIGURE 5-1 Washing a vehicle with pressure washer.

TABLE 5–1

Cleaning solvents for paint surfaces

Sherwin-Williams	Du Pont	Ditzler	Rinshed-Mason	Martin-Senour	Sikkens
1.ª R7K 156	3919S	DX440	900	6383	M600
2.ᵇ R1K 213	3939S	DX330	—	6387	—

ªUsually used to degrease and dewax enamels. If used on acrylic lacquer, soak rag with water first, wring out half dry, and apply degreaser and dewaxer to rag and slightly wring out before using. Using the product full strength could mar the finish.

ᵇUsually used to degrease and dewax acrylic lacquer.

scratches in the paint, and the edge of the paint where body repairs were performed. Table 4–4 should be consulted as to the grit of sandpaper to use for either wet or dry sanding methods. For featheredging, 80D to 120D or P80 to P120 grit production paper used on a vibrator sander or a circular foam disc sander on which the sandpaper is glued will do a good job. Featheredging means to wear the paint surface to a taper (Fig. 5–3). A good rule for featheredging a paint surface is to taper the surface 2 in. (51 mm) for every coat of paint. The edge is tapered gradually until no edge is felt on the break in the paint film.

Of course, there is always an exception to some procedures. When a paint film is very thick, the edge is featheredged or ground out to a sharp angle, or if a deep enough imperfection is present, it should be filled with a plastic body filler, which is then sanded level to the paint surface. This sanding will help to remove any rust, but the surface should also be treated with metal conditioner. These areas might require some filling with primer-surfacer and putty. This is followed by back

FIGURE 5–3 Featheredging with dual-action sander.

sanding of the area with No. 180 or P180. Once all featheredging and back sanding have been done, it is now necessary to sand the vehicle to prepare the surface for the application of the new coat of paint. The type of finish and the application method determine the type and grit of sandpaper to use (see Table 4–4).

If the paint surface is in good condition, sand with either No. 320 (P400) wet and dry sandpaper or No. 280 (P360) free-cut sandpaper if alkyd enamel is to be used for the topcoat. However, if acrylic enamel or urethane enamel is to be used, No. 360 (P500) wet and dry sandpaper should be used. For acrylic lacquer, a No. 400 (P800) wet or dry sandpaper should be used. Usually, one series lower of free-cut sandpaper can be used when dry sanding (Fig. 5–4).

The reasons for sanding a paint film are to smooth out the surface, reduce the film thickness, and remove the hard surface of the paint film. Sanding is done either wet or dry depending on the methods used in the shop. In the wet sanding method, the sanding should be started at the highest part of the vehicle that requires sanding.

FIGURE 5–2 Cleaning the surface with degreaser and dewaxer.

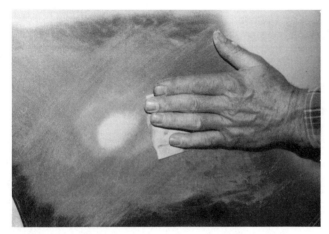

FIGURE 5-4 Sanding by hand.

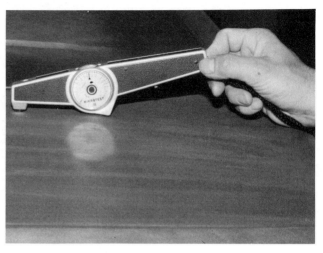

FIGURE 5-5 Using film thickness gauge.

As each part is sanded, the panel should be washed. Always use enough water when wet sanding, as the water not only cleans the sandpaper, but also provides a lubricant for the sandpaper to slide over.

When sanding a vehicle, all sanding should be done lengthwise as much as possible; this will help to prevent sand-scratch marks in the old finish from showing up if some of the sanding was done crosswise. Great care must be taken when sanding near moldings, door handles, and so on. All gloss must be removed from the old finish so that the surface has tooth. This allows the paint to mechanically adhere to the old finish. When the wet sanding of a panel is finished, a squeegee can be used to remove the excess water from the paint surface, leaving a nearly dry film behind.

The sanding may also be done by hand, but is more likely to be done by random orbit sander when the dry method is used. Whether wet or dry sanded, there are areas where a sanding block is advantageous and other areas where the hand is the only thing to use.

If wet sanded, the whole vehicle or affected area should be washed with water to remove the sanding residue. If dry sanded, the vehicle should *not* be blown off unless it is in the spray booth. The dust blown off the vehicle will settle on every surface it can cling to in the shop. This practice is also very dangerous as the dust in the air will be inhaled, causing harm to the lungs. If the vehicle is wet, blowing it off with air will speed up the drying time of the surface. Then the vehicle is masked off as required for the painting operations.

When preparing a surface in a poor condition, one of the first steps to take is to measure the thickness of the paint film (Fig. 5-5). The film thickness is very important because the application of excessively thick topcoats, a practice that is prevalent in many areas, may result in the paint film wrinkling or cracking, low gloss, water spotting, poor dry, and many other film defects that spoil what could be a first-quality refinish job. A thick topcoat could cause the vehicle to be redone, which will be very costly due to difficulties in removing the excessively thick topcoat by stripping or sanding.

If the paint film is not in good shape due to cracking, crazing, or other paint failure and has to be removed, a paint and varnish remover is used (Fig. 5-6). Before using the paint remover, all joints, moldings, and panel edges should be protected with masking tape and paper where appropriate. This will stop the paint remover from running into the joints, under the molding, or along the edges of the panels. It will also prevent the paint remover from removing paint where it is not required.

The paint remover is usually applied with a paintbrush in one direction only to eliminate breaking the film and trapping air in the remover. It must be applied thick enough to remain wet while it performs its task.

The paint remover should be allowed to stand for at least 15 minutes, depending on the temperature. For best results use at around 70°F (19°C). Some paint removers are designed to remove acrylic lacquer films without damaging the original baked primer. These paint removers will also easily remove air-dried alkyl and acrylic enamels (Table 5-2). They will lift these paints away from the primed coats rather than dissolving like lacquer. This will not destroy the baked-on primer on the vehicle.

TABLE 5-2

Paint removers and manufacturers' part numbers

Ditzler acrylic lacquer paint remover	DX525
Ditzler paint remover	DX587
Du Pont	5662S
Martin-Senour	68D1
Rinshed-Mason	815
Sherwin-Williams	V3K168

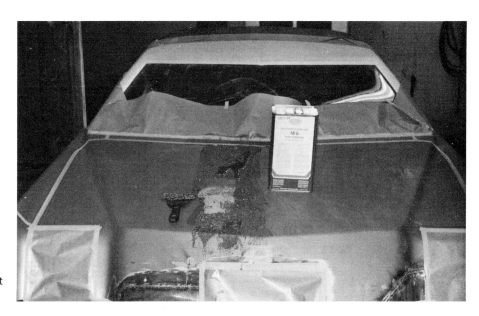

FIGURE 5-6 Removing paint with paint remover.

All-purpose paint strippers are fast-acting water-rinsable paint and varnish removers. Most of these strippers are noncaustic; but whether caustic or not, they should only be used in amply ventilated rooms. These paint removers are mostly nonflammable and are designed to quickly remove any paint finish or primer on any metal surface. This type of paint remover will remove alkyd enamel, acrylic enamel, acrylic lacquer, acrylic urethanes, and topcoats. However, it must be remembered that cooler temperatures lengthen the reaction time of paint removers, and cold temperatures will stop the removal action completely.

When the old paint surface is completely dissolved, a rubber squeegee or plastic spreader may be used to remove it. If the residue is lacquer, wash it off with a (medium) dry thinner or lacquer-removing solvent; other types of materials can be rinsed off with a strong stream of water. Before applying any paint remover the can should be well shaken to mix all the ingredients. The hands should be protected by neoprene or polyethylene gloves and the eyes with goggles.

Paint remover should not be used on ornamental plastic, anodized aluminum, fiber-glass bodies, or flexible parts or allowed to come in contact with rubber fabric, upholstery, and Plexiglass. After paint removal, the parts of the vehicle that have paint removed should be cleaned with a dewaxer and degreaser before sanding the original primer and repriming. Depending on the type of remover used, some primers, such as epoxy primers or baked enamels, will not be lifted or dissolved by paint remover. The vehicle or panel affected should then be rinsed off thoroughly using water; this neutralizes the paint remover.

When the panel is dry, the metal is sanded with a random orbit sander or an orbital vibrator using No. 80D to No. 120D (P80 to P120) grit production paper or free-sanding paper.

Paint remover should always be used in a well-ventilated area, as the fumes are quite toxic. If necessary, wear a proper respirator.

The solvents in Table 5-3 are often used to help featheredge bruised areas in acrylic lacquer; they will have no effect whatsoever on factory acrylic enamels. To apply, a small round ball is formed with a shop paper towel or a throwaway piece of rag. The ball is saturated with the removing solvent and then applied to the stone bruise or small nick in the paint surface. The ball is held against the surface for a few seconds and, with a circular motion, the solvent is rubbed on the affected spot for a few more seconds. If required, the operation is repeated until the metal shows up through the primer (Fig. 5-7). The spot is allowed to dry when sufficient color has been removed, while the painter prepares more spots as required. Then, by using No. 400 (P800) or 500 (P1000), the repair spot is sanded to complete the featheredge.

A surface in poor condition requires the most work to repair the damage to the paint film, so as to provide as good a surface as possible to which to apply the new

TABLE 5-3

Featheredging solvents for acrylic lacquer by part number

Sherwin-Williams	R7210
Du Pont	3907
Ditzler	DX525
Rinshed-Mason	830
Martin-Senour	6805

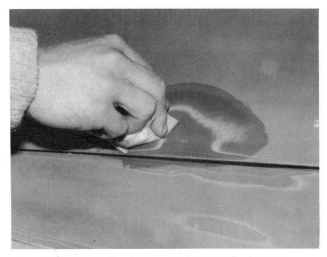

FIGURE 5-7 Featheredging acrylic lacquer with solvent.

coat of paint. A new paint job is only as good as its foundation; if the work is not done well, the new finish will soon deteriorate and fail. The shop then has an unhappy customer and faces the loss of future business.

Stripping a Vehicle

When removing the paint from a vehicle, certain methods should be followed; otherwise, it can turn out to be a very messy situation. The job must be carefully planned to achieve the least possible mess to clean up afterward, with no damage to areas that are not to be stripped. The vehicle must be prepared with care; otherwise, the paint remover will run down on flat areas such as between the hood edge and fender edge and trunk lid opening, causing damage to the paint. To prevent this, these areas should be taped to seal off the opening between the two panels; also, as on a hatchback, the reveal molding should be taped, with some of the tape going over the painted area (Fig. 5–8). This is done to prevent the paint remover from penetrating between the hatchback panel and the molding. Paint remover should be used at a temperature of around 70°F (19°C) or slightly warmer; it should never be used in the hot sun.

If the whole vehicle must be stripped, the work should be started on the roof panel, which must be masked properly. The masking tape should be applied approximately 1 in. (25 mm) inboard; then two thicknesses of a pretaped apron are applied on all four sides. This is to prevent the paint remover from running under the reveal moldings and other areas. The floor should also be covered with paper, as stripped paint does not readily clean off the floor.

All areas to be stripped should be masked off, such as the space between the doors and adjoining panels; everything must be protected (Fig. 5–9). All molding and nameplates that can be removed are taken off; this will prevent trapping paint remover, water, and dirt. Be sure to put all removed moldings, screws, nuts, and clips in a safe place as they will have to be reinstalled. When moldings and nameplates cannot be removed, they should be covered adequately, with the tape extending beyond them and covering the paint 1 in. (25 mm) beyond the nameplate or molding.

The label on the container should be read for directions on the use of the particular brand of paint remover. Paint remover is usually applied in as thick a film as possible on a vertical surface. With a thick film, the wax will float to the surface and form a seal on the

FIGURE 5-8 Preparing hatchback for paint stripping.

FIGURE 5-9 Masking side for paint stripping.

surface. This seal keeps the active chemical ingredients against the paint surface, allowing them to penetrate and dissolve or lift the paint film.

The paint remover is applied to the roof panel in a thick film using a paintbrush of sufficient size. It is applied and brushed going only one way; never go over the film again with the brush as this will break the wax seal that has formed on the surface. Only cover an area that is comfortable to work with. Let the paint remover work for approximately 10 to 15 minutes; then check to see if paint is soft. If the paint is soft, remove with a squeegee and then do the whole area. Repeat the procedure until the roof panel paint film is removed; then wash off the residue with medium dry thinner or lacquer-removing solvent.

If the paint is of an enamel type, the paint remover will lift the film in a series of bubbles. The paint film is ready to remove if it is all lifted in the treated area. If some of the paint has not lifted and the paint remover has dried, reapply another coat of paint remover to lift the affected area. When it is lifted, scrape off with a rubber squeegee as this will not damage the undercoat. Repeat the procedure until the old paint film has been removed from the panel. To help lift the old paint film off the vehicle once it has been removed, a flat piece of metal or a dustpan can be used to collect the residue; put it in an appropriate garbage can lined with old newspapers or masking paper.

When doing the hood and trunk lid, the same procedure may be followed as for the roof. All gaps between the panels should be double-masked with the tape extending at least ¼ in. (6 mm) onto the painted sur-

face. The paint remover should be kept away from the masking tape as much as possible. All plastic and chrome parts should be double-masked because certain paint removers could tarnish some of the plastic or anodized aluminum parts. All nameplates and emblems are either removed or double-masked with the tape extending onto the paint film. Then the paint remover is applied one section at a time and cleaned up as the job proceeds. The flexible plastic filler panels should be double-masked at both the rear and front bumpers.

When stripping the side of a vehicle, all the gaps between panels should be masked, extending the masking tape at least ¼ in. (6 mm) onto the painted surface. All nameplates, moldings, emblems, and wheel opening moldings that are removable are removed; if they cannot be removed, they are masked off with the tape extended onto the painted surface for 1 in. (25 mm). The wide windows which are on the doors and quarter-panels are masked off with the tape extended onto the painted surface for ¼ in. (6 mm). The door handles, lock cylinders, rear-view mirrors, and side marker lights are masked off the same way. The floor should then be covered with double paper to catch the paint as it is stripped and falls off the side of the vehicle.

When using paint remover on a vertical position, it is always best to start applying it at the highest point of the surface to be stripped. The paint remover, which is usually transferred from a large container to a pan holding about 1 quart or liter, is applied with an appropriate-sized paintbrush. The paint remover should be applied with the brush moving in an upward direction only. Brushing must be kept to a minimum and, depending on the thickness of the film applied or the thickness of the paint film, it may be necessary to apply another coat of paint remover to remove the paint film. Any paint remover that falls on the paper on the floor can be reapplied to the paint film. When the paint film has been dissolved or has lifted, it is removed with a scraper or squeegee, allowing the paint to fall on the paper.

When an estimate is made on a strip job, the thickness of the paint must be checked carefully as extra material is used when the paint is thick. This will raise the amount of material and labor and therefore increase the price for the paint job.

When the color has been removed, the panels should be washed thoroughly with a medium dry thinner and rag if the paint surface was acrylic lacquer. The thinner is applied and removed while still wet, and only a small area should be done at a time, approximately 4 ft² (0.4 m²), and overlapped as required.

The vehicle is unmasked and the remaining color hidden by the tape is then removed. On acrylic lacquer vehicles it is sometimes best to use a lacquer-removing solvent, but an orbital sander and appropriate grit of sandpaper can be used as long as it does not turn too fast and melt the lacquer remaining. On enamel vehicles the rest of the film is removed using a random orbit or orbital sander with either No. 80 or P80 production-type sandpaper; the same can be used on lacquer finishes. Once the vehicle surface has been cleaned of the color, it should be cleaned thoroughly with a dewaxer and degreaser (Table 5–1).

Safety Rules and Precautions When Using Paint Remover

Adequate ventilation must always be used, and prolonged breathing of the vapor and contact with the eyes or skin should be avoided. Paint removers can irritate the skin and should be washed off the skin immediately with clear water. Toxic vapors may be produced if remover comes in contact with a flame or hot surfaces. If paint remover is swallowed, a physician should be called immediately and the person must be given adequate medical care as prescribed. If paint remover comes in contact with the eyes, they should be flushed immediately with clear water for 15 minutes and get medical attention.

Since paint removers may contain chemicals such as alcohols, dichloromethane, propylene dichloride, ammonia, and methylene chloride, great care must be used when working with them and storing them. The containers should always be kept closed when not in use and out of the reach of children.

Sanding the Metal

If the paint remover does not remove the affected material, another method to use is a circular rotation sander polisher with a foam pad and sandpaper disc that has adhesive on the back of it that will stick to the pad. The sandpaper disc is replaced when it is worn out. Usually a No. 36 (P36) grit disc is used to sand the paint off. This is then followed with a No. 80 (P80) grit, which will leave the surface smooth. Care must be taken not to gouge the metal with the disc (Fig. 5–10). The sander is applied to the metal surface and should be moved quickly enough so that it will not create enough heat to warp the sheet metal, such as on hoods, trunk lids, roof panels, or any flat panel.

Sand scratches are probably the most annoying problem around a paint shop. Many otherwise beautiful paint jobs are spoiled because of some sand scratches in a prominent place. Unfortunately, they do not show up until after the color coat is applied, and then it is usually too late to correct them. If we understand what causes them and do not try to hurry the job too much, most of them can be avoided.

The first and prime requisite for a good paint job is smooth metal. The metal finisher or bump man can make it doubly hard for the painter if the metal is not properly finished. Careless filing or bearing down too hard on the coarse disc will leave furrows that are hard to fill. The best practice is to sand the rough spots and welds down with a coarse disc and finish off with a fine disc. Do not worry about getting the metal too smooth; metal that appears smooth will have plenty of tooth for

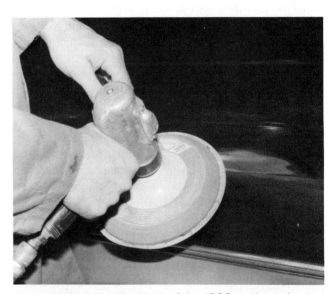

FIGURE 5–10 Using 8-in. (200-mm) sanding pad and disc to remove paint.

the primer to adhere to. Furrows and deep scratches create uneven shrinkage of the filler coats and therefore require a great deal more sanding. Also, more surfacer will have to be applied, and the more coats that are applied, the slower the drying time, thereby prolonging the operation.

Sandblasting

Due to the increase of rusted metal in many areas of the continent due to humidity or the use of salt on the roads, sandblasting the affected areas is now used quite extensively. It is the most efficient and fastest method of removing rust and contaminants from metal surfaces and even areas that are not easily accessible to regular sanding methods. Jobbers and many hardware stores sell different types of sandblasters, such as suction feed, pressure feed, and pressure feed with vacuum recovery of the sandblasting sand (Figs. 5–11 and 5–12).

Sandblasters, as in Fig. 5–11, have a reservoir to hold the sand, an airtight cover, hose and air line fittings, and a sandblasting gun with an air control valve. Many different types of sand are sold by jobbers for sandblasting purposes depending on the location of the shop and the country. Some sandblasting sand is made from the residue left from nickel mines, and silica sand is also used. Silica sand is sharp and removes rust

FIGURE 5–12 Pressure-feed sandblaster plus vacuum cleaner.

FIGURE 5–11 Suction-feed sandblaster.

quickly and is usually available at paint jobbers or any sand supply company.

When using a pressure-feed or suction-feed sandblaster, it is imperative that the operator use a positive-air-supplied hood and cape. No negative-type respirator can stop the fine silica dust that is a by-product of sandblasting with silica sand. Employees must be warned that repeated inhalation of respirable silica dust for extended periods of time may cause lung injury. OSHA safety and health regulations and standards should be followed.

Because of the dust that occurs when sandblasting in a body shop, great care and attention should be addressed to controlling the dust from the sandblasting operation. This operation should only be done in an area where the dust can be removed safely. To recover usable sand, a fine sieve is required to remove large particles that would block the nozzle of the sandblaster; this is not usually very economical as labor rates are too high to achieve a saving. Sand is usually swept up and thrown away in the garbage. The size of the nozzle determines the grit of the sand that will be used when sandblasting.

Low-cost sandblasters work on the suction principle. As the trigger is pulled or the valve turned, air passes through a hose and to the sandblasting nozzle. The air creates a strong suction as it passes the sand feed valve, which pulls the sand out into the hose to deliver it to the nozzle. On a suction-feed type, atmospheric pressure and gravity cause the sand to go down in the reservoir as long as the operation continues.

On a pressure-feed type, the compressed air is also delivered to the reservoir; this air causes turbulence in the reservoir, and a valve at the bottom controls the amount of sand that is mixed with the compressed air. The sand and air move through the hose with great turbulence and out through the nozzle of the gun. The greater the pressure, the more turbulence and force that are created, and the sand leaves the nozzle with great force. When the sand strikes the surface, it cuts away the surface rust condition in front of it. Usually, between 50 and 80 psi (345 and 550 kPa) of air pressure is used when sandblasting.

Recently, a new sandblasting system appeared on the market (Fig. 5–11). This unit can be operated at up to a maximum of 150 psi (1030 kPa). The blasting gun is a high-performance ejector type with a coaxial abrasive feed line. The abrasive is accelerated into the feed hose and barely touches the inside of the hose before entering the blasting gun. The final acceleration of the sand occurs in the mixing chamber of the blasting gun; this is done to optimize the value of the abrasive's projectile energy and speed of sandblasting.

With the built-on vacuum system, the sandblasting abrasive and dust are pulled back into the machine by the vacuum system. The vacuum and airflow in the machine are generated by an electric motor turbine. The turbine's capacity exceeds the sandblasting gun's air volume manyfold. The air washing system incorporates four phases. The first is a metal screen in the main body to prevent large objects from entering the reservoir of the machine. The abrasive and dust are first separated by a cyclone action. Then, the air compression and expansion, decreasing and increasing in speed depending upon the amount of air entering the vacuum nozzle, will result in the collecting of the larger particles in the built-in dust container. An industrial type of microfilter element is used for efficient filtration of particles; this element eliminates micron-sized dust from the atmosphere.

Abrasive that is suitable for another sandblasting cycle is collected in the lower part of the machine. The sandblasting gun is fed directly from this reservoir through a metering orifice. As a result of the vacuum created by the airflow through the sandblasting gun, the abrasive is fed into the gun from the reservoir. The abrasive, accelerated to a very high speed, thoroughly cleans the surface of corrosion and dirt. The abrasive and debris are pulled back by the continuous vacuum action in the machine.

Metal corrosion or rust occurs when the metal surface is exposed to the elements when the paint film is broken due to stone bruises, nicks, or sharp dents causing the paint film to crack. Under a microscope, metal corrosion resembles a lunar landscape with its many craters (Fig. 5–13).

Rust is like a sponge; it soaks up dirt, aggressive chemicals, and oxygen. If it is not stopped, rust will

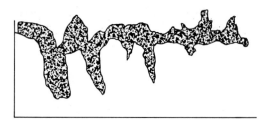

FIGURE 5–13 Microscopic view of metal edge that is rusted.

penetrate deeper into the metal until it disintegrates. A grinder is used only to remove the surface rust; to remove it all with a grinder, the metal must be ground as deep as the deepest crater. In most cases this would weaken and thin out the metal's structure, causing warping to occur due to the heat caused by the friction of the grinding disc (Fig. 5–14).

Therefore, it can be seen that grinding and sanding are not the solution. The rusting problem is only temporarily delayed and will break through the paint film. With a sandblaster, the rust is removed from the deepest pits in the metal, and with vacuum equipment the sandblasting can be performed while keeping the working area safe and clean without having to use special facilities. The abrasive hits the surface to be cleaned at a high velocity and is shot in all directions, which removes all surface impurities (Fig. 5–15). It does not break down the base metal but just slightly peens it so as to increase the area for adhesion. The airflow will cool the surface being sandblasted, somewhat eliminating thermal expansion of the metal. This can be very important on new vehicles where the sheet metal is thinner, such as hoods or door panels. Sandblasting prepares the metal so that it can be primed and get good paint adherence.

FIGURE 5–14 Grinding or sanding of metal.

FIGURE 5–15 Clean metal after sandblasting.

With sandblasting equipment, some safety precautions should be taken. Items that do not require sandblasting should be protected by masking or covered with suitable materials such as heavy cloth or cloth-backed vinyl or plastic. The parts that sometimes require protection are plastic parts, chrome parts, glass, grille parts, aluminum parts, and vinyl tops. When doing door jambs, it is necessary that the entire door opening be masked to prevent the sand from penetrating into the vehicle.

Due to the hazards when sandblasting, always wear a NIOSH-approved dust respirator to protect the lungs, tight-fitting goggles over the eyes, gloves to protect the hands, and suitable clothes for this type of work. Before using a sandblaster, make sure all safety precautions as well as the method of use are known. A sandblaster uses a lot of air, which must be clean and free of oil and water.

The container or reservoir is cleaned if required and then filled with the proper sand; usually a 60 to 100 grit is used depending on the equipment. All controls must be adjusted and the area to be sandblasted checked for the method to be used. The sandblasting gun, if not the vacuum type, should always be aimed at an angle to deflect the sand and air stream from the operator. Short overlapping strokes are used, and a small area is worked at a time.

Direct the gun so that the sand will hit the panel at an angle; this causes less heat and creates less distortion in the metal when using a regular sandblasting gun. When rust is being removed, a little more time may have to be spent on bad areas to bring them back to a dull gray appearance. After completing the job, all equipment should be cleaned and put away in its proper location. The area in which the sandblasting was done is thoroughly swept up and the sand disposed of. In most shops there is no area to clean up the vehicle, and it certainly should not be done in a spray booth because it will be contaminated with silica or sand and paint dust. The best method is to use a vacuum cleaner and a pressure washer to wash and cleanse the vehicle completely of all sand and dust.

If a sandblaster is not available, small pits in the sheet metal can sometimes be repaired by either thinning and soldering with body solder or by brazing. These operations are usually done by the people working in the body shop. There are also on the market some very effective chemicals that will neutralize and kill rust in small areas.

Shop Towels

Many different types of towels are used in the body and paint shop, such as rented towels, throwaway towels, and paper-reinforced towels. Rented towels are available from local suppliers, who pick them up, launder them, and deliver them for a certain charge per towel. The supplier usually furnishes them in a certain color, which makes them easy to spot in the shop. Clean towels should be kept in a clean area such as the stockroom; soiled towels should be placed in an appropriate container to be returned for cleaning. These towels are useful for cleaning cars but should not be used to clean areas or equipment that have wet paint on them, because they will be practically impossible to clean once the paint has dried.

Many shops use the throwaway type of cheesecloth or miscellaneous white rags that are bought in different sizes from jobbers or towel suppliers. These types of rags are ideal for any cleaning purpose as they can be used and then discarded. Disposable paper-reinforced towels are very popular due to their low cost, absorption capacity, and ease of use. They come in different sizes in boxes or on rolls and once used they are discarded. These towels are usually lint free and can be obtained from the local paint jobber.

Preparing Bare Metal

After the vehicle is cleaned and repaired, it is brushed and blown off to remove dirt and dust. It should then be masked as required so the preparation can be started. Spray painting, like brush painting or any other type of finishing, requires that the surface be properly prepared before paint is applied. Therefore, rust, oil, grease, and water must be removed from all surfaces that are to be spray painted. Any carelessness in surface preparation will result in a defective paint job. Also, where a high quality finish is required, paint will not hide or eliminate bad defects in the original surface, including holes or bumps. The life of a finish and the appearance of that finish depend considerably on the conditions of the surface over which the paint is applied. Students or apprentices should learn the steps to a perfect finish thoroughly, step by step.

It is important to realize the necessity of having the metal absolutely clean before applying any undercoats. Some painters rub their hands over the area to determine the effects of sanding without realizing that they are transferring oil from their hands to the surface. Oil comes from the skin and shop tools; even if one's hands are freshly washed, a fine oily film will be left on the surface.

If there is any rust on the metal or a suspicion of rust because the bright steel has been allowed to stand for a day or so before being primed, no priming should be done until the metal has been treated with a metal conditioner that will neutralize the rusting action. This

TABLE 5–4

Selection of proper conditioners and conversion coatings

Metal	Code	Reduction with water		Reaction	Rinse	Dry
		Conditioner	Water			
Steel	DX-579	1 Part	3 Parts	1–2 min.	On large areas, flush with water.	Blow off with air or wipe with a clean cloth.
Then use:	DX-550	1 Part	3–4 Parts	3–4 min.		
Aluminum (new)	DX-533	1 Part	10 Parts	2–3 min.		
Aluminum (old)		1 Part	3 Parts			
Then use:	DX-501 OR	1 Part	1 Part			
	DX-503	Do not dilute.				
Galvanized, galvanneal, plymetal and other zinc-coated metals	DX-589	1 Part	10 Parts	1–2 min.	On small areas, use a water wet clean cloth.	
Then use:	DX-512	Do not dilute.		1 min.		
Stainless steel and chrome plating	DX-579	1 Part	10 Parts	Use as a chemical cleaner only.		

Courtesy of Ditzler Automotive Finishes, PPG Industries, Inc.

step is essential if peeling and having to do a job over again are to be avoided. Manufacturers use different types of metals, such as galvanneal, galvanized, zincrometal, HSS and HSLA steel, hot- and cold-rolled steel, and aluminum, and some of these require special metal treatments. See Tables 5–4, 5–5, and 5–6.

All manufacturers do not use the same systems, methods, or products to produce a high degree of corrosion resistance and to promote adhesion of the paint film (Table 5–4). As can be seen from Tables 5–4 and 5–5, different materials are used to prepare metal before it is to be coated with a paint film. The shop and the

TABLE 5–5

Recommended Du Pont products for the treating of unpainted metal surfaces

Surface	Cleaner	Metal conditioner	Conversion coating
Aluminum		225S	226S
Brass	3812S	5717S	227S
Bronze	3812S	5717S	227S
Chrome	3812S	225S	
Copper	3812S	5717S	227S
Galvanized	3812S	5717S	227S
Iron	3812S	Sand, 5717S	224S
Magnesium	3812S	None required	226S (5 parts water)
Nickel	3812S	5717S	227S
Stainless steel	3812S	Sand, 5717S	224S
Steel (hot or cold rolled)	3812S	5717S	224S
Tin	3812S	225S	
Zinc	3812S	5717S	227S

Courtesy of Du Pont Company.

TABLE 5–6

Paint suppliers' metal conditioners by ordering number

	Sherwin-Williams	Du Pont	Ditzler	Rinshed-Mason	Martin-Senour
For flat or rolled steel					
Acid cleaner	W4K263	5717S	DX579	801	6879
Phosphate cleaner	W4K289	224S	DX550	—	6877
For galvanized steel					
Acid cleaner	W4K263	5717S	DX589	801	6879
Phosphate cleaner	W4K289	227S	DX512	802	—
For aluminum panel and parts					
Acid cleaner	W4K263	225S	DX533	801	6877
Phosphate cleaner	WHK289	226S	DX501	—	6879

area of the country determine the system used. The two-part metal conditioning method closely resembles the system used in factories, but the other system works very well if done properly. Metal conditioning is part of a system, along with the primers and topcoats, that when used together provide durability of the paint film.

Metal conditioners sold by the manufacturers are shipped in plastic containers and are inactive in this form. To activate them, they are mixed with water to the proper ratio as recommended by the manufacturer. Table 5–6 shows some of the different manufacturers' products as well as part numbers.

It is important to read the instructions on the labels not only for the reduction but for the method of use. When using the two-component system, the bare metal is cleaned by reducing the metal conditioner with water and then applying as recommended on the label. The bare metal is then treated with the other or part B metal conditioner, as directed, allowing the proper amount of time so that the chemical reacts properly. The bare metal areas are then washed, as well as adjacent parts, with a water-soaked cloth and clean water; these areas must be wiped dry. To simply put the conditioner on the bare metal and wipe dry is useless, because it will not have time to react. If any soldering has been done on the job, the soldering acids must also be neutralized; otherwise, blistering and peeling will occur.

When using the one-part metal conditioner, it is first reduced as required and then applied as directed; wait for the proper reaction time and then wash with clean water and dry. These materials are designed to etch the metal (usually the metal will change color slightly) and they also leave a phosphate coating to promote adhesion of ground coats.

When metal conditioner is used improperly, such as with no reduction or insufficient reduction with water, it is just like applying a soapy film of inactive acid. This causes the film to be hard to remove and clean off the surface. Acid will be trapped between the metal

and the following coats of primer, and if the primer is wet sanded, it is possible that enough moisture could penetrate through the primer and make the acid active. This condition could also occur when the vehicle is being used after painting. If the trapped acid reacts, it can affect the paint film; as the acid reacts and dries it will form a powder between the metal and primer, which will cause a loss of adhesion, blistering, and generally a poor paint film.

When the metal has been conditioned, it should not be washed with a cleaning solution since it is very likely that the protection on the metal will be removed and the job will have to be done over. The conditioned metal should be primed as soon as possible because if the atmosphere is very damp, rust will soon start forming and the surface will gather other contaminants. When reducing metal conditioner, the solution should be poured into an appropriate container and marked as to its use. Reduced metal conditioner can be kept for long periods as it will not spoil.

5–2 PRIMERS

The major reasons a vehicle or equipment is painted are first to make it attractive to the eye and, second, to protect it from the elements of nature and industrial pollution, which would cause deterioration of the equipment rather quickly.

The outside color is what gives the items beauty. The color coat is usually bonded to an undercoat called a *primer*. Primers are designed so that they will adhere to many different surfaces, such as steel, aluminum, fiber glass, and plastics (Fig. 5–16). The color topcoat is designed to adhere and reinforce the ability of the paint film to be able to resist many types of weather conditions.

A good paint film must be able to resist and withstand the elements and keep excellent color retention and

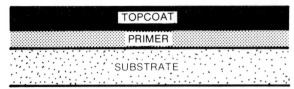

FIGURE 5-16 Primers are generally applied in a thin coat and do not require sanding. Primers are applied over bare substrates. *(Courtesy Du Pont Co.)*

FIGURE 5-18 Primer flow into the irregularities.

gloss for a long period of time. The paint film must be able to prevent breakdown of the surfaces it protects due to high humidity, snow, water, and rain. The paint film must be able to adhere to the many surfaces it is applied to, assuming, of course, that the preparation was well done. After drying, the paint film must be able to resist damage from gravel, sand, and many forms of contact when under normal use and driving conditions. It must also be easy to repair in a local paint shop when damaged. Primers are applied on bare substrates to provide for better adhesion. Primers are usually applied in a thin coat and do not require sanding.

After the surface has been properly prepared, the undercoat must be applied. It is of the utmost importance that the right undercoat for the job be applied promptly when the surface preparation is complete. The use of a proper undercoat is the required part for a good foundation for a durable topcoat (Fig. 5-17). If the undercoat or undercoats are not of the proper type, the appearance of the topcoat will suffer and could possibly peel or crack.

Primers are applied to the metal to achieve maximum adherence. Primers are a fairly thin material, and this allows them to flow into grooves cut into the metal by the grinding disc. The primer flows into these cavities when applied wet and follows the contour of the sand scratches and irregularities of the surface (Fig. 5-18).

Primer or Undercoats

Most manufacturers now use a seven-stage zinc phosphate metal treatment; then the bodies are primed with

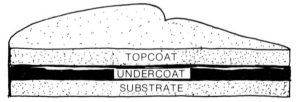

FIGURE 5-17 Undercoats can be compared to sandwich fillers that hold two slices of bread together. The bottom slice of bread is the substrate, and the top slice of bread is the topcoat. *(Courtesy Du Pont Co.)*

either polyesters or epoxy esters, using an electric deposition system. These types of primers are usually baked at 350° to 400°F (176° to 205°C) for 30 to 40 minutes. Some companies apply a surfacer, which is also baked for the required time. These are then wet sanded using a 400 (P800) grit sandpaper.

The changes in vehicles that have occurred in the last few years have meant that the industry has had to make many changes. Some of these have already been introduced, some are being introduced as the materials are ready for the marketplace, and many will continue to be introduced as they are perfected. Many of these new products originated in Europe, where they have been used for many years.

The range of different products on the market is immense and some of these will be discussed. The different materials will be identified mainly by their generic name. Many manufacturers provide products for the same markets, and it is impossible to mention them all (see Table 5-7).

The first products discussed are primers; there are different types of primers made for different applications. Zinc chromate is used especially on new construction and overall priming of truck bodies. This product can also be used as an insulator between different metals to prevent fast corrosion due to electrolysis; it also prevents corrosion because of moisture and has good rust-inhibiting qualities.

Another primer is a vinyl wash primer (Fig. 5-19), which is applied to bare substrate prior to primer-sealer or primer-surfacer. This treatment or application provides maximum protection and adhesion for most substrates. It can be used as a treatment on properly cleaned aluminum, steel, fiber glass, and certain zinc-coated steels. It provides very good adhesion for the paint films that will subsequently be applied over it. It is a two-component material and has a limited pot life of approximately 8 hours. If vinyl wash primer is not recoated before 4 hours with the next choice of material, it must be recoated with a new coating of vinyl wash primer. If this is not done, the next material to be applied will not adhere properly and will most likely peel off.

Epoxy primers (Fig. 5-20) are a two-component material used for priming aluminum body steel, zinc-coated metals, plastic fillers, and fiber glass. This primer

TABLE 5-7

Primers, primer-surfacers, epoxy primers, acrylic urethane primers, polyester primers, and polyvinyl primers

Primers	Sherwin-Williams	Du Pont	Ditzler	Rinshed-Mason	Martin-Senour	Sikkens
Vinyl wash	E2G 973	825S	DP-401	848A	8827	Metalflex WR Primer EP
Catalyst reducer	V6V 979	836S	DP-401	848B	8837	Metalflex WR Hardener EP
Epoxy enamel zinc						
Chromate yellow	E2Y 36	20855S	DPE-1537	—	8829	W/F580 S15/55 black
Black			DPE-1538	—		W/F Hardener C25/41
Self-etching vinyl wash primer surfacer	E2G 980	810 R	DX 1791	283-1501-1 (2-pak)	8847	
Catalyst primer-surfacer	R7K 981	815R	DX1792		8857	
Acrylic urethane	P6H49	1020R	K-200	512-5000	5100	
Catalyst	V6V79	125S	K-201	590-0100	5150	
Primer-surfacers, acrylic type						
Gray	P2A43	131S	DZ3	832	3254	Autocryl 3 + 1 beige
Red oxide	P2N44	110S	DZ7	831	3255	Autocryl filler beige
Beige						680
Primer-surfacer PX						
Lacquer gray	P2A32	30S	DZL-32	APS-423	3252	Auto fine
	P2A40	70S	DZL-34	APS-428	3257	Beige
	P2N39	80S	DZL-72	APS-422	3258	
Primer-surfacer						
Epoxy gray		8245S	DP40			
Red oxide	E2G-973	825S	DX-1791	889	8827	
Activator	V6V-979	826S	DP-401	EP-897	8837	
Polypropylene primer	P3C24	329S	DPX800	864	6242	Plastoflex
Primer-surfacer, enamel alkyd						
Red oxide		3012S		SS7 + SS53	8094	
Light gray	E3A4801	3055S	DZE27	SS54		
Medium gray		3011S				
White		3010S				
Polyester						
Primer surfacer		Evercoat				Polystop LP
Sealer lacquer						
Nonsanding	P1A38	2129S	DL-1970	870	3060	Transparent sealer
	P1C41	22S	DL-1947	PS6	3045	
	19	1984				
		1985				
		1986				
Enamel sealers						
Nonsanding						
Gray	E2A28	1858S	DPE1338	PS21	8098	Autocryl Filler beige
Clear			DPE-1020			
Red	E2R34	1697S			8821	Transparent only
Precoat sealer	V2V278		DXR1050		8822	
Acrylic urethane						
Sealers	E6H59			530-1106	5105	
Catalyst	V6V79			540-0116	5150	

gives an excellent corrosion film resistance and can be top-coated with any topcoat, but it is especially recommended for use under urethane and polyurethane topcoats. When mixed with its catalyst, this primer must be given induction time; follow the manufacturer's label directions.

An alkyd enamel primer-sealer (Fig. 5–21) is an all-purpose body primer for enamel topcoats. It is used as a sealer over old finish to minimize sand-scratch swelling, sink-in, or dulling of the enamel topcoat. This primer-sealer inhibits rust; it dries in 20 to 30 minutes and can be applied over old lacquer or enamel surfaces that are properly dried out and cleaned. This product may be lightly scuffed to remove dirt nibs if required.

Some of the plastic materials used in a vehicle require painting; special primers (Fig. 5–22) have been de-

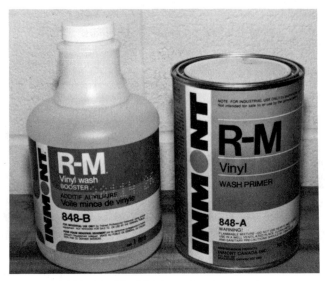

FIGURE 5-19 Vinyl wash primer and catalyst reducer.

FIGURE 5-20 Epoxy primer and catalyst.

veloped for adherence of the paint film to some of the different types of plastics. One is a polypropylene primer. It is used as a base on rigid polypropylene and polyethylene plastics. It can be top-coated with acrylic lacquer or enamel.

Primer-surfacers

The answer to a refinisher's dream would be a paint that would stick to anything (grease and dirt included), that would fill out all file marks, dings, and scratches, and finally that would flow out absolutely smooth without any sags and would require no rubbing or polishing. Unfortunately, no one has yet discovered a paint with all these qualities.

To design a paint that will stick to everything is a large order. In fact, to produce a paint that will stick to clean metal and remain bonded to it is by no means a simple problem. Adhesion is not a temporary proposition. Many materials will adhere to metal for a short period; but as soon as they begin to harden, the bond is destroyed.

FIGURE 5-21 Alkyd enamel primer-sealer.

FIGURE 5-22 Polypropylene plastic primer.

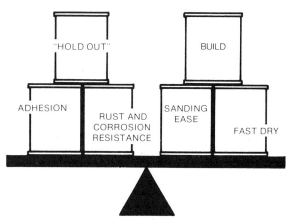

FIGURE 5-24 A balance of properties is vital in a primer-surfacer. The three on the left build the proper foundation for the topcoat; the three on the right make the job fast and easy. *(Courtesy of Du Pont Canada)*

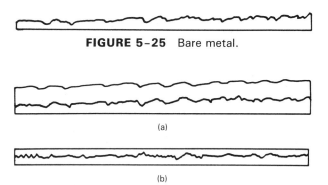

FIGURE 5-25 Bare metal.

(a)

(b)

FIGURE 5-26 (a) The metal is coated with primer-surfacer, which follows the approximate contours of the metal when it is dry. (b) Sanding will produce a flat smooth surface leveling off high spots. If it is not thoroughly dry before sanding, shrinking will occur over deep fills, producing uneven surfaces and showing file marks. *(Courtesy of Du Pont Co.)*

A primer-surfacer is recommended to improve the surface condition by filling the surface imperfections. Filling is a matter of placing sufficient materials on a surface so that after it dries and shrinks the surplus material may be sanded off to the level of the low spots (Fig. 5-23). To accomplish this, fillers or surfacers carry a very high solid content that includes pigments, as well as other materials, and the fillers are so formulated that when sprayed on a surface they build up the film thickness very rapidly.

Priming materials or finish coats cannot be formulated with such high solid contents without sacrificing other qualities. The one exception to this statement is a modern primer–surfacer, where a surfacer has been formulated to possess the adhesive properties of a primer (Fig. 5-24). Regardless of whether lacquers or synthetic enamels are used as a finishing coat, the paint will not materially improve the roughness of the original surface (Fig. 5-25). To obtain a smooth job means to start with a smooth surface, so we use a primer for good adhesion and a surfacer or putty for filling the rough surface (Fig. 5-26a). All the high spots are brought down to the level of the low points. If some of the metal shows before we reach the low spots, we have to spray more primer-surfacer and resand until the surface is smooth (Fig. 5-26b). Primer-surfacers should be re-

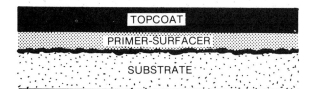

FIGURE 5-23 Primer-surfacers are unlike primers. They may be applied over bare metal or sanded old finishes. *(Courtesy Du Pont Co.)*

duced according to the manufacturer's recommendation and using a good-quality thinner.

There are different types of primers. In the average shop the most popular is the nitrocellulose primer-surfacer (Fig. 5-27), primarily because it fills well, dries fast, and is easy to sand. But it lacks the rust and corrosion resistance of an alkyd, acrylic, or urethane primer-surfacer and does not provide the tough flexible film of an alkyd acrylic or urethane surfacer; consequently, it is recommended for smaller repair areas.

Another lacquer-type primer is the acrylic lacquer primer-surfacer. It has very good filling qualities and good adhesion to automotive finishes, and it offers very good protection from corrosion (Fig. 5-28).

FIGURE 5-27 Nitrocellulose lacquer primer-surfacer.

FIGURE 5-28 Acrylic lacquer primer-surfacer.

Alkyd enamel primer-surfacer (Fig. 5-29) is excellent in all aspects but one; it has good adhesion and good filling qualities, and it offers excellent protection against corrosion of the metal. It can be applied on passenger vehicles or commercial trucks. It can be used to prime small areas that could lift on a fresh paint film if coated with lacquer primer-surfacer. It requires approximately 4 hours drying time before sanding.

Among the new developments is a urethane primer-surfacer now on the market (Fig. 5-30). It is a two-component type of material and gives a very high build on repaired areas. It has excellent adhesion and color holdout and is easily sanded; it also resists or eliminates featheredge sand-scratch swelling. Being a two-component material, it requires around 3 hours to dry depending on film thickness and temperature. This type of material has no film shrinkage and no overnight loss of gloss of the paint film, thus helping to eliminate expensive redoing of the repaired area. Being a urethane, it has tougher resistance to stone chips, corrosion, and

FIGURE 5-29 Alkyd enamel primer-surfacer.

FIGURE 5-30 Urethane primer-surfacer, catalyst, and reducer.

impacts. It can be applied over any properly prepared metal surface, as well as properly prepared plastics. This primer can be used for normal buildup as a primer-surfacer or as a high-fill primer when using a gravity feed gun. It can be used under any topcoat, but is especially recommended for basecoat/clearcoat systems. Since this material is catalyzed for use, read the manufacturer's label carefully for its pot life and for the materials it is compatible with.

Polyester primer-surfacers (Fig. 5-31) are used on new work and repairs; they fill surface flaws or heavy scratch marks in one operation. Since this product is catalyzed, it has a fast dry time and high buildup capabilities to fill imperfections found in steel or fiberglass refinishing operations. It can be used over properly cleaned and prepared steel, aluminum, fiber glass, wood, and previously painted surfaces. Since this material is catalyzed, read the manufacturer's label as to its pot life. This type of primer-surfacer can be used under basecoat/clearcoat systems as it will not allow bleaching or staining problems from solvent penetration.

Sealers

Paint sealers are manufactured from different types of resins, such as acrylic epoxy, acrylic lacquer alkyd, and urethane resins. The purpose of the sealers is to provide adhesion between the new coat of paint and the old painted surface (Fig. 5-32). Depending on the type used and amount of time between being recoated, some will have to be sanded. Another purpose of using sealers is that they act like a barrier to prevent the solvents from penetrating or to retard the penetration of the solvents

through to the old finish, which could cause a sinking in of the gloss of the new paint film or sand-scratch swelling. When a primer-surfacer has been used, there could be a difference in the holdout between the old paint film and the primer-surfacer. This condition can be corrected by applying a sealer before topcoating with

FIGURE 5-31 Polyester primer-surfacer.

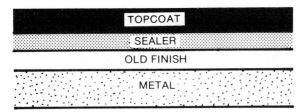

FIGURE 5-32 Sealers improve topcoat adhesion. They may be applied over primers, primer-surfacers, or (in this case) old finish. *(Courtesy of Du Pont Co.)*

the new paint film (Fig. 5-33). This type of primer-sealer (Fig. 5-34) must be allowed to dry approximately 30 minutes before recoating. If allowed to dry overnight, some of these primers must be scuff-sanded before painting with enamel. They should never be used under a new lacquer or acrylic lacquer film.

The acrylic lacquer type of sealers (Fig. 5-35) can usually be used on cured or OEM alkyd enamel, acrylic enamel and acrylic urethane enamel, and acrylic lacquer. Always check the manufacturer's label on the container as to method of using and drying time. If improperly used, sealers can cause problems, because they have what is called a recoat time; if not recoated during that time, the paint will likely peel off. The shop would have to redo the job, usually at no cost to the customer. All paint films must be properly prepared before sealing because sealers do not hide poor preparation methods. This type of sealer can also be used when changing the type of topcoat on a vehicle, such as going from an enamel undercoat or acrylic lacquer to acrylic enamel (Fig. 5-36).

Urethane sealers (Fig. 5-37) are two-component sealers that have universal use, since they can be used under any topcoat on the market. This sealer practically eliminates sand-scratch swelling and also provides excellent color holdout; it minimizes loss of gloss and featheredge lifting. It seals porous substrates quickly, minimizes topcoat buffing, and gives improved toughness for chip and impact resistance. Since this is a two-component material, the manufacturer's label should be checked as to the pot life of the material, the drying time, and the recoat time.

Putties

Lacquer primer-surfacers will cover small imperfections but should not be used to fill gouges, deep scratches, or similar defects. When these conditions are present, two different methods of repair can be used. When the scratches are a bit too deep for primer-surfacer, glazing may be applied in thin coats. Two or three applications of putty, allowing 15 to 20 minutes between coats, will produce better filling than one heavy coat. Glazing putty is usually applied by using a wide glazing knife or a squeegee (Fig. 5-38). Always remember to apply enough pressure to obtain adherence.

Another type of glazing putty is polyester glazing putty (Fig. 5-39), which is very smooth putty designed especially for final finishing over body filler, fiber glass, or bare metal. It fills minor imperfections, such as pinholes, and can be applied directly to clean metal with excellent adhesion and no shrinkage. It can be applied over aged paint films or primer-surfacers or sanded topcoat paint films. As with any glazing putty, it has its limits, and when the gouges or scratches are too deep (Fig. 5-40), they should be filled with body filler (see Table 5-8).

5-3 THINNERS AND REDUCERS

Thinners and reducers are specially developed thinning and reducing agents that are used with lacquer and enamel finishing materials. Generally, thinners are used to thin lacquer-based products to spraying viscosity. Reducers are used to reduce enamel products to a spraying viscosity. These products should never be intermixed because they are formulated to do specific jobs.

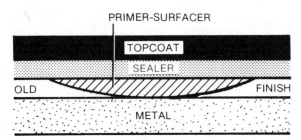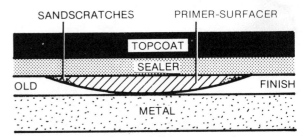

FIGURE 5-33 If a primer-surfacer has been used, there may be a difference in the holdout between the two types of finishes (left). If so, a sealer will solve the problem. Likewise (right), the use of a sealer may prevent show-through of sand scratches. *(Courtesy of Du Pont Co.)*

FIGURE 5–34   Alkyd enamel primer-sealer.

FIGURE 5–35   Acrylic lacquer type of sealer.

Enamel reducers and lacquer thinners are necessary for the application of lacquer and enamel automotive finishes. Since they become dissipated by evaporation, they do not become part of the paint film. The solvent value and the rate of evaporation of the thinners and reducers play an important part in the durability, appearance, and application of the paint film.

When using a poor thinner formula, a painter is at the mercy of variations in temperature and humidity. If the conditions are not perfect, the weak slow solvent will be the last to dry in the undercoat. This will kick the undercoat out of the solution and the adhesion will be very poor. In Table 5–9 it is shown that large amounts of strong fast and strong medium solvent are used in a good thinner. This will dissolve the topcoat well. In the poorer thinner, the 20% strong fast solvent will make it borderline for solvency.

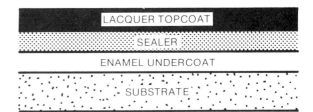

FIGURE 5–36   When a different topcoat than the old finish (in quality as well as color) is applied, a sealer should be used. *(Courtesy of Du Pont Co.)*

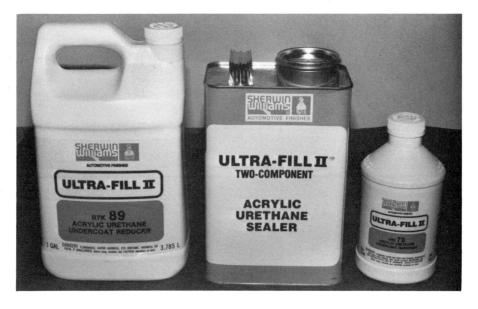

FIGURE 5–37   Urethane sealer, catalyst, and reducer.

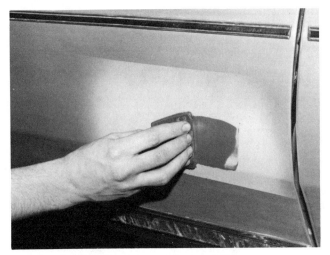

FIGURE 5-38 Applying glazing putty.

FIGURE 5-40 Applying the polyester glazing putty.

FIGURE 5-39 Polyester glazing putty.

The biggest problem in a top-coat thinner is in the slow and medium solvent area. The strong slow solvent in the good thinner will give good flow-out and gloss. The poor or cheaper thinner has only 20% slow solvent, but half of it is weak in solvency, which will cause poor gloss, flow, and adhesion. In the poor thinner, if the weak medium and weak slow solvent are the last to evaporate, the lacquer job will fail.

Strong solvents are more expensive to produce than weak solvents. Therefore, economic considerations tend to force manufacturers to produce solvents of various qualities to be sold at different prices.

A poor thinner or reducer can cause a multitude of problems for the painter because it must dissolve or reduce the coating through the entire solvent evaporation phase. A poor thinner or reducer can cause curdling or kickout, seediness, dulling gloss, chalking, cracking or splitting, sand-scratch swelling, blushing, poor adhesion, blistering and pinholing, poor settling properties, and poor color matches.

TABLE 5-8

Glazing putties and two-component fillers

	Sherwin-Williams	Du Pont	Ditzler	Rinshed-Mason	Martin-Senour	Sikkens
Lacquer type Glazing putty	D3A2749	2288S	DFL-17	76	639D	Auto-fine Stopper
Spot putty	D3R2748	2286S	DFL-5	92	6394	
Polyester two-component glaze Evercoat						Polystop

TABLE 5–9

Thinner, reducer, retarder, and catalyst chart

	Sherwin-Williams	Du Pont	Ditzler	Rinshed-Mason	Martin-Senour	Sikkens
Acrylic lacquer						
topcoat and lacquer undercoat fast for cold weather, 50° to 70°F (10° to 21°C)	R7K205	3613S	DTL-151	PNT-48	3088	Auto Fine Fast
Lacquer primer, medium dry for primer-surfacers, 65° to 80°F (18° to 26°C)	R7K6128	3642S	DTL-10	PNT-88	3093	
	R7K214	3608S	DTL-16		3092	
Slow for color, 75° to 95°F (24° to 35°C)	R7K203	3602S	DTL-135	PNT-90	3095	Auto Fine Slow
		3696S	DTL-105			
Medium dry, 65° to 80°F (18° to 26°C)	R7K248	3661S	DTL-876	PNT-88	3099	Thinner X
				6290		
Retarder		3979S				
Alkyd enamel reducer						
fast for cold weather 50° to 70°F (10° to 21°C)	R4K183	3812S	DTE-101	ER-59W	8005	ABC Fast M600
Very fast, 68° F (20°C)	R7K6220	8508S	DTE-201	ER-59	8008	
Completes and panels:						
70° to 90°F (21° to 35°C)	R4K183	8522S	DTE-202	ER-60	8004	ABS Slow
55° to 85°F (13° to 30°C)		3864S	DTE-303			Auto Flex Thinner
Completes high gloss		3832S	DTE-447	ER-61	8003	
Alkyd enamel color						
Blender	R4K179	3920S	DX-464	898		
Retarder	R4K239	RAC7007S	DXE-1807		8037	
Catalyst	V6V252	77S	DXE-123	829	8010	Aktivator
				895		
Acrylic enamel reducer						
fast for cold weather, 50° to 70°F (10° to 21°C)	R7K227	8034S	DTR-601	MS-5	8831	
Medium dry, 70° to 95°F (10° to 35°C)	R7K212	8022S	DTR-602	MS-6	8832	
Slow dry, 85° to 110°F (30° to 43°C)	RTK244	80935	DTR-607	MS-7	88331	
Retarder	R7K6251	8100S	DTV-1140	MS-8	8840	
Catalyst overall	V6V292	793S	DXR-80	MH-2	8870	
Spot repair	V6V292	792S	DX9-79	MH-1	8871	
Polyurethane reducers						
fast for cold weather, 50° to 70°F (10° to 21°C)	R7K6200	8485S	DTV-801	UT-1100	8431	
Medium, 65° to 85°F (18° to 29°C)	R7K6202	8485S	DTV-802	UT1100	8432	
Slow, 80° to 100°F (26° to 37°C)	R7K608		DTV-507		8455	
Retarder	R7K6251	8100S	DTX-1140	UT-11005	8840	
Catalyst activator	V6V769	192S	DAV-2		8450	
Accelerator	V6V766	189S	DXR-81	U892	8452	
Acrylic urethane reducer fast for cold weather, 50° to 70°F (10° to 21°C)		1025S	DTV-501			Tempo 1 ABC Fast
Medium dry, 65° to 85°F (18° to 29°C)	R7K89		DTV-504	5110		Tempo 11 ABC Fast
Slow dry, 80° to 100°F (26° to 37°C)			DTV-505			ABC Slow M368
Catalyst	V6V79					

Only with a balanced mixture of active and latent solvents and dilutents will reducers and thinners have the ability to dissolve various ingredients in enamels and lacquers. It is also necessary that they evaporate at the proper rate for ease of application and good flow-out without sags or runs. Each agent has a very specific function to perform.

Active solvents are the base for all thinners and reducers. They have the ability to dissolve or reduce completely the viscosity of lacquer or enamel finishes as received from the manufacturer.

In a refinish shop, a good grade of thinners and reducers should always be used. Low-priced thinners and reducers often contain an excess of cheap dilutents, which will cause lack of adhesion, brittleness of the paint film, or chalking and checking. If too much cheap, fast-evaporating solvent is used in a thinner or reducer, it will seriously affect the gloss and flow-out of the product being applied, as well as cause orange peel and blushing problems in lacquer.

The use of too much cheap, slow-evaporating solvent or dilutent may cause slow drying and other application problems. The thinners and reducers used in a shop should always match the conditions, such as cold or heat, of the different shops.

The latent solvents are the slower-acting solvents, which are relatively weak when used alone. They are blended with the active solvents to provide the extra measure of control necessary for the application of lacquers and enamel products.

The dilutents are a nonsolvent type of material and are primarily used as extenders. They also help the re-ducer and thinner to be more effective when the proper types are used in the right proportions.

To produce well-balanced lacquer thinners and enamel reducers, the blending of the proper types in the proper proportions of solvents and dilutents must be done very carefully, because each product has its own characteristics and many different types are available.

Topcoat Additives

Urethane hardeners (Fig. 5–41) have been used for quite a few years. This product can be used when so designed for alkyd, acrylic, and urethane enamels. When this additive is added to enamels, it changes them to a urethane type of enamel. This gives these enamels a mirrorlike, longer-lasting gloss that resists scratches and cleans easily. It also provides toughness to resist stone bruises and chipping, as well as chemical and solvent resistance. This additive improves the dry time through cure, cuts tape time, and eliminates wrinkling of the paint film (see Table 5–9).

Safety Measures

These products contain isocyanates, are considered hazardous materials, and may cause lung irritation and allergic reactions. They should not be used by any person who has chronic (long term) lung or breathing problems or who has ever had a reaction to isocyanates. These materials are to be used only with adequate ventilation. Where overspray is present, a positive pressure air supply respirator (TC19C NIOSH, MSHA) is recom-

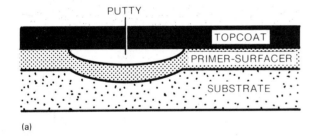

(a)

(b)

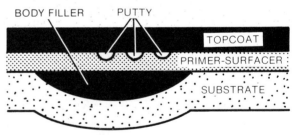

FIGURE 5-41 (a) Where scratches are too deep for primer-surfacers (left), you may have to use putty after application of the primer. When scratches are too severe for putty (right), you will have to use body filler on the surface and then the primer-surfacer. *(Courtesy of Du Pont Co.)* (b) Enamel hardener additives.

TABLE 5–10

Flex additives

Sherwin- Williams	Du Pont	Ditzler	Rinshed- Mason	Martin- Senour	Sikkens
V2V297	355S	DX1798	891	3082	Plasto Flex

mended. If not available, use a vapor particulate respirator that your respirator supplier recommends as effective for isocyanate vapors or mists. In all cases, follow manufacturer's directions for respirator use, and wear the respirator for the whole spraying time and until all vapors and mists are gone.

First Aid. In case of skin contact, wash with plenty of water. For eye contact, flush immediately with plenty of water for at least 15 minutes. If affected by inhalation of spray mist or vapor, remove to fresh air. If breathing difficulty persists or should occur later, a physician should be consulted; have the label instructions available.

Flex Additives or Elastomeric Paint Finishes

Some flex additives are designed to be used only when applying acrylic lacquer and others are designed to be used with all paint systems. These products are used to refinish exterior flexible parts such as bumpers, filler panels, and decorative fascia. They give excellent adhesion and flexibility to flexible parts while still maintaining superior gloss retention and a fast dry time (see Table 5–10).

Flattening Compounds

Flattening compounds are universal flattening materials that are used to lower the gloss of alkyd, acrylic enamel, acrylic lacquer, and urethane enamels. There are two types of flattening compounds, one for urethane finishes and one for nonurethane paint. This product may

be used when painting interior parts that require lower gloss levels. It cannot be used with success in alkyd or acrylic enamel if the hardener additive is used unless the proper urethane additive is also used (see Table 5–11).

Retarders and Antiwrinkling Additives

Retarders are used in the acrylic lacquer or the acrylic enamel painting systems when the temperature, humidity, and evaporation rates are high. The retarder prevents blushing of the lacquer film because it has a tremendous affinity for water. As condensation takes place on a panel with a freshly applied acrylic lacquer paint film with retarder in it, the retarder prevents a kick out or a blushing condition by absorbing the humidity and preventing it from mixing with the paint materials.

The advantages of using retarders are that they prevent blushing in acrylic lacquers and slow down the drying and evaporation rate in hot humid weather. The retarder used in acrylic enamel slows down the evaporation rate and gives a good flow-out of the paint film to increase the gloss. In both acrylic lacquer and enamel, when used in the mist coating of a complete paint job, a retarder will help dissolve overspray and also increase the gloss of the paint film. Through experience, the qualified painter knows when a retarder is required to achieve good results when painting. Retarders made for acrylic and urethane enamel are used to slow the drying and increase the flow-out and gloss.

Antiwrinkling additives are used in alkyd enamel when being force dried or sprayed in hot weather; they help eliminate wrinkling. They are used only when a hardener is not used (see Table 5–9).

TABLE 5–11

Flattening compounds

	Sherwin- Williams	Du Pont	Ditzler	Rinshed- Mason	Martin- Senour	Sikkens
Flattening compound for nonurethane	TIF270	4528S	DX265	850	3022	Matting paste
Alkyd enamel		903S				
Flattening compound for ure- thane			DX685			

TABLE 5–12

Topcoat clears

	Sherwin-Williams	Du Pont	Ditzler	Rinshed-Mason	Martin-Senour	Sikkens
Acrylic lacquer	TIC275	380S	DCA468	827	3072	Auto base clear
Acrylic enamel	TIC276	580S	DAV75	893	3073	Auto clear
Polyurethane enamel	TIC1000	500S			8454	Auto clear
Acrylic lacquer blending clear	TIC259	300S	DCA468	890	3081	
Acrylic enamel blending clear		1700S				

Topcoat Clears, Acrylic Lacquer Clearcoat Enamel, and Polyurethane

Acrylic lacquer clearcoat is used when repairing OEM basecoat/clearcoat finishes over acrylic lacquer base color coats.

Polyurethane clearcoat is used over acrylic lacquer base color coats of vehicles that are painted with OEM color coat/clearcoat paint film. It may also be used to clear acrylic enamel after waiting for the proper drying time before recoating.

Uniforming acrylic lacquer clear is used when blend coating acrylic lacquer for doing spot repairs on lacquer or enamel finishes (see Table 5-12).

5–4 SPECIALTY ITEMS

Vinyl Guard

Several manufacturers produce different types of vinyl guard. This material is used to repair and protect behind the wheel opening on the front lower fenders, lower portion of door panels, and lower sections on quarter-panels. Each manufacturer has its own method of application; some require that their product be top-coated with paint and some do not require any painting after application because their material is transparent. Therefore, the repairperson must follow the directions on the label. Figure 5-42 shows a quart of vinyl guard and a lower section of an automobile finished with vinyl guard.

The area to refinish is usually governed by a styling edge or sometimes a molding, which is used as a natural cutoff line to mask off the area that does not require refinishing. If there is rust on the outer panels or if the paint is badly chipped, it will probably be necessary to strip the paint off, sandblast the rust, and then use metal conditioner on the affected areas. A vinyl wash primer should be used to prime the metal. When

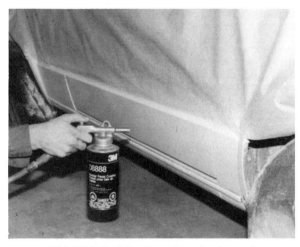

FIGURE 5–42 Spraying vinyl guard.

the area is dry, a primer-surfacer is used. After this has thoroughly dried, a pressure-feed gun is used to apply the vinyl guard to the panels. This usually takes about 2 hours to dry. Then, if required, the area can be painted the color of the automobile using the proper materials. Care must be taken to mask the required areas properly so that only the areas requiring refinishing will be painted with vinyl guard.

Trunk Splatter

When sections such as quarter-panels or trunk lower panels are changed, they must be refinished as they were finished in the factories. Many manufacturers use a multicolored interior finish that resists abrasion and moisture. This product is designed to duplicate original finishes in passenger car trunks.

The area to be painted is masked and, for best results, the paint is poured into the cup of a pressure-feed gun. The paint is sprayed at package consistency on the required parts (Fig. 5-43). The area is unmasked when the paint is fairly dry. A factory-type finish is left over

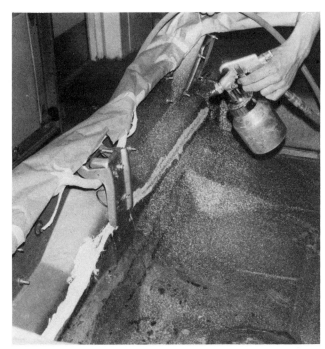

FIGURE 5-43 Spraying trunk splatter.

the repaired areas. When spraying operations are finished, the gun is cleaned thoroughly by following the instructions on the paint can label.

Rubbing Compounds

Rubbing compounds are used to remove dirt nibs, spray dust, and orange peel and to improve gloss in lacquer finishes. They can also be used on fully cured enamel surfaces. The rubbing compound is a fine abrasive in a neutral medium of creamy consistency. It can be used either by hand or by machine to polish a surface. It can also be used to clean the surface of the paint when it is to be blended in or spot repaired.

Tack Rag

A tack rag is made from a piece of cheesecloth that is dipped into a nondrying varnish. It is put into a special paper envelope to stop the varnish from drying out. The automobile body should be rubbed properly from end

to end with the tack rag, for it will pick up dust remaining after the body has been blown off.

Fisheye Eliminator

This product is used in alkyd, acrylic, and urethane enamels. The purpose of this product is to prevent fisheyes in the enamel paint film as it is being sprayed as necessary to overcome minor silicone contamination. One type is used for nonurethane paint and the other is used in urethane-type paint, that is, any paint that has a urethane hardener added to it (see Table 5–13).

Paint Strainers

Paint strainers (Fig. 5–44) are used to strain the paint when it is poured in the cup. They are manufactured in three different mesh sizes: 200 microns, 280 microns, and 400 microns.

The extra-fine 200-μm mesh size is used to strain highly thinned paint such as nonmetallic lacquer. The fine 280-μm mesh size is used to strain metallic paint, and the medium 400-μm mesh is used to strain coarse metallic paint. Straining the paint removes any particle of paint or dirt that could plug the gun or leave a dirt nib in the paint job.

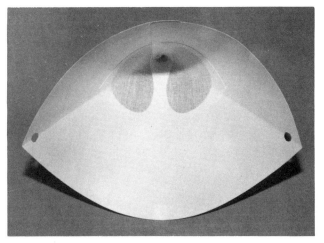

FIGURE 5-44 Paint strainer.

TABLE 5-13

Fisheye eliminator

	Sherwin-Williams	Du Pont	Ditzler	Rinshed-Mason	Martin-Senour	Sikkens
Nonurethane paint	V3K265	FEE	DX-66	803	77B	
Urethane paint	V3K780	2595	DX-77	819	87	

Paint Thickness Gauge

Paint thickness gauges are important tools in a paint shop because they are used to measure the thickness of the paint film on a vehicle. How else can an estimate be properly done but by measuring the film thickness? If the film is too thick, extra funds will be required to cover the cost of stripping the vehicle before repainting.

Many different types of gauges are sold by industry, but very common and inexpensive is the gauge with a magnetic rod that is attracted to ferrous metals (Fig. 5-45). To use, the protective cover is removed; a window on each side of a housing is exposed in which a magnetic rod is attached at the end to the housing by a spring (Fig. 5-46). One side of the rod is marked in thousandths of an inch (or mils); the other side is marked in the SI equivalent.

The gauge is held at right angle to the surface as in Fig. 5-45. The area to be tested must be free of dirt, grease, oil, or ferrous metal chips. The magnet end of the rod in the gauge is touched to the surface, and the gauge is then lifted smoothly and slowly away from the surface. The rod marking must be watched as the gauge is pulled up. When the magnet end releases from the surface, its location shows how thick the paint film application is on the metal underneath the paint film. On heavily coated metal, the magnetic attraction is less and the rod will let go sooner. On bare or very thinly covered metal, the magnetic strength is greater; therefore, the housing will have to be pulled higher before it releases and registers the mil thickness. The paint should be measured in several areas.

Paint film thickness gauges are available from some paint jobbers and for different prices depending on their construction.

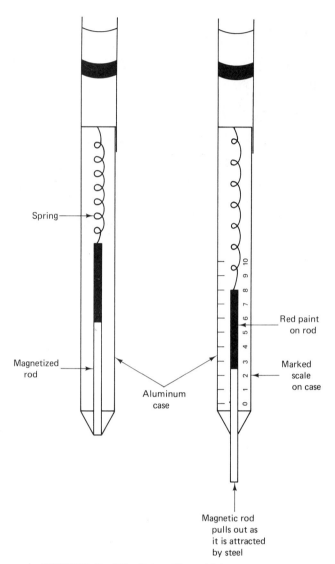

FIGURE 5-46 Paint film thickness gauge construction and use.

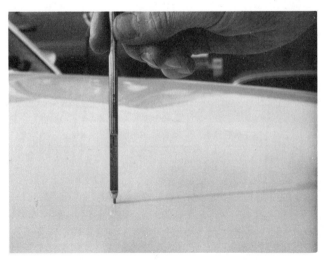

FIGURE 5-45 Using paint film thickness gauge.

5-5 MASKING

The masking tape and masking paper companies have a tremendous market to supply. They not only supply the body and paint shops but also the vehicle manufacturers. Masking tape is also used by home owners and a multitude of uses have been found for it. The conditions under which these products must be able to perform are varied, from the hot arid desert to cold and damp shops. Therefore, weather variability plus the dirt and dust that are always present in a refinish shop accounts for the exacting requirements that are placed on masking tape to accomplish the job successfully. Some tapes are made for special use, such as air dry paint conditions. Other tapes must be able to be used in baking operations and to perform the task properly.

A good tape must possess special qualities, such as the proper amount of adhesion. The adhesion must be instantaneous, but yet not so strong as to be hard to remove or so weak as to fall off by itself. The tape must stick at a touch without hard pressure to the moldings, nameplates, windshield, and so on. The tape should unwind without too much effort so as not to affect the strength and flexibility of the backing. A controlled unwind is necessary for good performance for hand masking or use on apron tapers. The tape must be strong enough not to rip easily or break when being applied. The tape must have the ability to stretch when going around mild curves or when force must be applied to it. This stretch must also remain in the tape so as to prevent edge lifting around sharp curves. The tape must have the ability to remain in place when stress is present due to shrinkage of primers or to cold and hot temperatures. The strength of the adhesive on the tape must be balanced so that the adhesive is removed with the tape and leaves no residue.

Due to the many uses and climatic conditions under which masking tape is used, the refinishing market must certainly be one of the most critical users of masking tape. Due to the many varied conditions, problems will certainly arise at the shop level that may not be the fault of the tape. The following problems are the most frequently encountered; the causes and remedies are based on experience gathered in the field.

Masking Tape Problems

Low adhesion, edge curl, or fall off are most frequently caused when the edges of the tape are not pressed down properly. These problems also occur when the tape is applied on a surface contaminated by moisture, wax, dirt, silicone, or grease but can be prevented by properly cleaning the surface prior to masking and making sure the edges are pressed down properly. When primer-surfacer dries, it can curl the edge of the tape if it is not applied properly.

When removing masking tape at cool temperatures, adhesive transfer can occur due to greater adhesive bond at these temperatures. Adhesive transfer may also occur from long exposure to sunlight, excessively high temperatures during the bake cycles, or the excessive use of solvents when cleaning the vehicle prior to painting. To help remedy these problems, remove the tape at above 60°F (16°C) and avoid sunlight exposure, hot, long bake cycles, and excessive use of solvents. When a bake oven is used, a high-temperature tape should be used.

Removing the masking tape at low temperatures may cause the tape to sliver; that is, the tape either tears or breaks when being removed from the surface. When masking tape is removed at low temperatures, the adhesion is greater and the rubber treatment in the backing is more brittle. This could cause the bond to be stronger than the strength of the backing, thus causing the tearing or slivering. It is possible to make the backing strong enough to prevent slivering, but then the desirable properties of easy tear and stretching would be destroyed. Therefore, the only solutions are never to leave masking tape on longer than necessary and to remove it at a temperature above 60°F (16°C). Removing the masking tape at slow speed and at a 90° angle or less to the surface will reduce the risk of slivering.

When primer-surfacer flakes or cracks off the backing of the masking tape when removed from a surface, the following reasons are the major causes. The backing of the masking tape is contaminated by wax or grease, the primer was sprayed on with too little solvent, or too heavy a coat of primer was used. To eliminate these problems, the masking tape should be removed at a 90° angle or less (this will reduce the risk of flaking); also, use a good quality masking tape that has a treatment on the backing to help reduce the risk of primer flaking.

The staining or yellow discoloration of a painted surface, which usually occurs more often on light-colored shades of paint, is a chemical reaction or migration of ingredients from the tape into the paint. Most paints and tapes used on the market today in the automotive field are resistant to staining. This problem can be overcome by the proper choice of tape and paint. Staining tendencies increase with the length of time the tape is in contact with a freshly painted surface; the tape and masking paper should be removed as soon as possible after painting. Remove all tape and masking paper before force drying or baking a paint job. Before taping over fresh paint, be sure that the surface is dry enough so that the tape will not mark the finish when the tape is removed.

Rolls of masking tape should be stored at temperatures of 75°F (24°C) or slightly lower. The stock of rolls of masking tape should always be carefully rotated to prevent old stock being kept in the shop. When masking tape gets old, the rolls may become distorted and out of round. Low winding tensions will also increase roll distortion.

Types of Masking Tape

When masking a vehicle, the method and care used will make the difference between a good and a poor job. All surfaces such as glass, moldings, light lenses, bumpers, and so on, should be cleaned of dust or any accumulation of any contaminant. When masking tape is put on a molding or any other part, it should not be stretched if at all possible.

A good masking tape is water resistant so as to be able to withstand the water used when wet sanding and show no failure in either adhesive or backing.

Masking tape is manufactured and sold in many sizes: 1/8, 1/4, 1/2, 3/4, 1, 1 1/2, 2, and 3 in. (3.6, 12, 18, 24, 36, 48, and 72 mm) are common. The 1/4 and 3/4 in. (6 and 18 mm) are the sizes used most often when masking. The rolls are usually 180 ft (55 m) in length.

Another type of tape available is a fine-line masking tape manufactured by 3M. This tape is used for cutting out a two-tone paint job or custom painting (Fig. 5–47) because it is very flexible and thin. This masking tape with its special polypropylene backing allows the tape to be used sooner on freshly painted enamel or lacquer surfaces, with less danger of showing tape imprint marks when removed. It is also very resistant to solvent penetration. This tape is available in rolls of 1/16, 1/8, 3/16, 1/4, 3/8, 1/2, and 3/4 in. (1.5, 3, 5, 6, 10, 12, and 18 mm).

The major masking tape manufacturers also provide the shop with a specially treated masking paper. This paper comes in rolls 1000 ft (305 m) long and in widths of 3, 6, 9, 12, 15, 18, 24, and 36 in. (8, 15, 23, 30, 38, 46, 69, and 91 cm). One side of this paper is treated with a special material and is shinier than the other side. This paper should always be applied with the smooth shiny side out as it will not shed any impurities if not applied in this manner. Some manufacturers also provide masking paper that is a polyimpregnated paper on each side. This type of masking paper is virtually bleed-through proof. It also nonsheds dirt, and so is ap-

plicable for doing basecoat/clearcoat or custom finishes.

Other Masking Materials and Equipment

Many other types of materials are used for masking large areas; some of these materials are wallpaper, Kraft paper, newspaper, sheets of polyethylene, and specially built maskers that cover large sections of the vehicle. When using newspaper it must be handled carefully as it tears easily; it should not be used on lacquer panels due to the chance the solvents will dissolve the ink and allow it to discolor the panel being protected.

When the wheels have to be covered, most shops use a manufactured wheel cover (Fig. 5–48). These covers are usually made from heavy cloth or vinyl material, which is sewn in a nearly complete circle with a spring wire inserted into it in the form of an arc to hold it on the wheel.

Manufacturers also provide equipment that holds different widths of masking paper and a roll of masking tape (Fig. 5–49). These units are made so as to be able to apply masking tape to the edge of masking paper as required. They also have a cutting bar to cut the paper to the desired length. These units help to speed up the work as they can be brought to the job; they can also provide pretaped aprons for the painter or apprentice.

Some shops do not have automatic apron tapers. Then the painter, when he or she has to do filler masking, should clean a large area on a flat surface such as a bench or a hood. Large enough sections of paper for the job are laid on this area; then a strip of tape is applied to one edge of the paper, half on the paper and

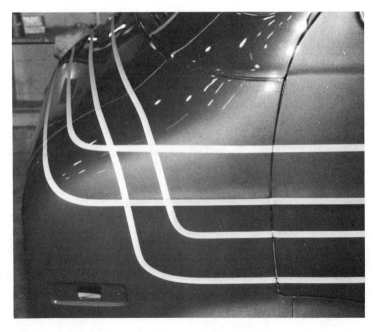

FIGURE 5–47 Masking with 3M fine line tape.

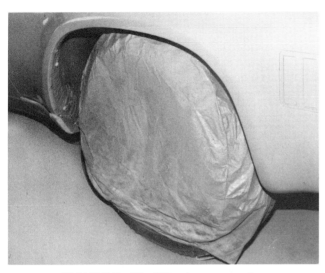

FIGURE 5-48 Wheel cover masker.

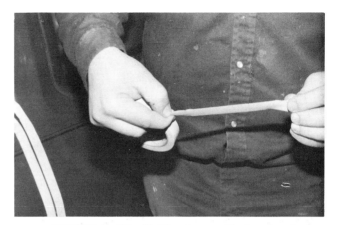

FIGURE 5-50 Cutting tape with thumbnail from roll.

half off for its full length or as required. This apron is then lifted and applied in the normal fashion to the area to be masked.

Some painters make themselves favorite tools to help apply tape or to remove it. A narrow paintbrush with short bristles can be used to apply tape on hard to reach places. A tongue depressor or a revel stick can be shaped to help scrape dirt in hard-to-reach places that was not removed when the vehicle was washed. A small flat screwdriver can be bent to put a hook in it and then used to help remove masking tape in hard-to-reach areas by scraping it and lifting the edge to enable the fingers to pull it off.

Applying Tape

On many occasions when masking a vehicle, short pieces of tape have to be cut to tack the masking paper in certain areas. The roll is held in one hand as in Fig. 5-50, and with the fingers of the other hand a length of tape is cut off the roll by using the thumbnail as the cutting edge. Quite often the masking tape must be applied to an edge and here also, as in Fig. 5-51, the thumbnail is used to cut the tape at the desired location on the panel.

When taping a freshly painted area to mask it off for more painting such as two-toning, the tape is unwound off the roll slowly and the fingers are rubbed on the adhesive (Fig. 5-52). This is done to reduce the adhesive strength and to help to prevent pulling the fresh

FIGURE 5-49 Portable masking unit.

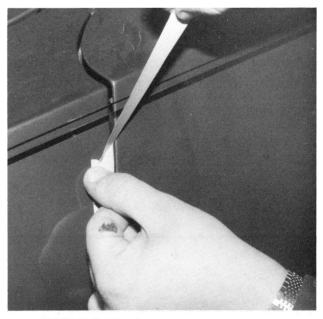

FIGURE 5-51 Cutting tape with thumbnail on panel.

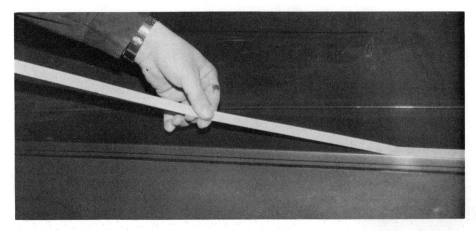

FIGURE 5-52   Rubbing adhesive with fingers.

paint off the panel when the tape and masking paper are removed.

When holding a roll of masking tape to mask a molding or other area, the roll of masking tape is held in the left or right hand as appropriate. The roll is held with the fingers inside the roll and the thumb on the outside of the roll. As the roll unwinds, the adhesive should not be facing the painter, but away from him. The roll is held fairly loosely and the end of the tape is unwound and applied on the molding or a wheel opening (Fig. 5-53). The distance of the tape from the surface to be painted should be at least approximately 1/32 in. (0.7 mm). The roll of tape is allowed to roll on the fingers while being applied to the correct area on the molding. The width of the molding governs how many strips need to be used. Always remember to leave a small gap between the molding and the area to be painted as the paint could bridge the gap, especially with lacquer. The tape is applied with enough pressure to make it stick, but it must not be stretched more than required when going around curves. If the masking tape should be too wide for an emblem or molding, it can be split to the proper size by using scissors or a razor blade.

Masking the Vehicle

The masking tape and paper are applied on the vehicle to protect areas from the paint that will be applied. The area to be painted should never be contacted or overlapped by the tape or paper as this will lead to edge lifting of the new coat of paint. A painter or apprentice must always use good judgment when masking as a shoddy method of application will lead to a shoddy looking job.

When painting with lacquer, the area to be protected should usually be masked with two layers of masking paper to stop the thinner from seeping through to damage the original finish. All masking tape and paper should be removed as soon as possible after painting

(a)

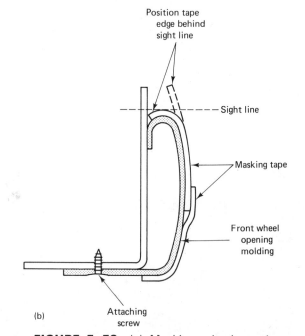

(b)

FIGURE 5-53   (a) Masking wheel opening molding. (b) End view of tape position on wheel opening molding.

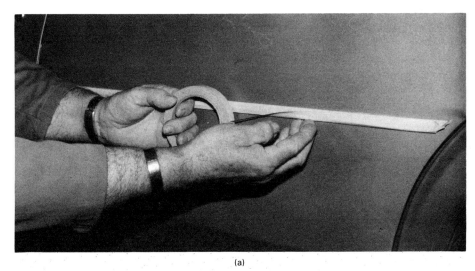

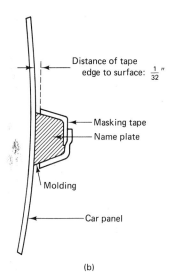

Distance of tape
edge to surface: $\frac{1}{32}$"

Masking tape
Name plate

Molding

Car panel

(a)   (b)

FIGURE 5–54   (a) Masking a door molding. (b) End view of tape on
door molding.

when the paint is dry enough. The dryness of the paint can be checked by rubbing the back of a finger on a part of the job that would not easily show a slight defect if the paint is not dry enough. The first test should always be done on the masking beside the new paint film. Masking tape should not be allowed to touch or contact a freshly painted surface when it is removed as the tape could possibly remove the paint.

When masking moldings, a ¾-in. (19-mm) tape is used, and the first tape is applied on the top part of the molding, leaving enough of an edge to cover the top of the molding and just enough to leave a narrow gap so

that the paint will not bridge between the panel and the tape. A finger or other instrument is used to press the tape in position on the top edge of the molding (Fig. 5–54). The tape is unrolled and applied while the fingers of the other hand position the tape correctly. When a corner has to be masked, it should be started with a fresh end of masking tape.

When a nameplate has to be masked, the masking tape is positioned on the top part first, leaving the required gap, and then it is bent down and pressed on the nameplate. The bottom part of the nameplate is taped by putting the masking tape on the bottom of the molding and then folding the tape up (Fig. 5–55); pressing firmly on it will assure proper adherence.

Certain areas require that a strip of tape be applied around the perimeter of the area (Figs. 5–56 and

FIGURE 5–55   Masking a nameplate.

FIGURE 5–56   Masking the perimeter of a
side window.

FIGURE 5-57 Masking the perimeter of the tail lights.

5-57). Then an apron of the approximate size is used, the bottom edge is taped to the bottom perimeter tape, and the paper with the right side facing outside is folded neatly with the folded edge on the inside. This is tacked down with short pieces of tape and then completely taped down to the perimeter tape. This leaves a clean, smooth sheet of paper that will be easy to keep clean and not catch or trap any dust (Fig. 5-58).

Always mask the driver's door separately so that it can be opened if the vehicle has to be moved. Doors with a regular frame around the glass will have the glass masked separately. On vehicles that have no pillar in the center, the glass can be masked as one unit as long as all weather strips or other sealing devices are covered with tape.

To mask a vinyl top, it is necessary to first put a strip of tape around its perimeter; then the vinyl top is covered as in Fig. 5-59 with an appropriate size and

FIGURE 5-59 Masked vinyl top.

amount of aprons to completely cover the top. All the aprons should be applied as smooth as possible, with the extra edges tucked in. All seams must be taped together to prevent any paint or dust from penetrating inside the masked area.

Windshields and rear windows are masked by applying a strip on the perimeter; then a 24-in. (610-mm) or a combination of a 12- and 16-in. (305- and 406-mm) apron will cover most rear windows or windshields (Fig. 5-60). The taped edge of the apron is applied to the top of the windshield; sometimes the paper is folded to make it follow the curve of the glass. At other times it is cut to shape to fit the area to be masked before applying any tape to it; then it is taped in place. The extra paper at the edge is folded inward and toward the window; the loose edges are fastened with a ¾-in. (19-mm) tape. If two aprons are used, the top one must always overlap the lower apron to prevent spray or dust seepage. If any creases are present, they must be taped down to prevent dust from accumulating in them while cleaning and

FIGURE 5-58 Filling in the perimeter with an apron to mask the window.

FIGURE 5-60 Masking the windshield.

FIGURE 5-61 Masked door handle.

painting are going on. If the glass is retained by a rubber weather strip, it may be necessary to clean it with a cleaning solvent to remove impurities so that the tape will stick to it. It is sometimes important that a window be cut in the paper on the driver's side if it is to be moved after masking operations.

Most door handles are masked using ¾-in. (19-mm) masking tape, which is applied lengthwise as in Fig. 5-61. On the older style of handles the tape is applied around the handle close to the panel, but as soon as possible it is applied lengthwise.

On most late-model vehicles the grille is masked separately from the bumper (Fig. 5-62). A perimeter tape is applied to the grille and the area is then filled in with a masking apron of the appropriate size. Whether the bumper is plated, of shiny aluminum construction, or a urethane type of fascia determines how it is masked. If the bumper is made of metal, it is masked with the

right size of apron and the lower edges are folded under and taped to the lower part of the bumper (Fig. 5-62).

On some vehicles it is possible to mask the grille and bumper together except for the areas where the flexible plastic filler panel is between the bumper and front part of the fender. These parts are usually painted at the same time as the rest of the vehicle.

When a vehicle is painted with two different colors, one color must be applied and left to dry. When it is dry, the section that must be protected is masked off to prevent the application of the next coat of paint from covering the previous coat. A perimeter tape is applied where required; some painters use ¾-in. (19-mm) tape, but others use fine-line tape because it is thinner

FIGURE 5-62 Grille and bumper masking.

FIGURE 5-63 Masking side for two-tone paint job.

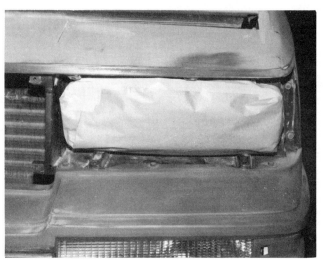

FIGURE 5-66 Masked rectangular seal beam.

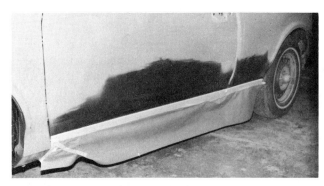

FIGURE 5-64 Masked rocker panel molding.

FIGURE 5-65 Masked round seal beam.

FIGURE 5-67 Masking an aerial.

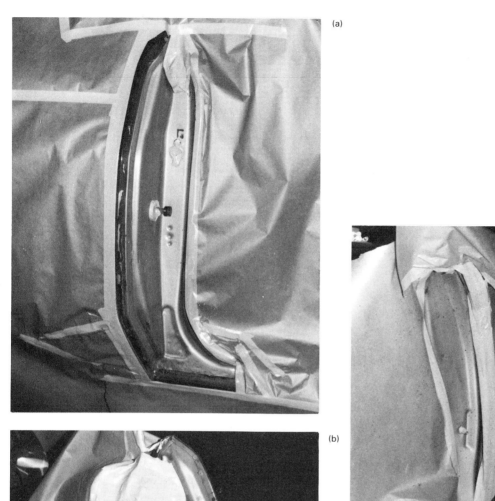
(a)

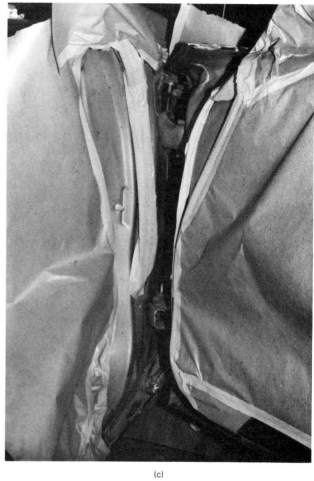
(b)

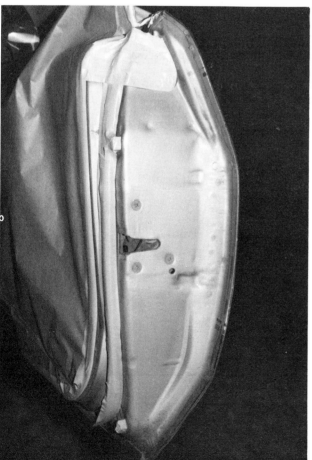
(c)

FIGURE 5-68 Masking (a) door, (b) jambs, and (c) upholstery.

and will cause less of a buildup where the tape separates the two colors. After the perimeter tape has been applied, the area is filled in with the proper size of apron. The tape on the apron is applied at the top part of the perimeter tape; the excess at the bottom and the ends is folded under and tacked. Then a strip of masking tape is run along the bottom and ends as required, leaving an area that is masked somewhat like that shown in Fig. 5–63.

Wide molding on the rocker panels can be easily masked by using a pretaped apron of the proper width. The pretaped apron is applied to the molding by using the taped edge of the apron and leaving enough gap so the paint will not bridge across (Fig. 5–64).

The masking tape and paper are removed as soon as possible after finishing the paint job and should never be left on overnight, as the solvents in the paint under the paper will evaporate. Since the solvents cannot escape, they will soften the paint film and the masking paper may stick to the paint and usually mark the paint film.

To mask headlights, use a 6-in. (152-mm) apron. The tape edge is applied to the edge of the seal beam or its retaining ring, forming a circle (Fig. 5–65) or a rectangle (Fig. 5–66). The paper is then folded toward the center, and a strip of tape is pressed down from edge to edge across the center to hold the paper flat. The same method can be used for taillights and parking lights, but for some a 3-in. (76-mm) apron or less is very often sufficient.

A tube used to hold brazing rods or a tube made of paper is slipped over the aerial and taped to the bottom (Fig. 5–67). Another method is to use a tape of the proper width, which is run up one side and then up the other and pressed together.

Miscellaneous Masking

When the door jambs have to be painted, it is necessary to cover the upholstery, windlacing, weather stripping, lock, and striker plate (Fig. 5–68a, b, c). A 6-in. (152-mm) or wider pretaped apron is ideal for this operation. If the rubber is not perfectly clean, it might be necessary to coat it with clear lacquer before applying tape. With the edges covered, a spray gun can be used to paint the area.

Door jambs are quite often sprayed with acrylic lacquer as it is quick drying, but acrylic enamel is used also even if it is slower drying. On a complete paint job, the door jambs, trunk lid gutter, inside fender edges, and hood edges should be painted first if so required. A 6-in. (152-mm) pretaped apron with ½-in. (13-mm) pleats every 4 to 6 in. (101 to 152 mm) is used to mask

a wheel quickly (Fig. 5–69). The taped edge of the apron is placed on the tire next to the rim. Short strips of tape are used to fasten the paper to the tire.

Reverse masking or styling edge masking is used especially when spot repairs have to be done on a panel. This type of masking is done by using sharp styling edges on the panel to be spot repaired. Figure 5–70 shows one method where the top of the fender and part of the hood are covered by a pretaped apron. The tape is applied just very slightly before the bend in the styling edge. Then another strip is bent over. This will create enough turbulence in the paint stream so that no appreciable paint line will show once the masking is removed.

Reverse masking along sharp styling edges can also be achieved by using a pretaped apron. The pretaped apron is aligned with the sharp part of the styling edge of the panel where the masking tape and paper join (Fig. 5–71a). The masking paper that naturally falls down is then lifted up and folded gently over, allowing reverse curvature of the paper to extend ½ to ¾ in. (12 to 20 mm) beyond the styling edge. The masking paper is then tacked to the panel to hold it in place (Fig. 5–71b).

When it is required to mask along a curved styling edge, it is necessary to use masking tape. Place ¾-in. (19-mm) strips at a right angle along the curved styling edge. These strips should be 4 to 5 in. (10 to 13 mm) long and are overlapped as required and applied to the panel above the crease line (Fig. 5–72a). Each masking paper strip is then turned over in a gentle circle, starting with the last strip applied to the tape (Fig. 5–72b). A strip of tape should be used to hold this section of curved masking while the rest of the masking operation is finished.

FIGURE 5–69 Masking wheels.

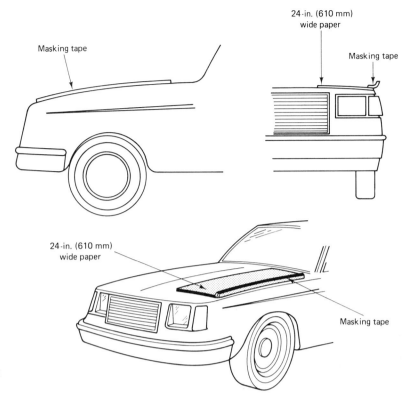

FIGURE 5-70 Reverse masking with tape and masking paper.

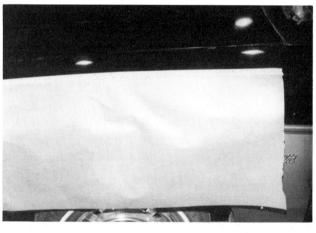

FIGURE 5-71 Reverse masking with tape using masking paper and tape.

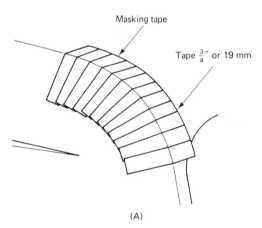

(A)

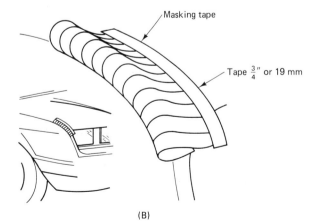

(B)

FIGURE 5-72 Reverse masking with tape.

REVIEW QUESTIONS

5-1. Describe a paint surface that is in good condition.

5-2. Describe a paint surface that is in poor condition.

5-3. What does a painter use to find out if the paint film is acrylic lacquer or enamel?

5-4. Describe how a vehicle is degreased properly.

5-5. Describe how featheredging is done.

5-6. Describe how a vehicle should be wet sanded.

5-7. What product is used to remove paint chemically and how is it used?

5-8. Describe how a hatchback must be masked prior to paint-removing operations.

5-9. Why is sandblasting used to remove rust from the metal surface?

5-10. What type of sand may be used when sandblasting operations are carried out?

5-11. Why are metal conditioners used on metal?

5-12. What is the purpose of using a primer?

5-13. What type of primer should be used in shop repairs on bare metal?

5-14. What is used as a primer when repairing polypropelene plastic?

5-15. What is the purpose of primer-surfacer?

5-16. What type of primer is used on commercial trucks?

5-17. What is the name of a new two-component primer-surfacer that should be used when repairing a basecoat paint job?

5-18. What are sealers used for when painting?

5-19. What are the qualities of a urethane sealer?

5-20. What is used to fill small imperfections in a paint finish?

5-21. What is thinner used for?

5-22. What is used to slow down the drying of acrylic lacquer?

5-23. What safety precautions must be taken when using materials that contain isocyanates?

5-24. What is the purpose of a flattening compound?

5-25. What is vinyl guard used for?

5-26. Describe how a pencil magnetic type of film thickness gauge works.

5-27. What causes low adhesion, edge curl, or fall off of masking tape?

5-28. What causes masking tape to sliver?

5-29. What is the difference between masking paper and newspaper?

5-30. What is meant by perimeter masking?

5-31. Describe how to mask a windshield.

5-32. Describe how to mask a rectangular headlight.

5-33. How is a two-tone paint job masked?

5-34. Explain how reverse masking is done with paper.

CHAPTER SIX

The Application of Paint Materials

SAFETY HINTS

All paint and solvents should be stored in approved cabinets or in storage rooms that have explosion-proof lights and adequate ventilation.

All solvent drums must be grounded and bonded to containers while being used.

High-flash paint solvents should always be used when possible.

Adequate ventilation must be provided to remove any solvent fumes.

Always read directions on labels to find the safe way of using the products and for first-aid instructions.

Care should be used to prevent spilling of solvents or liquids.

Used cloth or paper towels should be stored in a covered container and then removed from the shop at day's end and stored in a proper garbage bin or tank.

6–1 METAL CONDITIONING AND PRIMING

The proper treatment of metal in every successful automotive paint shop is a very critical step. But in many shops it is ignored or carried out in a haphazard, careless method. By doing this, a paint shop can expect to receive customer complaints about poor adhesion and corrosion.

Metal that is bare of any protective coating such as paint must be chemically cleaned to provide maximum adhesion for the primer. This treatment is a three-step operation. The metal must be cleaned with a degreaser to remove grease, oil, or any other contaminants. Then the metal is chemically cleaned with the appropriate metal conditioner to remove corrosion and rust. The last step, if required, is the application of the recommended conversion coating so as to provide maximum adhesion.

When applying the degreaser or a nonoily solvent or reducer, the area to be treated should be wet down thoroughly. The product is usually applied with a clean cloth, and while the surface is still wet a second cloth is folded and used to wipe the area dry. This cloth should be disposed of after completing a section. Only areas that are comfortable in size to work with should be done at one time; repeat the same method over and over again until the whole area has been cleaned.

The metal conditioner is mixed to the proper ratio following directions on the label. It is mixed in a plastic pail or jug with the appropriate amount of water as per

directions. The metal conditioner is applied with a sponge or cloth; the area must sometimes be worked with steel wool, a wire brush, or an abrasive pad if rust is present (Fig. 6–1). Then, depending on the type, the surface is either washed with water before it dries or is wiped dry according to directions.

The conversion coating, if used, is poured into a plastic pail or jug; using steel wool, an abrasive pad, a rag, or brush, the coating is then applied to the metal surface. This solution is left on the surface for 2 to 5 minutes and then rinsed off before the solution dries. If it should dry before it is rinsed off, the area must be treated and rinsed off again. The coating is flushed from the surface with cold water using a rag or a sponge rinsed in clean water. The area is then wiped dry with a clean cloth and allowed to air dry. When applying these chemicals, it is sometimes necessary to wear rubber or neoprene gloves to protect the skin from the acid.

Priming the Surface

The bare metal must be primed as soon as possible to prevent a recurrence of rusting and oxidation. Some paint shops use either zinc chromate primer or vinyl wash or epoxy primer on the bare metal. Zinc chromate is reduced with a reducer as per label directions and sprayed on either steel or aluminum at a gun pressure of 40 to 45 psi (276 to 310 kPa) of air pressure. It is sprayed from a distance of approximately 6 to 8 in. (152 to 200 mm) between the metal surface and the gun. This

FIGURE 6-1 Applying metal conditioner.

material must be sprayed on in a see-through coat because too thick a film will cause it to lift off the surface and result in a paint failure. This primer is usually reduced 4 parts primer to 1 part reducer; approximately 1 mil is applied, and then there is a 10-minute wait before recoating and a 30-minute wait period before applying a topcoat material. Always check the manufacturer's label on the container for directions.

A vinyl wash or epoxy primer should be used as a first primer on all bare metal; it should be stirred properly as the solids in the binder have a tendency to settle to the bottom of the can rather quickly. It must be reduced according to the manufacturer's recommendations. Only enough to do the job should be mixed as it is a catalyzed material when mixed and has about an 8-hour pot life.

The vinyl wash or epoxy primer has excellent adhesion and will provide corrosion protection for most substrates. It is applied in a thin see-through coat; the metal should be fairly visible through it. It can be used over steel, aluminum, fiber glass, plastic, galvanized, and Zinco sheet metal. It is sprayed at a pressure of 40 to 45 psi (276 to 310 kPa) of air pressure at the gun keeping a distance between gun and metal of approximately 6 to 8 in. (152 to 200 mm). These primers are drawn by capillary action to coat the surface of the metal, which has either been sanded or is fairly smooth. Figure 6-2 shows how the primer will follow the scratches or valleys and peaks of the metal surface to be primed.

Primer or primer-surfacer should always be reduced according to manufacturer's recommendation (Fig. 6-3). Most lacquer-based primer-surfacers are re-

FIGURE 6-2 Primers covering the substrate.

FIGURE 6-3 Mixing and reducing the viscosity of primer-surfacer.

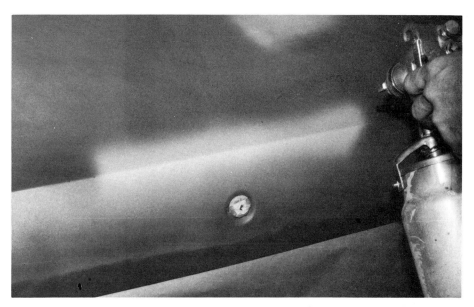

FIGURE 6-4 Spraying primer-surfacer.

duced with 1 part of primer-surfacer to 1 to 1½ parts of thinner. The thinner used should be the right type for the shop conditions present, whether slow, medium, or fast evaporating. This mixture is then sprayed on the bare metal in light coats to obtain sufficient film thickness for satisfactory sanding (Fig. 6-4). Heavy coats should not be applied, and sufficient time should be allowed to let the primer-surfacer flash off between coats. Between 40 and 45 psi (276 to 310 kPa) of air should be used at the gun. Undercoats form the important *middle layer* of the refinishing system. They must provide good adhesion to the surface and form a solid foundation for the color coats at the same time.

The key to the selection of the undercoats is *compatibility.* Consideration must be given to the surface on which they are to be applied and to the type of color coat that is to follow. Furthermore, if several undercoats are used to form the complete undercoat system, they must be compatible with one another.

Vinyl wash or epoxy primer should be recoated with a primer-surfacer for most uses after allowing it to dry for 20 to 30 minutes. If it is not coated within 4 hours, it will have to be resprayed with vinyl wash or epoxy primer all over again, a waste of material. Vinyl wash or epoxy primer should always be the first step in coating the surface; it will save having to redo some jobs due to its great adhesion and corrosion resistance.

Primer-surfacers are applied to basic types of substrates as an undercoat; these are rough surfaces, repairs of painted substrates, auto body steel, most plastic, and fiber glass. A primer-surfacer must not only prime the surface to improve adhesion of the top coat, but it also fills feathered areas and other imperfections in the substrate (Fig. 6-5). Primer-surfacer must be sanded to

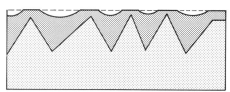

FIGURE 6-5 Primer-surfacer applied over sanded metal simulates the contours of the metal, shrinkage being more over deeper fills. (*Courtesy of Ditzler Automobile Finishes, PPG Industries, Inc.*)

provide a smooth surface with the appropriate grit according to the topcoat to be used. If the primer surfacer is sanded before all the solvents have evaporated, further evaporation will cause sand-scratch marks in the finish (Fig. 6-6).

A good lacquer primer-surfacer is easy to sand smooth, has a fast film buildup, holds out for the topcoat, and must be fast drying, usually around 30 minutes if applied properly.

If it is applied too thickly, one coat on top of the

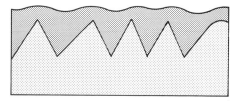

FIGURE 6-6 If sanded level before all the solvents have evaporated, further evaporation of solvents will cause shrinkage, leaving furrows over sand marks in the metal. (*Courtesy of Ditzler Automobile Finishes, PPG Industries, Inc.*)

other, the top layer will dry, trapping solvents in the material. This will cause sand-scratch swelling and also could cause solvent popping at a later date.

Refer to the paint label for the proper reduction percentage so there will be no danger of over- or underreducing. Table 6–1 shows how to convert these percentages to the proper proportions of paint and thinner.

Nitrocellulose primer-surfacers are quick drying and are used in many shops. They are economical to purchase but offer poor durability compared to factory-type primers and primer-surfacers. They are more prone to failure in areas that get very cold or cold and very humid, such as the northern United States or Canada. They can possibly crack from the cold or allow corrosion in salt-air environments or on roads on which salt is used during the winter.

Depending on the manufacturer's directions, the nitrocellulose primer-surfacers are reduced or thinned 100% to 200% (see Table 6–1) and usually sprayed at around 25 to 45 psi (175 to 310 kPa) of air pressure at the spray gun. The spray gun is held 6 to 8 in. (152 to 200 mm) away from the metal surface to be sprayed. The first coat is sprayed as a light, wet, thin coat and allowed to flash off; then a heavier coat is applied for building up the paint film. More primer-surfacer may be applied if required, but always allow enough flash-off time between coats. Generally, no more than four medium coats should be applied.

The first coat should not go beyond the feather-edged area; the additional coats applied should extend or overlap slightly beyond the last coat. This must then be allowed to dry for 20 to 40 minutes, depending on the temperature and humidity before sanding. If sanded prematurely, the top film will most likely break and expose damp primer-surfacer underneath this top surface. Also, if the coats of primer are applied too rapidly, this will cause solvents to be trapped in the finish. As these solvents dry they evaporate, and this shrinks the top of the surface (Fig. 6–6), which shows sand scratches in the finish. This primer when dry can be sanded with 320 or P400 wet and dry sandpaper or, if the painter prefers, it can be dry sanded with 360 or P500. After sanding the whole area, all featheredges should be water sanded with 400 or P800 sandpaper or compounded so as to remove all sand scratches.

Acrylic lacquer primer-surfacers were developed to be a fast-drying easy-sanding type of primer-surfacer. This surfacer offers excellent adhesion, fast-filling characteristics, high build, easy featheredging, and good color holdout. It can be used over properly cleaned and treated steel, aluminum, sanded rigid plastic (except polyethylene and polypropylene), and previously painted substrates. This material offers excellent corrosion protection when applied over a 2-mil thickness after sanding.

The reduction and air pressure at which it is sprayed will vary according to the manufacturer of the material that is to be applied. It should be applied in two or more coats and sufficient time should be allowed to flash off before recoating. It should be allowed to dry a minimum of 15 to 20 minutes before sanding the surface. This type of a primer-surfacer should not be mixed with other primer-surfacers and should not be applied in a thin film and used as a sealer. Always follow the manufacturer's directions as to application and use.

With the coming of the basecoat/clearcoat systems, a multitude of new materials have and are still appearing on the marketplace. The latest primer-surfacer is the two-component *urethane primer-surfacer*. This primer-surfacer can be used two different ways; one way is as a normal build as a primer-surfacer (2 to 3 mils = 5 μm to 7.5 μm), and the other is as a high fill primer (8 to 10 mils = 20 μm to 25 μm) when using a gravity feed gun. These new primers are all slightly different in their reduction ratios, depending on the manufacturer's method of application. Drying times vary greatly depending also on the method of use and application. These primers offer excellent adhesion to prepared substrates, except some plastics; no shrinkage; good moisture, corrosion, and stone chip resistance; and good hiding qualities.

When preparing these primer-surfacers for application, they must be well stirred; then the appropriate reducer is used at the proper ratio, and then the catalyst is added as required while stirring. Since this is catalyzed material, it has a certain pot life that will vary with the temperature, the reduction method used, and the manufacturer's material. When applied with a syphon-type spray gun, the air pressure varies from 30 to 50 psi (205 to 345 kPa) at the gun. With a gravity fed gun, the reduction ratio is different and also the air pressure, which can be from 20 to 35 psi (140 to 240 kPa).

TABLE 6–1

Paint reduction chart

Reduction percentage	Proportions of thinner to paint
25%	1 Part thinner to 4 parts paint
33%	1 Part thinner to 3 parts paint
50%	1 Part thinner to 2 parts paint
75%	3 Parts thinner to 4 parts paint
100%	1 Part thinner to 1 part paint
125%	5 Parts thinner to 4 parts paint
150%	3 Parts thinner to 2 parts paint
200%	2 Parts thinner to 1 part paint
250%	5 Parts thinner to 2 parts paint
300%	3 Parts thinner to 1 part paint

Source: Sherwin-Williams Canada Ltd.

The drying time when this primer-surfacer is used as a normal build is approximately 5 minutes for dust-free time and 3 hours at normal temperatures with a 2- to 3-mil or 5 to 7.6 μm thickness. High build will require approximately five full wet coats with a 15-minute flash-off time between coats to build up a film thickness of 8 to 10 mils or 20 to 25 μm. These materials may be force dried to shorten the drying period before sanding. The sanding time, if not force dried, will be from approximately 3 hours to an overnight dry for best sanding and topcoat appearance. For high build, which is 8 to 10 mils or 20 to 25 μm, usually 16 to 24 hours of dry time is required before wet or dry sanding and top coating. For basecoat/clearcoat systems, to get the topcoat best results, it should be wet sanded with 280 or P360 or finer sandpaper and finish sanded with 400 or P800; if dry sanded, start the sanding with 320 or P400 sandpaper.

When priming is being done over lacquer substrates, only complete panels should be done; spot priming lacquer finishes should not be attempted as lifting will occur when topcoated with a product that uses or contains strong solvents. Do not let overspray go into the door jambs; if they are to be painted with a topcoat containing strong solvents, the door jambs should be masked off or washed off as required. It would also be wise to check which materials the type of urethane primer being used is compatible with.

Some of these materials have a limited time for topcoating after being sanded (wet sanded, 4 hours; dry sanded, 24 hours). As these materials are new on our market, it is very wise to read the manufacturer's label of directions before using so as to be able to obtain the desired results from the product. The spray gun should be cleaned immediately after use with a good-quality thinner.

Alkyd enamel primer-surfacers can be used on rough substrates with bare spots. This primer-surfacer is usually reduced to 2 parts of primer to 1 part of reducer, which is added to it while stirring. When repairing an enamel surface, the bare metal featheredged areas are filled by spot spraying by using a smaller pattern and 25 to 35 psi (170 to 240 kPa) of air pressure for application.

Then for the larger panels or area a large spray pattern with an air pressure of 40 to 45 psi (255 to 310 kPa) is used for the application. The entire area to be painted should be sprayed with at least two wet coats, allowing each coat to flash before recoating. This material should be allowed 2 to 3 hours dry time before applying putty or sanding. An overnight dry should be allowed for wet sanding or where the topcoat is going to be lacquer. The sanding should be done with 320 or P400 by hand, block, or orbital sander. If the topcoat is to be lacquer, it must be sealed with a universal lac-

quer sealer first. This product should never be sandwiched between two lacquer-type finishes.

Alkyd nonsanding primer-sealers can be used for two purposes; the first is as a primer where the material is reduced approximately 8 parts primer-sealer to 1 part of the appropriate reducer. This type of primer-sealer is applied where the surface is smooth and the topcoat is to be alkyd or acrylic enamel. It is applied in one uniform medium coat and allowed to dry for at least 30 minutes under good drying conditions. If it dries longer, it will increase sealing effectiveness over old finishes. If necessary, the primer-sealer can be scuff sanded lightly to remove dirt nibs before applying topcoat. It is sprayed at 45 psi (310 kPa) of air pressure at the gun.

When used as a sealer, it is reduced 40% to 50% with an appropriate reducer. This is sprayed at 45 psi (310 kPa) of air pressure at the gun. A medium wet coat is applied, but it is not necessary to achieve full hiding; this wet coat must be allowed to dry 30 minutes and then tack wiped before applying the enamel or acrylic enamel topcoat.

An *epoxy primer* used as a primer-surfacer is usually applied to rough substrate enamel or lacquer topcoats. This primer is activated or catalyzed according to manufacturer's directions and then reduced as required with the appropriate solvent and stirred thoroughly. There is a time wait of between 1 to 2 hours before using and it has a specified pot life. It is sprayed in one or two full wet coats to give a dry film thickness of 1.5 to 1.8 mils or 3.8 to 4.6 μm. It is applied with an air pressure of 45 to 55 psi (310 to 380 kPa) at the gun, depending on the manufacturer's directions. It is usually allowed to dry for 6 hours before topcoating, but if maximum corrosion and chemical resistance are desired a second coat may be applied; an overnight dry before topcoating is then required. The equipment should be cleaned promptly after using.

Acrylic or universal lacquer sealers are used to seal paint film such as acrylic lacquer or baked or aged air-dried enamel. This sealer may be used for spot repairing or overall refinishing. It may also be applied over factory primers or replacement parts and then followed by the topcoat as required. The material is stirred and strained while being poured into the gun cup. The sealer is usually applied at a pressure of 35 to 45 psi (240 to 310 kPa), and a medium wet coat is applied. When doing spot repairs, the same air pressure is used, but the sealer is applied by blending the repair area just beyond the featheredge. The area where the topcoat is to be blended should not be sealed as it will only make the blending operation harder to do. It is allowed to dry for 15 to 45 minutes, which depends on the sealer applied and the temperature in the spray booth. When the sealer dries too quickly, a retarder can be added to it to slow the drying. It is then tack wiped when dry to remove overspray and dirt nibs as required. The sealer is then top-coated with the appropriate, recommended topcoat.

A *urethane sealer* is catalyzed with the appropriate hardener as it is a two-component material. It is then reduced as recommended and strained as it is poured into the gun. To apply, the air pressure is adjusted to 40 to 45 psi (275 to 310 kPa) for a syphon feed gun or 30 to 35 psi (205 to 240 kPa) for a gravity fed gun. The sealer can be sprayed in one full wet coat or one medium double coat of activated and reduced sealer. It should be sprayed to a complete hiding, 1.5 to 2 mils or 3.8 to 5.1 μm thick, for maximum film performance when dry. If additional flow-out is required or desired, the sealer may be reduced up to 25% by volume using the appropriate reducer. This reducer may be added to previously partially reduced material as long as the total does not exceed 25%; then the sealer is sprayed to achieve hiding. Make certain that the spray gun is immediately cleaned with a good-quality lacquer thinner.

Since this product has been catalyzed, it has a certain pot life as well as a recommended drying time. When used on lacquer substrates, the complete panel or overall sealing should be done. Always read the directions on the label of the container before using the product.

Lacquer-type putties are used to fill slight imperfections in the metal-finished surface. They are usually applied in thin coats with a glazing knife or squeegee (Fig. 6-7). Putty is applied over primer-surfacer; if applied in thin coats, it will dry in a few minutes. If it is applied in a thick coat, the surface will dry, but solvents will be trapped underneath. This will cause shrinking as the solvents evaporate. If too thick, the putty could also split and open up the surface. Some putties require coating with primer before painting, but others need not be primed. Putties are sanded with anywhere from 80D (P80) production paper to 320 (P400) wet or dry sandpaper, depending on the product, the shop, and the method used.

Another type of glazing is the *polyester resin glazing putty*, which is applied on areas free of dirt, rust, wax, and water. This product is activated by a catalyst to harden it and dry it out. It should only be mixed in quantities that can be used before the catalyst reacts. A squeegee or glazing knife may be used to apply the putty in a thin layer onto the surface to be repaired. Maximum fill should not exceed 1/8 in. (3 mm). The repaired area is usually sandable in 30 minutes; very thin applications over paint or primer will most likely take longer to harden and dry. The first sanding should be done with 180 or P180, and the putty is finish sanded to the desired smoothness. To prevent possible discoloration or staining of the topcoat on basecoat/clearcoat systems, the use of a catalyzed primer-surfacer or sealer is recommended. This product should also be used with care as the vapors are harmful and they can irritate the skin and eyes. In case of skin or other contact, flush with lots of water.

6-2 COLOR AND TYPES OF PAINT

Color may be explained as an effect that is formed on the part of the eye called the retina; the effect is created by light of certain wavelengths. The shape of an object or part of an object can be recognized due to the contrast between the color or colors of the object and the background. In normal daylight the light from the sun

FIGURE 6-7 Applying glazing putty.

is composed of a spectrum of colors; they are red, orange, yellow, green, blue, indigo, and violet. These different colors can be seen when light rays go through a medium, such as from air to water or from air to glass, and is bent, such as in a rainbow or a prism.

Many materials such as pigments have the ability to absorb part of the white light and reflect the balance. If the pigments in a paint selectively absorb blue and green rays, the paint color will be red. When an object appears blue to a person, all the light rays of the spectrum are absorbed except the blue, which it reflects. When all the colors of the spectrum are being reflected, the color is white, and when they are all absorbed, the color is black.

The compositions of automotive coatings are similar in some respects, whether they are acrylic lacquer, acrylic enamel, or conventional enamel. They are all composed of a pigment or pigments dispersed in a vehicle composed of a resin or resins and solvents.

The acrylic lacquer vehicle or binder contains more ingredients than an enamel. Synthetic enamel consists of an alkyd resin and pigment or pigments and solvents. Acrylic enamels consist of an alkyd resin fortified with an acrylic resin and solvents. An acrylic lacquer consists of an acrylic resin, cellulose resin, a plasticizer, and solvents.

How do these ingredients differ and what are the differences? The resins in both synthetic enamel and acrylic enamel are chemically related. Alkyd resin in a synthetic is a combination of a drying oil, such as linseed oil, a polyhydric alcohol, such as glycerine, and a dibasic acid such as phthalic anhydride. This resin is soft and sticky even when there are no solvents present. It will react with the oxygen in the air to become a hard, tough material.

Acrylic enamel resin is an alkyd resin similar to that used in synthetic enamel, but it is further modified with an acrylic resin. In contrast to an unmodified alkyd resin, this resin is not soft and sticky when no solvents are present. However, it further reacts with oxygen to become harder and tougher. Both synthetic resin and acrylic enamel resin are no longer soluble in solvents after a few days exposure to the air.

The resin used in acrylic lacquer is a hard nonsticky material that tends to be slightly brittle. This deficiency is overcome by the use of a plasticizer, a liquid that is a solvent for these resins and softens them slightly and makes them tough and flexible. An acrylic resin is chemically any polymer whose basic monomers are chemical derivatives of acrylic acid. An acrylic acid resin can range from soft resins soluble in mineral spirits to very hard resins, such as Plexiglass, that are insoluble (or essentially so) in any type of solvent. Those useful in lacquers are readily soluble and about midway in

hardness. A cellulosic resin is any resin derived from cellulose (pure cotton). These vary from hard and brittle to hard and tough.

You may wonder why industry does not use one or the other of these resins and have a simple formula. Industry could, but it would sacrifice some desired properties. The proportions of components are selected to give best exterior durability with desired adhesion, flexibility, and polishing characteristics under varying circumstances.

The other component of the vehicle is the solvent. The types in use are classified chemically as follows:

1. Aliphatic hydrocarbons: mineral spirits, naphtha
2. Aromatic hydrocarbons: tuolene-xylene
3. Esters: ethyl acetate, butyl acetate
4. Ketones: acetone, methyl ethyl ketone

Selection of the proper solvent is a matter of knowing which resins are soluble in which solvent and then blending fast-evaporating, medium-evaporating, and slow-evaporating types to give the desired drying rate. This is not a simple operation and requires a great deal of skill and knowledge.

The pigmentation of automotive paints requires a great deal of knowledge and experience. About 90 different pigments are used in manufacturing plants to obtain factory package colors. These pigments can range from inexpensive earth colors such as oxide yellow to chemically complicated vat drystuffs, which are very expensive.

Acrylic and alkyd enamels contain certain solvents that evaporate rapidly after spraying. This evaporation gives the initial *set* to enamels. Then, as oxygen is "breathed" into the paint film, it creates a reaction with the dryers that starts the cure cycle for the film. Although the film is apparently dry within a few hours, the total cure process requires several weeks (Fig. 6-8).

The knowledge gained from experience enables the manufacturer to blend these various ingredients to come up with very high quality enamels and lacquers that enable the body shop to produce high-quality repairs.

The paint used in shops generally consists of thinners or reducers, the binder, and the pigment. The thinners and reducers evaporate quickly, depending on the way they are formulated. The binder is the part that carries the pigment and that forms the protective film. The pigment is the part that gives the paint the color, as well as its hiding qualities.

Nitrocellulose or acrylic lacquers dry by the evaporation of the thinner (Fig. 6-9). Each is fairly soluble even when dry and when recoated with the same prod-

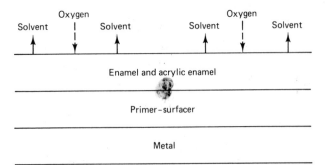

FIGURE 6-8 How enamel dries. *(Courtesy of Sherwin-Williams Automotive Finishes, Inc./ Finitions Automobile Sherwin-Williams, Inc.)*

uct. They usually form a good bond between recoats without having to be sanded too much. Lacquer dries from the top down to the bottom surface, sets up fast, and becomes hard in a short time. These factors are important for the shop that is usually cool and that has a problem with dust.

Lacquers have a hard finish and good gloss; but if they are applied too thickly, they are liable to crack, especially when subjected to a considerable change of temperature. Acrylic lacquers have better gloss retention and provide a harder and tougher finish than nitrocellulose lacquer. Consequently, they are better suited for the glamour colors used today.

Synthetic or acrylic enamels dry first from the evaporation of the reducer; then the binder is oxidized and polymerized by the oxygen in the air and the heat from the sun. Enamels dry from the inside out and to a full gloss; they do not need to be polished. They are usually soft because they require a long time to dry; once dry, however, the film becomes very hard and practically insoluble to ordinary solvents. In recent years manufacturers have introduced chemicals that when added to the paint speed up the hardening to eliminate lifting when recoating. These catalysts also improve the gloss, appearance, adhesion, flexibility, and flow of the paint film. The sanding of the old surface must be well done to provide a suitable base for the adherence of the new paint film. The paint area must also be clean, for enamel does not dry very fast.

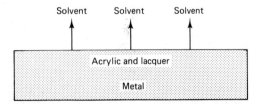

FIGURE 6-9 Acrylic and nitrocellulose lacquers require solvent evaporation only to attain film hardness. *(Courtesy of B.A.S.F. Inmont Canada, Inc.)*

The pigments used in the binder make the paint more durable by screening out the sun's ultraviolet rays; they also provide the color and hiding power of the paint film. Metallic particles have been added to paint for many years, but now manufacturers are adding mica, pearl, and, in custom paints, micro sequins.

The paint is also provided with an ultraviolet screener to protect the paint from the sun's ultraviolet rays. This helps the paint to last longer with less chalking, fading, and loss of gloss. Metallic colors have an additive that helps to prevent mottling to a great degree. These additives make it easier to get trouble-free paint jobs because they prevent the flakes from mottling as the paint is applied.

Automotive paints are generally divided into two types, solid colors and metallic colors. Solid colors are manufactured with a great amount of opaque pigments. Opaque pigments block the light rays from the sun and reflect the light; this gives us the color we see. Opaque pigments keep the ultraviolet light out of the paint film and do not let the light pass through them and are thus more durable. It is a known fact that a light color is much cooler than a dark color when exposed to the sun.

Metallic colors and also what is known as the basecoat/clearcoat type of finish use a high amount of metallic particles, mica, or pearl mixed in a clear resin with special pigments. These colors are more transparent than the solid colors, and some are much more transparent than others and have less hiding strength. Metallics allow the light to penetrate the paint film and reflect off the metallic flakes, mica, pearl, and pigment to give us the final color and shade. These colors have more sales appeal to the buying public, and when viewed from different angles or under different types of light the color will change (Fig. 6-10). These colors are harder to match when being spot repaired or when only one or two panels are being repainted.

As seen in Chapter 1, the types of paints used by the different manufacturers vary to a certain degree. The thermoplastic type of paint is used mainly by General Motors; most manufacturers apply a clear coat on top of the color coat. This clear coating protects the paint film from pollutants such as acid rain and ultraviolet

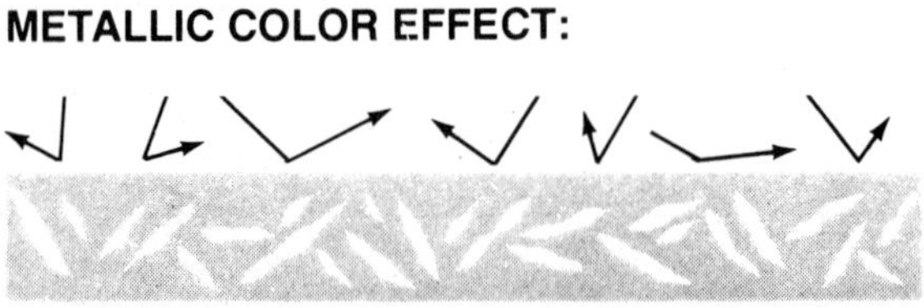

METALLIC COLOR EFFECT:

FIGURE 6-10 In metallic finishes, the light enters the finish and is reflected by metal flakes to produce metallic color effect. *(Courtesy of Du Pont Co.)*

rays from the sun. The clearcoat applied makes the color look deeper and richer and provides greater sales appeal.

6-3 SHOP REPAIR MATERIALS

With all the materials available, a good painter must be very versatile to use all of them successfully.

Topcoats

When the vehicle is to be refinished, the first thing to note is the kind of paint on it. It could be acrylic lacquer, acrylic enamel, enamel, or polyurethane enamel. A general rule is to use the same product as that already on the vehicle unless the vehicle is stripped to the bare metal.

Different manufacturers use different types of paints, such as alkyd enamel, acrylic enamel, urethane enamel, waterborne acrylic enamel, or acrylic lacquer. All these paints are types that can be baked at high temperatures. They also use what is called a basecoat/clearcoat system, which is formulated from many different types of paints and is used mainly for metallic colors. The basecoat/clearcoat system makes the paint richer looking, retains its gloss longer, and has a deep look that is very attractive to customers. The clearcoat also protects the paint film from the contaminants in the air such as acid rain or other chemicals being emitted from different sources.

Acrylic lacquer need not necessarily be sanded when it is recoated with acrylic lacquer. As a rule, the surface is not free from imperfections; therefore, it should be sanded to give the surface good bond and appearance. If acrylic lacquer is to be used over baked enamel, the surface should be sealed with a sealer.

Acrylic enamel or synthetic enamel has to be sanded and prepared properly before repainting in order to provide the necessary adhesion to resist peeling and chipping of the film. Without this preparation, a new coat of enamel would not be very satisfactory. Enamel can be spot painted if the proper techniques and products are used in certain cases.

A customer's desires will probably dictate what type of topcoat will be used. The customer should be informed as to the results that can be expected with the different materials. In this way, satisfaction is usually assured.

One of the most important jobs in the painting process is the mixing and matching of colors. To find the color required to repaint a vehicle, the plate on the body must be checked for the original finish (see Chapter 1). If the customer wants a different color, it is mixed according to his or her wishes. Once the painter has this information, he or she either orders the paint from a supplier or mixes it. The code book that is supplied with a paint-mixing system is consulted to find the amount and type of colors that have to be mixed together to produce the desired color.

Mixing the Colors

When using a power mixer, the paint should be mixed for at least a minute. Some pigments are heavier than others, and they have to be mixed enough so that they

FIGURE 6-11 Mixing and reducing paint.

are mixed thoroughly in the binder. Pigments give the color and opacity and they vary in weight. Some pigments are many times heavier than the vehicle, a factor that makes them settle faster than some of the others. The heavier the viscosity of a paint, the slower the pigment will settle. When a color has been reduced to spraying consistency, the heavier pigments will settle to the bottom. This fact will change the shade of the color unless it is used immediately after mixing.

Factory-mixed paint is used by some refinish shops because the colors are usually a good match to the paint that is on the car. These colors are very carefully formulated at the factory. If the paint has been in stock for a long time, the pigments have probably settled to the bottom and become hard. The binder should be poured out and then the pigment should be broken up and remixed into the binder.

The viscosity of the paint shipped by manufacturers is usually heavy and it has to be reduced to spraying viscosity. When reducer or thinner is added, it should always be poured in slowly, stirring the paint at the same time (Fig. 6–11).

Manufacturer's recommendations should always be followed as to the amount of reducer or thinner to be used in their products. Using the wrong amounts could ruin the paint job.

Spraying Viscosity (Viscosity Cup)

Altogether too many painters fail to concern themselves with the spraying viscosity of paint materials. The average painter pays little or no attention to the paint manufacturer's recommendations of the amount of thinning or the type of thinners specified. The painter uses a number of so-called systems of reduction, such as adding reducers until the paint runs off the stirring stick at a certain rate that has been pre-established in the painter's mind. Unfortunately, the viscosity varies considerably from job to job and is sometimes reflected in poor gloss, poor hiding, excessive fade, and poor metallic color shades.

What is viscosity, and how can it be checked? Viscosity is frequently stated in terms of the length of time it takes for a known quantity of paint to flow through a certain size of orifice.

Temperatures strongly influence viscosity, and therefore paint should be stored at room temperature. If this is not possible, remember that paint must be brought to room temperature before reducing. A cold paint will be thick. When thinner is added to bring it down to spraying viscosity, we usually obtain a paint that has poor hiding qualities or paint may run off the job, especially on a vertical surface.

Several easy-to-use viscometers are manufactured,

and one of them should be part of the refinisher's equipment. Perhaps one of the most popular is the No. 4 Ford Cup. This cup holds 100 cc and has a cone-shaped bottom with a ⁵⁄₃₂-in. (4-mm) orifice (Fig. 6–12).

Method of Using Viscosity Cup

1. Check the temperature of the material; it should be approximately 70°F (21.1°C).
2. Read the paint manufacturer's directions for proper reduction. Add the reducer, stirring until the thinner and material are well mixed.
3. Place a finger over the orifice in the bottom of the cup and fill with material at hand. A stop watch is used to time the number of seconds it takes the cup to empty or the flow of material to break.

Different materials have different spraying viscosities. For example, acrylic lacquer will spray best and give good hiding and flow-out at 18 to 22 seconds. Alkyd enamel will show its best qualities at 20 to 23 seconds, acrylic enamel at 18 to 21 seconds, and polyurethane enamel at 18 to 22 seconds.

Unfortunately, a number of paint shops never use a viscosity cup, but the importance of measuring the amount of thinners according to the paint manufactur-

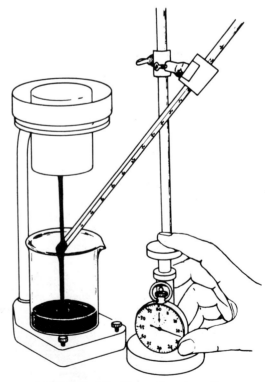

FIGURE 6–12   Using the viscosity cup.

er's directions cannot be stressed too strongly. Consistent control will give each job uniform hiding, gloss, better flowout, and good gloss retention. It is interesting to know that car manufacturers and paint companies control viscosity to within a variation of 1 second from the desired viscosity.

Overreduction and underreduction of paint result in a good many cases of excessive orange peel, sags or runs, mismatches with metallic shades, and poor hiding.

When mixing colors to match, add only a small amount of color at a time. This is very important when mixing metallic colors. Sometimes, when adding extra color to metallics, it is necessary to add some extra-clear vehicle to the paint in order to keep the high gloss.

Stirring

For years paint manufacturers have stressed this one point: *stir thoroughly before using.* Yet many in the refinishing field fail to do so, and 95% of complaints of color fading and the like are a result of this failure.

Do not use sharp sticks or screwdrivers for stirring. Use at least a 1 in. (25 mm) wide, flat, clean stirring stick or steel spatula, and mix from the bottom up, making sure that all pigments are in suspension and completely mixed.

Another method sometimes employed is to box the material, that is, pour it from one container to another until all pigments are mixed.

Spraying Metallics to Match

Almost everyone will agree that by employing different gun techniques they can create infinite numbers of shades from the same can of paint. Dry spray will cause the color to lighten, whereas wet spraying will cause it to darken. Consequently, if the operator can predetermine the correct gun technique for a certain finish on an automobile, he or she can in all probability cut down rework time considerably. The painter does so by testing the color on a panel, creating two or three variations and then allowing the panel a short drying period. The painter can then match this panel against any flat surface of the original finish. There is a possibility that not one of the variations will match, but one will be closer than the others. And by using the same technique, although changing enough to allow for the difference on the panel, the painter should come very close. This process is suggested where there is considerable trouble in matching due to excessive fade.

This method will prove itself on cars that (1) have been exposed to the elements for some time, (2) have been stored inside most of the time, and (3) have been parked outside all the time. Although the color is the

FIGURE 6-13 A wet spray allows sufficient time for the metallic particles to settle in the paint film, which will produce a strong pigment color effect.

same, there will be a distinct difference in shades that will necessitate a different technique.

Metallics are very sensitive to reduction, film thickness, and changes in air pressure. To achieve good matches, a painter must be on guard against all these hazards and eliminate as much guesswork as possible, especially in film thickness, uniformity of metallic particles, viscosity, gun technique, and atomizing air pressure.

The material in the can is usually a good match to the manufacturer's standards, but it may still be a poor match if it is not properly prepared and applied. There are two very basic causes of mismatch. The first is the painter's failure to stir the paint thoroughly before and after reducing the viscosity. Any flakes or pigment left in the bottom of the can or the spray cup will affect the sprayed-out color.

The second cause is the painter's failure to apply the same degree of wetness as was applied to the original finish. If the original color was sprayed wet and the repair is sprayed drier, it will lighten the color. The reason for this is that when a wet coat is sprayed the metallic flakes have time to position themselves deeper in the paint film before it flashes. This method produces a darker and stronger shade of color (Fig. 6–13).

When the paint is sprayed dry, the metallic flakes remain trapped closer to the surface of the drying film. This produces a lighter shade and a more metallic-looking finish (Fig. 6–14). Most new vehicles are sprayed with a wet spray, and some manufacturers use a clearcoat on top of the regular paint to produce what is called the "wet look." The color shines more and is of a darker shade.

FIGURE 6-14 Using a dry spray method traps metallic particles at various angles near the surface of the paint film; this will cause a high metallic effect.

FIGURE 6–15a Alkyd enamel system.

FIGURE 6–15b Acrylic enamel system.

Different methods are used to achieve the desired result. Gun adjustments, spray techniques, and using proper reducer or thinner are all different ways of controlling the wetness of the spray material. If a couple of coats have been applied over the repaired area and the color is too light and metallic looking, the color is darkened by spraying a few wet coats. This can be done by using different spraying techniques or adjustments, for example, decreasing the spray gun pattern or distance, opening the fluid adjusting valve slightly more or reducing the spray pattern height, using less flash-off time between coats, or slowing down the speed of the stroke.

If the repair area is too dark, a few lighter, drier coats are applied so that the color will become lighter and will look more metallic. This can be achieved by reversing the techniques used to darken the color: in-

creasing the spray gun pattern or distance, closing the fluid adjusting valve or increasing the width of the spray pattern, using more flash-off time between coats, or increasing the speed of the stroke.

If these techniques do not solve the dryness or wetness problem, then a different evaporation rate of thinner or reducer should be used. The amount of air pressure used will also cause different shades of color. The higher the pressure air used, the lighter the color will be; the lower the air pressure, the darker the color will be.

When making a metallic repair, it is difficult to foresee how accurate the match will be. Before spraying the color on the vehicle it is wise to spray some color on a piece of sheet metal and let it dry a bit and then compare the color with the color on the car body.

FIGURE 6-15c Urethane enamel system.

FIGURE 6-15d Acrylic lacquer system.

Paint Types

Many different types of paints are available on the market and they are used as required by the paint shops. Table 6-2 shows the general names given to these different paints by the manufacturers.

Alkyd enamel is still used extensively as a topcoat material for many different types of vehicles. It is durable and has good gloss. It is used to repaint panels as well as for complete overall paint jobs. It gives an economical two-coat paint system that hides small surface imperfections better than newer enamels. The addition of a urethane hardener has made it more versatile by shortening the dry time and recoat time. This material is reduced between 25% and 30% and is usually sprayed at between 45 and 55 psi (310 and 380 kPa) of air pressure at the gun, depending on the manufacturer's directions on the container label.

Acrylic lacquer, which was introduced in 1956, quickly replaced nitrocellulose lacquer because acrylic lacquer dried to a higher gloss and retained its gloss much longer. It is used for spot repairing and overall paint work; but when acrylic lacquer is used on cured or baked enamel, a sealer should be used on the old surface before applying it. This material is thinned by a ratio of 100% to 150% of thinner for the right temperature. It is very adaptable to spot repairing and is sprayed at 20 to 35 psi (135 to 240 kPa) of air pressure at the gun when doing spot repairs. For panels, acrylic lacquer is sprayed at 40 to 45 psi (275 to 310 kPa) of pressure at the spray gun.

Acrylic enamel was developed in the 1960s; it is a

TABLE 6-2

Paint names by manufacturer

	Sherwin-Williams	Du Pont	Ditzler	Rinshed-Mason	Martin-Senour	Sikkens
Alkyd enamel	Kem transport	Dulux	Ditzco	(Per-Max) (Super-Max)	Synthol enamel	Auto Flex RX
Acrylic lacquer	Acrylic lacquer	Lucite	Duracryl	Alphacryl	Acrylic lacquer	Auto Fine
Acrylic enamel	Acrylyd	Centari	Delstar	Miracryl 2	Acrylic enamel	
Polyurethane enamel	Sunfire	Imron	Deltron	Bonacryl	Nitram	Autocryl

more durable finish than alkyd enamel and dries faster. Acrylic enamel dries to a full gloss and therefore does not require the compounding step that is involved when using acrylic lacquer. Acrylic enamel is recommended for panel and complete overall repainting and may be used to spot repair original finishes. This material is reduced with the appropriate reducer for the ambient temperature; the reduction will vary from manufacturer to manufacturer. Acrylic enamel may be reduced from 50% to 75% and sprayed at a pressure of 40 to 65 psi (275 to 410 kPa) at the gun as recommended by the manufacturer. A urethane additive is usually added to the enamel; this additive gives higher gloss, a faster through cure, excellent durability, and resistance to water spotting, cold cracking, or softening by heat. It is highly recommended to read the instructions on the container label.

Polyurethane enamel, which was introduced in the early 1970s, is one of the toughest finishes available on the market today. It has a high gloss, has excellent resistance to chemicals, and is much more durable than air-dried enamels. It has been primarily used to paint trucks, marine fleets, heavy equipment, farm equipment, and aircraft. Some car manufacturers are now using polyurethane enamel in their plants, and some paint companies offer the different colors required to refinish these vehicles. An activator is required to activate this type of paint and must be mixed thoroughly. To speed up the drying time, an accelerator may be used to cut down dry time and cure time. (Typical paint mixing systems are shown in Fig. 6-15.)

CAUTION: When using any type of paint to which a catalyst is added, an appropriate respirator as approved by NIOSH should be used. Failure to do so could damage your lungs and have other effects on your body; read the label very carefully and use the required protection.

REVIEW QUESTIONS

6-1. Describe how metal conditioners are applied.

6-2. What type of primer should be used as a first coat for maximum adherence?

6-3. What is the pot life of vinyl wash primer?

6-4. At what air pressure are primers usually sprayed?

6-5. What different types of primer are most commonly used in paint shops?

6-6. What is meant by 150% reduction percentage?

6-7. How is nitrocellulose primer-surfacer applied to the surface?

6-8. Describe how urethane primer is prepared for application.

6-9. For high build when applying urethane primer, what type of spray gun should be used?

6-10. What thickness in mils can urethane primer be sprayed at for high build and how long must it dry before sanding?

6-11. Can urethane primer be used to spot prime acrylic lacquer and if not why?

6-12. How long must alkyd enamel primer be allowed to dry before sanding when topcoating with enamel?

6-13. What is the purpose of applying a sealer?

6-14. Explain how a urethane sealer is prepared for application.

6-15. How should lacquer glazing putty be applied and why?

6-16. What is meant by the term color?

6-17. How does an enamel type of resin dry?

6-18. How does a lacquer type of resin dry?

6-19. What is added to paint to protect it from the sun's ultraviolet rays?

6-20. What is the main difference between solid color paint and metallic paint?

6-21. What is the purpose of applying a clearcoat on a paint film?

6-22. What is meant by viscosity?

6-23. What is the reduction of acrylic lacquer?

CHAPTER SEVEN

Painting the Vehicle

SAFETY HINTS

A well-ventilated, safe, and clean spray booth will keep the skilled personnel healthy; they are the most precious assets.

Well-lighted and neat working areas encourage and improve the performance of employees.

When spray painting, always wear a respirator of the appropriate type for the materials used, especially when using isocyanates.

High-flash paint solvents should always be used when possible.

All floors should be kept clean; any paint, oil, or other materials should be cleaned up immediately, and any holes in the floor should be repaired.

Used cloth or paper towels should be stored in a covered container and then removed from the shop at day's end and stored in a proper garbage bin or tank.

7-1 METHODS, TOOLS, AND MATERIALS REQUIRED

Before a vehicle is to be painted, several factors must be taken into consideration before starting to spray the paint. Before the vehicle is put in the spray booth, it should be checked to see if any dust or dirt has accumulated under the engine hood, around the door jambs, and in the gutter around the truck lid opening. The vehicle is inspected very carefully to assure that when it was masked the paper was folded neatly and taped down as necessary. Also, check carefully that the glass was cleaned properly to remove dust and dirt before masking. Every item that was masked must be checked carefully to see that the tape does not overlap the old paint finish.

The surface of the vehicle should also be checked carefully to find if there are any deficiencies in the preparation work, such as the featheredging, sanding, glazing, priming, and sanding of the primer for a smooth finish. Deficiencies in any of these areas must be repaired immediately because paint cannot fix bad preparation work. It is wise to use a water-dampened towel or rag and to dust the door jambs, trunk lid opening gutter, and fender and hood edges; sometimes it is necessary to scuff them as required on the edges.

The spray booth must then be checked and cleaned if necessary. Cross-draft spray booths are often washed, including the walls, to remove dust and dirt particles. Down-draft spray booths are usually swept out and washed down slightly, taking care not to pour water in the pit where the air is exhausted. The seals on the doors should be checked periodically, as well as both the ex-

haust and intake filters; this need not be done for each job, but periodically. The joints of the panels that make up the booth should also be checked for leakage where the caulking has broken down. On negative-pressure-type booths, streaks of dust show where there is a leak problem on the inside. On positive-pressure booths a more careful examination is required to find the leaks, as they usually show on the outside of the panel. The air transformer and hoses should be checked and hung up on hose racks provided on the side wall of the spray booth.

Many items required in the paint mixing room must meet OSHA standards. The following items should be available: tinters, scale, microfiche, tinter mixing system, driers, catalyst, fisheye eliminator, containers for soiled rags, trash container for throwaway paper towels and rags, measuring cup, viscosity cup, 3-gallon (12-liter) plastic or metal paint container to be used for reduced paint, 1-gallon (4-liter), 1-quart (1-liter), and 1-pint (500-ml) containers, paint strainer stand, paint strainers, paint stirring sticks, masking tape, and a few small paint brushes to clean the equipment.

All shops should have a good stock of quality thinners and reducers as required for the different jobs to be done and for the different evaporation rates that will be encountered. Retarders, catalyst blending solvents and clears, and fisheye additives are also required. Some measuring cups or containers should always be close at hand so as to be able to measure quantities of paint or solvents as needed.

In some areas lacquers are used predominately, but in other areas enamel is used to a greater degree. Since lacquers dry quickly, these are often used for spot repairs, where conditions are slightly dusty, or where cool temperatures prevail. Enamels require a dust-free atmosphere and a fairly constant warm temperature to be used successfully. When doing enamel jobs, the spray booth must be clean and the filtration system must remove the dirt in the air going through the spray booth. When painting enamel, a bit of dust or dirt particles will mar a glossy finish and perhaps require the job to be redone to sastify the customer.

When the painter is ready to use the paint, it must be stirred (Fig. 7–1 a and b); if the stirring is to be done by hand, the container must be opened (Fig. 7–2) with a proper can opener. To help prevent spillage, a pouring spout can be made by using masking tape on the container opening (Fig. 7–3). Then, as required, a portion of the paint in the container is poured into another container; then a stirring stick is used to stir the paint (Fig. 7–4). The stirring stick should be moved in such a way that it not only moves the paint in a circular motion, but also in an up and down fashion. This will force the

FIGURE 7–2 Removing friction lid.

pigment at the bottom to rise up to mix with the resin at the top. When both halves have been well agitated, they are poured back and forth from each container to equalize the paint mixtures and also further mixing. When the shop has a mechanical agitator, the container is put in the screw-type vise on the agitator (Fig. 7–5) and mixed for the required time; the paint will be well stirred when finished. If the paint has been sitting around for a while, it is always wise to check for settling at the bottom. If some of the pigment has settled and

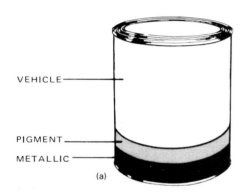

FIGURE 7–1 (a) Failure to thoroughly mix pigment and metallic flake may result in a mismatch. (*Courtesy of Du Pont Canada*)

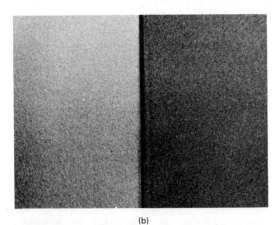

(b)

FIGURE 7–1 (b) These two panels were sprayed with the same color. The left panel was sprayed dry and the right panel wet. Note how much lighter the left one is. (*Courtesy of Du Pont Canada*)

FIGURE 7–3 Shaping a pouring spout on container using masking tape.

FIGURE 7-4 Stirring paint with flat stirring paddle by hand.

FIGURE 7-6 Measuring the amount of paint required.

FIGURE 7-5 Paint container in a powered agitator.

become slightly hard, it is broken up before putting the container on the power agitator. The paint is agitated for the required period, which can be for up to 15 minutes for metallics that were well settled at the bottom of the container. The paint container is then removed from the agitator and is ready to be used for the next operation, which is measurement of the amount of paint required (Fig. 7-6).

The required amount of paint is measured and poured into a mixing container; the thinner or reducer must also be measured according to the percentage of solvents required for the particular paint. When pouring paint from a square container, the spout of the container should always be at the highest point as in Fig. 7-7. This allows air to enter the container smoothly and allows the solvent to flow out smoothly with very little splashing.

Before reducing any type of paint materials, the painter must always check the container label. The reduction rates are not the same for all manufacturers, and changes can occur due to changes made in the resins or pigments used to formulate the particular material. The painter must know how many ounces or milliliters of unreduced paint to put into the mixing container or graduated cup (Fig. 7-8). From this, the painter must be able to figure out the amount of solvents required for the proper reduction of the paint material for spraying purposes (see Table 7-1).

Some paint manufacturer's supply paint-stirring

FIGURE 7-7 Pouring and measuring paint reducer from a gallon container.

TABLE 7-1

Reduction methods and what they mean

Reduction percentage	Proportions of thinner to paint
25	1 Part thinner to 4 parts paint
33	1 Part thinner to 3 parts paint
50	1 Part thinner to 2 parts paint
75	3 Parts thinner to 4 parts paint
100	1 Part thinner to 1 part paint
125	5 Parts thinner to 4 parts paint
150	3 Parts thinner to 2 parts paint
200	2 Parts thinner to 1 part paint
250	5 Parts thinner to 2 parts paint
300	3 Parts thinner to 1 part paint

Source: Sherwin-Williams Canada Ltd.

paddles that have the different mixing or reduction ratios marked on them. They are very handy to use and make the reduction very easy to figure out. When a painter has properly reduced the paint, it should be checked against the standard the particular manufacturer recommends that the material be sprayed at. This is where a viscosity cup is a very useful tool (Chapter 6). It is also useful to measure the viscosity of paint in containers in which the paint has been reduced to find out if the viscosity of the material can be used as is or must be reduced more (Fig. 7-9).

The reduction of paint material is always important because, when using metallic, mica, or pearl type of paints, reduction may change the color by several shades. Matching of paint cannot be done accurately by dipping a stirring stick into a container of paint and then pulling it partially out to compare the color (Fig. 7-10). Automotive paint must always be reduced and sprayed to assure a color match with the paint on the vehicle, especially when using metallic, mica, or pearl type of paint.

Lacquers require no catalyst to dry and become hard quickly as they dry and harden from solvent evaporation. Enamels, on the other hand, dry by solvent evaporation, polymerization, and oxidation. To speed up the process and to improve the durability of the resins, manufacturers provide urethane hardeners that act as a catalyst and speed the through cure of the paint film (see Table 5-10). This is mixed 16 ounces (262 milliliters) to 1 gallon (4 liters) of paint; this is a ratio of 8 to 1 and is standard among all manufacturers. Urethane materials are added to the enamels while stirring them so that the paint is properly mixed. Only enough enamel should be catalyzed at one time to do the job required, because any excess material will have to be thrown out due to its restricted pot life.

When the paint has been reduced, it should be strained through a paint strainer as it is poured into a

FIGURE 7-8 Pouring paint in a measuring cup.

FIGURE 7–9 Measuring the viscosity of paint material.

FIGURE 7–10 Checking for color match, the wrong way.

gun cup or other container to clean it of impurities (Fig. 7–11).

When the paint has been poured into the gun cup, the spray gun should be attached to it and the clamp made secure. The vent lid in the cap should be checked to see if it is open; if it is plugged, it must be opened with a sharp, round, pointed tool. The gun is then held in a horizontal position as when spraying a horizontal panel; this is done to check to see if there is a leak between the cup and the lid. If there is a leak, remove the gun from the cup and check the gasket for breaks. A new antidrip gasket may be installed if necessary and then the spray gun is attached to the cup and rechecked for leaks. Tie a small piece of rag around the cup edge if it is an old type of cup to catch any drips.

Most new guns have either special gaskets or dripproof lids, which make the spraying of horizontal surfaces fairly free of dripping paint. The spray gun is then connected to the air hose and the pressure is set for the material to be sprayed (see Table 7–2).

The spray gun should be adjusted to a full open

FIGURE 7–11 Straining reduced paint.

TABLE 7-2

Spray gun air pressure chart

REFINISH MATERIAL	AIR PRESSURE RANGE (p.s.i.)												
	20	25	30	35	40	45	50	55	60	65	70	75	80
ACRYLIC LACQUERS													
Acme Pro-Kril				▓	▓	▓							
Ditzler Duracryl				▓	▓	▓							
Dupont Lucite (Overall Refinishing and Panel Repair)				▓	▓	▓							
Dupont Lucite (Spot Repair)	▓	▓	▓	▓									
Martin Senour Acrylic Lacquer				▓	▓	▓							
R-M Alpha-Cryl				▓	▓	▓							
Rogers Acrylic Lacquer				▓	▓	▓							
Sherwin Williams Acrylic Lacquer				▓	▓	▓							
Sikkens Auto Fine							▓	▓	▓				
ACRYLIC ENAMELS													
Acme Acrylic Enamel (Non-metallic)							▓						
Acme Acrylic Enamel (Metallic)									▓				
Ditzier Delstar (Overall)								▓					
Ditzler Delstar (Spot Repair)									▓				
Dupont Centari (Overall and Panel Repair)								▓	▓	▓			
Dupont Centari (Spot Repair)			▓	▓	▓								
Limco								▓					
Martin Senour Acrylic Enamel (Non-metallic)								▓					
Martin Senour Acrylic Enamel (Metallic)									▓				
Nason Acrylic Enamel								▓					
R-M Miracryl 2 (Standard Colours)					▓	▓							
R-M Miracryl 2 (Base Coat)								▓					
Rogers Acrylic Enamel (Non-Metallic)								▓					
Rogers Acrylic Enamel (Metallic)									▓				
Sherwin Williams Acrylyd (Non-metallic)							▓						
Sherwin Williams Acrylyd (Metallic)									▓				
URETHANES													
Acme Miralon										▓	▓		
Ditzler Deltron					▓	▓	▓						
Ditzler Durethane					▓	▓	▓						
Dupont Imron (Non-metallic)								▓	▓				
Dupont Imron (Metallic)										▓	▓		
Martin Senour Nitram									▓	▓			
R-M Bonacryl							▓	▓					
Rogers Monarch									▓	▓			
Sherwin Williams Sunfire 421									▓	▓			
Sikkens Auto Cryl									▓				
SYNTHETIC ENAMELS													
Acme Fleet X (With 61 Reducer)								▓	▓				
Acme Fleet X (With 62 Reducer)								▓	▓				
Acme Fleet X (With 65 Reducer)					▓	▓							
Ditzier Ditzco								▓					
Dupont Dulux								▓					
Limco								▓					
Martin Senour Synthol (With 8004 Reducer)								▓					
Martin Senour Synthol (With 8005 Reducer)								▓					
Martin Senour Synthol (With 8008 Reducer)					▓	▓							
Nason Astron and Nasco										▓	▓	▓	▓
R-M Super-Max								▓					
Rogers Synthacote (With 4061 Reducer)								▓	▓				
Rogers Synthacote (With 4062 Reducer)								▓	▓				
Rogers Synthacote (With 4065 Reducer)					▓	▓							
Sherwin Williams Kem Transport (With 179 Reducer)								▓					
Sherwin Williams Kem Transport (With 183 Reducer)								▓					
Sherwin Williams Kem Transport (With 6220 Reducer)					▓	▓							
	138	172	207	241	276	310	345	379	414	448	483	517	552
	AIR PRESSURE RANGE (kPa)												

trigger position; the first thread of the fluid adjustment valve should be visible. Then the spreader adjustment is opened to give a maximum spray pattern (check Chapter 3), which should be tested on a spray check stand or a section of the wall masked off for this purpose. The pattern should be equal and of proper width and height, giving enough paint to provide a smooth, full, even application of paint.

The painter must control the spray gun hose so that it does not interfere with the spraying process or touch the freshly painted vehicle. The hose should always be cleaned off as required; then it is run under one armpit and over the neck, using long enough hose to extend to the spray gun held in the other hand. This will enable the painter to reach over and paint roof panels, hoods, and trunk lids without the hose touching these areas while painting. Once these areas are done, the hose is usually held with one hand and allowed to extend to the other hand holding the gun.

The painter must finish preparing the vehicle after it is in position in the spray booth. After a careful examination for defects, the vehicle, if ready, must be blown off with compressed air while rubbing the surface with a clean dry rag. The cleaning procedure is always started from the area where the air enters the spray booth and continued toward the exhaust fan. In cross-draft booths this is done from the back to the front, and in a down-draft booth from the top to the bottom of the vehicle or section to be painted. The blowgun is held in such a way that it blows compressed air at high pressure into the spaces between the roof and door gaps as well as any other gaps between other body panels and all the surfaces of the vehicle which must be cleaned out thoroughly of any loose dirt and dust (Fig. 7–12). The whole vehicle is done in this fashion, and it must be remembered that the exhaust fan must be on and all the doors closed.

Once this operation has been done, the vehicle should be washed with a final wash of nonoily solvent to finish cleansing the surface to be painted (see Table 7–3). This is done with a similar type of towel or rag and method as for degreasing and dewaxing, but the paint film should not be oversoaked. The solvent should be applied and wiped almost immediately; this will clean the paint film without making the sand scratches swell.

FIGURE 7–12 Blowing dust off the vehicle with compressed air.

When the vehicle is dry, it must be wiped with a tack rag, which is a cheese cloth impregnated with a nondrying varnish. Remove the cloth from its package, unfold, and refold in a fashion so that the outer two surfaces are on the inside. This is done because, when it is in the package, the weight of the other packages on it has a tendency to force the varnish out onto its outer surfaces. Turning it over helps to prevent the transfer of the resin to the paint film. The tack rag is unfolded, used as in Fig. 7–13 to dust the whole vehicle lightly, and turned over as required, taking care not to press too hard and leave traces of varnish on the surface. If some varnish is left on the paint film, the same cleaning solvent used for the final wash may be used to clean the surface. The vehicle is then ready for painting with a new coat of paint.

7–2 APPLYING THE PAINT FILM

Sealers are used by many shops, depending on the products used to refinish the vehicle. Most paint manufacturers recommend various methods that should be used with their undercoat preparation before the color coat

TABLE 7–3
Paint-cleaning solvents by part number

Sherwin-Williams	Du Pont	Ditzler	Rinshed-Mason	Martin-Senour
RIK 213	4105S	DX330	884	6387

FIGURE 7-13 Using tack rag to wipe the vehicle before painting.

is applied. Sealers are used to prevent sand-scratch swelling and gloss sinking in and to increase adhesion when refinishing over sanded, air dried, or baked enamel and acrylic lacquer. The sealer should be strained when poured in the paint cup. The sealer is reduced if required and then is usually sprayed in one medium wet coat, using an air pressure of 35 to 45 psi (240 to 310 kPa) at the gun. The sealer should then be given the proper amount of time to dry before it is topcoated with the appropriate color coat. When the sealer is dry enough, it should be tack wiped to remove any overspray on the surface of the vehicle.

When applying the first color coat, fisheyes may appear (see Chapter 9). This is caused by silicones that are still on the surface of the paint film even after careful cleaning. Silicones are used in grease, oil, rubber lubricants, and car polishes and are very slippery. Silicone has many uses and is used widely by many industries, but it is an impediment for a painter that must be overcome. If the vehicle has been well cleaned previously with silicone remover, the chances of trouble are rare. Silicones present on the surface prevent the new paint film from sticking to the surface causing the paint film to part in the shape of a fisheye.

When the painter encounters fisheyes on the first coat, the problem can sometimes be solved by dry spraying without using an additive. The spray gun trigger is pulled slightly back and a dry spray coat of paint is applied over the affected areas; this should be done at least twice and should make the fisheyes disappear. Allow to dry for approximately 15 minutes, and if the fisheyes are covered continue with the paint job. Applying the paint in a dry state allows it to act as a sealer. Then it is coated in the regular way.

If this does not succeed, fisheye eliminator is added to the paint in the required amount; follow manufacturers' directions. Table 7-4 shows the proper additive to use in different types of paint. The active silicone remains on the surface and would cause fisheyes, but the additive causes the paint to flow over and cover the areas that would be affected. The additive is silicone and when added to the color to be sprayed the paint is completely saturated with silicones. The fisheyes are prevented because the additive causes a uniform tension on the surface of the new paint film.

Due to the different types of spray booths, different methods or techniques are used when applying paint on a vehicle, especially a topcoat. The painter should paint in a fashion or method that will enable him or her to keep a wet edge on the paint film and not have overspray fall on the wet film.

The airflow in the booth must be considered when painting. When using a cross-draft booth, a method such as in Fig. 7-14 may be used; also refer to Chapter 3. In a down-draft spray booth in which the air is moving from the ceiling down toward a pit in the floor from which it is exhausted, the painting must proceed similarly. The roof panel, hood, and trunk lid areas are done first; then the sides and rear and front areas. The painter must always keep a wet edge to enable him or her to apply a paint film that will be glossy once it is finished (Fig. 7-15).

When painting a complete vehicle, the spraying operation is usually started by doing the roof panel first. It may be necessary to have suitable benches or scaffoldings of the proper height to enable the painter to

TABLE 7-4

Fisheye eliminator by part number

	Sherwin-Williams	Du Pont	Ditzler	Rinshed-Mason	Martin-Senour
Noncatalyzed paint, lacquer, and enamel	V3K265	FEE	DX66	803	77B
Catalyzed and urethane enamels	V3K780	259S	DX77	819	87

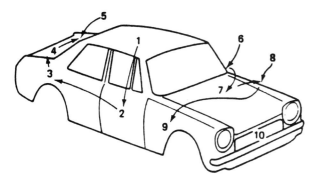

FIGURE 7-14 Spraying a complete automobile in a cross-draft spray booth

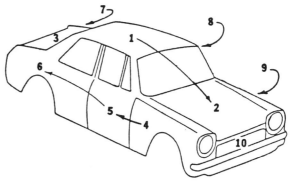

FIGURE 7-15 Spraying an automobile in a down-draft spray booth.

reach and paint the roof panel. Wearing an approved respirator and holding the spray gun in the appropriate hand, the roof panel is banded at each end. Then the first paint stroke is applied to the side edge near the painter; the next stroke is applied from right to left and left to right with a 50% overlap (Fig. 7-16). Then, as the distance increases due to the width to be covered, the overlap will have to increase to 60% or 70% as the gun angle changes from perpendicular to a slight angle. Each pass brings the painted surface closer to the center and the painter must observe if the paint is being applied with the right wetness required.

Once the first side is done, the painter moves to the other side and bands the ends; then she or he starts painting from the center to the outside edge. The roof windshield pillars are also painted at the same time. This method enables the painter to keep a wet edge at all times. A freshly painted surface should always be viewed at an angle so that the light reflection will show the degree of wetness of the paint film. The hood is usually done using the same system, but sometimes, depending on the size of the trunk lid, a different method may be used. For long trunk lids, the back window lower panel

is banded and then the trunk lid is painted using the same system as the roof panel. Smaller trunk lids or hatchbacks are usually painted from the back, moving the gun from side to side until completed.

The spray gun is refilled as required and always checked after filling so that it is not leaking or dripping. When painting lacquer, the gun distance is usually from 6 to 8 in. (150 to 200 mm) from the spray gun fluid tip to the surface being painted. A constant speed, overlap, and distance must be kept at all times to assure that the proper degree of wetness is applied at all times. The spray gun must be kept perpendicular or at right angles at all times to the surface being painted.

The sides of the car should be done with the least amount of sideway overlap possible; this means that the painter should stretch as far as is comfortable when painting the side of a vehicle. By doing this, the chances of runs at paint side overlap will diminish. Also, the spray gun should be arced slightly to feather out the overlap in the paint surface (Fig. 7-17).

Most painters start at the wet edge from the trunk lid or top fender edge and paint downward as this helps

FIGURE 7-16 Spray painting the roof panel.

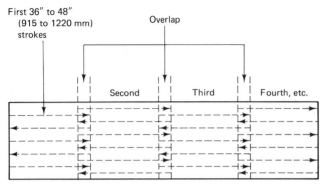

FIGURE 7-17 Method of spraying the side of a vehicle.

eliminate overspray around the painter's face. The paint is applied from left to right and back, and a single wet coat is applied (50% overlap) to the area that is reachable until it is fully coated. The painter moves to the next area and repeats the same operation until the whole side is done, watching for side overlaps so as not to spray them too dry or too wet. The painter must look at the amount of paint being applied to judge the speed of travel required, and when finished the painter should inspect it at an angle, using light reflection to show if there are any dry spots present, which should be touched up immediately.

To paint the wheel opening flange, the painter should be positioned so that in one motion he or she can spray the flange. This is done by positioning the spray gun at a slight angle to reach the flange around the bend of the wheel opening. With the gun placed either on the right or left side of the wheel, the opening trigger is pulled to half-trigger and the spray gun is moved following the half-circle the wheel opening makes.

To paint the rocker panels, usually the gun is tilted slightly to the side and the gun is triggered to a half- or full-trigger position, depending on the skill of the painter. The application of the paint should be medium wet to avoid flooding the area, and the painter must pay attention to how much paint is being applied. The rest of the vehicle is finished using this method. The painting of valances is done in much the same way as the rocker panels.

The methods of applying different types of paints with a spray gun are fairly similar, but they all have their differences. The methods of preparation are very similar; sandpaper grits are somewhat slightly different (Table 4-4). The reductions are different from one product to another, as are the solvents used and the air pressure required to atomize them (Table 7-2).

When a vehicle is painted at the factory, it has 1.0 or 1.5 mils (or 2.5 μm to 3.7 μm) of primer and 1.5 to 2.5 mils (or 3.7 μm to 6.3 μm) of topcoat applied on it.

Out in the refinish field, many painters apply excessively thick topcoats, which can result in cracking, poor dry, water spotting, wrinkling, low gloss, and many other defects that could spoil a good paint job. If the vehicle has to be repaired, it will increase the cost of the repair due to having to remove the paint film by sanding or stripping. The air dry time of enamels is extended greatly with varying film thicknesses (Table 7-5).

The regular baking schedule of 20 to 30 minutes at 180°F (83°C) is usually no longer effective for water spot resistance and proper hardness due to the thick paint film. Solvents that have been trapped in the paint film will cause it to soften again when placed in a warm environment such as direct sunlight.

Once a certain film thickness has been exceeded, the danger of paint failure increases. If the topcoat exceeds more than 5 mils or 12 μm due to repainting, it would be wise to sand the vehicle well to remove some of the excess thickness, or it should be stripped so that when the vehicle is repainted the total paint film will not exceed 5 mils or 12 μm in thickness.

The various types of paints are designed to approximately build the film to a certain degree. This build will depend on the type of spray equipment, painter application speed, temperature in the spray booth, viscosity of the material, and atomization air pressure used (see Table 7-6).

Automotive Enamels

Automotive topcoat must always be strained before using. Straining can be done when the paint is poured into the paint cup. It should then be reduced with the proper reducer, made to match the conditions of the shop (Fig. 7-18). If the temperature is under 70°F (21°C), a fast evaporating reducer should be used. If the temperature is between 70° and 85°F (21° and 29.4°C), use a medium-evaporating reducer. When the temperature is above 85°F (29.4°C), a slow-evaporating reducer is used (see Table 7-7).

When the slow-drying reducer is not available, an antiwrinkling additive can be used in hot and humid weather. This additive is also used when the car is to be

TABLE 7-5
Recommended paint film thickness

Film thickeners (mils)	Print-free time at 70°F or 24°C
1.5–2.5	6–8 hours
2.5–3.0	16 hours
3.0–5.0	24–48 hours
5.0–10.0	1 week
10.0 mils	1 week plus

Source: BASF Inmont, Inc.

TABLE 7-6

Paint film thickness guide

		Metric units
Acrylic lacquer	½-¾ mil per double coat	1.3 μm to 1.9μm
Alkyd enamel	¾-1½ mils per double coat	1.9 μm to 3.8 μm
Urethane enamel	1¼-2 mils per double coat	3.7 μm to 5.1 μm
Acrylic enamel	¾-1¼ mils per double coat	1.9 μm to 3.77 μm
Specific film recommendations for topcoat finishes depending on color and metal size		
Acrylic lacquer	2-3 mils max.	5.1 μm to 7.6 μm
Alkyd enamel	3-4 mils max.	7.6 μm to 10.1 μm
Urethane enamel	3-4 mils max.	7.6 μm to 10.1 μm
Acrylic enamel	3-4 mils max.	7.6 μm to 10.1 μm

Source: BASF Inmont, Inc.

Note: Acrylic lacquer may check if these film thicknesses are exceeded.

These measurements include all paint material from the substrate to the top of the paint film.

baked after painting. Follow manufacturer's recommendations for the amount to add.

Reduce the alkyd enamel to the proper spraying viscosity and apply a medium wet first coat; follow this in 10 to 20 minutes by a full wet coat. This coat is sprayed at a pressure at the gun of 50 to 60 psi (345 to 419 kPa) (Fig. 7-19). If the color is metallic, it has to be mist coated with a mixture reduced by 1 part of enamel to 1 part of reducer. This mixture is sprayed on to obtain the desired uniform metallic finish. Or, after spraying two to three panels with the regular second-coat material, the panels painted previously can be blended in by spraying a light coat on them if they are still wet enough to absorb the paint. This gives the painter good color control if done properly. If the whole vehicle is mist coated with a high solvent ratio to paint, the painter must be careful not to overdo the mist coat as this has a tendency to wash the resin off the pigment

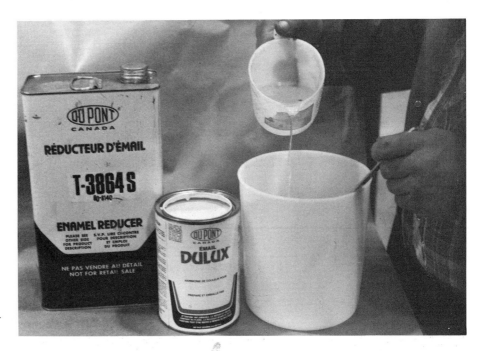

FIGURE 7-18 Mixing and stirring enamel.

TABLE 7–7

Recommended temperature ranges for use of enamel reducers

	4.4	7.2	10.0	12.8	15.6	18.3	21.1	23.9	26.7	29.4	32.2	35.0	37.8		82.2	°C
SHOP TEMPERATURE	40	45	50	55	60	65	70	75	80	85	90	95	100	TO	180°F.
FAST-FLO REDUCER			/////	/////	/////	/////	- - -	- - -	- - -	- - -	- - -	- - -	- - -	- - -	- - -
MEDIUM DRY							/////	/////	/////	- - -	- - -	- - -	- - -	- - -	- - -
SLOW DRY								/////	/////						
LOW BAKE										/////	/////	/////	/////	/////	/////
SHOP TEMPERATURE:	40	45	50	55	60	65	70	75	80	85	90	95	100	TO	180°F.
	4.4	7.2	10.0	12.8	15.6	18.3	21.1	23.9	26.7	29.4	32.2	35.0	37.8		82.2	°C

Source: CIL of Canada Ltd.

and metallic flakes, which will expose them to the elements and cause the paint job to fail prematurely.

Alkyd enamel dries dust free in 20 to 40 minutes and tack free to handle in 6 to 8 hours; overnight drying will give a fairly hard surface. If a super hardener or catalyst is used, the enamel dries much quicker and can be fairly hard in 2 to 3 hours; this helps to speed up production as the paint is tack free in about 1 hour after painting is finished. If the paint is force dried, it is usually tack free to handle in 30 minutes to 1 hour, depending on the size of the baking oven.

Table 7–7 can be followed to find the proper reducer for the temperature.

NOTE: When the temperature is above 85°F (29.4°C) and the relative humidity is high, add 1 1/2 to 2 1/2 ounces (33 to 71 grams) of antiwrinkling additive to each 1 quart (1 liter) of enamel. Then the enamel is reduced in the normal ratio with the proper reducer for air-dry or force-dry application. Remember that thinners should never be used in enamel. Thinners are likely to make the film brittle and give a poor gloss. Enamel may be polished with a paste wax after 90 days.

Metallic Colors

A major problem confronting the automobile refinisher today is metallic colors. It is well-known that the gun technique, mixing, reduction, and distance the gun is held from the surface all play a major role when spraying these glamour shades. Metallic color has a great deal of acceptance and eye appeal with the buying public,

FIGURE 7–19 Spraying enamel.

and as long as the demand for these shades exists, car manufacturers will continue to use them.

It is not our intention to say that these colors are delicate and troublesome. If a refinisher is familiar with the difficulties and, in some cases, follows a few simple recommendations, she or he can overcome a good many of the problems.

Alkyd Enamel. Metallic color must be sprayed exactly opposite to straight color. That is, the first coat applied is medium wet, or what could be termed a *flow coat*, with the gun held 8 to 10 in. (200 to 250 mm) from the surface, followed by one or two medium coats with the gun held 12 to 14 in. (305 to 356 mm) from the surface. The reason for the greater gun distance is to eliminate dappling streaks and shadows.

Certain metallic colors are very transparent and often give the painter problems. Transparent colors have poor hiding qualities. If a color change is being done using one of these transparent colors, the body of the car must be all the same color. This can be achieved by priming the body completely and taking care not to cut through during sanding operations so that there will be the same color throughout. Another method is to use a nonsanding pigmented sealer and coat the body completely. Or the body of the car can be based with a solid color to hide the old paint film.

Care must be taken to tack off the car body to keep it clean. Primer-sealers must be recoated within a certain amount of time to achieve maximum adherence of the paint film. When the same color is being used and primer spots are present, a first coat is applied, but not so heavy as to cause runs or sags. Then the primer spots showing through are sprayed with a fairly dry spray. One spot is done per application. The spots are done one after another by applying successive coats and moving from one spot to another between coats in order to allow the reducer to flash off. This procedure is followed until the spots are well hidden. Then the second coat is applied at the regular distance or three panels are done one after the other. Usually the paint has set up enough so that these panels can be blended in to eliminate all traces of irregular metallic variations. The gun is usually held from 12 to 14 in. (305 to 356 mm) from the surface. The paint job is done in this fashion until it is completed. The repairperson should then check for uniformity of the metallic flakes in the paint film throughout.

Sometimes the last panel painted looks different from the other panels. To overcome this, it is sometimes necessary to open the front door to a half-open position and repaint the door with one coat. This stops the overspray from going onto the adjacent panel, which is too dry to absorb the last coat of spray. This procedure usu-

ally gives a very satisfactory job and a uniform metallic pattern.

Acrylic Enamel

Acrylic enamel is more widely used today than ever before in the refinish field. Over the past few years it, and some of the products used with it, have been greatly improved. Figure 7-20 shows some of the products used to repaint a vehicle.

The preliminary steps for preparing the car are the same as those for enamel, but some manufacturers require that a finer paper be used. After the car body has been cleaned and is ready to receive the acrylic paint, care should be taken to follow the methods and recommendations on the can label. Some manufacturers insist that a sealer be used over all substrates, that is, over all paint films except enamel. On a good enamel surface it is not absolutely necessary, but to ensure a good bond between the paint films it is strongly recommended that a sealer be used at all times.

First, the paint is stirred thoroughly and then the proper catalyst is poured into the paint following the manufacturer's recommendations as to the amount required per quart (liter) of enamel. The paint is then reduced according to the manufacturer's recommendations using the proper reducer for the temperature. Products from other companies must not be intermixed because one product may react with another product.

The reduced material is then poured through a strainer in the gun cup to ensure that there will be no dirt in the paint. The right amount of air pressure (Table 7-3) must be used. This varies from one manufacturer to another. Some acrylic enamels are applied by using a two-coat system and others are applied using a three-coat system. The one shown in Fig. 7-20 requires a three-coat system. The first coat, which is a medium wet

FIGURE 7-20 Acrylic enamel materials.

coat over the primed or sealed surface, is allowed to dry for 20 minutes. This coat is followed by two medium wet coats. For metallics, a final mist coat can be applied if necessary to eliminate streaking and mottling or to lighten the color. This final mist coat is made of the same material as used previously. No additional reducer is required. It should be applied immediately after the last coat to prevent a hazy, pinched effect and also loss of gloss.

Once the catalyst has been added to the acrylic enamel, the mixture should be used as soon as possible (within 3 hours under normal shop conditions). The pot life can be increased by reducing the paint immediately after the catalyst has been poured in and stirred. Pot life decreases as the temperature and humidity increase and it also varies depending on the color. If the viscosity should begin to increase, additional reducer can be added as required.

Most acrylic enamels can be baked once the catalyst has been added without adding any further additives. They are usually baked at a temperature of 180°F (or 83°C) maximum for not more than 20 minutes. The solvents should be allowed to evaporate for 15 minutes before baking is started. A 20-minute bake at 180°F (83°C) is approximately equivalent to 24 to 48 hours of air dry time.

Most acrylic enamels will dry dust free in 30 minutes under normal conditions and tack free in 2 hours. Under most conditions, the painted vehicle may be moved within 2 hours and put outside in 4 hours if the weather permits. If the weather is not good, the unit should be left inside overnight.

When two-toning is required, the vehicle can usually be taped within 5 to 7 hours. Most acrylic enamels may be recoated after 5 to 7 hours under normal drying conditions. The masking tape should be removed immediately after the final color has been applied to prevent tape marking. All possible masking paper contact with fresh material should be avoided.

The spray gun and equipment should be cleaned immediately, preferably with a lacquer thinner. All catalyzed paint should be disposed of in the proper manner because it will harden and be of no use.

Acrylic enamel and alkyd enamel do not easily lend themselves to spot repairing except on a recent paint job. If the acrylic enamel has dried overnight, it can be spot repaired with acrylic lacquer or acrylic enamel. If there are any dry areas in the paint job, they can usually be compounded after 24 hours; a check should be made first on a small area by using a fine-grit polishing compound. If there are any fisheyes, the proper fisheye eliminator should be used. When painting with a paint that has a catalyst, hardener, or accelerator added to it, proper respirating equipment should be used and the painting should be done in a well-ventilated booth.

Polyurethane Enamel

Alkyd enamels have been used on fleet equipment for many years, but today polyurethane enamel is being used by many fleets. Polyurethane enamel gives a faster drying time to speed ease of repair, gives better initial gloss, resists fading, resists chemicals, gasoline, and solvents, has a harder surface, washes better, and since it tends to shed dirt easier, fewer washings are needed.

The metal is prepared by following the proper methods. Usually, a vinyl wash primer is applied to a thickness that is still transparent. Complete hiding is not necessary. This primer is allowed to dry 20 to 30 minutes at room temperature before recoating with the special epoxy primer. If the vinyl wash primer is allowed to dry more than 1 hour, it will be necessary to recoat again with vinyl wash primer.

Epoxy primer requires an activator, which is mixed in the required proportions and left to stand for the required time before using. This mixture is thinned with the proper thinner and in the recommended proportions. The pot life of epoxy primer is usually up to 3 days at room temperature. It must not be stored at below 50°F (10°C).

The primer is applied in one or two full wet coats to achieve a desirable dry thickness. It should be allowed to dry 2 to 4 hours. For best topcoat appearance, it is sanded. If it is allowed to dry more than 24 hours, it must be sanded prior to topcoating.

Figure 7–21 shows the materials used for this type of paint job. Imron takes an activator which is mixed as follows: one part activator to three parts pigmented Imron. If desired, a dry time activator may be added to the mixture at the rate of 5 ounces per gallon (140 milliliters to 4 liters approximately) to provide a faster hard dry and tape time.

This activator is recommended at all times but especially when using Imron metallics 500S clear or black. Usually, no more reduction is required, but, if necessary, the material may be reduced with the proper reducer at the rate of 4.7 ounces (139.7 milliliters) per activated gallon (4 liters). This will increase flow-out, leveling, and gloss (especially on large areas). The average pot life is approximately 8 hours at normal room temperature.

The solid colors are applied by using 50 psi (323 kPa) at the gun. A medium wet coat is sprayed first and is allowed to tack up. This is followed by a full second coat. On metallic colors, 65 psi or (420 kPa) is used at the gun and a light-medium coat is applied as a tack coat. This is allowed to set 20 minutes and then a second light-medium coat is applied. The material is then reduced 15% with the proper reducer and a light-medium coat is applied. If desired, another light-medium coat of the reduced material may be applied.

FIGURE 7-21 Polyurethane enamel materials.

Imron metallic colors should be clearcoated with the proper Imron clear material after an overnight dry (12 to 18 hours), but the metallic topcoat should not be sanded before the clear material is applied.

All these materials are very toxic. Therefore, a painter should always wear the proper respirating equipment and painting should always be done in a well-ventilated spray booth.

The dry time for two-toning at 68°F (20°C) with accelerator is approximately 2 to 4 hours and without accelerator it is approximately 6 to 10 hours. This paint can be force dried without additives to a temperature up to 250°F (121°C). If there are any fisheyes, only fisheye eliminator made for this product should be used.

The instructions for the Imron materials apply to a certain degree to other manufacturers' materials since reduction and application are similar; for air pressure, see Table 7-2. For more information, read the manufacturer's label on the container; this will contain the application, reduction, and air pressure required.

As soon as the paint job is finished, the spray equipment should be cleaned immediately with lacquer thinner. All unused paint that has accelerator in it should be disposed of properly because it will harden and be of no use.

Acrylic Lacquer

Acrylic lacquers provide a superior finish because they combine the advantages of lacquer and the qualities inherent in acrylic resins. Acrylic lacquer dries by evaporation and requires compounding and buffing in order to bring out the gloss.

The most outstanding characteristics of acrylic lacquer are its superior gloss retention and its exceptionally good resistance to color fade under exposure. The main reason acrylic lacquers are used is because they can tolerate larger amounts of aluminum in their formulation, thus offering a wide color selection.

The basic steps for preparing are the same as those for other paints, but a finer grit of paper is used and a sealer sometimes has to be used. A fresh can of acrylic lacquer must be stirred thoroughly and then it must be reduced with the recommended thinner and in specified amounts. Most manufacturers recommend a reduction rate of 100% to 150% for this type of material. The reduction of this product can greatly affect the final color; the less thinner used the darker the color will be, and the more thinner used the lighter the color will be (see Table 7-8). At all times the previous color on the vehicle must be matched as closely as possible when doing panel repairs.

Temperature and humidity not only affect the evaporation rate but also the choice of thinner. On hot, humid days or in baking, a retarder is added to the mixture to prevent blushing of the lacquer film and to increase gloss (Fig. 7-22).

The lacquer is strained in the gun cup and then it is sprayed with a spray gun that doesn't have too many holes in the air cap. A pressure of 45 psi (310 kPa) (Table 7-2) is used at the gun. Usually, one or two coats are sprayed first and the solvents are given time to evaporate before more lacquer is sprayed on. This method allows the first and second coats to seal the surface, which helps prevent sand-scratch swelling. At no time should the spraying be done without allowing sufficient time for the solvents to evaporate. Succeeding coats can then be applied by allowing each coat to flash off before applying the next coat. Only as many coats as required to achieve proper hiding and the proper level of gloss should be applied, for too much thickness causes the paint film to crack or craze.

For metallic colors, a final mist coat consisting of one part lacquer to nine parts thinner is applied and spray techniques are adjusted to achieve the desired metallic effect. The lacquer will be tack free in approximately 15 minutes at 70° to 80°F (21.0° to 26.7°C) and it will hard dry in 1 1/2 hours. If force dried at 180°F

TABLE 7–8

Metallic color control guide

	For lighter color	For darker color
Spray equipment and adjustments		
Fluid tip	Use smaller size	Use larger size
Air cap	Use air cap with greater number of openings	Use air cap with lesser number of openings
Fluid adjustment valve	Reduce volume of material flow	Increase volume of material flow
Spreader adjustment valve	Increase fan width	Decrease fan width
Air pressure (at gun)	Increase air pressure	Decrease air pressure
Thinner usage		
Type of thinner	Use faster-evaporating thinner	Use slower-evaporating thinner
Reduction of color	Increase volume of thinner	Decrease volume of thinner
Use of retarder	(Do not use retarder)	Add proportional amount of retarder to thinner
Spraying techniques		
Gun distance	Increase distance	Decrease distance
Gun speed	Increase speed	Decrease speed
Flash time between coats	Allow more flash time	Allow less flash time

Source: BASF Inmont, Inc.

(82.2°C), the lacquer will hard dry in 30 minutes to 1 hour.

When a clear coat is being applied, the clear material is thinned according to the manufacturer's recommendations and two coats are usually sprayed on. Care should be taken to overlap properly because overlapping will give the desired gloss and deep look to the paint job.

7–3 ACRYLIC ENAMEL AND LACQUER BASECOAT/CLEARCOAT

Acrylic Enamel

Recently, manufacturers have introduced what is called basecoat/clearcoat paint on their vehicles. The base-coat/clearcoat system contains mica, or aluminum flakes, or pearl, commonly known as a pearl coat. Some paint manufacturers have acrylic basecoat/clearcoat materials in both acrylic enamel and lacquer. We will discuss the application of the acrylic enamel basecoat/clearcoat system (Fig. 7–23). The basecoat should not be sprayed to more than a 2-mil film thickness. The air pressure will be 50 to 60 psi (345 to 410 kPa) at the spray gun.

The preparation of the vehicle or part is the same or nearly the same as for the application of an acrylic enamel topcoat. To find out if the vehicle has a basecoat/clearcoat system, all that is necessary is to sand a small area. If the vehicle had a clearcoat sprayed on it when wet sanding, a whitish residue will be noticed in the water film; when dry sanding, a whitish powder will appear where the sanding is being done.

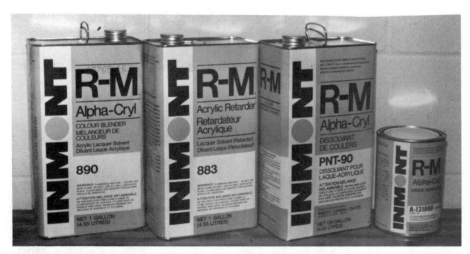

FIGURE 7–22 Materials required for acrylic lacquer paint job.

FIGURE 7-23 Acrylic enamel basecoat/clearcoat materials.

The surface must be sanded thoroughly, metal etched, primed, sealed, and cleaned as required. The type of paint that will be used will affect slightly some of the methods. For example, the reduction ratios vary greatly from one manufacturer to another, so the information on the container label should be read carefully.

The paint is applied in two or three light color coats, enough to achieve hiding and uniformity of the color. A 20-minute flash-off time should be allowed between coats; the basecoat will not be glossy. After a 2-hour drying time, it is coated with an acrylic urethane clear with catalyst added according to the manufacturer's recommendations. To increase flow-out, a retarder may be added to it. The pot life is about 6 hours. Maximum safe film thickness should not exceed 1.5 to 2 mils or 3.7 μm to 5 μm.

Sanding of the basecoat should be avoided; but if required because of dirt, the basecoat is resprayed where the area was sanded. Light controlled coats using a blending technique work best. Should imperfections show up in the basecoat after the first coat of clear is applied, the clear can be sanded if it is dry, which usually takes about 3 hours. Using heat, the affected area can be sanded 1 hour after coating. If there are dirt problems in the second coat of clear, the times are doubled.

Color sanding and buffing can be performed the next day. Use color-sanding ultrafine 1200 grit sandpaper to sand if required. To buff, a clean pad is necessary; buff at approximately 1800 rpm using a medium- to heavy-duty liquid compound followed by a polish.

Du Pont System

Figure 7-24a and b shows the method that should be used when doing a repair on an OEM finish using Du Pont Centari Base Coat. This product is mixed in an 8:1:16 ratio. Figure 7-24b shows a mixing chart. This shows that 1 quart (1 liter) of basecoat is activated by 1 cap of 782S Centari Activator; to this mix, 2 quarts or liters of basemaker 826OS and in case of fisheyes 1 ounce (30 milliliters) of 259S can be added to 1 gallon

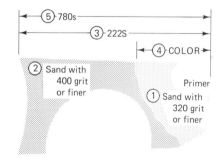

Proper use of 222S Mid-Coat Adhesion Promoter with the Centari basecoat/clearcoat system.

1. After priming, sand area where base coat will be applied with 320 grit or finer.
2. Sand the rest of the panel, which will be clearcoated only, with 400 grit or finer.
3. Apply 1 medium coat of 222S Mid-Coat Adhesion Promoter over entire panel.
4. Apply Centari base coat according to label directions.
5. Apply 780S Centari clear according to label directions.

(A)

FIGURE 7-24a Painting of a repair on a fender, steps 1 to 5. (*Courtesy of Du Pont Co.*)

Centari base coat
Mixing Guide

| 8 parts base coat color to |
| 1 part 782S to |
| 16 parts basemaker |

or 1 quart to
4 oz. (1 cap) to
2 quarts or,
2 quarts to
8 oz. (2 caps) to
1 gallon (4 quarts)

(B)

FIGURE 7-24b Mixing chart. (*Courtesy of Du Pont Co.*)

or 4 liters of mixed Centari. The basecoat is applied using 30 to 40 psi (205 to 275 kPa) of air pressure at the gun, applying a full wet coat of basecoat over the repaired area. This is allowed to flash 5 to 10 minutes and a second full coat is applied. It may be necessary to spray a very fast cross coat to even out the metallic effect. If it is required, the cross coat should be done immediately after the second full coat; it may be necessary to increase the air pressure slightly to even out the color effect.

When doing panel repairs that do not have a cutoff section or molding, the blend area should be scuff sanded with 320 or P400 grit or finer sandpaper. The first full wet coat of basecoat is applied slightly beyond the tapered edge and allowed to flash 5 minutes. Then the second full wet coat is applied beyond the first coat tapering into the adjacent area. This should be immediately followed with a fast cross coat to fix the metallic effect, which again must be tapered into the adjoining area. Heavy coats must be prevented on tapered edges to avoid possible excessive texture and poor appearance beneath the clearcoat. The basecoat is allowed to dry for 15 to 30 minutes before applying the clear.

Then the clearcoat is mixed as follows: to 1 quart or liter of 780S clear, one capful of 782S activator is added while mixing; if fisheyes are present use 259S as directed. Then, using an air pressure of 40 psi (275 kPa) at the gun, a medium wet coat of the clear is sprayed over the repaired area. This is allowed to flash for 15 minutes and then a second medium wet coat of clear is applied. On panel repairs where there is no cutoff line or section, the clear is applied with proper flash-off time, but each coat of the clear is tapered farther beyond the

basecoat area. Then 1700S Centari Blender is put in an empty gun cup and the blend tapered area is sprayed as required using a pressure of 15 to 20 psi (100 to 135 kPa) at the gun.

For overall refinishing the proper amount of basecoat is stirred thoroughly; then, while stirring, the proper amount of 782S activator is added to it. Then the proper basemaker, 826OS when temperatures range from 50° to 70°F (10° to 21°C), is used. When temperatures exceed 70°F (21°C), 828OS basemaker is used and mixed according to directions. The 259S Fisheye Eliminator® is added in the required quantity if needed; do not use an alkyd enamel fisheye eliminator. Then using an air pressure of 50 to 55 psi (345 to 380 kPa) at the gun, it is sprayed to hiding with two full wet coats. If required, the second coat is followed by using a fast cross coat to fix the metallic effect.

The clear is activated and sprayed using the same directions for the spot and panel repair. Then all the equipment should be cleaned immediately.

To match the OEM finish, basecoat/clearcoat systems should always be used; however, some refinishers, when doing an overall refinish job, want to use a single-stage acrylic enamel that has been formulated to give the best possible match to the basecoat color. This single-stage acrylic enamel matches in color only and should only be used for overall refinishing. But to add more protection against corrosive chemicals, chipping, and acid rain, and to increase gloss, the acrylic enamel is topcoated with a urethane clear, such as 780S clear. However, make sure that the proper catalyst is used in the acrylic enamel (Fig. 7–25), which should be allowed to dry for 1 to 4 hours, depending on shop conditions,

FIGURE 7–25 Materials used when clearcoating single-stage acrylic enamel with a clear urethane coating.

before applying the clear. The surface may have to be scuff sanded with ultrafine sandpaper before applying the clear, if dirt nibs are present in the paint film; the scuff sanding may only be done after an overnight dry to ensure that the paint film is hard enough to scuff ssand.

The vehicle topcoat must be clean before applying the urethane clear, which must be activated with the catalyst following the manufacturer's recommendations. Do not mix more than 1 quart (1 liter) of material or more than can be used in an hour. If additional flowout is required when refinishing large surfaces or in temperatures of 75°F (24°C), 5 ounces of flow reducer can be added if recommended by the manufacturer.

Two medium wet coats should be applied at 50 to 55 psi (345 to 380 kPa) at the gun with a temperature of 65° to 70°F (18° to 21°C). A third, medium coat may be applied if required, allowing a 5- to 10-minute dry time between coats under normal conditions; the time may be extended under cooler conditions.

Heavy coats of acrylic enamel should be avoided as this could affect through-dry and the appearance of the paint film. The finish should be allowed to set up before removing the vehicle from the spray booth. For the best film performance, the finish should be allowed to air dry overnight indoors or to bake 20 to 30 minutes at 140° to 160°F (60° to 70°C). The masking tape should be removed as soon as the clearcoat is touch dry or after baking to avoid the film pulling away from the edges.

If the finish has to be repaired, allow 24 hours of drying time. To minimize featheredge lifting, apply the repair primer, color, and clearcoat carefully, using faster solvents and light dry coats. All necessary steps to clean and prepare the area must be followed, and proper materials must be used.

Acrylic Lacquer Basecoat/Clearcoat

With the changes in technology, factory finishes (OEM) are glamorous and much more durable than ever due to the introduction of the lacquer basecoat/clearcoat system. Paint manufacturers have introduced similar materials that can be used in body shops (Fig. 7-26).

In the acrylic lacquer system, a concentrated acrylic color with special thinners and urethane clears with activator and flow reducer have been introduced. These materials are not hard to work with as long as instructions are followed.

The preparation of the area is the same as for lacquer except that the final sanding should be done with No. 600 or P1200 grit or finer sandpaper. For the newer finishes and waterborne acrylic enamel, a midcoat adhesion promoter must be used on (OEM) factory acrylic enamel on the complete panel or in a blend area if the panel has to be blended in. The panel or the area of the panel is prepared and masked as required. Figure 7-27 shows that the panel was masked to a sharp styling edge where a strip of masking tape was used on the edge and half of it was turned up to create turbulence in the air stream. By doing it this way, only part of the hood had to be painted.

The sealer is used on older finishes but should never be used together with 222S. Then the basecoat lacquer is stirred thoroughly and thinned with the appropriate medium. Coats are applied to a visual hiding and mottle-free appearance using 40 to 45 psi (275 to 310 kPa) at the gun and allowing sufficient dry time between coats. The basecoat is only applied to the area requiring it, and each coat is tapered outward more each time it is sprayed. Usually two to three coats are required for proper color (Fig. 7-28). The masking is pulled off as

FIGURE 7-26 Materials required for repair of basecoat/clearcoat.

FIGURE 7-27 Hood prepared for partial painting with basecoat/clearcoat.

required when dry enough to check the match (Fig. 7-29).

The film buildup should be kept to a minimum and heavy wet coats of base color should be avoided, as such coats could affect the final color and film appearance. The color coats should be tack wiped between coats, and if necessary a solid ground coat should be used for transparent basecoat colors.

The final color should not be overthinned, as it could affect the color match and the metallic orientation or color effect. The final basecoat color must not be sanded prior to clearcoating. Under normal shop drying conditions, allow the basecoat to dry for about 15 minutes before clearcoating with the clear. The urethane clear is activated according to the manufacturer's directions; in this case 1 part activator is slowly added to 4 parts clear while it is being mixed. No more material should be mixed than will be needed in a 1-hour period.

Under most circumstances no further reduction will be necessary, but if additional flow is required when refinishing large surfaces or in temperatures above 75°F (24°C), up to 5 ounces of flow reducer can be added per activated quart can or liter of clear.

The spraying viscosity of the clear should be between 17 and 19 seconds in the same cup. The pot life of the mixture may vary from 2 to 4 hours depending on the shop working temperature. It should be used within 1 hour after mixing and should always be strained before application.

The clear should be applied in two medium-wet coats at 55 to 60 psi (380 to 420 kPa) of pressure at the gun and can be followed with a third medium-wet coat

FIGURE 7-28 Spraying lacquer on area to bring it up to color.

FIGURE 7–29 Pulling tape and masking paper and checking for color match.

if it is required. A 5- to 10-minute dry time between coats should be allowed under normal conditions; in a cool shop, extend the dry time.

To ensure a proper cure, the temperature of the surface to be refinished should be at least 65° to 70°F (18° to 21°C). The finish should be allowed to set up before removing the vehicle from the spray booth. The masking tape is removed as soon as the clear is touch dry or after baking to avoid the film pulling away from the edges. It should be allowed to air dry overnight indoors or be baked 20 to 30 minutes at 140° to 160°F (60° to 71°C).

Where the tape had been turned at a right angle on the styling edge of the hood, the edge of the clear was so minute that it was polished to make it disappear.

Figure 7–30 shows a step-by-step procedure to repair a basecoat/clearcoat after it has dried for 24 hours.

It must be remembered that, after the area is compounded, it must be washed with a wash solvent and then tack wiped. If the clear must be blended into the area beyond the repair area, it should be compounded and then washed with a wash solvent.

To blend the clear, add 2 parts base coat thinner to 1 part activated clear, with air pressure set at 35 to 40 psi (245 to 275 kPa) at the gun. Blend out over the prepared area using light, thin coats. Thinner alone should not be applied to the blend area. The blend area should be left to dry overnight before compounding very carefully to prevent cutting through the clear.

In the case of two-toning, apply all colors first; then double-mask the required area to prevent penetration of the solvents through to the finish. The area is

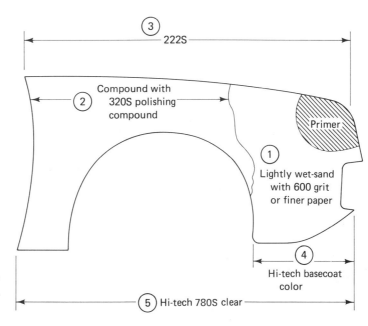

FIGURE 7–30 Basic steps for repair of basecoat/clearcoat. (*Courtesy of Du Pont Canada*)

then unmasked and the colors are tack wiped; then the clear is applied over the required areas.

A vehicle that has been refinished completely, or even one with only a fender refinished, should be cleaned thoroughly inside and out. A vacuum cleaner can be used to clean the inside of the body and the trunk. Windows and chrome should be cleaned of all overspray and dust. If necessary, the tires should also be refreshed with tire dressing. These steps will create a favorable impression with any customer, which will mean repeat business if all aspects of the job are done properly.

7-4 RUBBING AND POLISHING COMPOUNDS

The purposes of using rubbing and polishing compounds are many. To achieve good results they must be used properly. They are most often used to bring up to gloss and smoothness in blended areas in acrylic lacquer or enamels repairs. They are also used to remove sand-scratch marks from featheredge repair areas, to provide tooth for better adhesion, and also to polish and increase the gloss of acrylic lacquer. They are also used to increase the gloss of an old lacquer finish and remove slight paint imperfections from light scratches.

Rubbing compounds are similar to the paste and liquid cleaners that are used on a car before it is waxed. They come in either paste or liquid form. They contain an abrasive mixed in oils, water, and solvents; this abrasive comes in a few different grades of coarseness. Abrasives are mainly pumice and talc and are used in either form to level off the paint film and make it smooth and glossy. There are both hand rubbing or machine compounding materials of different grits of abrasives. The compounds used for hand compounding are oil based to provide lubrication, and the compounds used with machines are water based to help disperse the abrasive while the buffing wheel buffs the panel.

Usually, rubbing compounds have the coarser abrasive particles, and the polishing compounds contain fine particles of pumice. The rubbing compounds work in two ways; the pumice particles smooth and cut the surface being compounded, and this working action breaks down the pumice as it polishes into smaller particles. The lubricant the pumice is in helps to prevent scratching and eases the rubbing operation.

The main difference between the two compounds is that hand rubbing compounds use a slow-drying oil that dries slower than the water-based machine polishing compounds. For this reason the compound remains in a paste form longer; it should not be used with a machine as the compound will clog the buffing pad, which will cause it to become inefficient. The machine compound is designed to dry faster and changes to a powder. Hand compounds generally produce a better gloss than machine compounds due to the type of liquid and abrasives they contain.

Small areas, such as around a featheredge (Fig. 7-31), should be done by hand, but large areas should be done by machine. These areas must be cleaned with a cleaning solvent before any painting is done. When compounding styling edges, great care must be taken not to cut through them; a strip of masking tape applied along the edge will help to prevent this. After the compounding is finished, the masking paper strip is removed and the edge is compounded by hand just enough to produce a glossy finish. Styling edges usually retain less paint than flat surfaces and should only be compounded slightly.

A fresh acrylic lacquer film must be given the

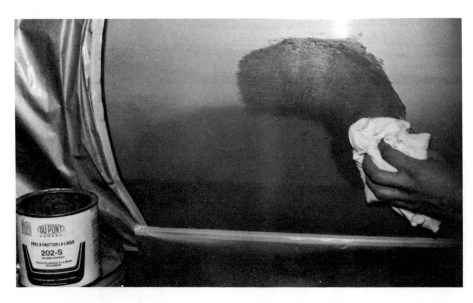

FIGURE 7-31 Using rubbing and polishing compound by hand.

TABLE 7–9

Rubbing and polishing compounds

	Sherwin-Williams	Du Pont	Rinshed-Mason	Martin-Senour	Ditzler
Machine rubbing compound	DIT122	303S	853	6361	DRX16
Hand compound:					
Light cutting	DIT273	606S	852	6358	DRX25
Medium cutting	DIT271	202S	851	6356	DRX45
Fast cutting	DIT13	101S	854	6360	DRX55

proper amount of time before being polished. If not force dried, usually an overnight dry is required for a complete paint job. Force drying at 165°F (74°C) for 15 minutes for spot and panel repair or 1 hour for overall repainting will give a satisfactory dry after cooling. For force-dried panels, usually a 4-hour drying time is sufficient. Acrylic lacquer must never be compounded too soon as this could cause dulling back or hazing of the paint film. Spot repairs and blend areas done with acrylic lacquer or catalyzed enamel may be compounded the next day if dry enough. These areas can be compounded by hand or machine as required. Table 7–9 shows the different compounds available from some manufacturers.

Each rubbing compound is characterized by a different cutting speed, method of use, and quality of gloss. If the painter chooses the wrong type, it will slow down the completion of a particular job and may also result in poor gloss. Before starting to use the compound the painter should check the paint film for orange peel, lack of gloss, dirt specks, and dry spots. Many times, if the painter had difficulty in applying the lacquer, the paint film may require sanding with 400 or P800, 500 or P1000, or 600 or P1200 grit wet and dry sandpaper. The sandpaper is sometimes used with mineral oil, water, or a slight soapy solution. This is done to remove the imperfections in the finish and to speed up the polishing operation.

Machine polishing and compounding is usually done with a lightweight air- or electric-driven tool similar to a disc grinder (Fig. 7–32), which turns at approximately 1400 to 2300 rpm. Before starting to machine compound, the painter should put on a smock or coveralls as this type of work will soon dirty clean clothes. A lightweight machine is preferred over a heavy one as it is not as tiring to use and produces excellent gloss of the paint film. For compounding, a compounding pad is used and wool pads are used for polishing. Great care must be taken when using the machine to keep it constantly on the move to prevent burn throughs or cutting through the paint film.

FIGURE 7–32 Machine compounding and polishing.

Compounding and polishing techniques are similar to sanding techniques, either by hand or machine. When compounding by hand, a soft lint-free cloth is folded into a thick pad to which a previously stirred compound is applied. The pad is applied to the surface, and the panel is rubbed and compounded using straight back and forth strokes while applying a medium to hard pressure (Fig. 7–33). An area approximately 24 × 30 in. (61 to 76 cm) is done at one time; if the compound is drying too quickly, a small amount of water may be sprayed on the area to keep it wet enough. To hand compound a panel is time consuming and uses up a lot of elbow grease. To keep compounding to a minimum, it is important to apply the paint film as wet as possible with the right thinner to obtain good after-the-gun gloss.

When machine compounding, the compound is applied to the panel using a squeeze bottle or a coarse bristle brush. Then the area is compounded using a compound buffing pad on the machine. The equipment and the type of pad will determine the method of fastening it to the power polisher. Compound only an area that is comfortable to reach at one time as the com-

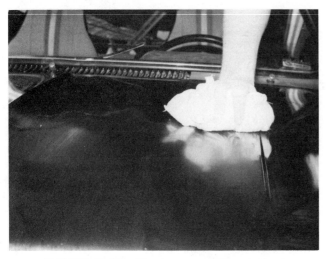

FIGURE 7-33   Hand compounding and polishing.

pound has a tendency to dry out; it should sometimes be sprayed with a small amount of water to keep it wet long enough, while observing the cutting action of the compound as the job progresses toward completion. A light, medium pressure is applied to the machine, if required, while it is turning and moving back and forth in a 50% overlapping stroke. The strokes are usually started with either a right-to-left or a left-to-right movement. The right side of the pad is lifted slightly when moving right and lifted slightly on the left when moving left. Or if going up and down or back and forth, the area of the pad closest to the operator is lifted slightly on the downstroke; the upstroke is done in the opposite manner.

The amount of compound applied to the panel should not be overdone and should never be applied to the pad directly. The compound should be applied to the panel and then the pad is applied to it, sliding it around to distribute the compound to the panel. Two left-to-right strokes and two fore-and-aft strokes should complete a compounding cycle. If an excess of compound remains after the compounding cycle, it shows that too much compound was used in the first place. If it disappears too quickly from the surface, then not enough was used. As each area is completed, a new area is started until the job is finished. The cutting action of the compound should be observed so that the entire area that was compounded has the same glossy effect. To avoid burn throughs or the cutting through of the film, always keep the machine moving.

The advantages of machine compounding are the time saving plus the nonclogging of the compounding pad. If the pad needs cleaning, a cleaning spur or dull screwdriver may be used to rub the pad while it is rotating; this action will unclog and clean the pad.

When the compounding is finished, the buffing

pad is removed and replaced by a polishing pad or lamb's wool bonnet, and the panel, area, or vehicle is polished in the same fashion but without using compound. To help remove swirl marks if they are present, corn starch can be used as a slight abrasive while polishing. Also, a polishing material such as in Fig. 7-34 may be used to fill the swirl marks and increase the gloss of the lacquer finish.

An acrylic lacquer film is polished until the final polishing gives a satisfactory gloss that is free of defects and very smooth to the touch. Compounding an acrylic enamel finish for a spot repair will slightly dull the finish.

Compounding Problems and Remedies

Cut throughs at panel or styling edges are usually caused by excessive compounding; to prevent this, tape all edges and style lines because they will have to be spot repaired to fix the damage. If excessive orange peel and overspray are present, wet sanding before compounding will save time; make sure to use the right thinner and good spray techniques on the next job. When rub throughs occur in the middle of a panel, this is usually due to insufficient film thickness. This will have to be either spot or panel repaired. If the pad clogs fast and poor

FIGURE 7-34   Another type of polishing material

results are being achieved, this is usually because a hand compound is used with a machine polisher. To correct this situation, the pad will have to be changed or cleaned as required; make sure to use proper compounds.

After polishing the vehicle, it will be necessary to wash it completely; this includes all crevices, chrome, glass, molding, and exterior plastic. All surfaces should be wiped with a chamois or good cloth; do not forget the inside of the windows, the dash and steering wheel, and the upholstery. All carpets and interior trim should be vacuumed and everything should be made clean for the customer.

REVIEW QUESTIONS

7-1. Why must paint be stirred properly and how should it be done?

7-2. Why should paint amounts be measured?

7-3. How should the color be matched before painting a panel on a vehicle?

7-4. What is the pressure at which urethane enamel is sprayed?

7-5. What technique should be used when spraying a vehicle in a down-draft spray booth?

7-6. What causes fisheyes in a paint job?

7-7. How should the side of a vehicle be sprayed?

7-8. How should a roof panel be sprayed?

7-9. What is the mil thickness of the paint on a vehicle sprayed at the factory?

7-10. Explain briefly how to apply alkyd enamel.

7-11. Explain briefly how to apply metallic colors.

7-12. For how long should catalyzed acrylic enamel be baked and at what temperature?

7-13. At what pressure is Imron applied?

7-14. Describe what can be done to match metallic acrylic without tinting.

7-15. What is meant by a basecoat/clearcoat paint system?

7-16. What is done to even out the metallic effect when spraying basecoat acrylic enamel?

7-17. What is used to promote adhesion on waterborne acrylic enamel?

7-18. How should a clearcoat be applied?

7-19. What is the purpose of rubbing and polishing compounds?

7-20. Describe the type of compound used for hand polishing.

CHAPTER EIGHT

Spot Repairing, Painting, and Matching Colors

SAFETY HINTS

All paint and solvents should be stored in approved cabinets or in storage rooms that have explosion-proof lights and adequate ventilation.

Never more than a day's supply of paint materials should be outside of an approved storage area.

All solvent drums must be grounded and bonded to containers while being used.

Always wear the appropriate respirator or dust filter masks when painting, machine sanding, or sandblasting. These respirators or dust filters protect your lungs from the harmful effects of solvents, dust, and fine silica sand dust.

8-1 SPOT REPAIR USING ACRYLIC LACQUER

Spot repairing with acrylic lacquer can be done, provided the right methods are used. It can be done on certain areas but should not be attempted on large flat panels.

Using panel edges, contour changes, or molding where possible, mask off to protect the remainder of the vehicle from overspray. Where there is no natural break, mask well beyond the area to be repaired to allow enough room for color blending and featheredging. The area should then be cleaned with a silicone polish remover by scrubbing a small area; wipe dry while the solvent is still wet. If the solvent should dry, rewet the surface and wipe dry while the solvent is still wet; change cloths frequently. The area should be wet sanded to remove all gloss; start by using No. 320 (P400) paper and give the final sanding with No. 400 (P800) or finer. Do not sand beyond the area to be covered with topcoat. If cut throughs occur during sanding, featheredge well back from bare metal areas.

If bare metal is exposed, treat with metal conditioner as usual; then prime by using lacquer-type primer or other approved primer surfacer (Fig. 8-1). A medium wet coat should be applied, using a medium spray fan and 15 to 20 psi (103 to 138 kPa) at the gun. The work should be done from the center of the repair area out toward the fringe (Fig. 8-2), building up with succeeding coats to bring the low area up level to the paint surface if necessary. Let the primer surfacer dry for the required time and then sand, using No. 400 (P800) paper. Next, apply a fine polishing compound reduced to creamy consistency with water (Fig. 8-3). A soft cloth or buffing pad moistened with water should be used to polish the area around the repair area to remove primer-surfacer overspray and prepare a blending edge.

It is also wise to prepare both the front part of the quarter-panel and the rear part of the front door with the grit polish and clean them with cleaning solvents before masking. Thus if the paint does not match properly, the paint can then be blended into these areas to spread the color difference. This method is used when the color is not an exact match and must be blended in. The polished area should then be cleaned with a silicone polish remover, using clean cloths, and the area should be tacked off with a tack cloth (Fig. 8-4).

The acrylic lacquer is then applied with the spray gun using an air pressure of 20 to 35 psi (135 to 240 kPa) at the gun. Using a medium fan, three wet coats are applied, with each coat being a little wetter than the preceding coat (Fig. 8-5). Each coat should have at least 5 minutes of flash-off time; then, after the third coat, a 10- to 15-minute flash-off time must be allowed. Then two more wet double-coats are applied, each extending well beyond the third coat. It is sometimes advantageous to tack wipe the blend area in between coats to remove the dry overspray (Fig. 8-6). This usually helps to keep the blend area cleaner.

After the final coat has flashed, two medium coats of a blending clear are applied around the blend area at a pressure at the gun of 15 to 20 psi (100 to 135 kPa) and then followed by two coats over the entire repair area (Fig. 8-7).

When doing a spot repair on aged acrylic lacquer,

FIGURE 8-1 Applying primer-surfacer with a medium fan.

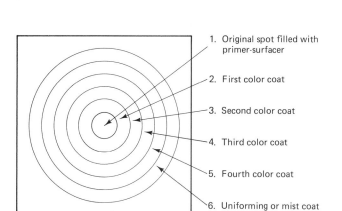

1. Original spot filled with primer-surfacer

2. First color coat

3. Second color coat

4. Third color coat

5. Fourth color coat

6. Uniforming or mist coat

FIGURE 8-2 Spot repairs blend into the old finish. (*Courtesy of Du Pont Canada*)

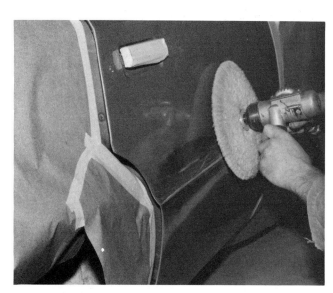

FIGURE 8-3 Applying the polishing compound.

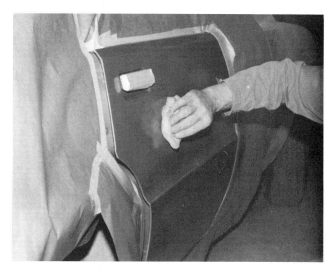

FIGURE 8-4 Cleaning surface with a tack rag.

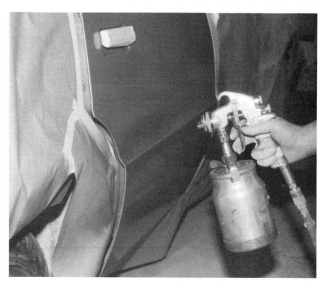

FIGURE 8-5 Applying the color.

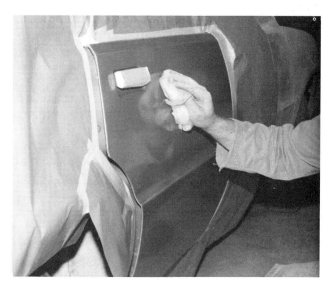

FIGURE 8-6 Tack wiping between coats.

FIGURE 8-7 Applying blending clear.

FIGURE 8-8 Color blended into quarter-panel.

a very fast drying solvent should be used to prevent sand-scratch swelling in the application of the first two or three coats. The evaporation rate or flash-off time should be 20 to 25 seconds; being this fast, the thinner makes very little penetration into the old film. This makes the lacquer coats act as a sealer. Then for the last two coats a mix with a slower drying thinner and retarder is used for achieving higher off-the-gun gloss. Paint manufacturers supply a thinner that when sprayed in the last two coats gives good off-the-gun gloss, but it should not be used in the first coats as the penetration is deep and the flash-off time is too slow.

An example of proper technique is shown in Fig. 8-8. Since the paint repair area was in the back part of the door, the masking tape was removed from the quarter-panel partially to compare the color match. There was a slight difference; therefore, the blend area was extended into the lower quarter-panel area. This eliminated the distinct color difference between the door and quarter and spread the blend of the color so that the difference in the color was eliminated.

After the panel has dried for approximately 4 hours, it must be polished with compound to bring out its gloss. This is either done by hand or by machine; but when polishing a panel with sharp style edges, there is always the danger of a cut line through the paint film. A piece of masking tape (Fig. 8-9) on the style line will avoid this, and this area can then be polished by hand after the panel is finished.

Other methods for repairing acrylic lacquer have been developed. When done properly, they provide excellent color matches. These methods are called the modified conventional method and the metallic color control method. The modified conventional method is used for partial panel repair; and the metallic control method is used for spot repair.

The preparation steps are the same as for the other methods, but featheredging solvent is used with a cloth to featheredge the broken area. The work is carried out from the center to the outer edges by sanding with No. 400 (10/0) paper. The edges are compounded to remove sand scratches and then washed with a rag that is soaked with a little water and silicone polish remover. The next steps are the same as for acrylic lacquer until the time has come for the color coat.

The modified conventional method requires that two guns be used. One gun contains the acrylic lacquer color, which is composed of the acrylic lacquer, plus the thinner and 5% of retarder. The second gun contains the same mixture of thinner but only 5% of color. The

FIGURE 8-9 Protecting styling edges in the panel.

purpose of adding 5% color is to allow uniformity of wetting the surface and to prevent beading of the thinner. An air cap with only a few holes should be used on both guns so that the material does not become over-atomized.

To help prevent sand scratches, a dry, dusty color coat from the first gun is applied on the primer edges. This dusty coat is obtained by closing the fluid valve completely and then opening it a quarter-turn. The spreader valve should be opened to give the widest fan possible in relation to the size of the repair area. A thorough wipe with a tack rag is required on this coat before proceeding. For large primed areas, it is advisable to apply a normal color coat first, followed immediately by a mist coat from the second gun. This mist coat is allowed to flash off before the next step is undertaken.

A medium wet coat from the mist coat thinner gun is applied and then followed with a color coat from the other gun. It will be noted that the wetter the color coat, the darker the color obtained. This coat is then sprayed with a medium wet mist coat; the two steps are repeated until the color being applied matches the color on the car. The final mist coat used will probably require a cross coat to obtain uniform wetness, and it should be applied to a larger area than the color coat to allow complete blending in with the factory finish. The finish is then allowed to air dry overnight or to air flash 30 minutes; it is then force dried for half an hour at 180°F (82.2°C) and allowed to cool before polishing.

The metallic color control is normally used for smaller body repairs and paint defects, such as mottling, streaks, and off color. If the existing defect reaches bare metal, the same preparation steps as for the other method should be applied.

Two guns are again necessary; the first gun contains the color and the second gun contains the mist coat. The thinner used is generally a different mixture than that used previously. The thinner or thinner blend used is a very important aspect of the metallic color control method. A thinner that will flash off in approximately 60 to 70 seconds when it is applied under the following conditions is necessary.

A specially prepared primed panel is used; one double pass of thinner is sprayed on the panel at an atomizing air pressure of 35 to 40 psi (241 to 276 kPa). A normal opening on the spreader valve is used. The fan in the booth should not be running when this check is made. The flash off is timed, and if necessary the blend is adjusted as detailed below. The acrylic lacquer thinner normally recommended should be used for this application. If the temperature and humidity conditions are such that an adjustment of flash-off time is required, up to 10% of retarder may be used to slow down flash time and up to 50% of a faster evaporating thinner may

be used to speed up flash time. This blend of thinner is used both in the color coat gun and in the mist coat gun.

Using the mist coat thinner gun, a medium wet mist coat is applied to the repair area as well as to the surrounding area. This coat is immediately followed with a dry, dusty color coat from the other gun. This dusty coat is obtained by closing the fluid valve completely and then opening it a quarter of a turn. The spreader valve should be opened to give the widest fan possible in relation to the size of the repair area. Two or three dry passes with the gun may be made, followed immediately by careful tack wiping of the surface to remove loose overspray. This step is followed again with a medium wet coat from the mist gun and then back to dry dusty color coat and a further tack off. This step is repeated until a suitable color match is obtained. The final coat is always a mist coat.

The metallic color control method offers about a 50% reduction in air-dry time compared with conventional repair methods. With lamps, the force-dry time is about 10 minutes. After the surface has cooled from force drying, compounding may be required . Use a fine polishing compound and then a polish to obtain a finish that is comparable to the original finish. Care should be taken in buffing because it is possible to rub through.

8–2 SPOT REPAIRING USING ACRYLIC ENAMEL

The vehicle in Fig. 8–10 was masked so that the door and a partial lower quarter-panel would be painted and the paint would be blended over the wheel opening. The front door and lower quarter-panel were painted with acrylic enamel and blended in the front part of the wheel opening (Fig. 8–11). The paint work was completed following the above-specified procedures, but because of

FIGURE 8–10 Masked vehicle.

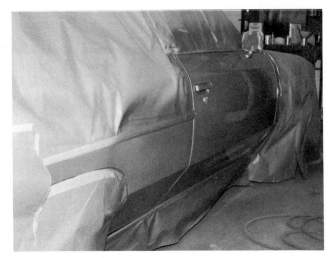

FIGURE 8-11 Blended area.

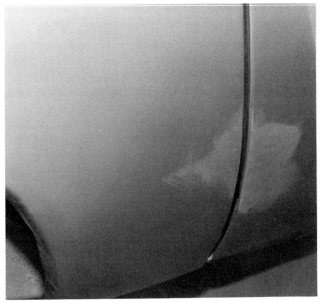

FIGURE 8-12 Prepared area for spot repairing.

a heavy application, a run developed on the rear lower part of the door and lower quarter-panel. This area was sanded after drying overnight, compounded, and cleaned lightly with a cleaning solvent and tack wiped (Fig. 8-12).

If the spot repair is done with enamel, add spot repair catalyst; the procedure is as follows. Reduce the enamel as usual; then apply it in medium wet coats, using a medium spray fan and a pressure of 25 to 40 psi (170 to 200 kPa) at the gun. Work from the center of the repair area out toward the edge. Each coat is applied in a normal manner, and each coat is extended beyond the previous coats to produce a tapered edge. Leave a small amount of paint in the gun cup and add an equal amount of blending clear. Using the same air pressure, a medium wet coat is applied out from the repair area on blend repairs; on spot repairs it is applied over the entire area to a tapered edge (Fig. 8-13). This is allowed to flash for 5 to 10 minutes and a second medium wet coat is applied, extending further into the original paint film. If more leveling is required, more blending clear is added to the mixture and this is sprayed farther out on the original paint finish. If a haze should appear on the blend area when it has dried overnight, it should be rubbed and polished with a rubbing and polishing compound. Make sure to clean all equipment when finished with lacquer thinner or enamel reducer. A liquid cleaner and polish can be used to remove any overspray left on the enamel surface after drying for 24 hours. This is done when the spot repair has dried for the required amount of time. A liquid cleaner should then be used for further polishing on the repaired area. The sanding job must be done as well for acrylic enamel as for enamel. Acrylic enamel needs a good surface to be able to provide good adhesion on the old surface. All these products can be either air dried or force dried.

FIGURE 8-13 Applying blending clear.

Acrylic Enamel Basecoat/Clearcoat Spot Repair

Figures 8-14 through 8-18 show the proper procedure for doing acrylic enamel basecoat/clearcoat spot repair. The preparation was basically the same as for other spot repairs except a polyester glaze was used to fill a slight imperfection. This was sanded off using a sanding block with 180 or P180 sandpaper (Fig. 8-14). Polyester glazing does not shrink once it is dry.

The vehicle was masked, but before masking the top part of the door was prepared for receiving a blend of color due to color variation. This area was compounded and washed with the appropriate solvent and then masked off separately. The area was then primed using a small fan (Fig. 8-15). This area was sanded, compounded, cleaned with the solvent, and tack wiped. Acrylic enamel basecoat was applied to cover the primed area and also tapered (Fig. 8-16). Once the basic coat had dried enough, the color was checked with the upper part of the door by pulling the masking paper off. Because the color was slightly off, the back part of the door was sprayed and each coat was sprayed farther than the other, giving a tapered effect (Fig. 8-17). After the basecoat had dried, the area was sprayed with the clearcoat using two coats. The second coat was extended beyond the first, giving a tapered edge to the clearcoat. This tapered edge was then sprayed with a blending clear and allowed to dry to a glossy finish (Fig. 8-18). A slight amount of rubbing and polishing was done on the tapered blend area once it was dry. This produced a quality finish and a good color match, as the color blend was sprayed to a taper to provide no discernible color change on the repaired panels.

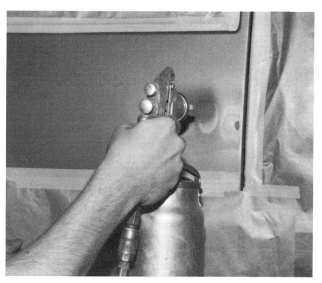

FIGURE 8-15   Spraying primer.

FIGURE 8-16   Applying the basecoat.

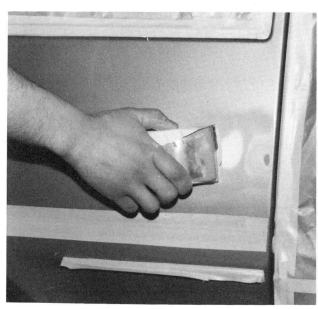

FIGURE 8-14   Sanding polyester glaze.

FIGURE 8-17   Spraying on door panel.

FIGURE 8-18 Area sprayed with clear and blending clear.

8-3 MATCHING COLOR FUNDAMENTALS AND TECHNIQUES

With over 20,000 classified colors used in the automotive industry, it is no wonder that matching colors is one of the biggest obstacles a painter must be able to overcome. Most of these colors come from approximately 30 different color groups. All the colors from these different groups can be made from basically three primary colors, which are blue, red, and yellow, plus white, black, metallics, mica, and pearl.

A successful, qualified painter must be able to recognize a paint mismatch and rectify the problem. The problem is that some painters are color blind to a poor match of certain colors. Another problem a painter will meet is trying to match a slightly faded paint finish. It is not possible to fade a new coat of paint; the shade can be changed slightly by certain techniques but never faded.

To discover how much the color has changed, always look at the door jambs and compare the color to the paint that is in the can. Another method is to clean the oxidized paint on part of the surface. A piece of paper with a hole in it can be used to restrict the area that is sprayed as a test. Comparing the colors should give a clue as to what changes must be made in the formulation.

To further explain the matching of colors, it must be realized that color is produced by different pigments and dyes mixed together to obtain a particular shade of a color. Car manufacturers choose a multitude of different colors and develop a standard for every color that will be used in the factory.

Paint manufacturers develop what is known as factory package paint. The rest is mixed on a tinting

system in either the jobber's establishment or at the body shop according to a formula. At the factory a computer is used, as well as the eye (which is the more sophisticated device), to tint a color to match the color standard.

With all this equipment and these formulas, a painter may think that painting a panel on a vehicle should be no problem, but Fig. 8-19, which shows samples of colors from just one vehicle manufacturer for one year, tells a different story. These vehicles are painted at factories which use precise and accurate methods and materials that are supposed to match the color standard. Vehicles are painted in spray areas that have the best of equipment and controlled temperature, ventilation, and humidity, but still there are great variations and colors that are off the standard.

Most problems occur with the metallic, mica, and pearl colors and it is up to the painter to match these finishes to the best of his or her ability so as to please the customer. In the refinish field these colors are applied by many different techniques. The repairs are done in many shops without temperature, ventilation, or humidity control, so it is no wonder that it is hard to control metallic, mica, and pearl types of paints.

The greatest problem with these colors is that they are formulated with a pigment, metallic flakes, mica, or pearl in a binder that allows the light to penetrate into the cured paint film. Metallics, iridescents, and polychromatics are all the same type of paint; different manufacturers use sightly different names for them (Fig. 8-20). The appearance of the paint film surface depends on the position of the metallic flakes within the paint film. The multitude of metal, mica, or pearl particles reflect the light in the paint film. Some of the light intensity is absorbed in the paint film as it travels to and from the flakes. If a vehicle is painted such that the me-

FIGURE 8-19 Color samples.

Polychromatic colors: These paints contain very small flakes of metal in the liquid.

FIGURE 8-20 Polychromatic, iridescent, or metallic colors. (*Courtesy of Martin-Senour, Inc.*)

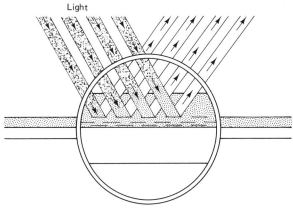

Light is reflected
Light is absorbed

FIGURE 8-21 Metallic particles are deep. (*Courtesy of Martin-Senour, Inc.*)

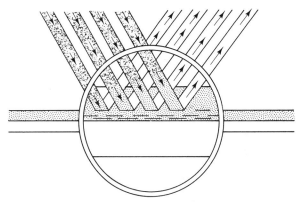

Uniform reflection of light. Heavy light absorption.

FIGURE 8-22 Dark shade of metallic color. (*Courtesy of Martin-Senour, Inc.*)

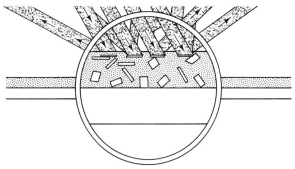

Nonuniform reflection of light. Low light absorption.

FIGURE 8-23 Light shade of metallic color. (*Courtesy of Martin-Senour, Inc.*)

tallics lie deep in the paint film and are all parallel to the surface, they will all reflect the light uniformly (Fig. 8-21). With the flakes lying deep in the paint film, a great portion of the light intensity is absorbed by the paint film as the light travels through the paint. Therefore, the paint film will appear dark and deep in color (Fig. 8-22).

When a vehicle is painted with a metallic paint in such a way that the metallics are dispersed at random and near the surface, the reflection of the light will not be uniform. The light has less film to travel through to get to the flakes and just a slight amount of that light will be absorbed in the paint film (Fig. 8-23).

These color variations may be caused by the painter. When the paint is applied in two coats, more flash time in between the coats will produce a lighter color. When the painter applies the two coats with very little flash time between the coats, it will produce a darker shade of the color.

A dry film occurs due to a lack of solvent in the paint or to a solvent that evaporated too quickly. This prevents a good flow-out of the paint film and causes a lighter color (Fig. 8-24).

A wet film occurs when the paint film contains slow-drying solvent or if there is enough solvent in the paint as it hits the surface to be painted. This allows the paint film sufficient time to flow out before all the solvent evaporates. This produces a smooth surface and is called a wet paint film; it produces a darker color (Fig. 8-24).

When the paint is applied in a wet film, the metal or any other particles, since they are heavier than the paint, will have time to settle into the paint surface as

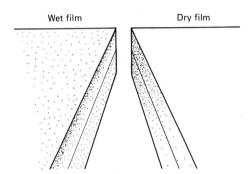

FIGURE 8-24 Different shades of a paint film. (*Courtesy of Martin-Senour, Inc.*)

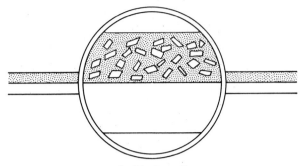

Particles trapped
where sprayed

FIGURE 8-26 Arrangement of metallic particles in a dry paint film. (*Courtesy of Martin-Senour, Inc.*)

the solvents leave the paint film through evaporation. When the paint has dried fully, the flakes will be arranged deep in the paint film, which will produce a dark shade of color. Therefore, a wet application of metallic types of paint produces a darker color (Fig. 8-25).

When a fast-evaporating solvent is used, it prevents the intermixing of the paint due to the fast drying of the paint film. This prevents the flakes from settling into the paint film. This application of a dry film produces a lighter color (Fig. 8-26).

A mist coat, which is the final application when painting acrylic lacquer, is an overthinned polychromatic color. The mist coat is usually reduced approximately 1 part of acrylic lacquer to 10 parts of acrylic lacquer thinner (Fig. 8-27). It is used to obtain the maximum off-the-gun gloss for acrylic lacquer.

A fog coat or blend coat of polychromatic acrylic enamel, reduced according to manufacturer's recommendations, is the final coat applied. This coat may be sprayed at a slightly greater gun distance and/or increased air pressure and reduced fluid flow. This method will produce a lighter color. The variables used to lighten a metallic color are the reduction, air pressure, faster reducer, and greater gun distance. To darken a metallic color, use less reducer, less air pressure, less gun distance, a slower evaporating reducer, and some retarder if required (Fig. 8-28). Table 8-1 gives the many vari-

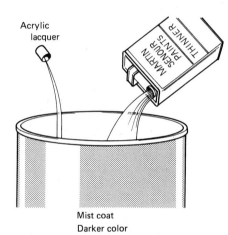

Acrylic
lacquer

MARTIN
SENOUR
PAINTS
THINNER

Mist coat
Darker color

FIGURE 8-27 Mist coat. (*Courtesy of Martin-Senour, Inc.*)

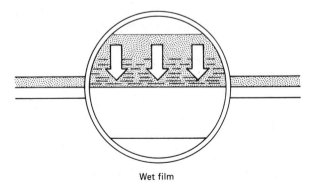

Wet film

FIGURE 8-25 Metallic particle arrangement in wet paint film. (*Courtesy of Martin-Senour, Inc.*)

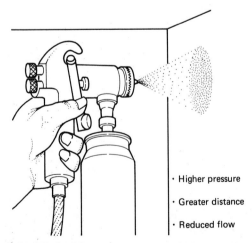

· Higher pressure

· Greater distance

· Reduced flow

FIGURE 8-28 Fog coat. (*Courtesy of Martin-Senour, Inc.*)

TABLE 8-1

Variables affecting color match

Variable	To make colors	
	Lighter	Darker
Shop condition		
Temperature	Increase	Decrease
Humidity	Decrease	Increase
Ventilation	Increase	Decrease
Spraying techniques		
Gun distance	Increase distance	Decrease distance
Gun speed	Increase speed	Decrease speed
Flash time between coats	Allow more flash time	Allow less flash time
Mist coat	(Will not lighten color)	Wetter mist coat
Spray equipment and adjustments		
Fluid tip	Use smaller size	Use larger size
Air cap	Use cap with more holes	Use cap with less holes
Fluid adjustment valve	Decrease material flow	Increase material flow
Fan adjustment valve	Increase fan width	Decrease fan width
Air pressure (at gun)	Increase air pressure	Decrease air pressure
Thinner usage		
Type thinner	Use faster-evaporating thinner	Use slower-evaporating thinner
Reduction of color	Increase amount of thinner	Decrease amount of thinner
Use of retarder	(Do not use retarder)	Add retarder to thinner

Source: Martin-Senour, Inc.

ables that affect any metallic color. The same color from a quart of paint sprayed by different painters will produce numerous different shades of the same basic color due to the many variables given in Table 8-1. Commonsense must be used when color matching. Use a factory package when possible as their quality control is much better because the paint is mixed in large batches to match the color standard.

When mixing in the shop, make sure the measuring equipment does not stick and is properly calibrated. The paint should not be over- or underreduced when comparing for match. Make sure that paint containing toners and metallics is properly agitated and that no pigment or metallic flakes are left at the bottom of the can. Colors dry darker, so on critical matches a spray test on a panel should be done and allowed to dry before applying the color (Fig. 8-29). Adjacent panels should always be cleaned and compounded. Colors should always be matched in natural light if at all possible.

When tinting is required, always use a small quantity of the paint color before trying to tint an entire quart (liter) or gallon (4 liters); then only add small amounts of toners at one time and remember dark colors will require more toners than light colors. When color is viewed at a 90° angle or perpendicular to the surface (Fig. 8-30a), this is known as the face angle. When viewed at a 45° angle or less to the surface (Fig. 8-30b),

FIGURE 8-29 Matching the color.

it is called the pitch angle or the side tone of the color. When tinting metallics, pearl, or mica paint, the viewing position is most critical as a dark face could have a light pitch, or vice versa. The same toners as used in the formula should always be used when tinting a color. After the color has been sprayed, it should always be checked for match before removing the masking paper partially (Fig. 8-31).

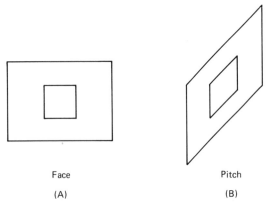

Face   Pitch

(A)   (B)

FIGURE 8-30   Terms used to describe methods of looking at a color. (a) Face of the color. (b) Pitch of the color.

Using the previous methods, there is just so much a painter can do to vary and adjust a color. Therefore, in many cases the color has to be changed by tinting. To do this, the painter must know how to use a systematic system for changing color by tinting. As mentioned before, certain pigments absorb light and others reflect it, and all colors are derived from the primary colors, red, blue, and yellow, and white, black, metallic flakes, mica, and pearl. When any two primary colors are mixed in equal amounts, they make the secondary colors. For example, blue and red = violet, red and yellow = orange, and yellow and blue = green.

If all three of the primary colors are mixed together in equal amounts, they produce a neutral gray. Whenever primary and secondary colors are mixed in equal amounts they will produce an intermediate color; for example, blue and green make a bluish-green color.

The numbers of combinations are infinite, and the addition of white, black, metallics, mica, and pearl to any of the combinations will produce even more variations.

Instead of dealing with all the variations, the focus must be on the color reference points, such as red or green, which are primary colors. A way must be found to move these colors from their reference points to a required or desired tint, shade, or intensity. Color has three qualities or dimensions to be considered when tinting is done:

1. *Brightness or depth lightness:* Expressed as darker or lighter, this value is a reference to the amount of black or white in a certain color.
2. *Hue or cast:* The hue or cast may vary in four ways: redder, bluer, greener, or yellower (for example, reddish blue).
3. *Saturation or cleanliness:* Describes the richness or purity of a color (for example, the greenest green).

To explain the dimensions of color, the color wheel (Fig. 8-32) is used to provide reference points for the four colors. The hue or cast is the easiest to see; is it redder, bluer, greener, or yellower? Equal parts of red and blue make a violet color and equal parts of green and blue produce a turquoise color. When matching a red, the color that has to be matched must be determined as having a bluer or yellower hue or cast; then small amounts of blue or yellow toner are added to achieve the desired hue or cast. Table 8-2 shows how a particular color will change a cast or hue.

FIGURE 8-31   Removing masking paper partially to check for color match.

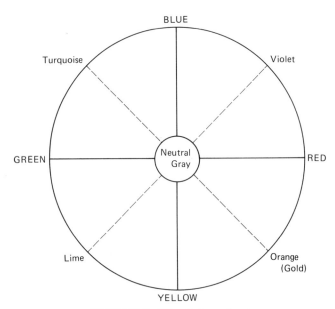

FIGURE 8-32   Color wheel.

TABLE 8–2

How colors change in cast or hue

Color	Variations of hue
Green	Bluer or yellower
Blue	Greener or redder
Red	Bluer or yellower
Yellow	Greener or redder
Gold	Greener or redder
Maroon	Yellower or bluer
Bronze	Yellower or redder
Orange	Yellower or redder
White	Yellower or bluer
Beige	Greener or redder
Purple	Greener or redder
Black	Yellower or bluer
Aqua	Bluer or greener
Gray	Yellower or bluer

Source: Martin-Senour, Inc.

TABLE 8–3

Changing cast or hue

	If a color is "too something in cast," the following kills will change the cast:		
Color being matched	Adding	Kills	Subtracting
Blue	Green	"	Red
Blue	Red	"	Green
Green	Yellow	"	Blue
Green	Blue	"	Yellow
Red	Yellow	"	Blue
Red	Blue	"	Yellow
Gold	Green	"	Red
Gold	Red	"	Green
Maroon	Yellow	"	Blue
Maroon	Blue	"	Yellow
Bronze	Yellow	"	Red
Bronze	Red	"	Yellow
Orange	Yellow	"	Red
Orange	Red	"	Yellow
Yellow	Green	"	Red
Yellow	Red	"	Green
White	Yellow	"	Blue
White	Blue	"	Yellow
Beige	Green	"	Red
Beige	Red	"	Green
Purple	Green	"	Red
Purple	Red	"	Green
Aqua	Blue	"	Green
Gray	Blue kills yellow		
	Yellow kills blue		

Source: Martin-Senour, Inc.

When tinting colors, sometimes the paint may have the wrong cast or hue. A blue color may have too much of a red cast or hue. To kill the red cast, a green toner must be added. The opposite cast or hue on the color wheel must be used to kill the undesired cast. Table 8–3 shows what colors or toners must be added to the mixture of paint to kill the cast or hue of the particular color.

Saturation or chroma refers to a color's purity and richness. Look at the color wheel in Fig. 8–33; the center represents the neutral color, which is gray, and any color in its weakest concentration will become gray or neutral. A line plotted from the center of the wheel to blue will change to a light blue, then to a medium blue, and then a dark blue. Also, a line plotted from the center of the

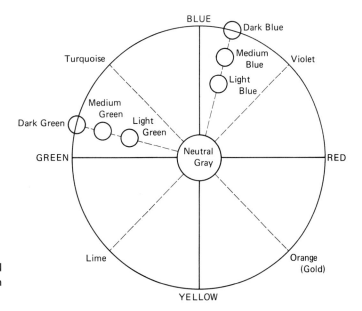

FIGURE 8–33 Color wheel showing the chroma or saturation effect.

wheel to green will change to light green, then to a medium green, and then to a dark green. Therefore, to darken a color a dark toner must be used. For instance, the bluest toner in the tinting system that is the richest and has the least amount of green or red cast must be added slowly. The same principle must be used for the green color; that is, use the greenest and richest toner that has the least amount of blue or yellow in it. Too often a painter, when trying to tint a medium color darker, will use black, when all that is needed is a darker toner of the same color. Also, many times white is used to lighten a color when a lighter toner of the same color family should be used.

Brightness or depth, also referred to as being brighter or grayer, refers to the amount of white or black in a given color. Brightness should never be thought of as light or dark, but as intensity. When tinting a color, its hue or cast and intensity can be maintained, while still changing the color with relation to its reflectivity by adding white or black.

It is sometimes very difficult to determine how to change the saturation of a color or the brightness of the color. This is where a painter with a good eye excels, but some general rules should be followed. A black color may be used to darken most colors but not make them richer; but the side effect of using black might be to gray or muddy the color. Adding black to a red will produce an oxide tone or a brown, so to darken a red, a maroon toner should be used.

When a black is added to yellow, it will darken the yellow but a grayish-green tone may be produced. White is used to lighten colors except red, maroon, browns, dark blues, and dark greens. When lightening red, brown, and maroon, orange and yellow should be used; to add white to these colors will produce a pink tone. Green or gold are used to lighten dark green depending on its cast. The richer or cleaner a color is, the less white and black that should be used.

When a close match has been achieved when tinting a color, the painter should stop tinting and blend to finish the repair. It often happens that the last little spot of a tinting tone will change the color too far, and this will cause a loss of time and materials, because the painter has to start all over. (See Table 8–4.)

The terms in Table 8–5, a color-matching glossary, should be learned and remembered by the painter as an aid in matching colors.

Tinting Metallic Colors

Due to the many angles at which metallic flakes may be suspended in the paint film, they will produce a variation of colors from the same container of paint (Table 8–4). Optimally, the painter wants to have the same size of flakes suspended in the same fashion that they are in

TABLE 8–4

Polychrome (metallic) mixing colors

Acrylic enamel		
9824	Bright	Clean and bright
9827	Fine	Slightly dirty and chalky
9819	Coarse	Big and bright
9817	Medium	Dirty
9833	Biggest	Clean sparkle
Synthol enamel		
9041	Fine	Clean and bright
9014	Finest	Dirty
9040	Coarse	Bright
9050	Biggest	Clean sparkle
Acrylic lacquer		
3008	Fine	Chalky
3012	Medium	Clean
3016	Coarse	Slightly dirty
3035	Coarser	Clean
3043	Coarsest	Clean
3048	Biggest	Diamond sparkle

Source: Martin-Senour, Inc.

the original paint film. This is hard to achieve, however, and even the manufacturers have difficulty with paint application at the assembly plants.

For a metallic color to match, it is important that both the face and pitch angles be the same as in the original paint film. There are many different sizes of metallic flakes and there are differences between foreign and domestic metallics. Foreign metallics flakes are polished on both sides and the domestic only on one side. This is why foreign metallics always look brighter than domestic metallics, and it is for this reason that foreign metallics are hard to match with domestic paint.

Using a medium or fine metallic instead of a coarse or sparkle metallic will give a darker pitch; but when using a coarse metallic, a more definite flop will be produced. More light is reflected from larger-sized metallics, and this will produce a lighter pitch in the color. More color will be shown on the pitch angle, whereas if a fine flake were used the color would show a grayer pitch angle (see Table 8–4).

The size of the metallic flake used in the color should be determined when tinting is to be done. Look at the color and notice the small black spots. These are upside down metallic flakes, and the bigger the black spot the larger the metallic flake. On foreign cars try to find the size of the flake by observing the paint; paint usually has only two sizes of flakes, which are polished on both sides and are coarse or fine. The finer the metallic used, the brighter the color will appear; but many times a color has more than one size of metallic flakes.

When tinting metallic colors, it is recommended that lower-strength or more transparent toners be used.

TABLE 8-5
Glossary of matching terms

Clean: The opposite of dirty. Describes a color with a bright appearance rather than one that has a drab appearance. The exclusion of black makes colors cleaner.

Dark: By eliminating white, solid colors become darker, while eliminating metallic flake makes metallic colors darker.

Dirty: The opposite of clean. Describes a color that has a drab appearance rather than one with a bright appearance. The addition of black makes colors dirty.

Face: The appearance of a color viewed straight on (at 90° angle). This term is most often used in comparison to the "pitch" of a color, which is the appearance of the color when viewed at any angle other than 90°. The face color is often different in lightness or darkness or in shade from the pitch, particularly when working with iridescent colors.

Flake: Particles added to a color to achieve a metallic or iridescent finish.

Flop: The appearance of a color when viewed from any angle other than straight on. The flop of a color is also referred to as its pitch.

Hiding: The ability of a color to cover up (hide) a primer. Poor hiding color will allow the primer spot to show through.

Hue: Describes the basic color. Is the color blue, red, yellow, green, violet, or orange? Hue is used to describe where the color would generally fall on the color wheel.

Iridescents: This term is used interchangably with the word metallic. It is used to cover all colors which contain aluminum, mica, or other particles that impart a metallic appearance to the color. Iridescent colors must be carefully matched on the face and the pitch in order to achieve a desirable appearance.

Light: The addition of white makes solid colors lighter, while the addition of metallic flake makes metallic colors lighter.

Mass tone: The color of a tinting base prior to intermixing with other bases.

Metallics: See iridescents.

Pitch: The appearance of a color when viewed from any angle other than straight on. This term is most often used in comparison to the "face" of a color, which is the appearance of a color when viewed at a 90° angle or straight on. Pitch is also referred to as the "flop" of a color. The pitch is often different from the face when working with iridescent colors.

Shade: This term is used to describe the variations of a color. Assuming that a color is generally blue, that is, the hue is blue, it can have a red shade or a yellow shade as well as being blue. Shade is also called undertone as it describes the subtle tone of a color.

Strength: High strength bases contain a lot of pigment. The additional pigment gives the bases good hiding.

Transparent: Bases that contain a small amount of pigment have poor hiding and are transparent. You can see through the base.

Source: BASF Inmont, Inc.

Red, white, orange, and yellow tones should not be used unless they are gold or oxides. It is possible to have a good face angle match, but the pitch or the flop will be too dark.

To rectify this condition, a small amount of low-strength white is added; this will lighten the pitch or flop but not change the color. If the pitch or flop must be darker, a small amount of low-strength black is added and also a bit of clear. The clear is used to brighten the color so that the face color will not be too gray. When tinting metallics or any color, compare the tinted paint to the color on the vehicle for brightness; the appropriate colors are added in small quantities while checking both the pitch and face angles. When the brightness has been corrected, the hue must be compared to the color on the vehicle. If the hue is not right, add toner to correct it. Once the brightness and hue are correct, the color must be checked for richness. If it is not rich enough, a small amount of toner of the same type as the mass toner is added. That is, to brighten a green, a green toner is added.

When tinting, always start with a small amount of paint and carefully keep track of the toners added by using a measuring spoon. Once the color is correct, the proportional amounts are added to the rest of the mix. By using this method it can be observed how much of each toner is added and how it changes the color. By taking the time required, there is less chance of changing the color too much. Each step should be done individually; this takes more time but hard colors to match require more time to be able to match them. The same method should be used when tinting solid colors.

Faded Colors

All colors fade with age, but they do not all fade the same amount as there are too many variables that affect this process. The panels on the top of a vehicle will fade faster than the sides. Orange, yellow, red, silver, and gold usually fade the most, and light-colored metallics will fade grayer. To compensate when painting metallics, add a little black and white to produce a grayer look. As reds fade lighter and bluer, small amounts of maroon and white or violet are added. The blues usually fade grayer and greener; offset this by adding a little white, black, and green. The brown colors usually fade grayer and yellower; offset this by adding white, black, and gold.

When applying the color, use lower reduction and low air pressure, apply medium wet coats, and use normal flash time to produce a grayer shade of the color. To produce a lighter gray shade, above normal reduction, higher air pressure, and medium wet double coats are used. Always compound and buff adjoining panels to remove as much oxidation as possible. But even after doing all this, a faded color may not give a good match.

Clears and How They Affect Color Matching

When having to match basecoat/clearcoat colors, a clearcoat should always be sprayed over the test spray panel, as the clear brightens the color. Brightness must not be confused with gloss. A color should never be matched without a clearcoat applied to it, because the clear will darken it. A clearcoat gives the color more depth and makes it appear richer.

Whenever tinting to match a basecoat/clearcoat, the basecoat should be tinted a shade lighter to compensate for the darkening effect when the clear is applied. At certain times a clear is used when solid colors are matched, and this will give more binder or vehicle to the paint. Adding extra clear helps to keep the metallic flakes in the toners in suspension. The suspension of the metallic flakes will add brightness, increase the flop effect, and make the color appear more saturated. The more clear that is added, the brighter and cleaner the color will appear.

When clear is added to nonmetallic paint, this will increase the brightness slightly, but not as in metallic colors. However, it must not be assumed that adding a clear to a color will alone be sufficient to change the saturation or brightness. To increase this effect, it is much better to use a toner and a small amount of clear.

TABLE 8-6
Common reasons and remedies for color mismatches

I. Reasons for color mismatches:
  A. Car manufacturer: car's color has drifted from standard.
    1. New finish being used.
    2. Different supplier of original-equipment color or material change by the supplier.
    3. Equipment problem at the plant: color not properly agitated or spray equipment faulty.
    4. Vehicle baked too long or not long enough, or oven temperature too low or too high.
    5. Too little or too much paint applied.
  B. Aftermarket supplier—paint company.
    1. Color was not originally matched to standard.
    2. Change in raw material—pigment.
    3. Not properly mixed at the factory.
  C. Jobber.
    1. Color not properly mixed.
    2. Wrong color mixed.
  D. Painter.
    1. Color not properly stirred.
    2. Improper paint technique.
    3. Too much paint or not enough.
    4. Wrong color ordered.
  E. Color is faded or the film is degraded from weathering. No matter what the reason or who is to blame, the problem becomes the painter's.
II. How to solve color match problems:
  A. Learn to describe color correctly and in the proper sequence.
    1. Lighter–darker.
      a. Side angle.
      b. Direct.
    2. Cast: the effect a color gives when looking at it.
      a. Redder.
      b. Bluer.
      c. Greener.
      d. Yellower.
    3. Brighter–grayer.
  B. Learn to compare the original paint to the color that is being sprayed.
    1. Say that the car's finish is darker than the color being sprayed: always allow the color to dry before making an adjustment. Test for color description.
  C. Adjust painter control variables.
    1. Before any color is tinted, adjust lightness or darkness.

  2. The cast will be slightly affected by changes in lightness or darkness. If the cast is right, then:
  3. Adjust for brightness or grayness.
  D. Adjust the color for lightness or darkness.
    1. Methods to lighten a color:
      a. After spraying a wet coat, follow with a coat at half-trigger or adjust the fluid control valve for less material flow.
      b. Raise the air pressure at the gun in 5 psi (35 kPa) increments.
      c. Add more thinner—at least 25%—and use a faster thinner than that currently in the mix.
      d. Let the thinned color set for 10 minutes in the spray cup; pour the top half off into a clean container, stir up the remaining material, and spray.
      e. Add additional poly to the color.
    2. Methods to darken a color:
      a. Double coat the panel, wetting the surface. Open up the fluid valve and reduce the fan size slightly.
      b. Lower the pressure at the gun in 5 psi or 35 kPa increments.
      c. Add 2 oz or 60 ml of retarder per thinned cup.
      d. Let the thinned color set for 10 minutes, pour the top portion off into a clean spray cup, stir, attach gun, and spray.
      e. Add the predominant dark color to the mix.
  E. If after adjusting the color for lightness or darkness, the cast is off, tinting for correct cast is required.
    1. Steps involved in tinting for correct cast:
      a. Decide how the original finish is off compared to the material you sprayed; for example, the original finish is redder than the material sprayed. In being off in cast, a color can only be described as being redder, yellower, greener, or bluer.
      b. Use the chart to decide on what tint color for the appropriate system should be used.
      c. Each color can vary in cast in only two directions. Refer to the Chart for Table 8-6 below.
  F. Once the color necessary to correctly adjust the cast is determined, the amount must be calculated.
    1. The first tinter should be determined from the chart, indicating the least amount of the particular tint necessary to effectively change the color.
    2. The color should be thoroughly mixed, the gun triggered to clear the chamber, and the small panel

(1) Colors either greener or redder in cast:
  (a) Blue   (c) Gold   (e) Beige
  (b) Yellow   (d) Purple   (f) Brown
(2) Colors either yellower or bluer in cast:
  (a) Green   (c) White   (e) Gray
  (b) Maroon   (d) Black
(3) Colors yellower or redder in cast:
  (a) Bronze   (b) Orange   (c) Red
(4) Colors bluer or greener in cast:
  (a) Aqua   (b) Turquoise

Materials you will need to be able to color match when using Sherwin-Williams paint

Acrylic lacquer colors	Acrylic enamel colors
Metallic L4 S 335	Metallic F S 69
White L4 W 301	White F5 W 80
Black L4 B 320	Black F5 B 81
Gold L4 N 314	Gold F5 N 85
Green L4 G 337	Green F5 G 79
Yellow L4 Y 310	Yellow F5 Y 89
Blue L4 L 339	Blue F5 L 70
Red L4 M 321	Red F5 P 92
Large L4 S 345, metallic	Large F5 S 101, metallic
Basecoat L4 S 349, metallic	Basecoat F5 S 102, metallic
Basecoat L4 S 352, metallic large	Basecoat P4 S 103, metallic large

Initial shading hits for acrylic lacquer metallics

Lighter: Use L4 S 335–L4 S 345:
  Light metallics 8 tsp
  Medium metallics 4 tsp
  Dark metallics 2 tsp
Redder: Use L4 M 321:
  Light metallics ¼ tsp
  Medium metallics ½ tsp
  Dark metallics 2 tsp
Greener: Use L4 G 337:
  Light metallics ¼ tsp
  Medium metallics ½ tsp
  Dark metallics 2 tsp
Yellower: Use L4 Y 310:
  Light metallics 1 tsp
  Medium metallics 6 tsp
  Dark metallics 15 tsp
Bluer: Use L4 L 339:
  Light metallics ¼ tsp
  Medium metallics ½ tsp
  Dark metallics 2 tsp

Grayer: Use L4 B 320:
  Light metallics ¼ tsp
  Medium metallics ½ tsp
  Dark metallics 2 tsp
Browner: Use L4 N 314:
  Light metallics ½ tsp
  Medium metallics 1 tsp
  Dark metallics 4 tsp
  L4 S 349–L4 S 352: For basecoat colors, use one-half the indicated amount.

All values based on 1 quart of reduced paint.
Initial hit of white L4 W 301 or F5 W 80 to metallics to lighten the side angle color:
Light metallics 1 tsp
Medium metallics ½ tsp
Dark metallics ¼ tsp

Initial shading hits for acrylic enamel metallics

Lighter: Use F5 S 69–F5 S 101:
  Light metallics 8 tsp
  Medium metallics 4 tsp
  Dark metallics 2 tsp
Redder: Use F5 P 92:
  Light metallics ¼ tsp
  Medium metallics ½ tsp
  Dark metallics 2 tsp
Greener: Use F5 G 79:
  Light metallics ¼ tsp
  Medium metallics ½ tsp
  Dark metallics 2 tsp
Yellower: Use F5 Y 89:
  Light metallics 1 tsp
  Medium metallics 6 tsp
  Dark metallics 15 tsp
Bluer: Use F5 L 70:
  Light metallics ¼ tsp
  Medium metallics ½ tsp
  Dark metallics 2 tsp
Grayer: Use F5 B 81:
  Light metallics ¼ tsp
  Medium metallics ½ tsp
  Dark metallics 2 tsp
Browner: Use F5 N 85:
  Light metallics ½ tsp
  Medium metallics 1 tsp
  Dark metallics 4 tsp
  F5 S 102–F5 S 103
  For basecoat colors, use one-half the indicated amount.

All values based on 1 quart of reduced paint.

sprayed, allowed to dry, and checked with the original-equipment (OE) panel. Add additional tint in the specified increments and repeat the process.
G. After the color is correct in lightness–darkness and cast, the final adjustment must be made.
  1. *Note:* It is impossible to make a color brighter without throwing the previous corrections off.
  2. The only way a color can go at this point is to the grayer or dirtier side.
  3. To gray a color, follow this procedure:
    a. Spray a wet coat followed by a coat that is sprayed at half-trigger at a slightly greater distance, lifting the metallic to the surface.
    b. Add a small amount of white mixed with a very small amount of black.
H. Once these three corrections are made in the proper sequence, the color will match the OE panel.
III. *Test* the color match as follows: On one corner of the OE panel, effectively blend the color into the panel.
  A. Use blending clear or blending solvent.
  B. Tape off one corner of the panel at least 6 in. into the panel and spray the color simulating a panel repair.

Source: Sherwin-Williams Automotive Finishes, Inc./Finitions Automobile Sherwin-Williams, Inc.

TABLE 8–7

Materials you will need to be able to color match when using Du Pont paint

Color family	Tint	Tint name	Color head-on	Color sidetone	Comments
White	401L/701A	Low-strength white	White	White	Will gray off metallics head-on and lighten sidetone. Lightens pastels head-on and sidetone.
Black	406L/705A 706A	High-strength black Low-strength black	Black	Black	Darkens head-on and sidetone. May effect color other than graying off. May also cause metallics to go green or yellow.
Aluminum (silver)	411L/710A	Medium aluminum	Medium fine aluminum		Will gray off metallics head-on and lighten sidetone. Normally used in high metallic colors.
	711A	Coarse aluminum	Medium coarse aluminum flake		Will lighten head-on and sidetone. Will move color very quickly. Normally used in the medium lightness range.
	713A	Bright aluminum	Coarse aluminum flake		Will lighten head-on and sidetone. Normally used in the darker metallic colors.
	447L	Bright aluminum	Fine, bright aluminum		Used primarily in CC/EC colors with a high metallic content. In silvers and light metallics, 447L will lighten both head-on and sidetone. 447L is quite concentrated so be careful not to overtint.
	494L	Bright medium aluminum	Medium fine aluminum with a small degree of brilliance		Will lighten metallic colors in medium color ranges. Will not lighten sidetone appearance as effectively as 447L.
	495L	Bright coarse aluminum	Very coarse, brilliant aluminum		Use where a high degree of sparkle is required for head-on appearance. Will not lighten sidetone. If a degree of brilliance is required, along with a lightening of sidetone, use a combination of 495L and 447L.
Blue	414L/723A 416L/721A 422L/722A	Purple/violet Fast blue Phthalo blue	Blue violet Reddish blue Slightly greenish blue	Blue violet Reddish blue Very greenish blue	Moves color very quickly. Moves color very quickly.

Color	Code	Pigment			Comments
Green	423L/730A	Green gold	Greenish yellow	Light reddish green	
Red	425L/742A	Fast green/blue green	Bluish green	Bluish green	Use in small amounts.
	428L/717A	Red oxide	Very opaque Red brown	Light yellowish red brown	Will give a chalky sidetone.
	432L/746A	Bright red	Bright bluish red	Bluish red	
	434L/749A	Maroon	Dark bluish red brown	Dark bluish red brown	Bluer than 441L and 716A.
	440L/748A	Violet/monastral violet	Red violet	Red violet	
	441L/716A	Dark violet/red	Red violet	Red violet	Lightens sidetone. In metallics, it washes out the color and masks the flake.
Orange	437L/731A	Orange	Yellowish red orange	Yellowish red orange	
Yellow	452L/737A	Yellow	Dark yellow	Greenish yellow	Lightens sidetone. Can cause metallics to go green. In metallics, it washes out the color and masks the flake.
	453L/732A	Ferrite yellow	Dark yellow Gold	Light reddish yellow	Lightens sidetone.
	454L/751A	Gold/iron oxide	Reddish gold	Reddish gold	Not as red as 455L and 752A.
	455L/752A	Red gold/transparent oxide	Rich reddish brown	Reddish brown	Basic in all beige, saddle, maroon, and bronze metallics.
	456L/750A	Amber oxide/yellow oxide	Reddish yellow gold	Gold	Greener than 454L and 751A.
	457L/736A	Irgazin yellow	Bright reddish yellow	Reddish yellow	Used in most yellow and gold metallics.

Source: Du Pont Co.

TABLE 8–8
Ditzler tinting guide

TINTING GUIDE
For — Delstar® Acrylic Enamel
Duracryl® Acrylic Lacquer
Deltron® Acrylic Urethane

THE ART OF KNOWING HOW A TINTING COLOR WILL TINT IN ALL DIFFERENT COLORS IS IMPOSSIBLE. THE ONLY WAY TO LEARN TO TINT PROPERLY IS PRACTICE. THIS GUIDE IS NOT A CURE-ALL, IT IS ONLY MADE AS AN AID TO ASSIST YOU.

SOME HINTS FOR COLOR TINTING.

1 — Always use small amounts of toners and tint a little at a time.
2 — Always match in outside light, artificial light sometimes cast colors.
3 — Always tint only what you need for the job. The next car may differ.
4 — Always spray to check for final match. Some colors will change if dabbled.
5 — Always tint on the light side as most colors change as they dry.
6 — Always select the tinting color closest to the direction you want to go.
7 — Always coarse polys will add sparkle to color without changing its darkness much.
8 — Remember fine polys will gray out a color.

TONERS NEEDED FOR DELSTAR				TONERS NEEDED FOR DURACRYL				TONERS NEEDED FOR DELTRON			
401	Weak White	410	Organic Blue	309	Thalo Green	317	Organic Green	610	Pthalo Blue	643	Light Chrome Yellow
431	Poly	435	Large Poly	311	White	323	Large Poly	625	Tran. Red Ox		
436	Fine Bright Poly	451	Dk. Perm. Red	322	Yellow	325	Fine Bright Poly	625	Quindo Violet	644	Indo Yellow (Red Shade)
440	Organic Green	484	Yellow	342	Org. Blue	346	Weak Black	631	Fine Alum.		
476	Trans. Red Ox.	491	Weak Black	349	Poly	360	Dk. Perm. Red	635	Very Coarse Alum.	646	Weak White
487	Organic Yellow			382	Tran. Yellow	383	Tran. Red Ox	636	Regency Alum.	648	Weak Black
								637	Pthalo Green (Yellow Shade)		

BASIC TINTS NEEDED TO DO VARIOUS JOBS		DELTRON	DELSTAR	DURACRYL
WHITES	to lighten	646	401	311
	to brighten	610	410	342
	to muddy or brown up	623 or 644	476 or 487	382 or 383
YELLOWS, GOLDS AND COPPERS				
	to lighten non poly colors	646 or 643	401 or 484	311 or 322
	to lighten poly colors	631 or 636	431 or 435	323 or 349
	to brighten or make deeper color	637, 623 or 644	440, 476, 487	309, 382, 383
	to brighten sparkle	635 or 636	435, 436	323, 325
	to gray up or fade color	631 or 648	431 or 491	349 or 346
GREENS	to lighten non poly colors	646, 643 or 644	401, 484, 487	311 or 322
	to brighten or lighten poly colors	635 or 636	435, 436	323, 325
	to darken or make greener	637 or 648	440 or 491	309 or 346
	to darken or make bluer	610	410	342
	to darken or make yellower-browner	623 or 644	476 or 487	382 or 383
BLUES	to lighten non poly colors	646	401	311
	to lighten poly colors	631 or 635	431 or 435	323 or 349
	to brighten poly colors	635, 636 or 610	435 or 410, 436	323 or 342, 325
	to darken or make greener	637 or 644	440 or 487	317 or 382
	to darken or make bluer	610 or 648	410 or 491	342 or 346
	to darken or add red cast	625	451	360
REDS	to lighten or brighten non poly colors	646, 643 or 644	401, 484, 487	311 or 322
	to lighten or brighten poly colors	631, 635 or 644	431, 435, 487	323, 349, 382
	to make orange non poly colors	643	484	322
	to make orange poly colors	644	487	382
	to darken	625 or 623	451 or 476	360 or 383

ALWAYS TINT WITH SMALL AMOUNTS AT ONE TIME. SOMETIMES A TINT WILL BE STRONGER THAN YOU EXPECT. IT IS MUCH HARDER TO COME BACK TO A COLOR ONCE YOU HAVE TINTED TOO MUCH SO **BE CAREFUL.**

Source: Ditzler Automotive Finishes, PPG Industries, Inc.

Alpha-Cryl (1 quart each) *(acrylic lacquer system)*		*Super-Max (1 quart each)* *(enamel system)*	
AT-114 — Bright Iridescent	AT-152 — Bon Red	TE-14 — Bright Iridescent	TE-51 — Medium Red
AT-117 — Firemist Iridescent	AT-174 — Ferrite Yellow	TE-17 — Firemist Iridescent	TE-74 — Ferrite Yellow
AT-125 — Cosmic Blue	AT-176 — Red Gold	TE-25 — Cosmic Blue	TE-76 — Yellow Toner
AT-136 — Organic Green	AT-180 — Yellow Gold	TE-31 — Organic Green	TE-85 — Red Gold
AT-141 — Black	AT-190 — Bright White	TE-41 — Black	TE-94 — Bright White

Note: A #996 Quart Hand Agitator and Pour Spout should be supplied for each tinting base to assure color uniformity and to make dispensing easier.

TABLE 8-9

Miracryl 2 Tinting Chart

COLOR TO BE TINTED		COLOR IS TOO LIGHT — TO MAKE DARKER ADD	COLOR IS TOO DARK — TO MAKE LIGHTER ADD	COLOR IS TOO YELLOW — TO MAKE BLUER ADD	COLOR IS TOO BLUE — TO MAKE YELLOWER ADD	COLOR IS TOO GREEN — TO MAKE REDDER ADD	COLOR IS TOO RED — TO MAKE GREENER ADD	COLOR IS TOO CLEAN — TO MAKE GRAYER ADD	COLOR IS TOO DIRTY — TO MAKE BRIGHTER ADD
GRAY	IRID	MB-451	MB-081	MB-212, MB-251	MB-711, MB-765	MB-557, MB-633	MB-335, MB-351	MB0-83, MB-431	MB0-85
	NON IRID	MB-451	MB-961	MB-212, MB-251	MB-722, MB-711	MB-553, MB-643	MB-335	MB-431	MB-961
BLUE	IRID	MB-451	MB-081	MB-212, MB-251	MB-711, MB-765	MB-553, MB-643	MB-335, MB-351	MB0-83, MB-431	MB0-85
	NON IRID	MB-451	MB-961	MB-212, MB-251		MB-553, MB-643	MB-335, MB-351	MB-431	MB-251, MB-253
GREEN	IRID	MB-451	MB-081	MB-212, MB-251	MB-711, MB-765		MB-351, MB-355	MB0-83, MB-431	MB0-85
	NON IRID	MB-451	MB-961	MB-212, MB-251	MB-711, MB-722		MB-351, MB-355	MB-431, MB-961	MB-351, MB-355
RED	IRID	MB-451	MB-081	MB-633, MB-643	MB-711, MB-763	MB-551, MB-557		MB0-83, MB-431	MB0-85
	NON IRID	MB-451	MB-961	MB-633, MB-643	MB-568, MB-722	MB-553		MB-568, MB-931	MB-553, MB-557
MAROON	IRID	MB-451	MB-081	MB-643	MB-711, MB-763	MB-557		MB0-83, MB-431	MB0-85
	NON IRID	MB-451	MB-961	MB-643	MB-722, MB-733	MB-553		MB-431, MB-643	MB-763, MB-568
YELLOW	IRID	MB-431	MB-081		MB-711, MB-765	MB-731, MB-763	MB-335, MB-351	MB-431	MB0-85
	NON IRID	MB-431	MB-961		MB-711, MB-718	MB-733, MB-566	MB-335, MB-351	MB-431, MB-722	MB-714, MB-718
GOLD TAN	IRID	MB-431	MB-081		MB-711, MB-765	MB-731, MB-763	MB-335, MB-351	MB-431, MB0-83	MB0-85
	NON IRID	MB-431	MB-961		MB-711, MB-722	MB-566	MB-335, MB-351	MB-431, MB-566	MB-711, MB-763
ORANGE	IRID	MB-431	MB-081		MB-711, MB-765	MB-557, MB-763		MB0-83, MB-431	MB0-85
	NON IRID	MB-431	MB-961		MB-718, MB-722	MB-553, MB-566		MB-431, MB-568	MB-731, MB-733
BROWN BEIGE	IRID	MB-451	MB-081		MB-711, MB-765	MB-557, MB-763		MB0-83, MB-431	MB0-85
	NON IRID	MB-431	MB-961		MB-711, MB-722	MB-566		MB-431, MB-568	MB-711, MB-722
WHITE	IRID	MB-431			MB-711			MB-431	MB0-85
	NON IRID	MB-431	MB-961	MB-233	MB-722	MB-566	MB-335	MB-961	MB-961

(cont.)

TABLE 8-9 (Continued)

Miracryl 2 Base Characteristics

MB-010 DRIER	This base is contained in all standard Miracryl 2 colors to produce a suitable dry film overnight. It is always 100 parts (10%) of the intermix formula and is never used in Miracryl 2 basecoat colors.
MB-040 FLATTING BASE	The addition of MB-040 makes metallic colors dirty on the face, less metallic flash, and also makes the pitch lighter.
MB-044 BASECOAT FIXE	A special "fixe" for metal control as well as an adhesion promoter of the basecoat color or sealers and primer-surfacers. MB-044 is never used in standard colors and it is always 200 parts (20%) of the basecoat color intermix formula.
MB-050 FORTIFIER	A clear fortifier used to adjust the tintometer formula for correct hiding. The amount used in standard Miracryl 2 formulas will vary depending upon the strength of the other bases used in that formula. MB-050 is never used in basecoat formulas or as a topcoat.
MB-066 PITCH CONTROL	The addition of MB-066 to an iridescent color will darken the pitch without making any substantial change in the face of the color. It will also help to reduce "metal movement" when applying the clearcoat. MB-066 should never exceed 300 parts (30%) of the intermix formula.
MB-073 WHITE MICA	A high strength white mica containing pigment which produces a bright flash in sunlight. Mica pigments are used in the same manner as aluminum flakes to produce iridescent effects. This base is used most frequently in transparent colors as well as charcoal, red and blue iridescents.
MB-075 RUSSET MICA	A high strength red-copper mica containing pigment which produces a bright red flash in sunlight. Mica pigments are used in the same manner as aluminum flakes to produce iridescent effects. This base is used most often in red or copper iridescents.
MB-081 FINE ALUMINUM	Fine particle size. Used to make iridescent colors lighter or more gray on the face and dark on the pitch.
MB-082 MEDIUM FINE ALUMINUM H.S.	Medium fine particle size. A highly concentrated base used in basecoat colors. Produces a bright face and slightly dark pitch.
MB-083 MEDIUM ALUMINUM	Medium particle size. Used to make iridescent colors lighter or more gray on the face and lighter on the pitch.
MB-084 MEDIUM COARSE ALUMINUM H.S.	Medium coarse particle size. A highly concentrated base used in basecoat colors. Produces a very bright face and slightly lighter pitch.
MB-085 COARSE ALUMINUM	Large particle size. Used to increase sparkle in the face of large flake iridescent colors. Will brighten the face and darken the pitch.
MB-212 INDO BLUE	A blue base with a very strong red shade. The reddest of the blue bases. Produces a red, dirty shade in solid and iridescent colors.
MB-214 VIOLET	Very strong violet color that will redden blue iridescent or solid colors.
MB-216 IRON BLUE	Produces a red face and green pitch in iridescent colors. Do not use in small quantities to tint. Used mainly in dark blue iridescent colors.
MB-233 RED BLUE L.S.	Produces a red face and a red pitch. This base is not as red as MB-212. A weaker version of MB-253.
MB-251 GREEN BLUE H.S.	Produces a very green face in blue colors without noticeably changing the pitch.
MB-253 RED BLUE H.S.	Produces a red face and a red pitch. This base is not as red as MB-212. A stronger version of MB-233.
MB-255 RED PITCH BLUE H.S.	Produces slightly less red in the face and slightly less red in the pitch than MB-253.
MB-335 BLUE GREEN L.S.	Produces a blue shade green in solid and iridescent colors. A weaker version of MB-355.
MB-351 YELLOW GREEN	Produces a yellow shade green in solid and iridescent colors.
MB-355 BLUE GREEN H.S.	Produces a blue shade green in solid and iridescent colors. A stronger version of MB-335.
MB-431 BLACK M.S.	Used to darken or dirty solid and iridescent colors. Produces a blue shade black.
MB-451 BLACK H.S.	Used to darken or dirty solid and iridescent colors. Produces a yellow shade black.
MB-455 JET BLACK H.S.	A high strength base used mainly in basecoat color. Produces high hiding colors.
MB-551 BRICK RED	A dark bluish/red base used in deep red iridescent colors when a blue shade is needed. Do not use in pastel or light red solid or iridescent colors.
MB-553 BRIGHT RED	A high strength opaque red used in bright red solid or iridescent colors. Use cautiously in iridescent colors as higher hiding properties will cover aluminum flake. This base is more opaque than MB-557.
MB-554 DARK RED	A yellow shade red used in bright red iridescent colors where a yellow shade is needed. Do not use in pastel solid or iridescent colors.
MB-557 CLEAN RED	A bright red base with a very blue shade for use in solid or iridescent colors. Not as opaque as MB-553.
MB-560 DARK BROWN	A yellow shade brown base used in light and dark brown iridescent colors. Do not use in pastel colors.
MB-566 RED OXIDE L.S.	A yellow shade brown base used to make light beiges and brown solid and iridescent colors. A weaker version of MB-568.

MB-568 RED OXIDE H.S. — A yellow shade brown base used to make solid colors with a yellow/red shade. Used in beiges and brown solid colors. A stronger version of MB-566.

MB-630 MAGENTA — Produces a clean bluish red shade in solid colors or iridescent colors. Not as blue as MB-643.

MB-633 MAROON L.S. — Produces a bluish red or purple shade in solid or iridescent colors. A weaker version of MB-643.

MB-643 MAROON H.S. — Produces a bluish red or purple shade in solid or iridescent colors. A stronger version of MB-633.

MB-711 YELLOW GOLD — Used mainly in gold iridescent colors to produce a red/yellow face and a clean, green pitch.

MB-714 YELLOW — A clean yellow used to brighten yellow solid colors. Produces a greener shade than MB-718. Do not use in iridescent colors.

MB-716 GREEN GOLD — A light green shade yellow used to produce clean, green iridescent colors. Used to make green/gold iridescent colors.

MB-718 BRIGHT YELLOW — A very clean yellow that has a redder shade than MB-714. Used often with MB-711 and MB-714 to make solid yellow colors. Do not use in iridescent colors.

MB-722 FERRITE YELLOW — A dark yellow with a dirty, red shade. Used often in iridescent colors to lighten and yellow the pitch.

MB-731 INDO ORANGE — A transparent orange used in iridescent colors to produce a clean red shade.

MB-733 BRIGHT ORANGE — A bright orange used to lighten red and maroon solid colors. Do not use in iridescent colors.

MB-763 RED GOLD — Produces brownish/red shades in solid and iridescent colors. Used to make red/gold iridescent colors.

MB-765 GOLD OXIDE — Used in iridescent colors to lighten the face and the pitch and produce a clean yellow shade. Used to make clean, yellow/gold iridescent colors.

MB-952 WHITE L.S. — Standard strength white used to lighten solid colors. A weaker version of MB-961.

MB-961 WHITE H.S. — A high strength white used to lighten solid colors. A stronger version of MB-952.

H.S. = High Strength   M.S. = Medium Strength   L.S. = Low Strength

(cont.)

TABLE 8-9 (Continued)

Miracryl 2 Tinting Tips

This tinting guide is meant to be of assistance to the automotive refinish painter who is attempting to adjust the color of a Miracryl 2 standard color or Miracryl 2 basecoat color. Attempts to tint Miracryl 2 colors should only be made with Miracryl 2 tinting bases. The use of other acrylic enamel colors or any other paint products to tint Miracryl 2 colors could be extremely detrimental to the adhesion, lightfastness and overall durability of the Miracryl 2 finish.

The following tips are intended to shorten the time necessary to arrive at a good color match. While some of the procedures may seem to be time consuming, if followed, these hints will make your work easier and faster in the end.

Steps to try before tinting a metallic color.

1. Reduction: the amount of reduction changes a color; more reducer will make the color light and gray; less reducer will make the color dark and rich

2. Solvent: select the correct solvent for shop conditions; hot & dry shops use a slow solvent; cold damp shops use a fast solvent; avoid cheap solvents they change a color

3. Air pressure: measure air pressure at the gun; use the recommended pressure — check the label; more air pressure will make the color light and gray; less air pressure will make the color dark and rich

4. Gun distance: generally eight to twelve inches; more distance will make the color light and gray; less distance will make the color dark and rich

If after trying the foregoing adjustments the match is still off, consider the following when you begin to tint the color.

When tinting with Miracryl 2 bases, keep in mind that the strength of the Miracryl 2 colors is generally much higher than colors in any other mixing system. These high strength bases were developed by R-M laboratories in order to allow for the matching of basecoat finishes with only .5 to 1.0 mils of paint, thus duplicating the OEM application. However, when tinting with these high strength bases remember that a little goes a long way.

Before attempting a color match with Miracryl 2, you should become familiar with the characteristics of each of the bases as outlined in this manual. You will note that many bases are available in two different strengths — a high strength version and a low strength version. When tinting with these bases it is recommended that adjustments to a color be made with the weaker version of a base in order to avoid over shooting the desired change.

In all cases, you should make small adjustments to a sample of the color. It is always possible to add additional color, but impossible to remove what you have added. Pour off some of the color to be adjusted into a separate container and make your changes to this small batch. Keep note of what you have added and how much. When you have a color that you think is a match, spray out a test panel and compare it to the car or body part. If you are satisfied with the match, use your notes from the small batch to make the necessary adjustments to the paint you are going to use.

It is always recommended that you spray test panels to make color evaluations. Most colors change significantly when they dry. Consequently, it is difficult to look at the wet color in a can or on a paint stick and compare it to the dry finish on an automobile.

Color matching should also be done in daylight whenever possible. Colors that appear to match under incandescent or fluorescent lighting frequently will not match when the vehicle is viewed in sunlight.

Whenever possible you should first try to adjust a color with the same bases that were used to make the original intermix formula. That is, you should first look to see which bases are used in the formula and then try to make your adjustments with those bases before trying to add something new.

Before trying to adjust the shade of an iridescent color, you should adjust the lightness/darkness of the color by adding the appropriated aluminum or mica to lighten it or adding black to darken it. Once the lightness/darkness of the match is satisfactory, then begin to adjust the shade of the color.

The use of MB-066 to darken the pitch of an iridescent color without noticeably changing the face of the color can save many hours of color matching. Do not overlook this unique base when color matching iridescent or metallic colors, particularly in basecoat/clearcoat systems. Note that no more than 30% of the final formula should be MB-066 — do not add more than 300 parts total!

Another base that is helpful in color matching is MB-040. This base makes basecoat/clearcoat colors dirty on the face and eliminates some of the metallic flash. It also makes the pitch lighter.

Attempting to match a basecoat color without applying the clear is often a tricky proposition. With Miracryl 2 a large part of the problem has been eliminated, as MC-1000 is nearly water-white in its final application. Still, it can be difficult to evaluate a dull basecoat color when you are trying to compare it to a high-gloss clearcoated finish. You will have better color matches if you spray the clearcoat over your test panel before you try to evaluate the match. With the extremely fast drying characteristics of Miracryl 2 colors (MC-1000 Clear can be applied after 15 minutes), the short wait will be worth your time in satisfied customers.

To summarize the three key steps to a good color match: 1. make small adjustments; 2. spray test panels; 3. match in daylight.

Suggested Tinting Kits for Miracryl 2

MB-083	Medium Aluminum	MB-431	Black	MB-722	Ferrite Yellow
MB-085	Coarse Aluminum	MB-551	Brick Red	MB-733	Bright Yellow
MB-251	Green Blue	MB-553	Bright Red	MB-763	Red Gold
MB-355	Blue Green	MB-714	Yellow	MB-952	White

Suggested Tinting Kits (courtesy of BASF Inmont Canada Inc.)

TABLE 8-10
Color Tinting Chart

COLOR TINTING CHART

Variations from color standards occasionally exist in the manufacture of assembly line built cars. Fade is a factor over which no one has control. Tinting and shading are often necessary to compensate for these color drifts. This color tinting chart will help you with your color problems.

Acrylic Lacquer (3000), Synthol Enamel (9000), and Acrylic Enamel (9800) base mixing colors shown in the chart below are not interchangeable or miscible. Each should be used only to tint colors of like material.

	°Lighter, Add—	Darker, Add—	Bluer, Add—	Greener, Add—	Yellower, Add—	Redder or Browner, Add—	°Grayer, Add—	(For Poly only) Brighter, Add—
YELLOW (Deep)	3001 9029 9800	3033 9036 9808		3032 9035 9807		3017 9038 9806		
ORANGE	3001 9029 9800	All colors except white				3017 9038 9806		
BLUE	3001 9029 9800	All colors except white or polychrome		3011 9030 9810		3021 9020 9812	3001 and 3002 9029 and 9023 9800 and 9801	3016 9025 9824
GREEN	3001 9029 9800	All colors except white or polychrome	3005 or 3009 9027 9818 or 9820		3010 or 3003 9021 or 9008 9809 or 9813	3004 or 3014 9018 or 9024 9805 or 9826	3001 and 3002 9029 and 9023 9800 and 9801	3016 9025 9824
IVORY or CREAM	3001 9029 9800	All colors except white			3010 9021 9809	3003 or 3004 9008 or 9018 9826 or 9828	3001 and 3002 9029 and 9023 9800 and 9801	
TAN or BEIGE or BROWN	3001 9029 9800	All colors except white or polychrome			3010 or 3003 9021 or 9008 9809 or 9813	3004 or 3014 9018 or 9024 9826 or 9828	3001 and 3002 9029 and 9023 9800 and 9801	3016 9025 9824
OFF WHITE	3001 9029 9800	All colors except white	3005 or 3009 9027 9818 or 9820	3011 9030 9810	3010 9021 9809	3014 9024 9805	3001 and 3002 9029 and 9023 9800 and 9801	
GRAY	3001 9029 9800	All colors except white or polychrome	3005 or 3009 9027 9818 or 9820	3011 9030 9810	3003 9008 9813	3004 9018 9826		3016 9025 9824
RED		3018 or 3021 9020 9812 or 9816			3017 9038 9806			3016 9025 9824
MAROON	3017 9038 9806	All colors except white or polychrome	3018 or 3021 9020 or 9026 9812 or 9816					3016 9025 9824

*To make all polychrome colors lighter, tint with polychrome preferably same used in the formula; to make grayer, use black and polychrome.

ACRYLIC LACQUER MIXING COLORS

3001 White	3009 Phthalo Blue	3017 Moly Orange	3033 Chrome Yellow	3041 Bright Maroon
3002 Black	3010 Indo Yellow	3018 Indo Maroon	3034 Light Gold	3042 Red Shade Gold
3003 Yellow Oxide	3011 Phthalo Green	3020 Carbon Black	3035 Ultra Polychrome	3043 Coarse Polychrome
3004 Red Oxide	3012 Polychrome Regular	3021 Violet	3036 Red Shade Blue	3044 Red Shade Yellow
3005 Blue	3013 Chinese Blue	3022 Flatting Base	3037 Yellow Shade Green	3048 Bright Aluminum
3006 Orange	3014 Gold	3023 Suede Univ. Base	3038 Amber Maroon	
3007 Clearmix	3015 Indo Blue	3025 L.T. Black	3039 Green Shade Blue	
3008 Polychrome	3016 Bright Polychrome	3032 Lemon Yellow	3040 L.T. Oxide Yellow	

SYNTHOL ENAMEL MIXING COLORS

9000 Syn-Mix	9020 Tinting Maroon	9030 Brill. Green	9041 Fine Polychrome	9049 Amber Maroon
9001 White	9021 P. T. Green Yellow	9032 Indo Orange	9042 Bright Maroon	9050 Sparkle Polychrome
9004 Toluidine Red	9022 P. Purple Blue	9034 Permansa Red	9043 Opal Yellow Oxide	
9005 Lemon Yellow	9023 Carbon Black	9035 Light Yellow	9044 Red Blue	
9008 P. T. Yellow	9024 P. T. Gold	9036 Chrome Yellow	9045 Yellow Green	
9011 Chinese Blue	9025 Brill. Polychrome	9038 Moly Orange	9046 Green Blue	
9014 Polychrome	9027 P. Medium Blue	9039 Violet Maroon	9047 Red Gold	
9018 Sienna	9029 Modern White	9040 Ultra Polychrome	9048 Medium Blue	

ACRYLIC ENAMEL MIXING COLORS

9800 White	9810 Green	9820 Green Blue	9829 Yellow Green	9837 H.S. Coarse Polychrome
9801 Black	9811 Blue	9821 Bright Maroon	9830 Red Shade Yellow	9838 H.S. Medium Polychrome
9803 Scarlet	9812 Violet	9822 Opal Yellow Oxide	9831 Red Orange	9839 A.E. Base Coat drier
9804 Orange	9813 Ferrite Yellow	9823 Medium Blue	9832 Magenta	9840 Brite Polychrome
9805 Gold	9814 Iron Blue	9824 Ultra Polychrome	9833 Bright Aluminum	
9806 Deep Orange	9816 Maroon	9825 Indo Blue	9835 Mix-Acryl	
9807 Medium Yellow	9817 Polychrome Medium	9826 Red Gold	9836 Mix-Clear	
9808 Lemon Yellow	9818 Red Blue	9827 Polychrome Fine		
9809 Indo Yellow	9819 Polychrome Coarse	9828 Amber Maroon		

(cont.)

TABLE 8–10   (*Continued*)

PAINTER CONTROLLED

In the Shop on the Spot

As a guide for in the shop on the spot color shading, we offer the following:

TO SHADE		USE	
Polychromatic colors lighter	9819	Polychrome Coarse	Acrylic Enamel
	3035	Ultra Polychrome	Acrylic Lacquer
	9040	Ultra Polychrome	Synthol Enamel
Non-Polychromatic colors lighter	9800	White	Acrylic Enamel
	3001	White	Acrylic Lacquer
	9001	White	Synthol Enamel
Dirtier and Bluer	9801	Black	Acrylic Enamel
	3020	Carbon Black	Acrylic Lacquer
	9023	Carbon Black	Synthol Enamel
Dirtier and Browner	9805	Gold	Acrylic Enamel
	3014	Gold	Acrylic Lacquer
	9024	P. T. Gold	Synthol Enamel
Greener in cast	9829	Yellow Green	Acrylic Enamel
	3037	Yellow Shade Grn.	Acrylic Lacquer
	9045	Yellow Green	Synthol Enamel
Yellower in cast	9809	Indo Yellow	Acrylic Enamel
	3010	Indo Yellow	Acrylic Lacquer
	9021	P. T. Grn. Yellow	Synthol Enamel
Bluer in cast	9820	Green Blue	Acrylic Enamel
	3039	Green Shade Blue	Acrylic Lacquer
	9046	Green Blue	Synthol Enamel
Redder in cast	9812	Violet	Acrylic Enamel
	3021	Violet	Acrylic Lacquer
	9039	Violet Maroon	Synthol Enamel

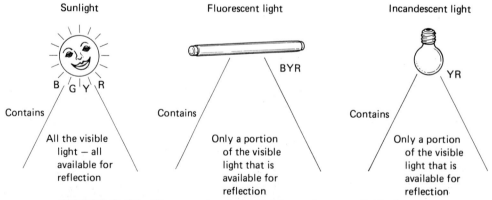

FIGURE 8–34 Those parts of the light spectrum available for reflection under different forms of light: B, blue; G, green; Y, yellow; R, red. When working inside the body shop, the most efficient lighting can probably be had with the color classer fluorescent bulb.

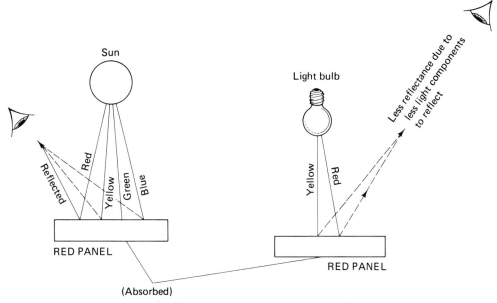

FIGURE 8-35 How we see color and why.

Tables 8–6 through 8–10 show tinting guides from Sherwin-Williams, Du Pont, Ditzler, Rinshed-Mason, and Martin-Senour.

The best light for a body shop to use when matching color is natural sunlight (see Figs. 8–34 and 8–35). These figures demonstrate a condition in color matching called metamerism, in which two colors appear identical under one lighting condition but not under another. For example, a painter sprays a panel inside a body shop. It looks pretty good for match, but the car is pulled out of the shop and the customer sees a glaring mismatch. The painter should be helped to determine the best location in the shop to view color match. Help him find the location where A and B are most likely to match. The painter should be shown why he should take the car outside to make a final *judgment*. Remind the painter of the quality match of the two manufacturers and that he or she take this condition into account when doing color matching.

Colors usually darken after drying, so a certain amount of consideration must be given when tinting the color, especially with enamel. Enamels dry much more slowly than lacquers, which creates a certain problem; it takes longer to find the true color. Another point to consider is the thickness of the film; light pastel shades will usually be lighter when a heavy film is sprayed.

Lacquers are usually sprayed to a film thickness of about 3.0 to 3.5 mils (7.6 to 8.8 μm); enamels are generally a little thicker, up to 3 to 4 mils (7.6 to 10.1 μm). This thickness includes the undercoat; more film thickness than this will at times make the film crack during great temperature changes. When the film is too thick, it loses elasticity and will crack as the metal expands and contracts.

The basic tinting bases listed in the tables should be made available by jobbers or painters so that tinting may be done in shops. Other tinting bases may be added to the basic kits as required.

REVIEW QUESTIONS

8-1. What method is used to build a ground-out metal area back to the paint film surface?

8-2. Why are adjoining panels prepared to receive paint when painting a center panel?

8-3. Explain how the spot repair is painted to make it match the original paint film.

8-4. Explain how the modified conventional method of spot repair is done.

8-5. How is an area prepared for an acrylic enamel spot repair?

8-6. Explain how the color shade will vary when spraying metallic colors.

8-7. Explain how a painter can vary the shades of a metallic color without tinting.

8-8. What is meant by a mist coat?

8-9. What is meant by the face angle?

8-10. What is meant by the pitch angle?

8-11. Name the three primary colors.

8-12. What is meant by brightness when used to tint paint?

8-13. How does a painter change the cast or hue of a color?

8-14. What is the difference between foreign and domestic metallic flakes?

8-15. Why are low-strength toners used when tinting metallic colors?

CHAPTER NINE

Painting Plastic Parts, Paint Failure Remedies, Wood Grains, Moldings, and Striping Tape

SAFETY HINTS

The shop should be kept free from debris, rags, and old parts to prevent a fire.

Care should be used to prevent spillings of solvents or liquids.

Always read directions on labels to find the safe way of using products and for first-aid instructions.

9-1 REFINISHING INTERIOR PLASTIC TRIM PARTS

Interior paintable plastic trim components are divided into three general types: polypropylene plastic, ABS plastic, and vinyl plastic (polyvinyl chloride). It is important that a painter be able to identify each plastic so that he or she can paint it satisfactorily. Manufacturers do not approve the complete painting of the soft seat cushion and seat back trim cover assemblies of vinyl construction. The plastic used most widely on the interior of bodies, with the exception of the soft seat cushion and back trim cover assemblies, is polypropylene.

Two tests will help the painter determine the identity of a given plastic.

1. *Test for ABS plastic polypropylene:* With a sharp blade, remove a sliver of plastic from a hidden backside portion of the part. Hold the sliver of plastic with tweezers or lay it on a clean noncombustible surface and then ignite the plastic. Observe the burning closely. Polypropylene burns with no readily visible smoke. ABS plastic burns with a readily visible black smoke residue that will hang temporarily in the air (Fig. 9-1 a,b,c).

2. *Test for vinyl plastic:* Using a suitable flame, such as provided by a propane torch or equivalent, heat a copper wire until the wire turns

red. Touch the backside or hidden surface of the part being tested with the heated wire. Some of the plastic will be retained on the wire. Return the wire and retained plastic to the flame. Observe for a green-blue flame, which indicates that the plastic being tested is vinyl (Fig. 9-1c).

To paint polypropylene plastic parts involves using a special primer (see Table 9-1 and Fig. 9-2). Because polypropylene plastic is hard, it should be color coated with conventional interior acrylic lacquer after the primer has dried. If the proper primer is not used on these parts, the color coat will usually fail and there will be peeling problems.

The parts must be washed thoroughly with a paint finish cleaning solvent such as Acryli-Clean, Pre-Kleano, Prep-Sol, or equivalent (see Table 9-2). All label directions should be followed. A thin wet coat of polypropylene primer is applied according to the directions on the label. The wetness of the primer is determined by observing the gloss reflection of the spray application in adequate lighting. The primer application must cover all edges. The polypropylene primer is applied at a pressure of 30 to 35 psi (205 to 240 kPa) at the spray gun. During the flash-off time period of usually 1 to 10 minutes, interior acrylic lacquer color is applied as required and is allowed to dry before the part is installed. Applying the color during the flash-off time range provides

(A) Polypropylene

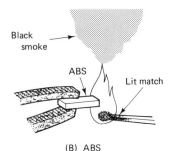

(B) ABS

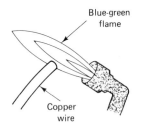

(C) Vinyl

FIGURE 9-1 Burn test to identify plastics. (Courtesy of Mitchell Information Services, Inc.)

the best adhesion of color coats (Fig. 9–3). The type of lacquer that must be used is the lacquer with the right amount of gloss for the particular item and its location. Most of the paint used is flat or semigloss or has a percentage of gloss printed on the color code chart.

The rigid or hard ABS plastic parts require no primer because conventional interior acrylic lacquers adhere satisfactorily to this material. The part is washed thoroughly with the proper paint finish cleaning solvent. The interior acrylic lacquer color is applied according to trim combination. Only enough color is applied for proper hiding and to avoid washout of the grain effect. The part is allowed to dry before installation.

To paint flexible parts such as filler panels between the bumper and fender or a bumper fascia, a flex agent must be used (see Fig. 9–4). The part is prepared as usual; then 355S or equivalent is sprayed on it and allowed to dry following manufacturer's recommendations. Then 1 part 355S is added to 1 part acrylic lacquer and 1 part thinner in the gun cup; this must be well mixed. This material is sprayed on the part in successive coats, with flash-off time in between coats. To spray this material a pressure of 25 to 35 psi (175 to 245 kPa) is used at the gun (Fig. 9–5).

The exterior flexible parts can also be repaired by using acrylic enamel and a urethane catalyst. The cleaning is done using the proper solvent; then the part is sanded with 320 or P400 sandpaper taking care not to break through the original primer to the flexible substrate. This is then cleaned as required before topcoat application. The proper amount of catalyst is added to the unreduced enamel; then it is reduced as per manufacturer's recommendations while stirring. The vehicle is masked and the area tack wiped as required; then paint is applied (Fig. 9–6) using an air pressure of between 50 and 65 psi (340 and 445 kPa) at the gun by

TABLE 9-1

Materials used to paint trim parts

	Sherwin-Williams	Du Pont	Ditzler	Rinshed-Mason	Martin-Senour
Cleaning solvents	R7K156	3919S	VK403	900	6383
	R1K213	3939S	DX330		6387
Vinyl conditioner			VK405		
Polypropylene primer	P3C24	329S	DPX800	864	6242
Urethane flex agent for acrylic lacquer	V2V297 or V6V299	355S	DX1798	891	3082
Flattening compound for nonurethane	T1F270	4528S	DX265	850	3022

FIGURE 9-2 Applying polypropylene primer.

TABLE 9-2

Materials used for treatment of unpainted nonmetal surfaces

Surface	Cleaner	Surface Prep
Fiber glass	3919S or 3929S	Sand
Gel coat	Soap wash, 3919S or 3929S	Sand
Plastic (flexible)	3919S or 3929S	Sand, 3812S or 3929S
Plastic (rigid)	3919S or 3929S	Sand
Plastic (rigid nonporous)	Soap wash, 3919S or 3929S	Sand
Polyester (fiber glass reinforced)	Soap wash, 3919S or 3929S	Sand
Rubber	3919S or 3929S	Sand, 3812S or 3929S
Vinyl	Soap wash, 3919S or 3929S	
Wood	None required	Sand, 3812S or 3929S
Wood (compressed fiber)	3919S or 3929S	Sand

Source: Du Pont Co.

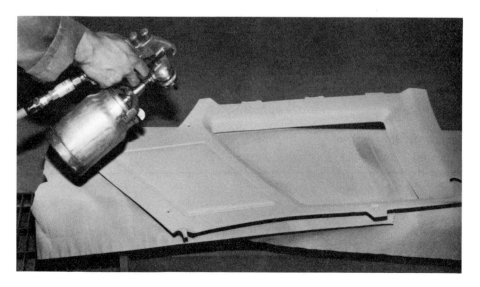

FIGURE 9-3 Applying the color.

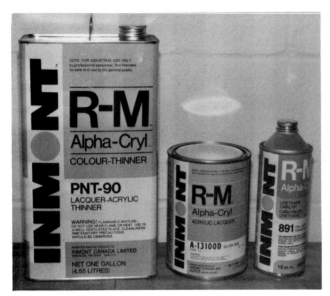

FIGURE 9-4 Materials used to paint flexible parts.

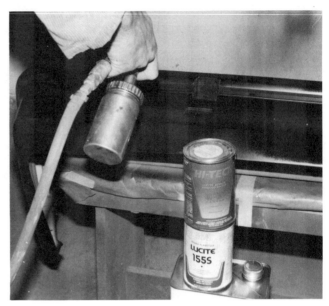

FIGURE 9-5 Applying the material.

applying a full wet coat to act as a sealer. This coat of paint should dry for 20 minutes, followed by two medium wet coats and allowing each to flash off. If the topcoat is a metallic type of paint, it may be necessary to apply a blend coat to even out the metallic flakes. Since the leftover material is catalyzed, it must be disposed of, and the gun should be cleaned using a good thinner.

Painting Vinyl and Flexible (Soft) ABS

The outer cover material on flexible instrument panel cover assemblies is made mostly of ABS plastic that is modified with PVC or vinyl. The same material is used on many padded door trim assemblies, but the soft cushion padding under the ABS covers is usually urethane plastic foam.

Flexible vinyls are most widely used in seat trim, some door trim assemblies, headlinings, etc. They are coated fabrics. Hard vinyls are used on seat back assist handles, coat hooks, exterior molding inserts, and some door trim panels.

The paint system for flexible ABS plastic and vinyl includes an interior vinyl color and a clear vinyl topcoat. Neither primer-sealer nor primer is required. The parts are washed thoroughly with a vinyl cleaning and prep-

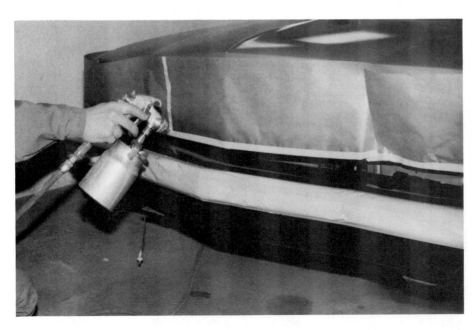

FIGURE 9-6 Painting a flexible bumper fascia.

TABLE 9-3
Plastic refinishing systems for interior use

Symbol	Plastic	Primer	Topcoat
ABS	Acrylonitrile/butadiene/styrene	None	A/L
CPE	Chlorinated polyethylene	P3C24	A/L
EP	Epoxy	P2A43-P2N44	A/L
E/P EPM	TPO, TPR (thermoplastic rubber)	P3C24	A/L plus V2V297
EP DM	Ethylene/propylene diene monomer	P3C24	A/L plus V2V297
E/VAC	Ethylene/vinyl acetate	P3C24	A/L plus V2V297
MF	Melamine	P2A43-P2N44	A/L
PF	Phenolic	P2A43-P2N44	A/L
PA	Nylon	P2A43-P2N44	A/L
UP	Polyester, thermoset	P2A43-P2N44	A/L
PE	Polyethylene	P3C24	A/L
PPYO, PPO	Noryl	P2A43-P2N44	A/L
PP	Polypropylene	P3C24	A/L
TPUR	Polyurethane, thermoplastic	None	A/L plus V2V297
PUR	Polyurethane, thermoset	None	A/L plus V2V297
PVC	Vinyl	None	Vinyl color
SAN	Styrene acrylonitrate	None	A/L
UF	Urea formaldehyde	P2A43-P2N44	A/L
PS	Polystyrene	P2A43-P2N44	A/L

Source: Sherwin-Williams Canada Ltd.
- A/L is Acrylic Lacquer
- P2A43-P2N44 is an acrylic-type primer-surfacer.
- P3C24 is a polyolefin in primer.
- V2V297 is a flexible additive for acrylic lacquer; use V2V297 when the plastic is flexible.

aration solvent, such as Vinyl Prep Conditioner, Vinyl Prep, or equivalent. The cleaner is wiped off with a clean, lint-free cloth while the cleaner is still wet. As soon as the surface is wiped dry, the interior vinyl color is applied in wet coats. Enough flash time must be allowed, and between coats all label directions must be followed. The proper color is found by using the trim color code, and only enough color is used for proper hiding and to avoid washout of the grain effect.

Before the color flashes off completely, one wet double coat of vinyl topcoat is applied. When this topcoat is being applied, care must be taken so that the appropriate level of gloss matches the adjacent parts. The instrument panel should be covered with a nonglare vinyl. A clearcoat is applied to control gloss requirements and to prevent the color from rubbing off after drying. The panel is allowed to dry before it is installed.

If unsure of the method to be used, check the part for the International Organization Code. Then compare to Tables 9-3 and 9-4 and find the proper materials for refinishing the different types of plastics.

If no code is present, a commonsense approach should be used; classify the types of materials, for example, for the exterior into flexible or hard, and for the interior, either flexible or hard. Exterior hard (rigid) parts should be treated as fiber glass when in doubt as to their makeup. Exterior flexible (semirigid) parts re-

quire the addition of a flexible additive to the paint. Interior hard (rigid) parts can all be painted except P.C. polycarbonate (lexan), as solvents will weaken the integrity of this material. The majority of the plastic parts that need refinishing will be polypropelene, which require the use of a plastic primer.

For interior flexible (semirigid) parts, the use of vinyl color is recommended. The second choice will involve the use of acrylic lacquer interior color and a flexible additive.

Vinyl Tops

Vinyl materials installed over roof panels may also require painting. The vehicle should be washed to remove dirt on the surface and then the surface should be dried. The vinyl material is then cleaned with a soapy water solution with a brush to remove any dirt left in its rough texture; this is rinsed off. When dry, the surface is cleaned with a vinyl cleaner (Fig. 9-7).

The area is then masked off as required (Fig. 9-8); a vinyl conditioner (Fig. 9-7) or other product as shown in Fig. 9-9 (check Table 9-3) is used to clean the material again. It should be applied with a rag and with strokes moving in one direction. This material is dried off the same way after 30 to 60 seconds to remove the contaminants. Use a lint-free cloth. When dry, it should

TABLE 9–4

Plastic refinishing systems for exterior use

Symbol	Plastic	Primer	Topcoat
ABS	Acrylonitrile/butadiene/styrene	P2A43-P2N44	A/L
		E2R34-E2A35	A/E
		E2R27-E2A28	CA/E
CPE	Chlorinated polyethylene epoxy	P3C24	A/L, A/E, CA/E
		P2A43-P2N44	A/L
		E2R34-E2A35	A/E
		E2R27-E2A28	CA/E
E/P EPM	TPO, TPR (thermoplastic rubber)	P3C24	A/L plus V2V297
			CA/E
EP DM	Ethylene /propylene diene monomer	P3C24	A/L plus V2V297
			CA/E
E/VAC	Ethylene/vinyl acetate	None	A/L plus V2V297
			CA/E
MF	Melamine	P2A43-P2N44	A/L
		E2R34-E2A35	A/E
		E2R27/E2A28	CA/E
PF	Phenolic	P2A43-P2N44	A/L
		E2R34-E2A35	A/E
		E2R27-E2A28	CA/E
PA	Nylon	P2A43-P2N44	A/L
		E2R34-E2A35	A/E
		E2R27-E2A28	CA/E
UP	Polyester thermoset	P2A43-P2N44	A/L
		E2R34-E2A35	A/E
		E2R27-E2A28	CA/E
PE	Polyethylene	P3C24	A/L, CA/E, or V2V297 plus A/L
PPYO, PPO	Noryl	P2A43-P2N44	A/L
		E2R34-E2A35	A/E
		E2R27-E2A28	CA/E
PP	Polypropylene	P3C24	A/L, CA/E, or V2V297 plus A/L
TPUR (TPU)	Polyurethane, thermoplastic	None	A/L plus V2V297
	If factory primed:	None	CA/E
	If unprimed:	E2G973-R7K242	CA/E
PUR	Polyurethane, thermoset	None	A/L plus V2V297
	If factory primed:	None	CA/E
	If unprimed:	E2G973-R7K242	CA/E
PVC	Vinyl	None	Vinyl color
SAN	Styrene acrylonitrile	P2A43-P2N44	A/L
		E2 R34-E2A35	A/E
		E2R27-E2A28	CA/E
UP	Urea formaldehyde	P2A43-P2N44	A/L
		E2R34-E2A35	A/E
		E2R27-E2A28	CA/E

Source: Sherwin-Williams Canada Ltd.

- Use flexible additive V2V297 in lacquer for flexible plastics.
- Use V6V241 or V6V247 Polasol in acrylic enamel for flexible plastics.
- A/L is acrylic lacquer.
- A/E is acrylic enamel.
- CA/E is catalyzed acrylic enamel.
- P2A43-P2N44 are acrylic-type primer-surfacers.
- V2V297 is a flexible additive for acrylic lacquer.
- E2R34-E2A35 are acrylic enamel primer-sealers.
- E2G973-R7K242 are vinyl wash primers for unprimed plastic.
- P3C24 is polyolefin in plastic primer and is recommended for limited automotive exterior plastic types where no other primer will gain adequate adhesion. The use of P3C24 for wider exterior applications must have laboratory approval.

FIGURE 9-7 Ditzler material for painting a vinyl or vinyl top.

be tacked off to remove any dirt particles still remaining on the surface of the fabric.

There are many manufacturers of the material that is used to recoat vinyl surfaces, such as vinyl tops. Each manufacturer recommends techniques that can be slightly different from one another. Therefore, before ordering the material for topcoating, check the trim code on the plate on the vehicle (Fig. 9-10). Then check for the code in a paint-chip book for interior colors to identify the color required (Fig. 9-11).

The color is ordered and directions for application should be checked; the material is stirred and strained when poured into the gun cup. If the material requires thinning, it should be done as recommended with a good-quality acrylic lacquer thinner. One thin coat is then applied to the vinyl surface and allowed to flash off as required, usually 10 to 15 minutes. Before applying the second coat, the adhesion of the first coat should

FIGURE 9-8 Masked vehicle ready for painting vinyl-top fabric.

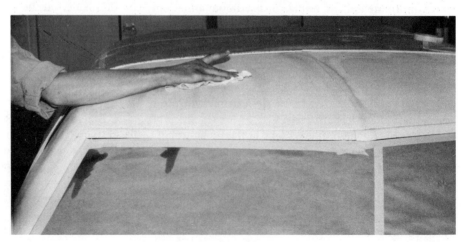

FIGURE 9-9 Using cleaning solvents.

FIGURE 9-10   Checking trim code.

be checked. This material has a high-hide capacity, and usually only one more coat need be applied to hide completely. When dry to the touch, all masking paper may be removed (Fig. 9-12).

Too many coats of this material may vary the color when trying to match factory colors. The material is applied with the spray gun using a pressure of 20 to 30 psi (135 to 200 kPa) at the gun (Fig. 9-13). When used under normal temperatures and conditions and on any surface that this material is made for, the color coat requires approximately 48 hours for maximum adhesion.

9-2 TROUBLESHOOTING AND PAINT FAILURES

The purpose of this section is to acquaint the new painter with paint failures so that he or she can recognize the causes and correct them.

Cracking. Fine minute cracks in the finish usually only appear on the surface of the paint film. This condition is generally caused by too heavy a film of lacquer topcoat or by sudden temperature changes. The surface has to be sanded and refinished (Fig. 9-14).

Shrinking and splitting. This condition is caused by the contraction and cracking of the material. Shrink-

ing and splitting is caused by applying material in heavy coats or by insufficient dry time between coats. The putty must be removed in the affected area and applied as directed (Fig. 9-15).

Blistering. This condition is caused by oil or moisture in spray lines or temperature variations between shop materials and surface to be painted or by high humidity conditions. To repair the area, remove the blisters and sand down to the metal. Treat the metal, prime, and topcoat (Fig. 9-16).

Cratering and crawling. Surface blemishes in a freshly painted surface where the paint has receded from small areas are usually found in the form of small round patches. This condition is caused by oil or moisture in spray lines or silicone contamination from products used in some surface operations. To repair on freshly painted surfaces, wash off with solvent, clean thoroughly, and repaint. If the surface dries before the condition is noted, sand and refinish damaged areas (Fig. 9-17).

Fisheyes. Small craters on the finished surface, sometimes as large as a dime and circled by a noticeable ring, are caused by silicone contamination on the surface. To repair, wash off while the paint is still wet; clean thoroughly and repaint (Fig. 9-18).

Pinholing. Breaks in a dry paint film no larger than the head of a pin, exposing the surface underneath, are caused by oil or moisture in equipment or material applied to a cold surface or by using too fast an evaporating solvent, causing surface dry or incorrect reduction. To repair, sand the damaged area and refinish (Fig. 9-19).

Runs and sags. A paint film that has drooped under its own weight and displays a thick edge or wrinkle at the lower part is caused by too heavy an application of paint or the paint reduced too much. To repair, wash off with solvent before the material dries and repaint. Should the surface dry, sand and refinish (Fig. 9-20).

Wrinkling. The buckling of a paint film at its surface causes a shriveled appearance; it occurs when the film is dry on the surface but remains soft underneath. This is caused by applying material in heavy coats, particularly in hot, humid weather, or by not adding retarder before force drying. To repair, allow to dry thoroughly, sand affected areas to remove surface wrinkles, and refinish (Fig. 9-21).

Sand-scratch swelling. Sand-scratch swelling is an exaggerated reproduction of sanding marks in the underlying finish of the new topcoat. The marks are distorted or swollen and usually occur over the original finish. They rarely appear on primed areas. They are caused by solvent penetration into the underlying surface, improper cleaning, using too coarse a grade of sandpaper, or using gasoline for wet sanding. To repair, allow to cure thoroughly and wet-sand with No. 400

DU PONT
CANADA
PAGE 1 OF 2 DE

PASSENGER CAR INTERIOR COLOURS
COULEURS D'INTÉRIEURS D'AUTOMOBILES **1986**

AMERICAN MOTORS

| 83P11/P27 LG/MG
GARNET/GRENAT
D8342 D8343 | 83P66 LG
BLACK/NOIR
99 | 84P6/P7 LG/MG
HONEY/MIEL
D8528 C8476 | 85P4 MG
BLUE/BLEU
D8530 | 86P3 LG
PEWTER/ÉTAIN
C8627 | 86P4 LG
TAN/TAN
C8626 |

LL - Windshield Frames, Instrument Panels, Steering Columns, and all plastic parts.
SG - Centrepost, Quarter Post, Window Mouldings, Jeep Tail Gate.

LL - Châssis de pare-brise, panneaux de bord, colonnes de direction, et toutes les pièces en plastique.
SG - Montant central, montant de custode, moulures de fenêtre, hayon de Jeep.

CHRYSLER

| AA3 SG
SILVER/ARGENT
C8247 | AA7 SG
DK.SILVER/ARGENT FONCÉ
C8248 | BB5 SG
BLUE/BLEU
C8318 | BT8 SG
BROWN/BRUN
C8317 | CS8 SG
CHARCOAL/CHARBON
C8439 | DX9 LL
BLACK/NOIR
44219 |

| EE8 SG
CORDOVAN/COURDOUAN
C8639 | EK1 SG
ALMOND/AMANDE
C8636 | EK3 SG
ALMOND/AMANDE
C8637 | FC5 SG
BLUE/BLEU
C8638 | SC9 LL
DK.BLUE/BLEU FONCÉ
45755 | TM6 LL
RED/ROUGE
C8094 |

FORD

| A (MJ 1724H) SG
BLACK/NOIR
99 | A (MJ 4149H) SG
BLACK/NOIR
D8302 | A (MJ 4172H) SG
BLACK/NOIR
D8501 | B (MJ 4153H) SG/F
BLUE/BLEU
D8310 D8504 | B (MJ 4177H) SG/F
BLUE/BLEU
D8502 D8503 |

| B (MJ 4184H) SG
BLUE/BLEU
C8605 | D (MJ 4158H) SG/F
RED/ROUGE
C8428 D8524 | D (MJ 4162H) F
RED/ROUGE
D8506 | F (MJ 4182H) SG
TAUPE/TAUPE
C8611 | F (MJ 4188H) SG/F
TAUPE/TAUPE
C8609 C8610 | P (MJ 4148H) SG/F
CHARCOAL/CHARBON
D8306 D8510 |

| P (MJ 4179H) SG/F
SMOKE/FUMÉE
D8541 D8542 | P (MJ 4163H) SG
WHITE/BLANC
C8432 | T (MJ 4175H) SG/F
BEIGE/BEIGE
D8511 D8512 | T (MJ 4178H) SG/F
BEIGE/BEIGE
C8606 D8572 | Z (MJ 4176H) SG/F
SABLE/ZIBELINE
D8515 D8516 |

Abbreviation Key/Légende: LL-Low Lustre/Faible lustre   SG-Semi-Gloss/Semi-brillant   F-Flat/Mat
Colour chips reproduced on paper cannot be considered fully accurate matches to either car maker standards or Du Pont material.
Les échantillons de couleurs sur papier ne s'harmonisent pas exactement avec les standards des fabricants de voitures ou les produits de Du Pont.

FIGURE 9–11 Interior trim color chips.

DUPONT
CANADA
PAGE 2 OF 2
DE

PASSENGER CAR INTERIOR COLOURS
COULEURS D'INTÉRIEURS D'AUTOMOBILES 1986

GENERAL MOTORS

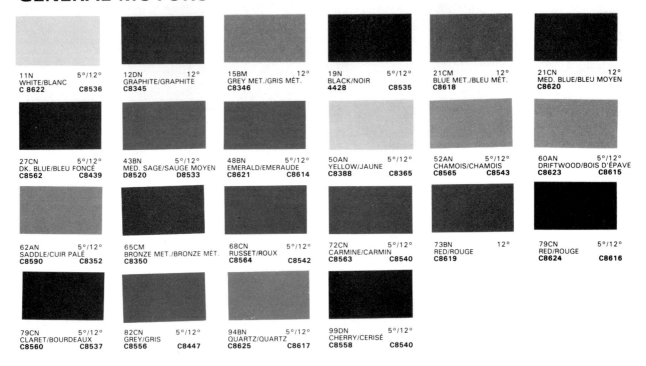

11N 5°/12°	12DN 12°	15BM 12°	19N 5°/12°	21CM 12°	21CN 12°
WHITE/BLANC	GRAPHITE/GRAPHITE	GREY MET./GRIS MÉT.	BLACK/NOIR	BLUE MET./BLEU MÉT.	MED. BLUE/BLEU MOYEN
C 8622 C8536	C8345	C8346	4428 C8535	C8618	C8620

27CN 5°/12°	43BN 5°/12°	48BN 5°/12°	50AN 5°/12°	52AN 5°/12°	60AN 5°/12°
DK. BLUE/BLEU FONCÉ	MED. SAGE/SAUGE MOYEN	EMERALD/EMERAUDE	YELLOW/JAUNE	CHAMOIS/CHAMOIS	DRIFTWOOD/BOIS D'ÉPAVE
C8562 C8439	D8520 D8533	C8621 C8614	C8388 C8365	C8565 C8543	C8623 C8615

62AN 5°/12°	65CM	68CN 5°/12°	72CN 5°/12°	73BN 12°	79CN 5°/12°
SADDLE/CUIR PALÉ	BRONZE MET./BRONZE MÉT.	RUSSET/ROUX	CARMINE/CARMIN	RED/ROUGE	RED/ROUGE
C8590 C8352	C8350	C8564 C8542	C8563 C8540	C8619	C8624 C8616

79CN 5°/12°	82CN 5°/12°	94BN 5°/12°	99DN 5°/12°
CLARET/BOURDEAUX	GREY/GRIS	QUARTZ/QUARTZ	CHERRY/CERISÉ
C8560 C8537	C8556 C8447	C8625 C8617	C8558 C8540

Abbreviation Key/Légende: LL-Low Lustre/Faible lustre   SG-Semi-Gloss/Semi-brillant   F-Flat/Mat
Colour chips reproduced on paper cannot be considered fully accurate matches to either car maker standards or Du Pont material.
Les échantillons de couleurs sur papier ne s'harmonisent pas exactement avec les standards des fabricants de voitures ou les produits de Du Pont.

FIGURE 9-11   (*Continued*)

FIGURE 9-12 Spraying the paint to the surface.

FIGURE 9-13 Vehicle with vinyl top unmasked after paint has dried.

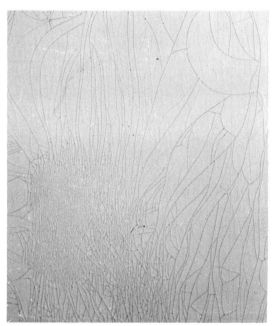

FIGURE 9-14 Cracking: fine, minute cracks. (*Courtesy of CIL of Canada Ltd.*)

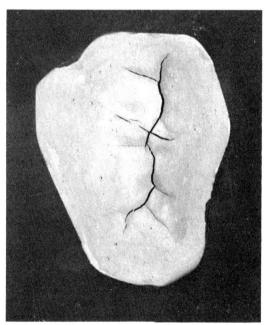

FIGURE 9-15 Shrinking and splitting of putty. (*Courtesy of CIL of Canada Ltd.*)

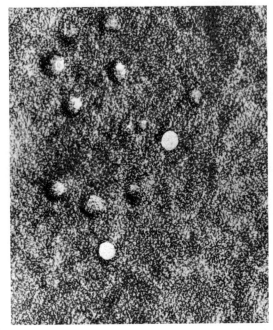

FIGURE 9-16   Blistering. (*Courtesy of CIL of Canada Ltd.*)

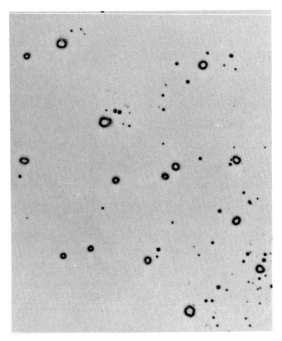

FIGURE 9-18   Fisheyes. (*Courtesy of CIL of Canada Ltd.*)

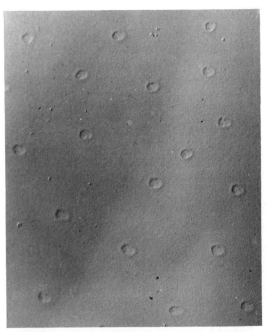

FIGURE 9-17   Cratering and crawling. (*Courtesy of CIL of Canada Ltd.*)

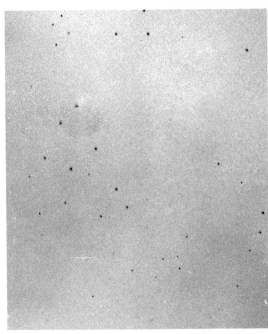

FIGURE 9-19   Pinholing. (*Courtesy of CIL of Canada Ltd.*)

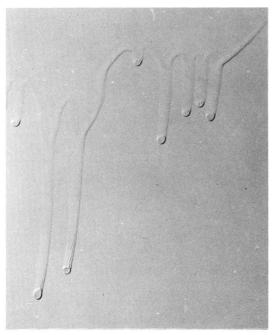

FIGURE 9-20 Runs and sags. (*Courtesy of CIL of Canada Ltd.*)

FIGURE 9-21 Wrinkling. (*Courtesy of CIL of Canada Ltd.*)

FIGURE 9-22 Sand-scratch swelling. (*Courtesy of CIL of Canada Ltd.*)

(P 800) paper. Apply one or two wet coats of sealer and respray with topcoat (Fig. 9–22).

Rub through. Burning of lacquer finishes through the primer during the compounding operation is caused by not applying enough material to allow proper compounding or excessive rubbing and compounding. To repair, sand the affected areas and repaint (Fig. 9–23).

Bleeding. Bleeding is the migration of soluble dyes or pigments from an old finish into a newly applied finish as a result of solvent action. This condition is caused by failing to test the old surface to determine if it is a bleeding color. To repair, use of a bleeder sealer will sometimes be sufficient to overcome the problem. In most cases, however, it is necessary to remove the paint in the affected area and resume refinishing procedures (Fig. 9–24).

Hand or finger prints. Hand or finger marks appearing in the finish are caused by touching or wiping the surface with bare hands prior to finishing. Avoid contacting the surface once it has been prepared for painting. To repair, remove the finish and repaint (Fig. 9–25).

Rain or water spotting. Small circular imprints in the finish that are low in gloss are caused by premature exposure of the freshly painted vehicle to rain or sunshine or washing the vehicle too soon after applying paint. To repair, allow to dry, wet sand, and refinish (Fig. 9–26).

Corrosion. Corrosion on metal surfaces is caused by improper cleaning and treatment of metal, by touch-

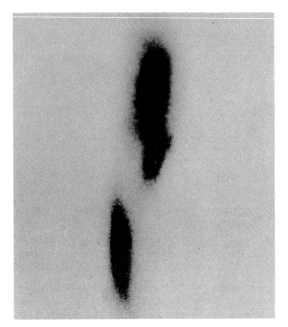

FIGURE 9-23 Rub-through. (*Courtesy of CIL of Canada Ltd.*)

FIGURE 9-25 Hand or finger prints. (*Courtesy of CIL of Canada, Ltd.*)

FIGURE 9-24 Bleeding. (*Courtesy of CIL of Canada Ltd.*)

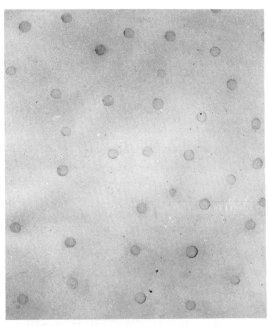

FIGURE 9-26 Rain or water spotting. (*Courtesy of CIL of Canada, Ltd.*)

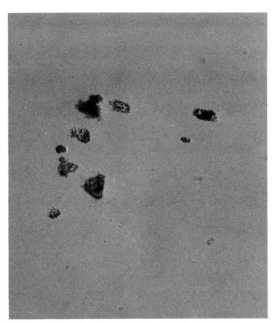

FIGURE 9-27 Corrosion (rust). (*Courtesy of CIL of Canada Ltd.*)

9-3 ADHESIVE-BACKED MOLDINGS

Most body side moldings are bonded with a urethane and hot melt adhesive system to the body panels. But some body side moldings are attached with foam or butyl adhesive tape to the body panels. Frequently, because of accidents, the adhesive-backed moldings on some panels have to be removed, repaired, or replaced with new moldings if they are damaged. If it is not damaged, the two-sided adhesive tape must be removed from the molding and the adhesive must be cleaned thoroughly with naptha or other nonoily solvent. Once the molding is dry, the two-sided tape is then applied to the back of the molding. Care must be taken not to touch the adhesive side or get any dirt on it. The protective film on the tape should not be removed until it is time to install the molding on the vehicle.

To ensure a quality repair or installation with new or old moldings, the panel surface should be between 70° and 90°F (21° and 32°C). The panels on which the moldings are to be applied must be free and clean of any wax or oil film. Therefore, the affected areas should be washed with detergent and water, wiped completely dry, and then wiped with oil-free naphtha or alcohol.

When moldings are to be installed on a vehicle on which there are no moldings, the repairperson must decide where the moldings should be installed. Figures 9-28 and 9-29 give different examples of where the trim moldings can be installed. The trim moldings are usually applied to the widest points on the contour of the car.

ing metal with bare hands after cleaning, or by moisture and chemicals attacking the metal through breaks in the film. This results in subsequent blistering or peeling. To repair, remove paint to the bare metal, clean thoroughly, and repaint. For more information, check a refinisher's manual (Fig. 9-27).

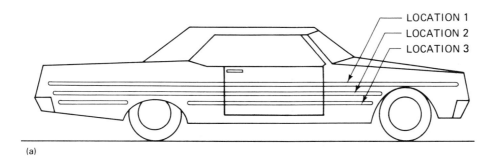

(a)

(b)

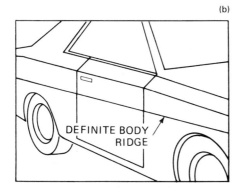

FIGURE 9-28 (a) Prepared location for molding. (b) Installing molding on a definite body ridge.

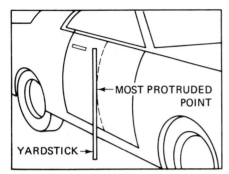

FIGURE 9-29 Installing molding on the most protuding point.

FIGURE 9-31 Cutting molding at a 45° angle at panel edge where required.

plied in a straight line. Then, using a soft cloth, the repairperson applies heavy pressure along the entire length of the molding (Fig. 9-33). The car should not be washed for one week so that the tape will set properly.

9-4 WOOD GRAIN TRANSFERS

Wood grain transfers have become popular on many types of vehicles. They have a semigloss finish, are made of vinyl, and are designed to adhere to an acrylic painted surface because they have a pressure-sensitive adhesive on the back.

Replacement transfers are available through the appropriate automobile dealers. In ordering transfers, it is important to state not only the make but also the style and the applicable panel. The transfers are usually sold in rolls that are long enough to cover a certain portion of the vehicle.

When a transfer has to be replaced because it has been damaged, all the parts affected and the adjacent panels and openings must be washed. In addition, all the moldings, clips, handles, side marker lamps, etc., and/or overlapping parts must be washed. A pointed or sharp instrument should never be used during transfer removal because it could gouge the underlying paint finish.

A heat gun facilitates the removal of the transfer because it softens the adhesive and the vinyl. The removal operation should be started at an edge by peeling back the transfer as a sheet from the surface of the panel. Too much force should not be used. Gradually heating the areas to be removed makes it easier to peel the transfer in most cases (Fig. 9-34).

In reinstalling a transfer, care must be taken so that the panel is clean and free from imperfections. If

If the car has a ridge, the trim molding is applied either directly below or above but never on this ridge. When an automobile has a ridge or styling line on the side panels that does not form a straight line, but sweeps up toward the rear and front over the wheel openings, the installation can be carried out as in Fig. 9-28. In other cases, the trim moldings can be installed on the most protruded points as in Fig. 9-29.

A yardstick and a felt pen or a piece of masking tape are used to mark the location where the trim molding is to be installed. Care must be taken to ensure that the molding is applied level to the ground surface. A length of masking tape can be applied in a straight line from the front to the back of the vehicle on the side panels either directly below or above where the molding is to be applied (Fig. 9-30).

Starting with either the front or back fender, the proper length required for the panel is cut. Care is taken to keep the tips at least 3 in. (80 mm) from the front or rear edge of the car. The required length is cut with a single-edge razor blade. The section at the doors should be cut at a 45° angle where required so that the door will open freely (Fig. 9-31).

The release liner or protective film is peeled off for approximately 6 in. (150 mm). Starting at the door edge opening, the repairperson lightly tacks on the trim molding along the guideline (Fig. 9-32). The other panels are all done the same way.

The trim is then checked to see if it has been ap-

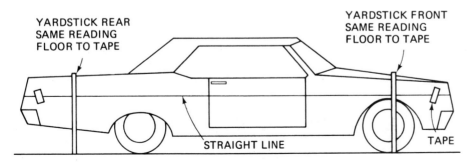

FIGURE 9-30 Measuring for height of molding.

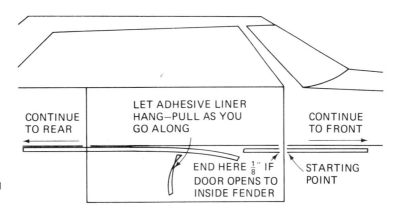

FIGURE 9-32 Installing molding on panel.

FIGURE 9-33 Rubbing molding with cloth to apply pressure so that adhesive sticks.

the panel has been repainted, it should be allowed to dry thoroughly. Solvents remaining in a fresh paint film can lead to subsequent blistering. Acrylic painted surfaces should be scuff-sanded with No. 320 (P400) or 400 (P800).

Acrylic painted surfaces should be cleaned by us-

FIGURE 9-34 Removing transfer with heat.

ing a good grade of dewaxing solvent. The surface is wiped with a cloth dampened with solvent and then with a dry, clean, absorbent cloth. The surface is allowed to dry, and then compressed air can be used to blow any dirt away from the affected area of repair.

The transfer is prepared for installation by first making a template as follows: Tack tape a suitable sheet of paper to the outer panel. Align it with the centers of the horizontal molding attaching clip holes. Following this line, the template can be marked and cut to the right size. With the template flush to the panel, mark the front, rear, and bottom edges of the panel on the template. On styles on which "planking" grain is used or on which lines run the whole length of the vehicle, the chaining or planking must be marked on the template.

Put the template on a table and draw another line of the front, rear, and bottom panel edges approximately ⅝ to ¾ in. (16 mm to 19 mm) from the panel edges. Trim the excess paper from the marked edges by cutting it with scissors. Mark the front of the template also on the underside of the template.

Unroll the service transfer and position it on a table with the backing paper on top and with the outer wood grain pattern running from left to right.

Position the prepared template on the service transfer and mark the perimeter cut lines on the backing of the service transfer. On styles that use planking grain or lines, mark the upper one, too. Make sure that the inner side of the template is up and that the wood grain pattern runs from left to right before marking the trim line on the service transfer. Then, following the marked lines, cut out the transfer.

Position the transfer on the repair panel and mark the center of the transfer and panel for proper vertical and lateral alignment (Fig. 9-35). Peel the paper backing from the transfer and lay the transfer face down on a clean table. Using a clean sponge, apply an ample wetting solution made of water and liquid detergent to the transfer adhesive and to the repair panel surface.

Center the transfer and align it with the center

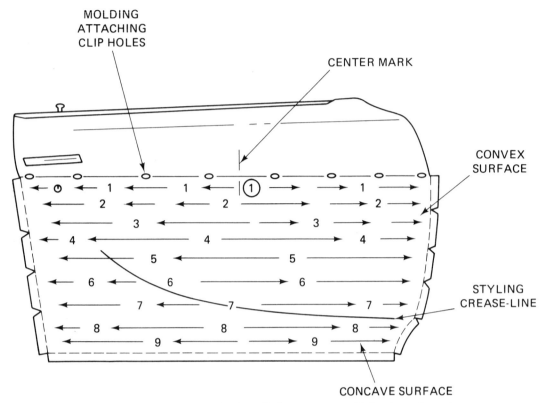

FIGURE 9-35   Transfer installation sequence (right door shown).

mark and the center of the horizontal molding clip holes. Press down lightly across the top. On styles using planking grain or lines, make certain that the upper plank lines or grain lines align with the lines on the adjacent panels. Use a squeegee on the center of the transfer. Press firmly at the center for a distance 3 to 4 in. (76 to 102 mm). Then squeegee upward over the same spot.

Raise one side of the transfer from the panel up to the secured spot at the center. Position the transfer close to the panel along the clip attaching holes. Working from the center, squeegee the transfer into place. Use firm, short, overlapping strokes. First squeegee laterally with overlapping strokes and then work horizontally across the top. Finish securing the opposite upper edge of the transfer the same way.

With one hand, lift the unsecured lower area of the transfer from the panel. If the transfer sticks prematurely, break the bond with a fast, firm pull. Position the transfer close to the panel at the center and squeegee at the center and downward approximately 2 in. (51 mm) and then laterally over the same area. Repeat this operation by working toward each end of the panel. Bonding of the transfer is made by means of firm overlapping strokes (Fig. 9–35).

It may be necessary to apply the wetting solution periodically to the panel to facilitate raising and positioning the transfer during squeegee operations. Con-

tinue progressively downward in small increments completely across the transfer until the bottom is reached. Cut 90° notches in the transfer edges as needed in the lower corners and cut V notches in the transfer sides where necessary.

Apply a light coating of vinyl trim adhesive to the door hem flanges or any surface that is covered at the back with transfer material. Do not use excessive amounts of adhesive. Heat the inboard side of the door hem flanges and transfer and then fold them over as required on the hem flanges. Apply pressure as required to the transfer and hem flanges. Do not pull or stretch more than necessary because tearing could result.

FIGURE 9-36   Applying heat to transfer.

FIGURE 9-37 Cutting excess transfer.

Apply heat to the transfer at the door handle holes or any other depression. Press firmly into these areas in order to obtain a good bond (Fig. 9–36). Using a sharp knife or razor blade, cut out the excess at the door handles or marker light holes or any other opening (Fig. 9–37).

Inspect the transfer from a critical angle. Use adequate light reflections to detect irregularities that may have developed during installation. Remove any air or moisture bubbles by piercing each bubble at an acute angle with a fine needle and then press the bubble down. Install all previously removed parts and clean the car.

9-5 STRIPING TAPE

For many years, stripes were applied on vehicles by a specialist using a specially designed paint brush and paint. Today methods such as tape with pull-out inserts are used to apply stripes with paint in some shops. Another type of tape is 3M Custom Striping Tape. This tape comes in a multitude of sizes (Fig. 9–38), lengths, and colors and is used on vehicles to beautify them. To apply this striping tape on vehicles that have been waxed, the vehicle must be totally degreased where the striping tape will be installed on the vehicle so that the tape will adhere properly. On new paint jobs, the striping tape may be installed as soon as the paint is dry enough; this method will result in excellent adherence.

Striping tapes are also used to separate two different colors on vehicles, such as in Fig. 9–39, which shows the tape being applied to the edge of the two-tone of the paint area. The paper strip on the back of the striping tape, which protects the adhesive, is partially removed; then the tape is applied to the designated area and only a slight pressure is applied to it. Notice the tape backing drooping downward in Fig. 9–39 as the striping tape is aligned to the paint edge; the straightness of the

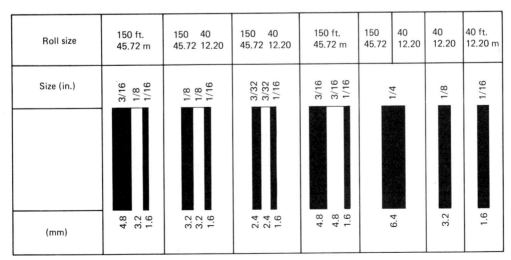

Roll size	150 ft. 45.72 m			150 40 45.72 12.20			150 40 45.72 12.20			150 ft. 45.72 m			150 45.72	40 12.20	40 12.20	40 ft. 12.20 m
Size (in.)	3/16	1/8	1/16	1/8	1/8	1/16	3/32	3/32	1/16	3/16	3/16	1/16	1/4	1/8	1/16	
(mm)	4.8	3.2	1.6	3.2	3.2	1.6	2.4	2.4	1.6	4.8	4.8	1.6	6.4	3.2	1.6	

FIGURE 9-38 Different sizes of striping tape.

FIGURE 9-39 Installing striping tape on edge of two-tone paint job.

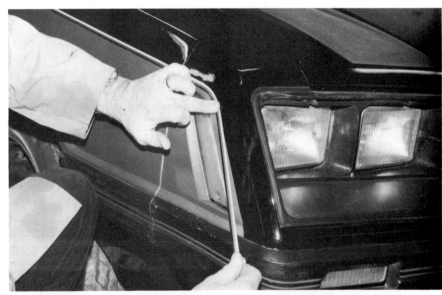

FIGURE 9-40 Stretching striping tape to follow paint line.

FIGURE 9-41 Removing clear plastic film on striping tape.

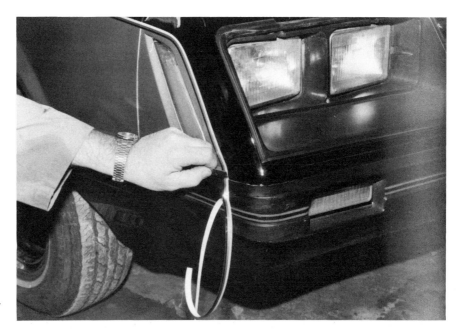

FIGURE 9-42 Cutting the striping tape.

FIGURE 9-43 Accent stripe being installed where it is stetched to form a gentle curve (Fig. 9-44).

FIGURE 9-44 Striping tape stretched to form a curve and cut to form a sharp point.

tape is checked by eye by following the styling line distance from the tape. The tape is applied on the front fender and, by carefully applying sufficient pressure to the tape with a finger, it is stretched gently to follow the curve (Fig. 9–40).

Usually one panel is done at one time and enough tape is left so that it can be rolled to the back of the panel for extra adherence to the panel. Once it is on the proper place, the plastic clear layer on the stripe should be rubbed with a soft cloth to increase adherence to the panel. Once this is done, the clear plastic layer on the stripes is lifted up gently, usually by using a sharp tool; then it is pulled off gently (Fig. 9–41). Once it is off, the ends of the tape, if on a door panel, are rolled back toward the inside for extra holding strength. When used on a fender, as in Fig. 9–42, the striping tape is brought to the flexible bumper fascia and cut with a sharp instrument such as a razor blade or Exacto knife. Care must be taken not to penetrate the paint film. Different companies sell different shapes of ends that can be installed at the end of the stripe, but most are installed on the vehicle as an accent color (Fig. 9–43). This stripe is installed in the same way except it will follow a styling edge from a certain distance and then curve up in the area behind the quarter-window. Once it has been installed properly except for the upper end on the quarter-panel, the colored stripes are separated from the clear layer and brought gently together, one on top of the other, to form a spear shape. The striping tape is cut on both sides very carefully, and this leaves a very neat end on the striped area (Fig. 9–44).

REVIEW QUESTIONS

9-1. Identify and explain the tests a painter may have to do to identify different types of plastics.

9-2. What is used to paint ABS type of plastics?

9-3. What material may be used to paint flexible parts besides a flex agent and acrylic lacquer?

9-4. What is used to paint a thermoplastic rubber?

9-5. What method is used to clean the vinyl fabric on a roof panel before topcoating?

9-6. Where is the trim code found for the color of the fabric top?

9-7. What causes a paint to blister?

9-8. What causes fisheyes in a paint film?

9-9. What causes sand-scratch swelling in a paint film?

9-10. What causes rain or water spotting in a paint film?

9-11. Describe how trim moldings are installed on vehicles that do not have any moldings.

9-12. With what material is an area cleaned before the molding can be reinstalled?

9-13. From what are wood grain transfers made?

9-14. Describe how wood grain transfers are installed on a panel.

9-15. Describe how striping tape is installed on a vehicle.

Conversion Tables

METRIC TABLES

Linear	One METER (m) : 10 decimeter (dm) : 100 centimeter (cm) : 1000 millimeters (mm)
	1000 meters : One kilometer (km)
Square	One SQUARE METER (m^2) : 100 square decimeters (dm^2) : 10,000 square centimeters (cm^2) : 1,000,000 square millimeters (mm^2)
Cubic	One CUBIC METER (m^3) : 1000 cubic decimeters (dm^3) : 1,000,000 cubic centimeters (cm^3)
Capacity	One LITER (l) : 10 deciliters (dl) : 1000 centiliters (cl)
	100 liters : One hectoliter (hl)
Weight	One KILOGRAM (kg) : 100 decagrams (dkg) : 1000 grams (g)
	100 kilograms : One metric cent (q)
	1000 kilograms : One ton (t)
Pressure	KILOGRAM PER SQUARE CENTIMETER (kg/cm^2)
	One kilogram per square centimeter : One ATMOSPHERE (atm)
Temperature	CENTIGRADE degree (°C) : CELSIUS degree (°C)

CONVERSION TABLE
INCH FRACTIONS AND DECIMALS TO METRIC EQUIVALENTS

INCHES Fractions	INCHES Decimals	m m	INCHES Fractions	INCHES Decimals	m m	INCHES Fractions	INCHES Decimals	m m
-	.0004	.01	-	.4331	11	31/32	.96875	24.606
-	.004	.10	7/16	.4375	11.113	-	.9843	25
-	.01	.25	29/64	.4531	11.509	1	1.000	25.4
1/64	.0156	.397	15/32	.46875	11.906	-	1.0236	26
-	.0197	.50	-	.4724	12	1 1/32	1.0312	26.194
-	.0295	.75	31/64	.48437	12.303	1 1/16	1.062	26.988
1/32	.03125	.794	-	.492	12.5	-	1.063	27
-	.0394	1	1/2	.500	12.700	1 3/32	1.094	27.781
3/64	.0469	1.191	-	.5118	13	-	1.1024	28
-	.059	1.5	33/64	.5156	13.097	1 1/8	1.125	28.575
1/16	.0625	1.588	17/32	.53125	13.494	-	1.1417	29
5/64	.0781	1.984	35/64	.54687	13.891	1 5/32	1.156	29.369
-	.0787	2	-	.5512	14	-	1.1811	30
3/32	.094	2.381	9/16	.5625	14.288	1 3/16	1.1875	30.163
-	.0984	2.5	-	.571	14.5	1 7/32	1.219	30.956
7/64	.1093	2.776	37/64	.57812	14.684	-	1.2205	31
-	.1181	3	-	.5906	15	1 1/4	1.250	31.750
1/8	.1250	3.175	19/32	.59375	15.081	-	1.2598	32
-	.1378	3.5	39/64	.60937	15.478	1 9/32	1.281	32.544
9/64	.1406	3.572	5/8	.6250	15.875	-	1.2992	33
5/32	.15625	3.969	-	.6299	16	1 5/16	1.312	33.338
-	.1575	4	41/64	.6406	16.272	-	1.3386	34
11/64	.17187	4.366	-	.6496	16.5	1 11/32	1.344	34.131
-	.177	4.5	21/32	.65625	16.669	1 3/8	1.375	34.925
3/16	.1875	4.763	-	.6693	17	-	1.3779	35
-	.1969	5	43/64	.67187	17.066	1 13/32	1.406	35.719
13/64	.2031	5.159	11/16	.6875	17.463	-	1.4173	36
-	.2165	5.5	45/64	.7031	17.859	1 7/16	1.438	36.513
7/32	.21875	5.556	-	.7087	18	-	1.4567	37
15/64	.23437	5.953	23/32	.71875	18.256	1 15/32	1.469	37.306
-	.2362	6	-	.7283	18.5	-	1.4961	38
1/4	.2500	6.350	47/64	.73437	18.653	1 1/2	1.500	38.100
-	.2559	6.5	-	.7480	19	1 17/32	1.531	38.894
17/64	.2656	6.747	3/4	.7500	19.050	-	1.5354	39
-	.2756	7	49/64	.7656	19.447	1 9/16	1.562	39.688
9/32	.28125	7.144	25/32	.78125	19.844	-	1.5748	40
-	.2953	7.5	-	.7874	20	1 19/32	1.594	40.481
19/64	.29687	7.541	51/64	.79687	20.241	-	1.6142	41
5/16	.3125	7.938	13/16	.8125	20.638	1 5/8	1.625	41.275
-	.3150	8	-	.8268	21	-	1.6535	42
21/64	.3281	8.334	53/64	.8281	21.034	1 21/32	1.6562	42.069
-	.335	8.5	27/32	.84375	21.431	1 11/16	1.6875	42.863
11/32	.34375	8.731	55/64	.85937	21.828	-	1.6929	43
-	.3543	9	-	.8662	22	1 23/32	1.719	43.656
23/64	.35937	9.128	7/8	.8750	22.225	-	1.7323	44
-	.374	9.5	57/64	.8906	22.622	1 3/4	1.750	44.450
3/8	.3750	9.525	-	.9055	23	-	1.7717	45
25/64	.3906	9.922	29/32	.90625	23.019	1 25/32	1.781	45.244
-	.3937	10	59/64	.92187	23.416	-	1.8110	46
13/32	.4062	10.319	15/16	.9375	23.813	1 13/16	1.8125	46.038
-	.413	10.5	-	.9449	24	1 27/32	1.844	46.831
27/64	.42187	10.716	61/64	.9531	24.209	-	1.8504	47

Millimeters

10 20 30 40 50 60 70 80 90 100 110 120 130 140 150

CONVERSION TABLE
INCH FRACTIONS AND DECIMALS TO METRIC EQUIVALENTS

INCHES Fractions	INCHES Decimals	m m	INCHES Fractions	INCHES Decimals	m m	INCHES Fractions	INCHES Decimals	m m
1 7/8	1.875	47.625	-	3.0709	78	-	4.7244	120
-	1.8898	48	-	3.1102	79	4 3/4	4.750	120.650
1 29/32	1.9062	48.419	3 1/8	3.125	79375	4 7/8	4.875	123.825
-	1.9291	49	-	3.1496	80	-	4.9212	125
1 15/16	1.9375	49.213	3 3/16	3.1875	80.963	5	5.000	127
-	1.9685	50	-	3.1890	81	-	5.1181	130
1 31/32	1.969	50.006	-	3.2283	82	5 1/4	5.250	133.350
2	2.000	50.800	3 1/4	3.250	82.550	5 1/2	5.500	139.700
-	2.0079	51	-	3.2677	83	-	5.5118	140
-	2.0472	52	-	3.3071	84	5 3/4	5.750	146.050
2 1/16	2.062	52.388	3 5/16	3.312	84.1377	-	5.9055	150
-	2.0866	53	-	3.3464	85	6	6.000	152.400
2 1/8	2.125	53.975	3 3/8	3.375	85.725	6 1/4	6.250	158.750
-	2.126	54	-	3.3858	86	-	6.2992	160
-	2.165	55	-	3.4252	87	6 1/2	6.500	165.100
2 3/16	2.1875	55.563	3 7/16	3.438	87.313	-	6.6929	170
-	2.2047	56	-	3.4646	88	6 3/4	6.750	171.450
-	2.244	57	3 1/2	3.500	88.900	7	7.000	177.800
2 1/4	2.250	57.150	-	3.5039	89	-	7.0866	180
-	2.2835	58	-	3.5433	90	-	7.4803	190
2 5/16	2.312	58.738	3 9/16	3.562	90.4877	7 1/2	7.500	190.500
-	2.3228	59	-	3.5827	91	-	7.8740	200
-	2.3622	60	-	3.622	92	8	8.000	203.200
2 3/8	2.375	60.325	3 5/8	3.625	92.075	-	8.2677	210
-	2.4016	61	-	3.6614	93	8 1/2	8.500	215.900
2 7/16	2.438	61.913	3 11/16	3.6875	93.663	-	8.6614	220
-	2.4409	62	-	3.7008	94	9	9.000	228.600
-	2.4803	63	-	3.7401	95	-	9.0551	230
2 1/2	2.500	63.500	3 3/4	3.750	95.250	-	9.4488	240
-	2.5197	64	-	3.7795	96	9 1/2	9.500	241.300
-	2.559	65	3 13/16	3.8125	96.838	-	9.8425	250
2 9/16	2.562	65.088	-	3.8189	97	10	10.000	254.000
-	2.5984	66	-	3.8583	98	-	10.2362	260
2 5/8	2.625	66.675	3 7/8	3.875	98.425	-	10.6299	270
-	2.638	67	-	3.8976	99	11	11.000	279.400
-	2.6772	68	-	3.9370	100	-	11.0236	280
2 11/16	2.6875	68.263	3 15/16	3.9375	100.013	-	11.4173	290
-	2.7165	69	-	3.9764	101	-	11.8110	300
2 3/4	2.750	69.850	4	4.000	101.600	12	12.000	304.800
-	2.7559	70	4 1/16	4.062	103.188	13	13.000	330.200
-	2.7953	71	4 1/8	4.125	104.775	-	13.7795	350
2 13/16	2.8125	71.438	-	4.1338	105	14	14.000	355.600
-	2.8346	72	4 3/16	4.1875	106.363	15	15.000	381
-	2.8740	73	4 1/4	4.250	107.950	-	15.7480	400
2 7/8	2.875	73.025	4 5/16	4.312	109.538	16	16.000	406.400
-	2.9134	74	-	4.3307	110	17	17.000	431.800
2 15/16	2.9375	74.613	4 3/8	4.375	111.125	-	17.7165	450
-	2.9527	75	4 7/16	4.438	112.713	18	18.000	457.200
-	2.9921	76	4 1/2	4.500	114.300	19	19.000	482.600
3	3.000	76.200	-	4.5275	115	-	19.6850	500
-	3.0315	77	4 9/16	4.562	115.888	20	20.000	508
3 1/16	3.062	77.788	4 5/8	4.625	117.475	21	21.000	533.400

Millimeters

10   20   30   40   50   60   70   80   90   100   110   120   130   140   150

METRIC CONVERSION EQUIVALENTS

Linear Measure

Inch to Metric				Metric to Inch		
1 inch	25.400	millimeters		1 millimeter	0.0393700	inch
1 inch	2.540	centimeters		1 centimeter	0.393700	inch
1 foot	304.800	millimeters		1 meter	39.3700	inches
1 foot	30.480	centimeters		1 meter	3.2808	feet
1 foot	0.3048	meter		1 meter	1.0936	yards
1 yard	91.4400	centimeters		1 kilometer	0.62137	mile
1 yard	0.9144	meter				
1 mile	1,609.35	meters				
1 mile	1.609	kilometers				

Area

Square Inch to Metric			Metric to Square Inch		
1 square inch	645.16	square millimeters	1 square millimeter	0.00155	square inch
1 square inch	6.4516	square centimeters	1 square centimeter	0.1550	square inch
1 square foot	929.00	square centimeters	1 square meter	10.7640	square feet
1 square foot	0.0929	square meter	1 square meter	1.196	square yards
1 square yard	0.836	square meter	1 square kilometer	0.38614	square mile
1 square mile	2.5889	square kilometers			

Cubic Measure

Cubic Inch to Metric			Metric to Cubic Inch		
1 cubic inch	16.387	cubic centimeters	1 cubic centimeter	0.0610	cubic inch
1 cubic foot	0.02832	cubic meter	1 cubic meter	85.314	cubic feet
1 cubic yard	0.765	cubic meter	1 cubic meter	1.308	cubic yards

Capacity

Imperial to Metric			Metric to Imperial		
1 fluid ounce	28.413	milliliters	1 milliliter	0.035195	fluid ounce
1 fluid ounce	0.2841	liter	1 centiliter	0.35195	fluid ounce
1 pint	0.56826	liter	1 deciliter	3.5195	fluid ounces
1 quart	1.13652	liters	1 liter	0.88	quart
1 gallon	4.546	liters	1 hectoliter	21.9969	gallons

Weight

Avoirdupois to Metric			Metric to Avoirdupois		
1 grain	64.7989	milligrams	1 gram	15.432	grains
1 ounce	28.35	grams	1 dekagram	0.353	ounce
1 pound	0.4536	kilogram	1 kilogram	2.2046	pounds
1 short ton (2000 lbs.)	907.200	kilograms	1 metric cent	220.46	pounds
1 short ton (2000 lbs.)	9.072	metric cents	1 ton	2204.6	pounds
1 short ton (2000 lbs.)	0.9072	ton	1 ton	1.102	short tons

Glossary

Abrasive: Substance used to wear away a surface by friction.

Abrasive coating: In close-coat paper, the adhesive is completely coated with abrasive; in open-coat paper, the adhesive is partially exposed, for the abrasive is not put on the paper close together.

Acrylic resin: A synthetic resin that has excellent color retention and clarity and that is used in both lacquer and enamel.

Active solvent: An ingredient of lacquer thinners that is a solvent for nitrocellulose.

Additive: A chemical substance that is added to a paint finish in relatively small amounts to improve or impart desirable properties.

Adhesion: Sticking together of two surfaces, such as topcoat to primer and primer to metal.

Air drying: A lacquer or enamel is said to be air drying when it is capable of drying hard at ordinary room temperatures without the aid of artificial heat.

Alkyd: A synthetic resin used in the manufacture of enamel finishes and usually derived from natural oils.

Alligatoring: Lacquer or enamel films in which the finish has cracked into large segments resembling alligator hide. Similar to checking, crazing, and cracking.

Aluminum oxide: Sharp and hard abrasive that is made by fusing mineral bauxite at high temperatures.

Anticorrosive and inhibitor: Protective coating applied on metal surfaces to retard or prevent corrosion and said to be anticorrosive or corrosion inhibitive.

Atomize: The extent to which air at the gun nozzle breaks up the paint and solvents into fine particles.

Baking: Application of heat to cure and dry a coating. In the refinishing trade, baking is used to speed up the drying of air-drying lacquers and enamel and is sometimes called force drying. The metal temperature in refinish baking usually does not exceed 180°F (82.2°C).

Banding: A single coat of paint applied to frame in an area to be sprayed.

Binder: The portion of the paint that helps to bind the pigment together.

Bleeding: The action whereby the color of a stain or other material works up into succeeding coats and imparts a certain amount of color. This is characteristic of certain red pigments used in lacquer and enamels. A nonbleeding color is one that is not soluble in materials used over it and, consequently, does not work up into succeeding coats.

Blending: Mixing together of two or more materials or the gradual shading off from one color to another. See *Tint*.

Blistering: A bubbling up of the paint film in the form of small blisters.

Blushing: White or grayish cast that sometimes forms on a lacquer film as it dries, particularly under conditions of hot, humid weather.

Body filler: A heavy-bodied plastic material that is used to fill small dents in metal and dries very hard.

Bodying: Thickening in the package, usually due to evaporation of solvents or volatile material because of excessive heat during storage.

Boiling point: The temperature at which the vapor pressure of a liquid exceeds the atmospheric pressure and the liquid begins to boil.

Bridging: The ability of an enamel or lacquer to cover a crack, void, or other small gap.

Bronzing: The formation on the paint film of a metalliclike haze.

Buffing compound: A soft paste containing fine abrasive in a neutral medium, used to eliminate fine scratches and polish lacquer.

Build: The amount of paint deposited in a film thickness.

Burning: Condition resulting from rubbing a lacquer film too hard. The heat generated by the friction of the rubbing pad may soften the lacquer and cause it to stick to the pad, thus permanently marring the finish.

Caking: Gathering of sanding dust into solid cakes sticking to sandpaper. Compare *Gumming.*

Cast: The tendency of one color to look like another.

Catalyst: A substance that causes or speeds up a chemical reaction when it is mixed with another substance and that does not change by itself.

Chalking: The formation of soft white powder on the surface of a finish, which may be removed by friction of the finger or similar methods.

Checking: Small, irregular cracks going partly or completely through a paint film. Like alligatoring, only very fine cracking. Compare *Cracking* and *Crazing.*

Chemical staining: Spotty staining or discoloration of the paint film topcoat caused by atmospheric conditions (acid rain).

Chipping: The condition where the finish is flaking off or chipping away from the underneath surface.

Clean: The opposite of dirty. Describes a color with a bright appearance rather than one that has a drab appearance. The exclusion of black makes colors cleaner.

Clear: A coating of paint that has no color.

Closed-coat disc: A disc on which the abrasive grains are very densely spaced. Used in disc sanding and polishing repaired sheet metal.

Coat double: Two single coats applied one after the other with little or no flash-off time.

Coat single: A coat produced by two passes of a spray gun when one pass overlaps the other 50% or by half-steps.

Cold cracking: Cracking of a paint job resulting from a sudden drop of temperature.

Color retention: A paint of a certain color, when it is exposed to the elements and does not change, is said to have good color retention.

Compatibility: The ability of two or more materials to blend into a homogeneous mixture and, upon drying, a homogeneous film.

Compounding: The use of an abrasive either by hand or machine to smooth out and bring up the gloss of an applied lacquer topcoat.

Compressor: A machine used to compress air from atmospheric pressure to a high pressure.

Cone mandrel: Special attachment used with an abrasive cone in sanding hard to get at concave surfaces around headlights, fender flanges, and trim moldings.

Connectors: Attachments used in coupling two or more extension tubes together or to various tools.

Contaminants: Any polish, wax, tree sap, tar, and the like that would damage the paint film or spoil the adhesion of a new paint film.

Conversion coating: Part of a metal treatment system that modifies a metal substrate to increase adhesion and corrosion protection.

Corrosion: The chemical reaction of air, moisture, or corrosive materials on a metal surface. Usually referred to as rusting or oxidation.

Coverage: (1) The quality some colors have to cover other colors and (2) the area a certain quantity of paint will cover.

Cracking: Crevices or ruptures going completely through a film. This is in contrast to alligatoring or checking, where crevices slowly work their way down from the surface.

Cratering: Surface blemishes in a freshly painted surface, usually in the form of small round patches.

Crawling: The action of a finishing material when it appears to creep or crawl away from certain spots and leaves them uncoated.

Crazing: Very fine minute cracks on the surface that are usually interlaced.

Cross coat: See *Double head coat.*

Curing: The final drying stage when a paint film reaches its full strength because of a chemical change.

Cut: Applied to surface coating, it denotes both the dissolving of solid material in a solvent and the reducing of the viscosity of liquid by the addition of a thinner. Can also refer to the sanding down of a film, as in "cut and polish."

Darken: By eliminating white, solid colors become darker; eliminating metallic flake makes metallic colors darker.

Dilutants: Volatile liquids that are not solvents for nitrocellulose. They are used in nitrocellulose lacquer to lower viscosity and give certain other desirable properties. In most cases, dilutants act as a solvent for the resins contained in the lacquer.

Dirt nibs: Small specks of foreign material in a dried film of finishing material. They should be removed by scuff sanding.

Dirty: The opposite of clean. Describes a color that has a drab appearance rather than one with a bright appearance. The addition of black makes colors dirty.

Disc sander: A power sanding tool used for grinding, sanding, and polishing repaired metal areas.

Disintegrate: The dried film of a finishing material completely breaks down.

Disk trimmer: A special tool used to cut down a worn-out sanding disk to a somewhat smaller size, giving it a fresh cutting edge.

Double head coat: Usually called one coat, but meaning an application of material sprayed horizontally and immediately followed by an application sprayed vertically. Also called a cross coat.

Driers: The salts of certain metals or metallo-organic compounds that when added to an enamel, paint, varnish, or oil hasten the drying or hardening of the film through proper ventilation.

Dry spray: A rough, dry finish that is a result of the atomized paint not being absorbed in the film.

Durability: The life of a paint film.

Dust free: Condition when a film has dried so that it will no longer allow dust to penetrate and stick to the finish.

Enamel: A pigmented alkyd varnish usually characterized by a glossy surface. Dulux is such a pigmented synthetic resin solution, which dries by evaporation of solvents but also cures through a chemical cure.

Epoxy resins: Resins obtained by the condensing reaction that occurs between phenols and epichlorohydrin.

Evaporation: The escape of solvents from the paint into the air.

Face: The appearance of a color viewed straight on (at a 90° angle). This term is most often used in comparison to the *pitch* of a color, which is the appearance of the color when viewed at any angle other than 90°. The face color is often different in lightness or darkness or in shade from the pitch, particularly when working with iridescent colors.

Fade: Denotes the change in the color of a surface coating as a result of exposure to sunlight. It is a dying away or bleaching action.

Fan: The spray pattern of a spray gun.

Fanning: Use of pressurized air through a spray gun to speed up the drying time of a paint finish; it is not recommended.

Featheredge splitting: Cracks or stretch marks along the featheredge; they occur while drying or shortly after the topcoat has been applied over a primer-surfacer.

Feathering (featheredging): Sanding down a surface to a very fine edge; that is, when one coat of material is made gradually thinner around the edge until it finally disappears.

Film: A layer of applied coating material.

Film thickness: See *Mil.*

Fisheyes: A kind of cratering appearing on the surface. Sometimes as large as a dime and circled by a noticeable ring.

Flake: Particles added to a color to achieve a metallic or iridescent finish.

Flaking: Condition when the finish does not knit properly to the undercoating, causing the finish to chip off the work by breaking into small pieces.

Flash off: The rate of evaporation of the thinner or reducer.

Flat: Designates a finish that has no luster or gloss.

Flint paper: An inexpensive but short working life abrasive paper, not used extensively in body shops.

Flood: The floating of a pigment to the surface of a coating, giving a changed color to the surface and lack of uniformity in color appearance through the film.

Flop: The appearance of a color when viewed from any angle other than straight on. The flop of a color is also referred to as its pitch.

Flow: The ability of paint droplets to melt or merge together to form a smooth paint film.

Fog coat: A thin, highly atomized coat applied in such a way as to obtain a fast flash off of the thinner and thereby achieve a minimum penetration of the thinner into the old finish.

Force dry: See *Baking.*

Garnet paper: A hard, sharp, red abrasive; more expensive than flint paper but will last much longer.

Gel: The general consistency of a jelly, the material being soft but not free flowing. Generally applied to a vehicle as contrasted to false body caused by pigmentation.

Glazing: The application of a filler by means of a putty knife; the material is filled into the depression but scraped off the higher areas.

Gloss: The shine, sheen, or luster of a dry film.

Gritty: A product is said to be gritty when it contains large particles, either from insufficient grinding, which would mean seed, or by the presence of large, hard particles of foreign materials.

Guide coat: A different color of a topcoat from the undercoat used as a guide for controlling sanding depth.

Gumming: The condition when the sandpaper becomes clogged by the abraded surface coating. Compare *Caking.*

Hairlining: Very fine lines or checks on the dried surface coating of a finished material.

Hardener: A special additive designed to promote a faster cure of the enamel paint film (isocyanates).

Hardness: The quality of the paint film that gives it resistance to surface damage.

Heaving: See *Lifting.*

Hide glue: Made from animal hides and used in making abrasives that can only be used in dry sanding and grinding work.

Hiding: The opacity or ability of a finishing material to cover solidly over another color so as to obscure or prevent the original color from showing through.

Hold out: The ability of a surface to keep the top coat from sinking in.

Hue: The basic color, that is, blue, red, yellow, green, violet, or orange. Hue is used to determine where the color would fall generally on the color wheel.

Humidity: The water vapor present in the air.

Industrial fallout: Airborne chemical compounds that are deposited on the surfaces of vehicles and that under certain circumstances affect the finish, particularly metallics.

Iridescents: All colors that contain aluminum, mica, or other particles that impart a metallic appearance to the color. Used interchangeably with the word metallic. Iridescent colors must be carefully matched on the face and the pitch in order to achieve a desirable appearance.

Knit: Adhere or bond together.

Lacquer: A refinishing material that dries by the evaporation of the thinner.

Leveling out: Flowing or settling to a smooth, uniform surface.

Lifting: Disruption of a paint film by the application of a succeeding coat, caused by the solvents of the succeeding coat penetrating and partially dissolving or swelling the preceding dried film.

Lighten: The addition of white to make solid colors lighter; the addition of metallic flake makes metallic colors lighter.

Livering: The coagulation of paint into a viscous liverlike mass.

Luster: Gloss, sheen, or brightness of a finish.

Masking paper: A paper designed to prevent paint bleed-through and resist water soaking to a certain degree.

Masking tape: A special paper coated with adhesive; it is used to protect body parts or to attach masking paper to the car.

Metal conditioner: An acetic acid preparation used to prepare metal, remove rust, and etch the metal slightly to provide good adherence between metal and paint.

Metallic: Finish containing aluminum particles.

Mil: Measure of film thickness; equal to 0.001 in. (0.025 mm).

Milkiness: Cloudy, whitish; not clear.

Mist coat: A light spray coat of lacquer thinner or other volatile solvent by itself or with very little color in it.

Mottling: A striped or spotty appearance that occurs in metallics when the flakes flow together because of poor spraying techniques.

Natural mineral abrasive: Abrasives made from materials found in nature.

Nitrocellulose: Gun cotton, pyroxylin; a compound of nitrogen and cellulose prepared from nitric acid and cotton or wood fiber.

Opaque: Impervious to light; not transparent.

Orange peel: An uneven, pebbly surface somewhat resembling the skin of an orange; appears in a paint film that has been applied by spray.

Original finish: The paint the car manufacturer applies at the factory.

Overall repainting: A refinish repair job in which the whole vehicle is completely repainted.

Overlap: The amount of the spray pattern that covers the previous spray swath.

Overspray: See *Dry spray.*

Oxidation: The drying of an oil, varnish, or synthetic resin by the absorption of oxygen from the air. The act or process of combining with oxygen.

Paint film: The coating of paint that is applied to a material.

Paint remover: A fast-acting blend of solvents used to remove enamels, lacquers, and varnish.

Panel repair: A refinish repair job in which only a complete panel is repainted.

Pebbling: Excessively large orange peel.

Peeling: Loss of bond or adhesion of a paint film from the surface to which it is applied.

Perchloroethylene: A solvent used in determining whether the finish is acrylic lacquer, nitrocellulose lacquer, or enamel.

Phenolic resin: A resin based on the reaction between formaldehyde and phenol.

Pigment: Any fine, insoluble, dry, solid particles used to impart color.

Piling: Heaping or applying too heavily.

Pinholing and pitting: Minute hollows or holes in a film no larger than the head of a pin and produced by the bursting of trapped air, moisture, or thinner during drying.

Pitch: The appearance of a color when viewed from any angle other than straight on. Most often used in comparison to the face of a color, which is the appearance of the color when viewed at a 90° angle or straight on. Pitch is also referred to as the *flop* of a color. The pitch is often different from the face when working with iridescent colors.

Plastic filler: A compound of resin and fiber glass used to fill dents on car bodies.

Polychromatic: Color coats that contain aluminum powder in flake form (used by some paint manufacturers).

Polyester filler: A special kind of puttylike filler used in filling slight imperfections and low spots on fiber glass panels.

Polyester resin: A bonding liquid that forms a good bond with fiber-glass surfaces only.

Polyurethane: A chemical structure used in the production of resins for enamel paint finishes.

Poor adhesion: A paint system that has poor bond to the underlying surface.

Pot life: The amount of time a paint will remain a liquid once catalyzed.

Powdered fiber glass: Processed fiber glass that has been crushed into a powder. It not only gives bulk but also strength to the filler.

Pressure-feed gun: A spray gun equipped with a separate paint container that is pressurized and connected to the spray gun by means of two hoses.

Primer: An undercoat applied to a bare metal or other substrate to improve the adhesion of the topcoat; it does not require sanding before recoating.

Primer coat: The first coat in a paint system; its main purpose is to impart adhesion.

Primer-sealer: An undercoat that improves the adhesion of the topcoat and seals the old painted surfaces that were sanded.

Primer-surfacer: A high-solid type of primer used to fill small imperfections in a substrate; it is usually sanded to smooth out the surface.

Putty glazing: A heavy-bodied nitrocellulose or polyester material used to fill small flaws that are in the surface and are too large to be filled by primer-surfacer.

Putty knife: Special knife used in applying glazing putty.

Pyroxylin: See *Nitrocellulose*.

Rain or water spotting: Marks on a surface due to rain or water absorption.

Reduce: Lower or make less in consistency. To cut.

Reducer: The volatile substance used to thin the viscosity of enamel prior to application.

Reflow: A heat process used to melt lacquer to produce a better flow or leveling.

Relative humidity: The condition of the atmosphere with reference to its content of water vapor at a given temperature.

Respirator: A filtering device worn over the mouth and nose to filter out particles and fumes and prevent them from reaching the lungs.

Retarder: A slowly evaporating thinner used to retard drying.

Rosin: A natural gum or resin; residue of the distillation of crude turpentine.

Rubbing and polishing compound: A special type of abrasive used to smooth out and polish a paint film.

Sander: A power-driven tool, some with a rotary action, others with an orbital motion, used with abrasives to sand car bodies.

Sander polisher: A power tool used to speed up the rate of polishing or sanding surfaces.

Sanding block: A hard rubber or plastic flexible block used to provide consistent backing for hand sanding.

Sand scratches: The reproduction in the topcoat of the sanding marks in the underlying surface.

Sand-scratch swelling: An exaggerated reproduction and distortion of the sanding marks in the underlying surface.

Sealer: A paint product used to prevent bleed-through of the previous coat or the sinking in of the new paint, resulting in loss of gloss.

Seediness: Being gritty or sandy or full of small grains.

Separation: Nonuniform mixture.

Setting up: The period during which solvent evaporation from the film flowing ceases, and the film surface becomes tack free.

Shade: The variation of a color. Assuming that a color is generally blue (that is, the hue is blue), it can have a red shade or a yellow shade as well as being blue. Shade is also called *undertone* since it describes the subtle tone of a color.

Shrinkage: Contracting of the surface.

Silicon carbide: An abrasive made by fusing silica and coke in an electric furnace. The abrasive is very hard, shiny black, and iridescent.

Silicone: An additive used in waxes and polishes that makes them easy to apply and smooth; also causes fisheyes.

Single coat: Usually refers to a coat of paint applied. Once over the surface with each stroke overlapping the previous stroke 50%.

Sinking in: When one coat is partially absorbed by the previous coat.

Skinning: The forming of a film on a thick topcoat before the solvents under the topcoat have evaporated.

Solids: The part of the paint that does not evaporate and stays on the surface.

Solution: A homogeneous liquid or mixture of two or more chemical substances.

Solvency: Ability or power of causing solution. Ability to dissolve.

Solvent: Any liquid in or by which a substance can be dissolved.

Solvent popping: Blisters that form on a paint film; caused by trapped solvents.

Specific gravity: The weight of a certain amount of liquid compared to the same amount of water at the same constant temperature.

Spot repair: A small refinish repair job in which a small section of a panel is refinished.

Spotting or spot repair: In repair work, the ability of a lacquer to blend in with the damaged film surface, thereby making the repair unnoticeable.

Spray gun: A device that mixes paint and compressed air to atomize and control the spray pattern as the paint leaves the fluid needle and cap.

Squeegee: A rectangular piece of rubber approximately 2 in. (51 mm) wide, 3 in. (76 mm) long, and 3/16 in. (5 mm) thick. It is used in applying glazing putty and plastic filler on concave surfaces.

Strength: Amount of pigment. High-strength bases contain a lot of pigment. The additional pigment gives the bases good hiding.

Substrate: A surface to be painted, whether an old finish or bare metal.

Suction-feed gun: A spray gun that has the paint container connected directly to it. It is designed to create a vacuum and thus draw the paint from the container.

Surface drying: The drying of the topcoat while the bottom coats have remained soft.

Sweating: Separation and appearance at the film surface of the oil in lacquer.

Synthetic resin: Any resin not produced by nature.

Tack coat: The first enamel coat. A full coat that is to dry only until it is quite sticky.

Tack free: That period of time in drying at which the surface of the film will not fingerprint, yet the film is not dry and hard throughout.

Tack rag: A cloth impregnated with varnish; used as a final cleanup to remove dust before applying the finishing paint.

Thermoplastic: Type of plastic that can be softened with the application of heat, can be reshaped, and can also be welded.

Thermosetting: Type of plastic that sets permanently; it cannot be softened with the application of heat, cannot be reshaped, and cannot be welded. Minor damage can often be repaired with a structural adhesive.

Thickness of film: The measurement of a film, usually expressed in mils; the distance from top to bottom or at right angles to its surface. A mil is 0.001 in. (0.0025 mm).

Thinner: Commonly known as a lacquer solvent; it reduces the viscosity of a lacquer to spraying consistency.

Tint: A mixture of two or more pigments. See *Blending*.

Tinting color: A finishing lacquer or enamel in which only one pigment or color is normally used.

Tooth: A roughened surface that affects the adhesion of the coating.

Topcoat: The final paint film application of a paint system.

Toxicity: Poisonous effect.

Transparent: Bases that contain a small amount of pigment have poor hiding and are transparent. You can see through the base.

Two tone: Two different colors used on a single paint job.

Undercoat: A material used to protect the underbody sections of a vehicle.

Urethane: See *Polyurethane*.

Vehicle: The liquid portion of a paint.

Viscosity: Consistency or body of a liquid.

Volatile: Capable of evaporating easily. The portion that readily vaporizes.

Water spotting: A condition caused by water evaporating on a paint film before it is thoroughly dry, resulting in a dulling of the gloss in spots.

Weathering: The change or failure in paint caused by exposure to the weather.

Wet spots: A discoloration caused where the paint fails to dry and adhere uniformly; caused by grease or finger marks usually.

Wrinkling: Buckling of a paint film at its surface, causing a shriveled appearance.

Index